# Equality

## From Theory to Action

Second Edition

John Baker
Kathleen Lynch
Sara Cantillon

and

Judy Walsh

*Equality Studies Centre, UCD School of Social Justice,*
*University College Dublin*

First edition published 2004

Second edition published 2009 by
PALGRAVE MACMILLAN

Palgrave Macmillan in the UK is an imprint of Macmillan Publishers Limited, registered in England, company number 785998, of Houndmills, Basingstoke, Hampshire RG21 6XS.

Palgrave Macmillan in the US is a division of St Martin's Press LLC, 175 Fifth Avenue, New York, NY 10010.

Palgrave Macmillan is the global academic imprint of the above companies and has companies and representatives throughout the world.

Palgrave® and Macmillan® are registered trademarks in the United States, the United Kingdom, Europe and other countries.

ISBN-13: 978–0–230–22717–0 (hardback)
ISBN-13: 978–0–230–22716–3 (paperback)

This book is printed on paper suitable for recycling and made from fully managed and sustained forest sources. Logging, pulping and manufacturing processes are expected to conform to the environmental regulations of the country of origin.

A catalogue record for this book is available from the British Library.

A catalog record for this book is available from the Library of Congress.

10   9   8   7   6   5   4   3   2
18   17   16   15   14   13   12   11   10   09

Printed and bound in Great Britain by
CPI Antony Rowe, Chippenham and Eastbourne

'This is a truly extraordinary book, combining sophisticated philosophical discussion of the fundamental moral issues linked to equality with solid sociological analysis of existing institutions and how they work to generate inequality, and provocative political analysis of strategies to transform those institutions...It provides a powerful framework for a new egalitarianism for the 21st century.'
– **Erik Olin Wright**, *Vilas Distinguished Professor of Sociology, University of Wisconsin, Madison, USA*

'The book is astonishing in its scope.'
– **Jonathan Wolff**, *Professor and Head of Department of Philosophy, University College London, UK*

**John Baker** is Senior Lecturer in Equality Studies at University College Dublin, Ireland, and was one of the founding members of the Equality Studies Centre and the UCD School of Social Justice. He is the author of *Arguing for Equality*. His main areas of research are theoretical issues of equality and democracy.

**Kathleen Lynch** is Professor of Equality Studies at University College Dublin, Ireland and was one of the founding members of the Equality Studies Centre and the UCD School of Social Justice. She is the author of *The Hidden Curriculum* and *Equality in Education* and co-author of *Schools and Society in Ireland, Equality and Power in Schools: Redistribution, Recognition and Representation* and *Inside Classrooms: The Teaching and Learning of Mathematics in Social Context*. Her main areas of research are equality in education, care and affective equality, emancipatory research, the role of the university in social change and theoretical issues in equality studies.

**Sara Cantillon** is Senior Lecturer in Equality Studies at University College Dublin, Ireland, a member of the Equality Studies Centre and a founding member of the UCD School of Social Justice. Her main areas of research are gender and poverty and intra-household distribution systems. Her publications include articles in *Journal of Social Policy, Radical Statistics* and *Feminist Economics*.

**Judy Walsh** is Lecturer in Equality Studies at University College Dublin, Ireland, a member of the Equality Studies Centre and a founding member of the UCD School of Social Justice. Her research interests and publications span various aspects of human rights law, discrimination law, and feminist and socio-legal theory.

The authors have also been active in a wide range of equality-related organizations and campaigns.

# Contents

*Preface*                                                                viii

*Preface to the Second Edition*                                            x

**Part I   The New Equality Agenda**                                       1

1   **New Challenges to an Unequal World**                                 3
     An unequal world                                                      3
     Responses to inequality                                             10
     Equality Studies as a response to inequality                        14
     Guide to the rest of this book                                      18

2   **Dimensions of Equality: A Framework for Theory
     and Action**                                                        21
     The idea of equality                                                21
     Basic equality                                                      23
     Liberal egalitarianism                                              24
     Equality of condition                                               33
     Applying the framework to social groups                             42

3   **The Centrality of Equality: Equality and Other Values**            47
     Aspects of equality                                                 47
     Freedom and equality                                                50
     Equality, solidarity and community                                  52
     Equality and the environment                                        53
     Genuine conflicts between equality and other values                 55

4   **Contexts of Egalitarian Change: Social Systems and
     Social Groups**                                                     57
     Social systems within which inequality is generated                 58
     Interactions between the key systems                                62
     Locating the generative causes of inequality across social
       groups                                                            65
     Implications for policy and politics                                70

**Part II   Putting Equality into Practice**                             73

5   **Towards Economic Equality**                                        75
     Economic inequality: a glance                                       76
     Economic perspectives on equality                                   78
     Economic inequality and economic growth: theory
       and evidence                                                      82

The equality–efficiency trade-off: theory and evidence       84
Routes to greater economic equality                          87

6   **The Challenge of Participatory Democracy**             96
Basic principles                                             96
Participatory democracy                                      98
Obstacles to participatory democracy                         101
Overcoming the intrinsic obstacles                           102
Overcoming the transitional obstacles                        113

7   **Equality, the Legal System and Employment Law**        118
How the legal system reinforces inequality                   118
Making the system more egalitarian                           123
Workplace anti-discrimination laws                           125
Towards equality of condition in employment                  132

8   **Equality and Education**                                140
Why equality in education matters                            141
Four major equality problems in education                    143
Equality of resources and economically generated
    inequalities in education: the primacy of social class   144
Equality of respect and recognition in education: recognizing
    diversity                                                154
Equality of power: democratizing education                   161
Equality of love, care and solidarity: the emotional
    dimensions of education                                  164

9   **Emancipatory Research as a Tool of Change**            169
Positivist methodologies and equality                        170
The conditions in which research is produced                 175
Emancipatory methodology                                     178
Emancipatory research in practice: research coalitions and
    learning partnerships                                    183

Part III   **Strategies for Change**                         189

10  **Class, Gender and the Equality Movement**              191
Two models of social change                                  191
How the equality movement stands today                       194
The achievements and challenges of the equality movement     199
Class politics and egalitarian change                        201
The gender order and the politics of change                  207

11  **Ideology and Resistance**                              212
The role of ideology                                         212
Egalitarianism as a mobilizing ideology                      218
Love, care and solidarity as political themes                220
Caring work and the women's movement                         224

**12 Strategic Issues for the Equality Movement** 229
Coordinating action 229
The role of political parties 232
Radicals and moderates 238
Ends and means 243

*Notes* 247

*Bibliography* 267

*Index* 307

# Preface

When the Equality Studies Centre at University College Dublin opened its doors in 1989, the prospects for equality looked bleak. It was a period of economic retrenchment in Ireland and of right-wing ascendancy in Britain and the US. The fall of communism in the USSR and central and eastern Europe made capitalism seem triumphant. In the academy, it was fashionable to dismiss an interest in equality as a 'grand narrative' of a bygone era. But resistance to inequality and domination has been a perennial feature of human societies and was never destined simply to disappear. In the last decade it has resurfaced on a global scale. Our aim in this book is to contribute to that struggle for equality. We want to show how cooperation across academic disciplines and among groups seeking egalitarian change can help to strengthen not just the theory of equality but its practical implementation and its political prospects.

We could never have written this book without the experience we have gained in the Equality Studies Centre. Most importantly, it has brought us into dialogue with the hundreds of activists who have enrolled on our postgraduate and outreach programmes out of a desire to reflect upon their own experiences of working for equality and to deepen their understanding of the issues they faced. We cannot overstate what we have learned from them and from the movements and organizations to which they belong. The existence of the Equality Studies Centre has also made it possible for us to interact with and learn from a wide number of other groups and individuals interested in egalitarian change. And it has given us the opportunity to learn from each other and from our colleagues associated with the Centre, with our different disciplinary and personal backgrounds.

It would therefore be truly impossible to name everyone who has contributed to this work. But we wish especially to thank our colleagues Alpha Connelly, Mary Kelly and Máire Nic Ghiolla Phádraig, who were involved in the research project from the start and shaped its overall conception and agenda, as well as our students and colleagues Carlos Bruen, John Bosco Conama, Maggie Feeley, Tarig Yousif, Mary McEvoy, Henry McClave, Pat McDonnell, Susan Miner, Maurice Murphy, Phyllis Murphy, Maeve O'Brien, Deiric O'Broin and Mary O'Donoghue, with whom we discussed a number of chapters and from whose own work we have learned a lot. We are also very grateful to many people for their generous comments on one or more chapters, including Chris Armstrong, Valerie Bresnihan, Harry Brighouse, Vittorio Bufacchi, Alan Carling, G.A. Cohen, Niall Crowley, Laurence Cox, Jurgen De Wispelaere, Marc Fleurbaey, Andrew Glyn, Keith Graham, Bernie Grummell, Niamh Hardiman, Ellen Hazelkorn, Iseult

Honohan, Cathal Kelly, Peter McDermott, Eithne McLaughlin, Mags Liddy, Ger Moane, Eadaoin ní Chleirigh, Shane O'Neill, Francis O'Toole, Anne Phillips, Andrew Sayer, Richard Sinnott, Bob Sutcliffe, Jennifer Todd, Louise Walsh, Tanya Ward, Gerry Whyte, Jonathan Wolff, Erik Olin Wright and Gillian Wylie, as well as participants in Equality Studies and Politics courses; we apologize to anyone whose comments we have overlooked. We also want to thank participants on occasions at which parts of this book were tried out, under the auspices of the American Political Science Association (1996), Queen's University Belfast (1996), the Political Studies Association of Ireland (1999, 2003), the UCD Politics Department (1999), the Tenth Anniversary Conference of the Equality Studies Centre (2000), the Fifth Summer School on Economics and Philosophy (San Sebastian, 2002), the Havens Center for the Study of Social Structure and Social Change (University of Wisconsin – Madison, 2002) and the Seamus Heaney Lectures (St Patrick's College, Dublin, 2003). This research was generously funded by The Atlantic Philanthropies. It also received institutional support from the Institution for Social and Policy Studies at Yale University (1998–99) and the Department of Politics, the Faculty of Interdisciplinary Studies and the Institute for the Study of Social Change at University College Dublin.

We would like to dedicate this book to our diverse families, from whom we have had object lessons in all of the dimensions of equality.

Earlier versions of various chapters or parts of chapters appeared as follows: Chapter 1: John Baker, 'Studying Equality', *Imprints* 2 (1997), pp. 57–71 and Iain MacKenzie and Shane O'Neill, eds, *Reconstituting Social Criticism* (Basingstoke: Macmillan – now Palgrave Macmillan, 1999), pp. 51–64. Chapter 2: John Baker, 'Equality', in S. Healy and B. Reynolds, eds, *Social Policy in Ireland: Principles, Practice and Problems* (Dublin: Oak Tree Press, 1998), pp. 21–42. Chapter 3: John Baker, 'Equality and Other Values', *Studies* 92 (2003), pp. 113–21. Chapter 9: Kathleen Lynch, 'Equality Studies, the Academy and the Role of Research in Emancipatory Social Change', *Economic and Social Review* 30 (1999), pp. 41–69.

Writing this book has been a genuinely collective enterprise, and the authors take joint responsibility for its contents. We wish to acknowledge primary responsibility for particular chapters as follows: John and Kathleen for Chapters 1, 2, 4 and 10, John for Chapters 3, 6 and 12, Kathleen for Chapters 8, 9 and 11, Sara for Chapter 5 and Judy for Chapter 7.

# Preface to the Second Edition

Since it took us many years to produce the first edition of *Equality: From Theory to Action*, it will come as no surprise that we are not yet ready to engage in a major reworking of this book. Within the text we have simply taken the opportunity to undertake some very minor amendments to the first edition. In this preface we respond to some of the comments that have been made about the book and then discuss briefly some of the ways that our thinking has developed since it was first published.[1]

## Responses to the first edition

Although reviewers and commentators have been generous in their reactions, they have raised several sets of issues that are worth responding to. The first concerns our limited focus, which was always on problems of inequality within well-off democracies. Our material is drawn largely from the experience and thinking of Ireland, Britain and the United States, although we also cite literature and evidence from many other countries. Undoubtedly this affects our perceptions and commitments, but since every author writes from a particular personal and intellectual experience and from a necessarily limited knowledge, all we can do is invite our readers to engage their experience with ours and make their own judgements as a result of the encounter. A related issue is the relative lack of attention we give to issues of imperialism, globalization, global inequality and global governance, even though these are often acknowledged in the text. In this case, it is not so much an issue of writing from a particular perspective, since everyone's experience is framed by global issues, but simply of not being able to talk about everything at once. As the opening pages of Chapter 1 indicate, it is perfectly possible to describe the many dimensions of global inequality, and in our view the theoretical frameworks set out more generally in Part I are as applicable to global as to national issues. The main normative question here is whether the ideal of equality of condition set out in Chapter 2 is justifiable as a conception of global justice, while the central empirical questions are how to apply the framework elaborated in Chapter 4, of four contexts of egalitarian change, at a global level and how to explain their interaction with more localized systems. A considerable amount of relevant work is being done in both of these areas and we fully acknowledge that such work is a necessary supplement to what we say in this book.

A rather different aspect of limited focus concerns the social groups that we have chosen to concentrate on as illustrations of equality issues. As

Chapter 1 indicates, the key social divisions that we return to repeatedly are class, gender, 'race' and ethnicity, disability and sexual orientation. These are the divisions that are particularly prominent in our own experience and therefore, again, reflect our situated perspective. What some commentators have found surprising is that the example of racism we concentrate on is the treatment of Irish Travellers rather than that of nonwhites. This is indeed a specific case, and it is importantly distinct from forms of racism that are marked by skin colour. However, we believed and continue to hold that it is both analytically and politically important to resist the view that racism only arrived in Irish society during its recent experience of net immigration, and we hope that readers in other countries will see both parallels and differences when they compare their own experience with what we say about racism and anti-racism in Ireland.

Despite our limited focus, many commentators have remarked on the breadth of the analysis here. As they have also pointed out, the price of breadth is sometimes lack of depth, and we acknowledge that on almost every question addressed in this book there is much more to be said and many difficult questions to answer. Since one of the central aims of the book is to exhibit the scope and coherence of equality studies as a field of inquiry, breadth was always going to have a high priority, and as a result we have often had to condense material. But we do not believe that we have over-simplified – that we have chosen breadth over accuracy. We have tried to be open about the many issues on which there is room for disagreement and for further analysis. We have also tried to deepen our own understanding of equality issues through further research. An area that we have been particularly concerned to understand is affective equality, and we draw on some of that work, as published in *Affective Equality: Love, Care and Injustice*, below.[2]

Part I of this book sets out our general theoretical framework, at the core of which is a commitment to what we call equality of condition, defined in terms of five dimensions of equality. But a number of thoughtful critics have suggested that we pay too little attention to the possibility of conflicts between different egalitarian goals. For example, it is sometimes argued that the celebration of cultural diversity is incompatible with a belief in gender equality, since some cultural norms are inimical to equality between men and women. Difficult choices need to be made, choices that the framework set out in Chapter 2 is claimed not to address. Our general answer to this criticism is to accept that in particular circumstances egalitarian aims may well be incompatible, and that choices do need to be made. The framework in Chapter 2 is not intended to rule out hard choices but to identify the range of principles that egalitarians can endorse, a range that has often been too narrowly construed. Yet although specific circumstances may force us to choose between egalitarian aims, our general position is that these circumstances arise most sharply in situations of severe inequality, and that therefore the practical task of making societies more equal also helps to alleviate the burden of choosing between egalitarian aims. In our view, the equalities constituting equality of condition are far from incompatible, and in fact reinforce each other. So, to return to the example, the conflict between celebrating cultural diversity and promoting gender equality arises most sharply in societies marked by gender inequality and the marginalization of cultural minorities, where such minorities are put on the defensive by dominant cultural traditions and by processes in the economic, political and affective systems that reinforce inequality. Greater economic, political and affective equality, together with a practice of what we call critical interculturalism, would, we think, promote both equality of respect and recognition and equality between men and women.

In Part II, we discuss the institutional and policy implications of equality of condition. We have always considered our views to be contributions to a broader egalitarian programme that is being developed all over the world by both researchers and activists. A number of people have suggested ways in which the ideas we put forward could be modified or supplemented. For example, our discussion in Chapter 5 focuses primarily on the distribution of earned incomes, and so says little about the very important issue of the distribution of wealth. The main point we would continue to stress about institutions and policies is the importance of looking at effects across all of the dimensions of equality. A change that generates greater equality of income may look very different in terms of its effects on work, power or love and care.

In Part III, we address political strategies for advancing the equality agenda. We point to a range of egalitarian movements and their combined potential for achieving social change. Some commentators have suggested that our stance is too optimistic – that there are too many divisions and conflicts among seemingly egalitarian movements to foster the kind of cooperation and common aims that are essential for political progress; indeed, that it is mistaken to talk of a shared equality agenda at all. We, in turn, think that these critics are too pessimistic, and in particular that they may not have fully appreciated the value of what we call strategic pluralism. There are of course many important differences among and within egalitarian movements, but these are not necessarily obstacles to changes in the broad direction of greater equality of condition.

## Developments in our thinking

In the five years since this book was first published, and in the longer period since most of it was written, there have been substantial changes in Irish and global society. Within Ireland, the main change has been the substantial increase in the number of non-Irish nationals living in the country. Although Ireland has been a country of net immigration since 1996, the expansion of the EU in 2004 led to a substantial jump in immigration in 2005. The first edition did recognize migration as an equality issue, but it has become a much more salient one and would now deserve more attention. At a global level, the continued economic growth of China and India has had an effect on global inequality, the invasion of Iraq has highlighted many equality issues, and the global capitalist economy is in crisis. Although we do not give much attention to global inequalities, these developments would affect some of what we say in passing. Another global factor that has become much more prominent in recent years is global warming. Although the first edition does refer to global warming, it does not receive an extended treatment. Now that it is much more familiar in public discourse, it could be used to develop the ideas on the relationship between equality and the environment set out in Chapter 3. Although everyone is affected by global warming, the fact that some are better placed to protect themselves than others is an important and perhaps under-recognized fact.

At the centre of this book is the conceptual framework set out in Chapters 2 and 4. Chapter 2 puts forward a multi-dimensional analysis of three conceptions of equality, called basic equality, liberal egalitarianism and equality of condition, and outlines their application to social groups. Chapter 4 sets out four main contexts of equality, namely the economic, cultural, political and affective systems.

In relation to the framework set out in Chapter 2, we would not yet propose any major changes. We continue to find the framework useful both in thinking normatively about equality and as a heuristic tool for empirical research. A number of relatively minor amendments now suggest themselves, however, particularly in relation to the dimension of love, care and solidarity, which we are continuing to conceptualize and to explore empirically. These are dealt with at greater length in *Affective Equality,* but broadly speaking they have to do with the scope and complexity of this dimension of equality. Although we always recognized that love, care and solidarity identify a family of related ideas rather than a single type of relationship, it is only in *Affective Equality* that we have analysed the differences in some depth, pointing out in particular some important differences between what we call primary caring relationships or love labour and what we call secondary and tertiary relationships. Another development has to do with the scope of this dimension of equality. In the first edition, our emphasis was on the positive: the value to people of relations of love, care and solidarity. We did not, in retrospect, give sufficient thought to their negative counterparts, such as violence, abuse, hatred and antagonism; our tendency was to treat these as issues of power rather than of love and care. Yet if there is an inequality of care between those who receive it and those who do not, there is clearly an even greater inequality in the same dimension between those who are cared for and those who are abused. We should therefore think of the range of the dimension of love, care and solidarity as extending in two directions and not just in one.

Within the dimension of respect and recognition, the main addition we would now make is to include liberal multiculturalism as a species of liberal egalitarianism. The more individualized idea of respect for persons clearly remains the dominant position among liberal egalitarians, and this led us in the first edition to confine group-based positions to the category of equality of condition. But 'multiculturalism' as it is understood in contemporary political discourse belongs much more to a liberal than a radical egalitarian mindset, because it emphasizes the toleration of difference rather than critical engagement. The criticisms that many liberal egalitarians have made of multiculturalism, based on its tendency to privilege the protection of cultures over the interests of individuals, motivated the group-sensitive but critically engaged understanding of difference that we meant to capture in the idea of critical interculturalism. But in the process the idea of multiculturalism itself dropped off of our map.

In the dimension of resources, our thinking has been informed by research and discussion in the Equality Studies Centre, which has often focused on particular contexts and social divisions. This has helped us to see more clearly that what counts as a valuable resource in one context is not necessarily valuable in another, and that characterizing and empirically investigating inequalities of resources is far from straightforward when dealing with resources like social and cultural capital. *Affective Equality* also pays attention to the idea of 'emotional' and 'nurturing' capitals, which refer both to external networks of support and internalized capacities. The idea of resources was always intended to be open-ended, so we are (naturally enough) inclined to see all this as confirming the fertility of the framework rather than its limitations.

In the dimension of power, the main issue that has emerged through our recent discussions has to do with the distinction between power over someone and the power to do something, a distinction common in the literature on power. Although from the point of view of the analysis of inequality, power over others remains central, not every inequality in the power of individuals or groups to do something is a case of power over; nor are such inequalities always reducible to the other dimensions of inequality, such as inequality of resources. The distinction between the two ideas of power comes particularly to the fore in relation to groups that are contesting subordination, where the ideas of personal and collective empowerment are important.[3]

We have also come to recognize a need for expansion in the dimension of working and learning. One might ask, for example, how it applies to the context of older people living in nursing homes. Some of them may not 'work' in any conventional sense; they may feel that they have learnt all they need to know. Yet their lives are still filled with activity – or inactivity – that can be satisfying and fulfilling or boring and stultifying. An analysis of inequalities in nursing homes would, among other things, consider the degree to which their residents have access to satisfying activities, making this question a further aspect of the dimension of working and learning.[4]

Chapter 4 of this book sets out a model of society in terms of four social systems: the economic, cultural, political and affective systems. Although the first three of these systems have been extensively investigated by social scientists, scant attention was paid to the affective system and its constituent inequalities before these were focused upon by feminist scholars, mostly since the 1980s. Even now, after at least two decades of scholarly attention, issues to do with love, care and solidarity and the work that goes into sustaining them are largely confined to branches of academic disciplines that are labelled as 'feminist' or 'radical' rather than being recognized as central issues. The theme of affective equality has still to become truly integrated into mainstream sociology, education, economics, law and political theory.

The aim of *Affective Equality* is to help to redress this imbalance. It is primarily concerned with the empirical analysis of equality within one aspect of the affective system, focusing on other-centred (primary care) relations: that sphere of social life that is primarily oriented to the care of intimate others. At its centre is a series of studies of primary care relations involving thirty Care Conversations and two focus groups, together with three further studies of mothers' emotional work in education, men's perception of masculinity and caring, and the relationship between care and literacy learning among people who had spent their childhoods in institutional care. It examines inequalities in the distribution of love and care labouring and, to a lesser degree, in the receipt of love and care. It also demonstrates inequalities of respect and recognition, of resources and of power in caring relationships and links these to the inter-relationships between inequality in the affective system and those in the economic, political and cultural systems. It reveals the depth and complexity of inequalities in the affective system and how these are shaped by key social characteristics, particularly gender, class and family status. Finally, *Affective Equality* draws attention to the primacy of loving care in life, and of the work that is involved (mostly for women at this time in history) in love labouring. It highlights the centrality of nurturing relationships to personal identities and provides extensive evidence showing how 'care-full' citizens are threatened and undermined by the lack of material supports, time and respect afforded to their labour in an increasingly 'care-less' public sphere.

We wrote *Equality: From Theory to Action* for many reasons, but most especially to contribute to the movement for egalitarian change. Four years after its publication, we remain committed to that aim, and we continue to hope that this book can help to achieve it.

## Notes

1. The responses in the next few paragraphs are motivated by reviews by Faith Armitage (*Feminist Review* 82 (2006)), Sandra Lilburn (*Australian Journal of Political Science* 40 (2005)), Uvanney Maylor (*Pedagogy, Culture and Society* 13 (2005)), Ronaldo Munck (*Irish Journal of Sociology* 14 (2005)), Harriet Samuels (*Feminist*

*Legal Studies* 13 (2005)) and Steven R. Smith (*Imprints* 9 (2005)); a review symposium in the *British Journal of Sociology of Education* 26 (2005) with contributions
from Tuula Gordon, Kevin Brain and Ivan Reid, and Kari Dehli; a symposium in
*Res Publica* 13 (2007) with contributions from Harry Brighouse, Joanne Conaghan,
Cillian McBride and Stuart White, with a reply by ourselves; and discussions with
a range of colleagues, students and activists.

2. Kathleen Lynch, John Baker and Maureen Lyons, with Sara Cantillon, Judy
   Walsh, Maggie Feeley, Niall Hanlon and Maeve O'Brien, *Affective Equality: Love,
   Care and Injustice* (Basingstoke and New York: Palgrave Macmillan, 2009).

3. The issue of empowerment is at the centre of Shari McDaid, 'Power, Empowerment and User Involvement in the Public Mental Health Services in Ireland' (PhD
   thesis: University College Dublin, 2008).

4. We are grateful to Errollyn Bruce for this point.

# Part I
# The New Equality Agenda

# 1
# New Challenges to an Unequal World

Inequality is a pervasive fact of our world. Yet in every country there is resistance to power and privilege, with people working at many levels to create more equal societies. What is equality? What would more equal societies look like? How can they be brought about? Those are the questions that have shaped this book. We treat egalitarianism as a practical project of developing new ideas, restructuring social institutions and achieving social change. We do not claim to answer all of the questions egalitarians need to ask, but we hope to show how these questions – and some of their answers – fit together within a coherent overall framework.

In this chapter, we review some of the obvious and not-so-obvious inequalities that exist in the world generally and in western, 'developed' societies in particular. We look at some of the responses they have generated from social movements, states and educational institutions. We go on to explain the general perspective from which we address equality and inequality in this book, the perspective of equality studies. The chapter ends with a guide to the rest of this book.

## An unequal world

All of us live in unequal societies in an unequal world. It would be a mammoth task to survey this inequality fully and systematically.[1] But a brief glance at some of the inequalities we are all familiar with is a useful starting point for what follows.

What stands out most sharply in the world as we find it is massive inequality in the life prospects of the rich and the poor. Life expectancy ranges from 49 years in Sub-Saharan Africa to 76 years in the OECD.[2] Of every 1000 children born in these two groups of countries, 174 die before their fifth birthday in Sub-Saharan Africa compared to 14 in the OECD (UNDP 2002, Table 8). These facts are stark reminders of global inequality. In every country the privileged have longer and healthier lives than the worse off. 'Unskilled' workers in the UK are three times as likely to die from heart disease and four times as likely to die from lung cancer as professionals (Acheson 1998, Table 2). African Americans are eight times as likely as whites to die from homicide (Keppel, Pearcy and Wagener 2002). These differences in how people's lives turn out reflect a range of inequalities in their circumstances – in the conditions of their lives.

**Inequalities of resources**

The most extensively researched inequalities of condition are those to do with income and other economic resources (Figure 1.1). A simple way of measuring income inequality is to compare the best-off tenth of the population with the worst-off tenth. In the United States, for example, the best-off tenth – the best-off 29 million people – have incomes of roughly 17 times those of the worst-off tenth. Income inequalities vary considerably among countries. In South Africa and Brazil, two of the most unequal countries, the best-off tenth of the population receive about 65 times as much income as the worst-off tenth. In the most equal countries, such as Finland and Japan, the ratio is only about five to one (World Bank 2003, Table 2.8). If we compare the best-off tenth of the *world's* population with the worst-off tenth, the figures show that those six hundred million best-off people receive about 60 times the income of the worst-off six hundred million (Sutcliffe 2002, p. 37). That is to say that global inequality is roughly of the same order as in the most unequal countries in the world.

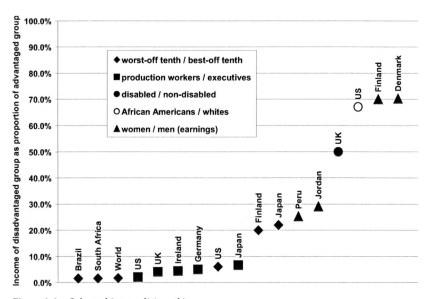

*Figure 1.1*   Selected inequalities of income
*Sources*: see text

Income inequality has several recognizable patterns. The most obvious is that income reflects social class. The richest people in the world, for example the 500 or so dollar billionaires (Kroll and Goldman 2003), belong to a class whose income derives almost entirely from investment. Among people who might loosely be called employees, there is a marked difference between the incomes of managers and workers, although this varies among countries. The average pay of high-level executives in Japan is around 15 times that of a typical production worker. In Germany the corresponding figure is 20, in the UK 25 and in the US 50 (Kenworthy 1995). The figure for Ireland[3] is 23 (Cantillon *et al.* 2001, p. 14).

In every country, men receive more income than women. In the most equal countries, like Denmark and Finland, women's share of earned income is about 70 per cent of men's. In the most unequal, like Jordan and Peru, women's earnings are less than a third of men's (UNDP 2002, Table 22). Another common pattern of inequality is its connection to 'race' and ethnicity. In the US, African American families receive on average less than two-thirds the income of non-Hispanic white families (Henwood 2002). Income inequality also reflects disability. The incomes of severely disabled people in Britain are only about half of average income, after taking account of the extra costs of impairment (Burchardt 2000).

Although income inequality is particularly obvious, there are other inequalities of resources. There is a resource inequality between the 1.2 billion people who have no access to safe drinking water and the people who do (UN 2002, p. 3). It is a resource inequality that health spending per person in Ireland and the UK is roughly 13 times as much as in Ecuador and Vietnam (WHO 2001, Annex Table 5). These and many other inequalities of resources are of course usually associated with inequality of income but may include a substantial amount of collective provision.

## Inequalities of respect and recognition

Inequalities in people's relations of respect and recognition are harder to quantify. There are some clear expressions of unequal respect, such as the fact that gay sex is illegal in more than 80 countries (ILGA 2003) or that there are at least 140 000 rapes or attempted rapes every year in the US (Bureau of Justice Statistics 2003). But the main expressions are more qualitative. One of the earliest issues addressed by the contemporary women's movement was the way that everyday speech privileges men over women. The use of male pronouns to refer to persons generally, the derogatory terms used by men to refer to women, the way that assertive behaviour gets praised in men but disparaged in women and the cautious ways that women are taught to express themselves are examples of this privileging (Baker 1979; Lakoff 1977; Strainchamps 1971; Vetterling-Braggin, Elliston and English 1977, Part III). Other movements have analysed similar features in relation to sexuality, 'race', disability and so on, giving rise to debates about 'political correctness'. The general reaction of members of dominant groups has been to belittle the complaints of subordinate groups and to appeal to freedom of speech, as though having the freedom to talk in ways that insult others somehow makes it less insulting (Dunant 1994). Inequality of recognition runs very deeply in many familiar settings. For example, it is an everyday practice to describe some students as 'smart' or 'brainy' and others as 'slow', 'weak', 'stupid' or 'duds', a pervasive inequality of recognition in the educational system (Lynch and Lodge 2002, pp. 71–82). Inequality of respect and recognition is also found in the celebrity culture fostered by the contemporary mass media, with status and adulation accorded to the 'stars' of selected fields of activity. This exaggeration and commercialization of the achievements of others has created an enormous gulf between celebrities – not just of sport and entertainment but of business and politics as well – and so-called ordinary people.

### Inequalities of love, care and solidarity

Inequalities in people's access to relations of love, care and solidarity are also hard to quantify, but they are perfectly familiar. The most striking inequalities of this type are found where the normal expectation of love and care is replaced by its opposite, as in the abuse of children by their parents and by those who have institutional control over them. In recent years there has been an explosion of publicity over such cases, with the result that there are currently 27 000 children on child protection registers in England (NSPCC 2003).

People in prison often suffer an extreme lack of love and care. Their ties of family and friendship are severely disrupted and typically replaced by their antithesis. 'Prisons and jails in even the richest and most developed countries were plagued [in 2001] by massive overcrowding, decaying physical infrastructure, inadequate sanitation, lack of medical care, guard abuse and corruption, and prisoner-on-prisoner violence. In many countries abysmal prison conditions were life threatening, leading to inmate deaths from disease, malnutrition, and physical abuse' (Human Rights Watch 2002, p. 608; see also Foucault 1991; Stern 1998). The ill-treatment experienced by prisoners is documented by such organizations as the European Committee for the Prevention of Torture and Inhuman or Degrading Treatment or Punishment, Amnesty International and Human Rights Watch. Other groups that suffer severe loss of love, care and solidarity include homeless people, refugees and asylum seekers (Fanning, Veale and O'Connor 2001).

For most people, relations of love, care and solidarity are important sources of comfort and support in their daily lives. But these relationships are put under severe strain by many of the features of contemporary life. It is increasingly expected that all parents should be in paid work, with the result that in Britain the employment rates for fathers and mothers in couples is 90 per cent and 69 per cent respectively. More than one and a half million people provide at least 20 hours of care per week to a sick, disabled or elderly person; of these carers, 51 per cent of the men and 26 per cent of the women do paid work as well. Yet the more flexible and family-friendly working arrangements needed by parents and carers are still not widely available, and are much more likely to be provided to professionals than to manual workers (EOC 2000). More generally, the pressure on many people to work long hours in paid employment imposes burdens on their personal relationships and limits the time and energy they can devote to loving and caring.

### Inequalities of power

Inequalities of power are most obvious in authoritarian states that deny their citizens even the most basic rights. These inequalities are regularly reported by Amnesty International, Human Rights Watch and similar organizations. Their reports also show frequent abuses of power in democratic states, particularly in relation to political offences and penal systems. Another example of unequal power is the under-representation of women and ethnic minorities in national legislatures. In Europe, women make up about 40 to 45 per cent of the most equal parliaments (Norway and Sweden) but less than 10 per cent in the least equal (France, Greece, Hungary and Malta) (FCZB 2003). In western countries with substantial racial and ethnic minorities, these minorities are consistently under-represented in legislatures. African Americans make up 13 per cent of the US population but only 7 per cent of members of Congress (Amer 2003; Ethnic Majority 2003).

Unequal power exists in a wide range of settings. In the economy, the unequal power relationship between boss and worker is almost universal: it is the bedrock of the capitalist system. Inequality of power is pervasive not just in openly hierarchical organizations like armies, police forces, prisons and bureaucracies but in hospitals, schools, universities and religions. Unequal power is also a feature of families in most cultures regardless of their variations, systematically subordinating women and children to the power of men.

### Inequalities of working and learning

Although work has many rewards, it is also a substantial burden for most working people. But there are large differences among both individuals and countries in the burdens of work. The best quantitative data concern paid employees, and show that 'an average worker in Hong Kong, Mexico City or Istanbul works about 600 more hours a year than her or his counterpart in Berlin or Copenhagen or Amsterdam' (Sutcliffe 2001, graph 7). Average paid working hours range from under 1400 in the Netherlands and Norway to over 2400 in South Korea (ILO 2002). Work inequalities are strongly related to gender. Time use surveys in a range of countries show that nearly everywhere women work longer hours than men and that they generally perform between two-thirds and four-fifths of a society's unpaid work (UNDP 2002, Table 26).

Within the paid workforce, women, disabled people, ethnic minorities and other marginalized groups are disproportionately represented among the peripheral and casualized workers in all societies (Sayer 1997). While the proportion of women in professional jobs has increased (Smith 1993) women are still disproportionately represented among part-time and low paid workers (Acker 1992; Blackwell and Nolan 1990; Drew 1990; Hakim 1995). This trend is particularly evident in Ireland, where 23 per cent of all women employees work part-time compared with 5 per cent of men (Fahey, Russell and Smyth 2000, p. 264).[4]

Studies of non-monetary job characteristics have shown up very marked inequalities between different classes of workers. Jobs vary considerably in factors like dirtiness, repetitive tasks, control over one's own hours and activities and opportunities for learning. Inequalities in these features are strongly connected to gender, 'race' and class (Jencks, Perman and Rainwater 1988).

These inequalities of work are in many ways closely related to inequalities in learning. Although formal educational attainment is only one aspect of learning, it has important connections to other goods. Yet throughout the world it is simply taken for granted that there will be a pyramid of educational attainment, with fewer and fewer people completing higher levels in the education system. This inequality of educational attainment is clearly related to social class. In Ireland about 80 per cent of children with fathers in 'higher professional' occupations enter third-level education compared with only about 20 per cent of children with fathers in 'unskilled manual' occupations (Clancy 2001, p. 74). Although gender inequalities have been considerably reduced in recent years, women have a lower literacy rate than men in most societies (UNDP 2002, Table 22). 'Race' and ethnicity are reflected in inequalities of educational attainment: only about 13 per cent of African Americans have had four years of college compared with 24 per cent of white Americans (Hacker 1992, p. 234). Disabled people have also been excluded from education in many countries, making up less than 1 per cent of the third-level student population in Ireland (Hoey 2000) and only about 2 per cent in the UK and Germany (Skilbeck 2000, pp. 42–3).[5]

## Patterns of inequality

As this short survey has indicated, inequality has some clear patterns: patterns that will occupy us throughout this book. Social class is a major, taken-for-granted factor in the shape of inequalities. Privileged classes have more resources, higher status, more power, better working conditions and greater access to education. Their privileges also help to protect them against the worst deprivations of love and care although they are by no means fully secure in that regard. As we have noted, gender is another pervasive feature of inequality. Women are on the whole worse off in terms of resources, status, power, work and education than men. It is harder to judge the gender gap in relation to love, care and solidarity, except to note that women demonstrably do much more of the work involved in sustaining these relationships while at the same time experiencing greater degrees of domestic violence.

'Race' and ethnicity are strongly implicated in how inequalities are patterned in most societies.[6] An example to which we will repeatedly refer in this book is the situation of Irish Travellers, an ethnic minority of about 30 000 people – just under 1 per cent of the Irish population. Travellers have a tradition of nomadism, and although about half of them now live in houses, the other half continue to live in caravans (mobile homes) located on roadsides or on government-provided sites of varying standards. While Travellers speak English, they also have a separate language, 'cant' or 'gammon', which is spoken among themselves. The needs of Travellers have been consistently ignored in Irish public affairs, resulting in exceptionally high levels of poverty, severe popular prejudice, an almost complete lack of influence on public policy, high levels of unemployment and low levels of formal education.[7] Although anti-Traveller racism is distinct from the forms of racism most familiar in the UK, US and other developed countries because of the absence of a 'colour line', it shares many of the same features and results in similar deprivations.

Another social division that plays an important role in structuring the inequalities of most societies is disability, on which we accept the general lines of analysis set out by the so-called 'social' (as contrasted with 'medical') model of disability. The fundamental distinction of the social model is between impairment and disability. Impairments are the physical and psychological differences between disabled people and people with 'normal' capabilities. By contrast, disability is the process by which societies prevent people with impairments from realizing their full potential and from participating as fully as possible in activities that others take for granted. Impairment does not necessarily result in disability: for example, many people with impaired eyesight are able to participate fully in society because they have access to eyeglasses. But social institutions are often designed in ways that exclude people with impairments, the most obvious case being the way in which buildings with steps have failed to accommodate people with mobility impairments. This social exclusion – this disabling – of people with impairments generates inequalities in all the dimensions we have referred to above.[8]

A fifth social division that features repeatedly in our discussion is based on sexual orientation. In predominantly Christian societies of the sort we are most familiar with, a sharp distinction has traditionally been made between the 'normal' practice of heterosexual relationships and 'perverted' sexual orientations towards members of one's own sex. Gay men, lesbians, bisexuals and transsexuals form a set of generally despised groups for which inequalities of respect and recognition – inequalities captured by the idea of homophobia – are central. These inequalities have legitimated discrimination, leading to inequalities of working and learning, of resources and of power. Homophobia has also had a severe impact on the opportunities of members of these groups for establishing relations of love, care and solidarity with others.

These social divisions do not exhaust the range of factors on which inequalities have been and continue to be erected. Age plays an important role in structuring inequality in every society. Differences between indigenous and settler populations are important in nearly all ex-colonial societies. Some of the factors that typically mark ethnic difference, such as language, nationality and religion, can be independently important. Other specific groups that suffer from inequality include prisoners and ex-prisoners, people with mental illnesses, refugees and asylum-seekers and economic migrants. We refer to some of the issues affecting these and other social groups in what follows. However, our aim is not to provide a comprehensive sociology of inequality but to pursue the more normative, practical questions of how to promote equality. We concentrate on inequalities of class, gender, ethnicity, disability and sexual orientation because these are divisions that are particularly prominent in our own experience and are likely to resonate with a wide variety of readers.[9]

## Responses to inequality

### Responses by social movements

The inequalities we have surveyed, and the catalogue of inequalities from which they are drawn, are not new, although their specific character has changed over time. Throughout history they have generated both covert and open resistance. In the modern era, resistance to inequality has been taken up by various social movements, often based on the social divisions already mentioned. Class inequality is at the centre of the labour and community development movements. Gender inequality is at the heart of the women's movement. Racism was at the core of the Civil Rights movement in the US and is the focus of anti-racist movements more generally. There are social movements in many countries centred on disability and sexual orientation. And there are movements concerned with ageism, the rights of indigenous peoples, religious equality and so on. Other social movements with an egalitarian agenda, such as the human rights movement, are not so closely tied to specific social divisions. We say more about egalitarian movements and the challenges they face in Part III of this book. But it is important to mention them here because we cannot understand the responses by either governments or academics to inequality without recognizing that these are not the result of their own goodwill but of the resistance of subordinate groups.

### Responses by states and interstate organizations

In recent years, egalitarian movements have extracted a number of concessions from governments, although these concessions have always been vulnerable to political changes and have often been reversed. The most prominent changes have probably been in the area of anti-discrimination legislation. In the US, the Civil Rights Act of 1964 was a milestone in the struggle to reverse racial discrimination. Although the attempt to incorporate gender equality into the Constitution in the form of the Equal Rights Amendment failed, there has been a considerable amount of legislation outlawing discrimination on the basis of gender. The Americans with Disabilities Act of 1990 set new standards for preventing discrimination against disabled people. Many US states passed anti-discrimination laws in relation to sexual orientation, and although some continued to criminalize gay sex, the Supreme Court declared such laws unconstitutional in 2003.[10]

In Europe, there has been anti-discrimination legislation at both EU level and within individual states. The EEC prohibited gender discrimination in pay from the start, in the Treaty of Rome. The biggest recent changes have been directives based on Article 13 of Amsterdam Treaty, which extended the scope of anti-discrimination law to a much wider set of grounds and in some cases a wider range of issues. Individual European states have varied in their approach to anti-discrimination legislation. In Ireland, the Employment Equality Act 1998 and the Equal Status Act 2000 consolidated and extended anti-discrimination legislation in relation to nine categories of people and established the Equality Authority and the Equality Tribunal.[11] In other countries, such as the UK, anti-discrimination policy is located in a set of laws dealing separately with 'race', gender and other forms of discrimination.

As we discuss in depth in Chapter 7, what is notable about most of this legislation is its concern with combating discrimination rather than with trying to achieve greater equality in the conditions of people's lives. At its best, it calls for positive action to help members of subordinate groups to access services and to compete in the labour market. But it does not challenge the inequalities of reward, power and prestige of different jobs and does little to change the social structures that produce inequality.

The laws normally referred to as equality legislation are only a fraction of the legislation that affects equality and inequality. For example, changes in tax codes and welfare provisions have profound effects on inequality of income. Tax cuts for people with high income and welfare reforms that, at best, fail to keep pace with average earnings and at worst remove support from the most vulnerable are clearly anti-egalitarian (Goodman and Shephard

2002, p. 31; Korpi and Palme 2003). Legislation that fails to control the disposal of hazardous waste has devastating effects on the environments of marginalized communities (Szasz 1994). International regulations promulgated by the World Trade Organization have major implications for the living conditions of countless people throughout the world. Of course it is impossible to generalize over all these different areas of state and interstate activity, but it would be hard to maintain that they have been strongly conducive to equality in recent years. Perhaps the most one can say is that egalitarian social movements have stopped them from being worse.

### Responses by the academy

Within educational institutions, the rise of egalitarian social movements has had some positive effects.[12] The most striking advance has been the development of women's studies as an interdisciplinary field. Because it is rooted in the women's movement, women's studies has always had an interest not just in analysing the experience of women but in transforming gender relations. Both the analysis and the transformation have been differently conceived according to the different forms of feminism that have developed over the last 40 years or so. The liberal feminism found in the work of Friedan (1963) and Kanter (1977), echoing the classical arguments of Mary Wollstonecraft (1792), Harriet Taylor Mill (1851) and John Stuart Mill (1869), sees the problem largely in terms of the exclusion of women from a public sphere dominated and defined by men; the solution is to provide women with an equal opportunity to enter that sphere. By contrast, radical feminists such as Millett (1970), Firestone (1970), Brownmiller (1975), Dworkin (1981) and Daly (1978, 1984) place women's sexuality at the heart of the feminist agenda. While some have seen a solution in the development of egalitarian heterosexual relations, others have promoted lesbian separatism and a women-controlled counter-culture. Another strand of feminist thinking has its origins in the Marxist tradition and specifically the work of Engels (1845). Focusing on the issue of women's paid and unpaid labour, socialist feminists such as Barrett (1980), Mitchell (1984) and Delphy and Leonard (1992) attempt to explain the interrelationships between capitalism and patriarchy in the oppression of women, developing the Marxist concept of exploitation and applying it to the family. On this analysis, the transformation that women need extends through both the family and the economy. These brief remarks only review the types of feminism prominent in the early years of women's studies, which has continued to develop new perspectives including psychoanalytic feminism, postmodernist feminism, global feminism and black feminism. They do, however, illustrate the diversity of approaches in the field of women's studies and the interplay between the empirical analysis of women's oppression and the normative commitment to women's liberation.

Another area in which an egalitarian social movement has produced important academic developments is disability. The study of disability traditionally occurred in several disciplines but especially in medicine, psychology, education and social policy. In all of these disciplines, the disabled person was traditionally defined as the 'Other', the person whom the researcher was not, but about whom the researcher could speak. Disability was presented as a social, psychological, educational or medical 'problem' which had to be resolved. Disability studies has emerged as a space where disabled people can speak for themselves and conduct their own analysis of the ways in which disabled people are excluded and oppressed. Developing the social model of disability to which we have already referred, writers such as Finkelstein (1980), Oliver (1990) and Barnes (1991, 1996) have shifted the focus from the individual, medical condition of disabled people to the disabling structures of society. Disability studies is not yet either as clearly defined or as intellectually diverse as women's studies. However, important new perspectives have developed particularly in relation to the interface between gender and disability (Deegan and Brooks 1985; Morris 1989, 1991), the role of culture in defining and reinforcing disability (Shakespeare 1994) and the interplay of impairment and disability (French 1997).

Other social movements have developed their own academic counterparts. For example, the anti-racist movement has generated ethnic and racial studies. Queer studies has emerged from the lesbian, gay and bisexual movement. The human rights movement has stimulated corresponding academic programmes. Even in the area of development studies, which had an essentially top-down origin against the backdrop of the Cold War, solidarity movements in the North and resistance movements in the South have had a significant impact, questioning western dominance over the definition of development and prioritizing the needs and perspectives of local communities.

A common feature of these areas of study is their interdisciplinary basis, reflecting an awareness of the multifaceted nature of inequality. Another common theme is their rejection of the tendency of the social sciences to make a sharp division between the normative and the empirical and to pretend that what academics do can be detached from their moral and political commitments. It is not a question of allowing those commitments to override the attempt to discover the truth about the social world, but rather about their providing a point and direction to research and teaching. This commitment to a synthesis of normative and empirical concerns has given a new impetus to attempts to articulate a coherent and defensible moral foundation for the types of study in question and to think about the types of social transformation necessary for creating a better world.

But there is a further common feature of these intellectual developments. It is that as each of these areas of studies has grown, it has come to recognize the importance of cross-cutting social divisions. This is most clearly marked in women's studies, where there has been considerable debate and agonizing over the suggestion that what feminist scholars were expressing in the early years was in fact the experience of white, middle class, heterosexual women living in rich countries. So women's studies has been pressed to find ways of incorporating the different experiences of women of colour, working class women, lesbians and women from the South. Similarly, feminists have complained about a gender bias in disability studies. It is clear that the same kinds of questions can be raised throughout the disciplines we have been discussing: questions about how to accommodate all the social differences that affect people's perspectives and agendas. One response to these challenges is fragmentation: to say that what we need is no longer women's studies or disability studies but a variety of studies focusing on ever more specific sets of characteristics. An alternative response is to develop an expanded set of studies that recognizes all of these issues within a coherent framework. That is what equality studies attempts to achieve.

## Equality Studies as a response to inequality

The deep, patterned inequalities of our world are there for all to see. If we think that these inequalities are wrong and want to change them, it is not enough to think of them solely from the point of view of workers or women or disabled people. We need to find a way of addressing them that incorporates all of these perspectives without attempting to ignore their differences. In this section, we set out the central questions of equality studies as it has developed in the Equality Studies Centre at University College Dublin.[13] We try to show that it is a coherent response to cross-cutting inequalities. As an interdisciplinary field that combines both normative and empirical enquiry and aims at transformation, it is similar to the fields of women's studies, disability studies and the like. What distinguishes it is its concern with the whole range of inequalities, its attempt to articulate and defend its normative commitments and its emphasis on how to achieve social change. While all of these features are to some degree present in other areas of study, they are central constituents of equality studies.

### Central questions of equality studies

The central concerns of equality studies can be expressed in terms of six interrelated sets of questions. Together they set out a new, coherent field of enquiry.

   1. *What are the central, significant, dominant patterns of inequality in our society, western capitalist society more generally, and, more generally still, the world at large?* An initial task of equality studies is simply to get a grip on

the scale and patterns of existing inequalities. How are income and wealth distributed among households and individuals? What are the differences in income and occupational status between men and women? How do different classes compare in access to education? Which ethnic groups are discriminated against and denied basic rights? What are the basic facts about the global distribution of resources? Who enjoys, and who is deprived of, relations of love, care and solidarity? We have cited some of the answers to these questions earlier in this chapter. Although this is essentially a descriptive task, it provides an indispensable backdrop for a wide range of egalitarian concerns.

2. *What are the best ways of explaining these inequalities, using which overall frameworks?* Contemporary social science is awash with explanatory frameworks: rational choice theory, systems theory, structuralism, poststructuralism, functionalism, hermeneutics, Marxism in its various versions, critical theory, psychoanalytic approaches and so on, each with their internal conflicts and sub-divisions. We cannot study inequality without making use of such frameworks, but there is certainly no consensus, even among egalitarians, on which of them are most helpful. So equality studies must operate pluralistically, encouraging work within different paradigms and learning what we can about the causes of inequality from each of many traditions. This part of equality studies is probably its most heavily researched area, although the explanation of inequality is sometimes hampered by disciplinary boundaries. Explaining inequality is a core concern in sociology, economics, political science, geography and the interdisciplinary fields we have mentioned above. For this reason, we do not devote much space in this book to explanatory research, although we rely on it when necessary. In Chapter 4 we do set out some of the key assumptions that we make in analysing inequality since these inform what we say in Parts II and III.

3. *What are the central principles or objectives of equality? What in principle are egalitarians trying to achieve? How strong are the arguments for and against these principles?* There are many possible conceptions of equality. It is clearly a central problem for equality studies to articulate these conceptions and explore their interrelations and relative merits. There has been a considerable amount of theoretical work in this area in the last 35 years.[14] A common feature of this work is to consider the relationship between equality and other normative concerns, such as freedom, community, cultural diversity, individual well-being, sexual difference, environmental values and so on. Although there is no consensus on either the formulation or justification of egalitarian principles, it is clear that these contributions nevertheless form a distinct theoretical family.

A great deal of egalitarian theory concerns the problem of defining the egalitarian ideal: an ideal that we will call, following Tawney (1964), 'equality of condition'. It is also worthwhile distinguishing more limited objectives that can be treated as intermediate steps to equality. Setting out an egalitarian ideal does not itself decide the case between radical and reformist political strategies, nor is it meant to distract us from urgent action to secure basic needs and other human rights. In Chapter 2, we attempt to provide a relatively inclusive framework for thinking about equality. In Chapter 3 we try to show how the framework relates to values that are not at first sight closely connected to equality.

As Sen (1992) has noted, setting out a coherent conception of equality is closely connected to setting out the case for equality so defined. That task has both a positive and a negative side. The positive side is to put forward the arguments in favour of equality, or to put it more precisely, to show why people should endorse a particular conception of equality as the right principle or set of principles for evaluating and governing our social relations. The negative side is to put the case against anti-egalitarian principles: to undermine the justifications that have been given for maintaining unequal social relationships. In this book we treat the case for equality as given. Although we occasionally mention arguments for or against equality, our concern is with questions that arise once equality is accepted as a goal. In Chapter 2 we sketch the logic of the argument that takes us from basic equality to liberal equality and from there to equality of condition. In Chapter 3 we draw connections and contrasts between equality and other values. In Chapter 5 we review evidence showing that equality is good for economic growth and efficiency. In Chapter 6 we respond to the claim that political equality is unrealistic. In Chapter 8 we review the case for equality in education. But for a full account of why equality matters, we refer the reader to other sources.[15]

4. *What are the best institutional frameworks for achieving equality in different spheres and contexts?* The institutional parallel to setting out egalitarian principles or objectives is to set out the case for corresponding social institutions, in the broad sense of economic and political structures, legal systems, educational systems, family forms and so on. Although there has been a tremendous amount of relevant work in this area, it has rarely had an explicitly egalitarian focus. There have been many discussions of models of socialism, and particularly of the use of markets within broadly socialist economies. But although issues about distribution usually arise at some point or other in these discussions, the egalitarian case for socialism is only given a central role by a few authors (e.g. Roemer 1994; Schweickart 1994). References to the idea of political equality are more prominent in the considerable literature on participatory democracy. Yet only a few treatments are based on an integrated conception of the role of participatory democracy in a wider egalitarian project (e.g. Bowles and Gintis 1987; Green 1985). Similar remarks could be made about work on other social institutions. Situating these discussions within an equality studies framework can help to bring out more clearly the purposes of alternative institutions and their role in a coherent vision of an egalitarian social order.

As with egalitarian principles, we can talk about both the social institutions necessary for a fully egalitarian society and other more limited reforms. The institutions of contemporary welfare states are not directed towards full equality, but do aspire to certain limited egalitarian objectives such as the elimination of poverty and the satisfaction of some basic needs. How these institutions can be reformed to achieve these limited goals more effectively is a perfectly legitimate question for contemporary egalitarians.

Because this area of equality studies is undeveloped, we have prioritized it for this book. In Part II, we discuss some of the changes equality calls for in economic, political, legal and educational institutions. Although each chapter takes up only a selection of the huge number of questions that arise, we hope that the range of institutional contexts and problems demonstrates the value of addressing these issues within an equality studies framework.

5. *Within a given institutional context, what policies would best promote equality?* Whether we are concerned with the 'utopian' question of a fully egalitarian society or the reformist question of improving the world as it stands, the state and other institutions face a range of policy options that may be more or less egalitarian. A large amount of contemporary work in social policy is concerned with this question, often in connection with limited objectives like equal opportunity and the relief of poverty. Well-known examples are debates around affirmative action and welfare reform. There is no precise borderline between major policy initiatives and institutional reform (question 4), but some issues are clearly on one side or the other. In Part II, we draw attention to the relation between broader institutional issues and more specific policy choices. For example, we note that the institutions of participatory democracy require policies on how political activity is financed. But we recognize that policy issues tend to be even more dependent on local contexts than institutional questions.

6. *What are the best political strategies for promoting equality, given our vision of equality, our understanding of the causes of inequality, and the (corresponding?) obstacles to achieving equality?* Work on egalitarian principles, institutions and policies is concerned with both the long-term goal of an egalitarian society and more immediate reforms. How are these changes to be brought about? To develop practical strategies for promoting equality, we need an understanding of social change rooted in the successes and failures of egalitarian movements. In Part III we put forward some ideas about these issues although our discussion is far from comprehensive. But if equality studies is to have any point, then these questions of political strategy are as much on its agenda as the more familiar tasks of describing, explaining and philosophizing.

The six groups of questions set out above are by no means definitive of a field that is only in its early stages of development, and they are in any case rather open-ended. For example, it might be suggested that equality studies should explicitly include questions about the history of equality and egalitarianism, treating these as a distinct branch of enquiry. Perhaps equality studies should also highlight the question of personal transformation: what changes do we have to make in our own lives here and now if we claim to take equality seriously?[16] It would be foolish to treat the six sets of questions as exhaustive, but they do establish a coherent core for the study of equality.

With such a wide range of questions to address, it is clear that equality studies has to be an interdisciplinary project that uses skills and knowledge drawn from political theory, empirical politics, sociology, education, law, economics, psychology and probably other disciplines as well. Like any co-operative project, it must operate on the basis of a certain division of labour – no one has to know everything – but it is important for its practitioners to listen to and learn from each other if their cooperation is to be as fruitful as possible. The fact that this book is the outcome of cooperation among people with different disciplinary backgrounds is intended to show both the necessity and the benefits of a cooperative, interdisciplinary approach.

But regardless of disciplinary origin, we believe that the study of equality entails a fundamental shift in how research is conducted. Egalitarians cannot be satisfied with traditional methods of research that are remote from and in many cases exploitative of the disadvantaged people academics have sought to examine. In Chapter 9 we set out an understanding of emancipatory research that involves partnership and dialogue with disadvantaged social groups. That process has had a profound effect on this book, since virtually all of the ideas we set forward here have arisen from and developed through the ongoing dialogues we have been privileged to be part of since 1989.

Equality studies aims not just to understand but to change the world. It is therefore essentially normative and sees knowledge as having a role to play in transforming social structures. As an unavoidably political form of enquiry, it is rooted in and aspires to express the understandings and priorities of egalitarian social movements. In these respects it shares many of the characteristics of, and is built on, similar projects such as Marxism, critical theory and the interdisciplinary fields of enquiry discussed above. Our aim is not to 'convert' practitioners in these fields to the idea of equality studies, but to show that there is a way of connecting up the work of these fields into a coherent overall project.

## Guide to the rest of this book

In the rest of this book, we focus on three of the central questions of equality studies. In Part I, we concentrate on the theory of equality. Chapter 2 compares basic equality and liberal egalitarianism with what we call equality of condition, and defines equality of condition in five key dimensions.

Chapter 3 explains why we take equality to be the central value of progressive politics. Chapter 4 analyses the contexts within which equality and inequality are created and reinforced, and sketches an account of the relationship between social systems and social groups.

In Part II, we turn to the institutional and policy implications of equality of condition. Chapter 5 considers some of the issues involved in promoting greater equality of income and puts forward an institutional proposal for doing so. Chapter 6 sets out a programme of participatory democracy as a way of institutionalizing equality in the political system. Chapter 7 considers some of the ways that the legal system has been used to protect, and occasionally to challenge, structured inequalities, and proposes some changes that would make it more amenable to the claims of subordinate groups, particularly in relation to laws about work. Chapter 8 turns to the education system and proposes a set of changes that would foster equality of condition in its various dimensions. Chapter 9 focuses on the field of research and sets out an egalitarian policy of emancipatory research. This choice of issues and contexts is of course only a fragment of the egalitarian agenda, based on what we feel we are best equipped to talk about. Some of the areas conspicuous by their absence are the global economic order, the family and criminal justice, and we have only touched on some other important areas such as the mass media. But we hope we have addressed a wide enough range of issues to indicate what a comprehensive treatment would look like.

In Part III, we turn to political strategies for advancing the equality agenda. In Chapter 10 we contrast the classic Marxist model of achieving social change with a social movement model, arguing that there is already a thriving, international equality movement that is rooted in a wide variety of struggles focusing not just on class but on gender, ethnicity, disability, sexuality and other relations of inequality. Chapter 11 addresses the ideological challenge facing the equality movement, and argues that we need to tap into those aspects of our shared beliefs that are currently downplayed by the dominant voices in the public sphere, in particular beliefs about care and interdependence. In Chapter 12 we discuss some strategic issues for the equality movement, including coordination problems, the role of political parties, working inside and outside the system, and the interplay of ends and means.

The struggle for greater equality belongs to a world-wide movement that has taken a variety of forms over the centuries. Although each of its participants engages in specific actions motivated by their own concerns and perspectives, we all have something to say and something to learn from others. In this book, we write from the experience of living in Ireland, which furnishes many of our examples. As a small country on the fringe of Europe with a post-colonial heritage, Ireland differs in many ways from large, powerful countries like the United States or Britain. But we do not think that the fundamental issues of inequality and oppression are all that different. Perhaps the greatest apparent difference is the degree of cultural homogeneity that has characterized Ireland since the 1920s, but even in this respect there are important cultural conflicts beneath the surface, the most striking of which is the treatment of Travellers by the settled population. There are much more important contrasts between the problems Ireland faces as a stable liberal democracy with a high standard of living and those faced by countries with very different political institutions or mass destitution. For that reason, and out of reluctance to join other privileged Northerners in preaching to the South, we address ourselves primarily to problems of inequality within well-off democracies. We very much hope that our ideas resonate with the experience of others, North and South, but we leave it to readers to judge that for themselves.

# 2
# Dimensions of Equality:
# A Framework for Theory and Action

In this chapter we provide a framework for thinking about equality, concentrating on the normative question: what ideals of equality should we believe in? We identify five dimensions of equality and use them to distinguish between what we call basic equality, liberal egalitarianism and equality of condition. What emerges is a spectrum of views with increasingly ambitious goals for developed societies and, by implication, for the relation between these societies and the rest of the world. We argue that there is a natural path from basic equality to the beliefs of liberal egalitarians and from those beliefs to equality of condition. We start by saying something about the idea of equality and why it generates so many different meanings. We then discuss each of the three views in turn, concentrating on comparing liberal egalitarianism and equality of condition in each of the five dimensions. Towards the end of the chapter we outline how this normative framework can be applied to different social groups.

## The idea of equality

Looked at in a very general way, equality is a relationship, of some kind or other, between two or more people or groups of people, regarding some aspect of those people's lives. If equality were a simple idea, it would be obvious what this relationship is, who it is about and what aspect of their lives it concerns. Unfortunately, none of these is obvious, and that is why there are many different conceptions of equality.

For a start, the idea of equality is sometimes applied to individuals and sometimes to groups. When the Universal Declaration of Human Rights states that 'All human beings are born free and equal in dignity and rights' (Article 1), it is referring to each and every individual person. But for good reasons, equality is often discussed in terms of groups, such as women or ethnic minorities. And of course there are many different and overlapping groups, even in relatively homogeneous societies. Equality between men and women, for instance, would not necessarily involve equality between middle class and working class people or equality between disabled and non-disabled people. So one question about equality is 'equality between whom?' (Young 2001a).

People can be equal or unequal in many different ways. Should we be interested in whether they have equally good lives overall – in their overall well-being or 'welfare'? Or should we have more tangible aims, like equality of income and wealth? Should we focus on outcomes such as educational attainment, or on the opportunities people have for achieving these? The question here is 'equality of what?' (Sen 1982).

Even the task of defining the relationship of equality can be approached in different ways. The clearest case is where two groups or individuals have the same amount of something, such as the same incomes. But this is a limited model of equality. The aim of ensuring that everyone's basic needs are satisfied is surely an egalitarian one, even though this may not involve an equal distribution of anything in particular. Again, it is widely considered egalitarian to give priority to the worst off, even if this does not go so far as to ensure that everyone is *equally* well off.[1] And it is a recognizably egalitarian position to say that there should be a much *more* equal distribution of income, even if no one thinks that incomes should be absolutely equal. To take a different kind of example, a relationship in which a husband dominates his wife is clearly an unequal relationship. But domination is not really a matter of having different *amounts* of something (Young 1990, ch. 1). So a third question is 'what type of relationship?'

Thus, equality can be defined in terms of both individuals and a wide variety of groups, it can relate to many different dimensions of people's lives and it can refer to many different types of relationship, all of these differences having some kind of basis in the idea of treating people as equals. It follows that far from being a single idea, equality refers to countless ideas, which may have very different implications and may even be incompatible (Rae *et al.* 1981). Another consequence of this variety of ideas of equality is that what we think of as an egalitarian political outlook may be better expressed in terms of a set of related principles of equality rather than in terms of a single principle. It may even be that different types of egalitarian consider their views to be based on the same fundamental principles of equality and differ most in terms of what they think these principles entail.

Over the last century, there have been many attempts to define equality and to classify types of egalitarianism. The framework developed here is only one alternative, which we think is particularly relevant to contemporary developed societies and to the interdisciplinary and practical project of equality studies. We try to relate it to some of the major theorists of equality, but they do not all fit in very neatly, for two main reasons. One is that a lot of recent theorizing has concerned philosophical questions about fundamental principles of equality. Our framework operates at a different level. It is intended for more practical use and is meant to be compatible with a variety of answers to those fundamental questions. A second, related reason is that our categories are meant to distinguish broad approaches to equality rather than to analyse particular theories, and broad classifications always involve a certain amount of simplification and generalization. Theorizing about equality is constantly challenged both by new academic work and even more importantly by social movements of the marginalized and oppressed. The framework below is meant for now, not forever. It is meant to be open enough to allow for different interpretations and perspectives. And it is designed to be relatively *à la carte*: to allow for someone to have liberal egalitarian views in one respect, while believing in equality of condition in another.

## Basic equality

Basic equality is the cornerstone of all egalitarian thinking: the idea that at some very basic level all human beings have equal worth and importance, and are therefore equally worthy of concern and respect. It is not easy to explain quite what these ideas amount to, since many of the people who claim to hold them defend a wide range of other inequalities, including the view that some people deserve more concern and respect than others. Perhaps what is really involved in basic equality is the idea that every human being deserves some basic minimum of concern and respect, placing at least some limits on what it is to treat someone as a human being. At any rate, that is how we will define basic equality here.[2]

The minimum standards involved in the idea of basic equality are far from trivial. They include prohibitions against inhuman and degrading treatment, protection against blatant violence and at least some commitment to satisfying people's most basic needs.[3] In a world in which rape, torture and other crimes against humanity are a daily occurrence, and in which millions of people die every year from want of the most basic necessities, the idea of basic equality remains a powerful force for action and for change. Yet taken on its own it remains a rather minimalist idea. On its own, it does not challenge widespread inequalities in people's living conditions or even in their civil rights or educational and economic opportunities. It calls on us to prevent inhumanity, but it does not necessarily couch its message in terms of justice as distinct from charity. These stronger ideas only arise in more robust forms of egalitarianism, of the sort to which the rest of this chapter is devoted.

It is surprisingly hard to provide any *arguments* for basic equality. Most people take it for granted that inhuman treatment and destitution are wrong; these ideas seem to be built into the very idea of morality. They are in any case the common assumptions of nearly all modern political outlooks. We will not survey all these outlooks here. Instead, we will concentrate on a variety of ideas that are particularly important for our times and that can all claim to be genuinely egalitarian.

## Liberal egalitarianism

Liberalism has itself been interpreted in many different ways, all of them embracing basic equality but varying quite a lot in terms of the other types of equality they believe in. We mean to include among what we call liberal egalitarians only those liberals who, on the one hand, move well beyond basic equality and, on the other, hold views that are clearly distinct from what we call equality of condition.[4] Their positions, which might be called 'left liberalism', are often found in social democratic political movements. Liberal egalitarians in this sense typically define equality in terms of individuals rather than groups. But beyond this common assumption, they hold a wide range of views.

### Equality of what?

Liberal egalitarians vary considerably in their replies to the question, 'equality of what?'[5] What ultimately matters, surely, is people's well-being: how well their lives are actually going. So in thinking about equality, one's first impulse is to call for equality of well-being. Unfortunately, that principle faces some serious problems. First of all, people have very different conceptions of what their well-being consists in – very different values concerning the good life. It would be wrong to define equality in a way that reflected only one view about what matters in life. A second major problem is to build into egalitarian principles an appropriate recognition of people's responsibility for their own lives. Even a basic respect for individuals implies a respect for their ability to make important choices in their lives, which may work out for better or worse. By contrast, strict equality of well-being would seem to commit us to taking collective responsibility for every aspect of people's lives. For these reasons, all contemporary egalitarian theorists have moved at least one step away from the idea of equality of well-being, emphasizing in one way or another the conditions that enable people to pursue their own aims rather than well-being itself. But they disagree on how these conditions should be specified.

Below, we identify some of the key factors that affect nearly everyone's well-being or quality of life. We treat these as five *dimensions of equality*, namely:

- respect and recognition
- resources
- love, care and solidarity
- power
- working and learning.

In choosing these five dimensions, we hope to provide a framework that not only helps to map the differences between liberal egalitarians and equality of condition, but also makes it easier to analyse inequality and to develop institutions and policies for the future. We recognize that the five dimensions do not necessarily pick out every aspect of equality and inequality that may be of sociological or political interest. But we think the categories are sufficiently broad to cover most of the issues that concern contemporary egalitarians.[6]

**What kind of relationship?**

A key assumption of the views we describe as liberal egalitarian is that there will always be major inequalities between people in their status, resources, work and power. The role of the idea of equality is to provide a fair basis for managing these inequalities, by strengthening the minimum to which everyone is entitled and by using equality of opportunity to regulate the competition for advantage.[7] Liberal egalitarians vary in both these respects. For some, the minimum to which all should be entitled barely differs from basic equality. Others have a more generous idea of the minimum, for example by using an expanded idea of what counts as a basic need or by defining poverty in relation to the normal activities of a particular society. The most ambitious liberal principle is Rawls's 'difference principle', which states that 'social and economic inequalities' should work 'to the greatest benefit of the least advantaged' members of society (Rawls 1971, p. 83; 1993, p. 6; 2001, pp. 42–3).

Liberal equality of opportunity means that people should in some sense have an equal chance to compete for social advantages. This principle has two major interpretations. The first, non-discrimination or 'formal' equal opportunity, is classically expressed in the French Declaration of the Rights of Man (1789) as the principle that all citizens 'are equally eligible for all positions, posts and public employments in accordance with their abilities' (Article 6). A stronger form of equal opportunity insists that people should not be advantaged or hampered by their social background and that their prospects in life should depend entirely on their own effort and abilities. Rawls calls this principle 'fair equal opportunity' (1971, p. 73; 2001, pp. 43–4).[8]

To make these ideas more concrete, we now look at the five dimensions of equality and at some of the ways in which liberal egalitarians have applied the ideas of a minimum standard and equal opportunity in each case.

## 1. Respect and recognition: universal citizenship, toleration and the private sphere

A fundamental element in the thinking of liberal egalitarians is their commitment to 'social' equality in the sense of recognizing the equal public status of all citizens and of tolerating individual and group differences, so long as they respect basic rights. The principle that in the public realm we all share an equal status as citizens is a long-standing democratic belief. The idea is that regardless of our relations in other, non-public spheres – the economy, religion, family life, private associations – we should relate to each other as equals when we are interacting politically as citizens. In this public sphere, we should abstract from all those differences of class, gender, ethnicity and so on that differentiate us from each other, and meet on the basis of our common identity as citizens. This principle of equal status is reflected in such practices as universal suffrage and the decline in the use of differentiating titles (Miller 1997, ch. 11; Walzer 1985, ch. 11). Although liberal egalitarians have differed to some extent over who should be granted the status of citizenship, the typical view is that citizenship should extend to all permanent residents regardless of gender or social background.

The idea of toleration is another deeply entrenched part of the liberal tradition, arising from the religious conflicts of the sixteenth and seventeenth centuries. The citizens of modern, pluralist societies disagree in many ways about what matters in life and how we should live, and these disagreements are embodied in their different religious commitments, cultural traditions, sexual preferences, family values and so on. We have different 'conceptions of the good', as it is sometimes put. Each of us may deeply disapprove of the values of others. But rather than act to suppress these values and impose our own, we should tolerate them and 'live and let live'. This toleration is embedded in freedom of conscience and opinion and in the protection of personal relationships from outside interference. It supports the idea that the basic constitutional arrangements of our societies should as far as possible be impartial among these different beliefs.

These elements of the thinking of liberal egalitarians are related to the distinction they make in the name of personal freedom between those aspects of human life that are subject to social and legal regulation and those that are protected against any such interference, a distinction sometimes phrased in terms of the 'public' versus the 'private'.[9] The idea of religious toleration was facilitated by thinking of religious belief and practice as a private concern that was not an appropriate object of public regulation. Another less explicit and now more controversial exemption was the realm of the family, allowing for male dominance of family affairs regardless of the degree to which women were able to achieve equality in other areas. Neither of these exemptions has been absolute – religions aren't allowed to perform blood sacrifices, husbands aren't allowed to murder their wives. But the public/private distinction, coupled with the principle of toleration, has protected important spheres of life from egalitarian challenges.[10]

Although these ideas of universal citizenship, toleration and the private sphere are meant to define a sense in which every member of society has an equal status, they are generally considered by liberal egalitarians to be compatible with huge differences in social esteem. Everyone has a right to the status of citizen, but social esteem has to be earned by achievement and is therefore inevitably unequal. In this regard, as in others, it is more accurate to think of liberal egalitarianism as combining the idea of a minimum entitlement with the idea of equal opportunity than to see it as committed to strictly equal respect (cf. Walzer 1985, ch. 11).

## 2.  Resources: poverty relief and the difference principle

The second dimension of liberal egalitarianism concerns the distribution of what can be called resources in a wide sense of the term. The most obvious resources are income and wealth, and these are the resources that liberal egalitarians typically concentrate on. Assuming that significant inequality in the distribution of resources is inevitable, liberal egalitarians again aim to regulate this inequality by combining a minimum floor or safety net with a principle of equal opportunity. The minimum floor is a logical extension of the basic egalitarian commitment to satisfying basic human needs and is an element of the modern welfare state. Quite where the floor should be and how it should be defined are continuing issues for liberal egalitarians, illustrated in debates about whether poverty is 'absolute' or 'relative' and whether it can be defined entirely in terms of income or has to include other resources. The key point is that most liberal egalitarians are more concerned with eliminating poverty than promoting equality of resources.

A more demanding liberal egalitarian principle, at least in theory, is Rawls's difference principle. Like other liberal egalitarians, Rawls assumes that there will be major inequalities of income and wealth, explaining that 'the function of unequal distributive shares is to cover the costs of training and education, to attract individuals to places and associations where they are most needed from a social point of view, and so on' (1971, p. 315). But rather than aiming simply at bringing everyone above the poverty line, the worst off should be brought as high up the scale as possible. How far this approach takes us towards full equality of resources depends on the degree of inequality necessary to perform the function Rawls sees for it. So it is hard to judge in practical terms quite how much the difference principle departs from an anti-poverty position.[11]

Because liberal egalitarians take inequality of resources to be inevitable, they are concerned to ensure that the competition for advantage is as fair as possible and that it is governed by equal opportunity. One of the most difficult problems for liberal egalitarians is that this is a forlorn hope. Major social and economic inequalities inevitably undermine all but the thinnest forms of equal opportunity, because privileged parents will always find ways of advantaging their children in an unequal society.[12]

## 3.  Love, care and solidarity: a private affair

The third dimension of equality we want to identify is conspicuous by its absence from the work of most liberal egalitarians. It is the dimension of love, care and solidarity. When we think of the conditions human beings typically need for even a minimally decent life, it is clear enough that relations of love, care and solidarity belong on the list, a point too obvious to labour. But when we turn to the work of liberal egalitarians, there is little discussion of these important goods. One line of feminist criticism of liberal egalitarianism has taken this absence to be a symptom of a misplaced emphasis on justice, and has contrasted this approach with the idea of an ethic of care (Benhabib 1992, ch. 6; Held 1995; Kymlicka 2002, ch. 9). But in our view, it is an important issue of equality, and therefore of justice, to ask who has access to, and who is denied, relations of love, care and solidarity, whether these relations are reciprocal or asymmetrical, and whether the ways societies operate help to satisfy or frustrate these human needs. Quite how to characterize equality in this dimension, and how to promote it, are difficult questions. But that is different from ignoring it altogether.

The most plausible explanation of the liberal egalitarian neglect of love, care and solidarity is that liberals tend to see these as private matters that individuals should work out for themselves. That stance sits uncomfortably with the fact that many of the institutions of liberal societies are both dependent upon and have a direct impact on these relationships. One of the central concerns of contemporary feminism has been to emphasize the degree to which all societies rely on the love and care typically provided by women to children and other dependants. More generally, the emotional support people get from family and friends plays a vital role in sustaining their capacity to function as workers and citizens. At the same time, the organization of work and transportation has an obvious impact on the amount of time workers can spend with their families. And the way the state organizes residential facilities for disabled people, or denies accommodation to Travellers or homeless people, has a huge impact on their personal relationships. So it is not surprising that this is an area of tremendous importance in the everyday lives of people in liberal societies. In this respect the concerns of ordinary people are ahead of those of liberal egalitarian theory.

Were we to construct a more adequate liberal egalitarian approach to love, care and solidarity, the natural place to start would be with the ideas of a minimum standard and equal opportunity. We would have to consider how to enable every member of society to develop an adequate range of loving, caring and solidary relationships, and to address those aspects of our societies that frustrate this important human need. We would also have to consider whether social arrangements systematically work in ways that make it harder for some groups of people to meet these needs than for other groups, since this would be contrary to equal opportunity. Attending to love, care and solidarity in this way would recognize these issues and the institutions that affect them as public concerns. But in keeping with the general shape of liberal egalitarian ideas, we would consider it inevitable that some people would have much more satisfactory access to relations of love, care and solidarity than others.[13]

## 4. Power relations: civil and personal rights and liberal democracy

The fourth dimension of liberal egalitarianism concerns relations of power. The protection of basic civil and personal rights against the powerful, particularly the state, is a central and longstanding idea within liberalism. These rights include the prohibition of slavery, of torture and of cruel, inhuman or degrading punishment. They encompass equality before the law, protection against arbitrary arrest and a right to the due process of law. Also included are such rights as freedom of movement, the right to own property, freedom of thought, conscience and religion, freedom of opinion and expression and freedom of association. These civil and personal rights are familiar features of modern liberal regimes and can be found in such documents as the American Bill of Rights (1789, although it took another 75 years and a civil war before slavery was prohibited), the Universal Declaration of Human Rights (1948), the European Convention on Human Rights (1950) and the International Covenant on Civil and Political Rights (1976). Quite what is included in these rights and how they are interpreted has varied. But taken overall, they are one way of setting limits on the degree of inequality of power any society should tolerate.

Liberalism also has a longstanding association with democracy and a certain conception of political equality. The principle that every citizen has an equal say through the ballot box, and the extension of this principle over the past two centuries to all social classes, to women and to ethnic minorities, is clearly an egalitarian idea, and it plays an important role both in reducing economic inequality and in expressing the equal public status of all citizens. But we need to contrast these equal political rights with the fact that economically and culturally dominant groups have much more influence on public policy in all liberal democracies than disadvantaged groups. Liberal democracy also assumes that there will necessarily be a power gap between ordinary voters and the people they elect. Elections are seen, primarily, as a method for choosing and limiting the power of decision-makers rather than as a means by which the people engage in self-rule in any meaningful sense. A further feature of liberal democracy is its concentration on what is generally considered 'politics', neglecting power inequalities (and often the violence through which they are expressed) in the economy, the family, religion and other areas. Liberal democracy and the conception of political equality that goes with it are thus themselves in line with the general idea that liberal equality is about regulating inequality rather than eliminating it. They provide, as before, both a basic minimum and a kind of equal opportunity – largely formal in character – for achieving and exercising power.

## 5.  Working and learning: occupational and educational equal opportunity

Work is a central fact of human life, but it is double-edged. In some respects it is a burden, something people have to be induced to do by threat or reward. In other ways it is a benefit, not just because it is a major factor determining status, resources and power but because it provides opportunities for social contact, personal satisfaction and self-realization. Work is immensely varied, consisting of all forms of productive activity, whether paid or unpaid and whether in the formal economy or not. It includes the work people do in households, voluntary bodies and political organizations. If liberal egalitarians were interested in equality with respect to work, they would need to consider these factors with care. But as with other dimensions of equality, they assume that there will be major inequalities of work.

Perhaps surprisingly, liberal egalitarians have paid little attention to minimum standards. The idea that everyone has a right to work, under minimally decent conditions, is common enough in the modern world. For example, the Universal Declaration of Human Rights states that 'Everyone has the right to work, to free choice of employment, to just and favourable conditions of work and to protection against unemployment' (Article 23, sec. 1). The International Labour Organization (ILO) has developed these ideas in its Constitution, its Declaration on Fundamental Principles and Rights at Work and in its promotion of Decent Work (ILO 1941, 1998, 1999, 2001). But that idea does not feature much in the writings of liberal egalitarian theorists. Nor, taking work as a burden, do liberal egalitarians have much to say about either the minimum or maximum burden any member of society should bear.[14]

The process of learning is closely related to work, because work always involves learnt abilities and therefore appropriate education and training is a necessary condition for decent work. But there are many other forms of learning, relevant to the whole range of human activities. Like work, learning is both beneficial and burdensome. It can be a joy and can open up all kinds of doors, but not all learning is fun: it often involves hard work. Another similarity with work is the wide range of contexts in which learning takes place, not just in the formal educational system but in families and playgrounds, in workplaces and politics. Learning has attracted considerable interest from both liberal and more radical egalitarians, particularly in relation to the formal educational system. As ever, the key liberal egalitarian concern is with equal opportunity, although the idea of achieving certain minimum educational standards – of a universal right to basic education – also features in the writings of liberal egalitarians (e.g. Gutmann 1987; Walzer 1985, ch. 8).

The central liberal egalitarian principle for dealing with working and learning, then, is equal opportunity. The 'formal' interpretation of equal opportunity inspires anti-discrimination legislation that makes it illegal to deny education or work to people because of their religion, sex or other specified characteristics. Rawls's principle of 'fair equal opportunity' has stronger implications, implying that the educational system should try to compensate for the obstacles faced by people from working class and other disadvantaged backgrounds in developing their talents. Since most educational systems do too little in this regard, another implication of fair equal opportunity is the development of 'affirmative action': policies for helping members of disadvantaged groups to compete for and obtain education and jobs. The reasoning is that if members of these groups are underrepresented in, say, universities or the professions, this must be because they have not had equal opportunities to develop their abilities. Affirmative action is a way of improving the balance at a later stage, ensuring greater equality of opportunity overall.

The emphasis placed by liberal egalitarians on equal opportunity means that it is left to the operation of 'fair' social institutions – in particular the market and the family – to decide who ends up in which occupations and how tasks are distributed among these occupations. The benefits and burdens attached to different kinds of work are taken as given, even though this has the effect of consigning some people to lives of unmitigated toil.

### Reform of existing social structures

The discussion so far has concentrated on the key principles endorsed by liberal egalitarians, but the picture would be incomplete without discussing how they think of these principles as being implemented: what social structures or institutions are necessary to put these principles into practice? The vision liberal egalitarians have of how the world operates and of the possibility of change seems to be based on the assumption that the fundamental structures of modern welfare states are at least in broad outline the best we are capable of. In saying this we do not mean to imply that liberal egalitarians think that we live in the best of all possible worlds or that there is little we can do to improve the way we manage our societies. But we think they are convinced that certain key features of modern welfare states – including representative government, a mixed economy, a developed system of social welfare, a meritocratic educational system, a specialized and hierarchical division of labour – define the institutional framework within which any progress towards equality can be made, and that the task for egalitarians is to make various adjustments to these structures rather than to alter them in fundamental ways.[15] It is partly because these structures inevitably produce inequality that liberal egalitarians think that inequality is unavoidable and that the egalitarian agenda must be defined in terms of regulating inequality rather than eliminating it.

## Justifying liberal equality

The views of liberal egalitarians represent a tremendous challenge not just to the inequalities of pre-capitalist societies but also to the entrenched inequalities of the contemporary world. Can this challenge be morally justified? Many of the arguments put forward by liberal egalitarians are rooted in the idea of basic equality, the claim of every human being to basic concern and respect. If we are to take these ideas seriously in the context of modern societies in which people have complex and diverse needs and differ profoundly in their moral and political beliefs, we must surely take steps to tolerate their differences, to protect their personal freedoms and to enable them to participate in decision-making. The ideas of concern and respect also support the principle that everyone should have a decent standard of living, including the resources necessary for exercising their rights and freedoms. The most distinctive idea of liberal egalitarians, equal opportunity, can be seen as a way of showing basic respect and concern for human beings as rational agents with differing talents and ambitions. Of course, these remarks are not a fully developed argument for liberal egalitarian ideas: they merely indicate the ways in which many authors have attempted to construct one. In any case, the principles of liberal egalitarians are in fact widely accepted in contemporary welfare states (Miller 1997, ch. 4). But are these principles strong enough? We argue below that they are not.

## Basic equality, liberal egalitarianism and human rights

One of the most powerful political advances of our times has been the development of an international movement in support of human rights. Defined over several decades of activism and international negotiation, the human rights agenda is widely seen as setting universal minimum standards for the ways people can be treated, particularly by governments. The idea of human rights is a fundamentally egalitarian idea, resting as it does on the Universal Declaration's commitment to equal dignity.

In relation to our spectrum of egalitarian views, the human rights agenda clearly encompasses basic equality. It is also closely connected to liberal egalitarianism because it is primarily concerned with the setting of minimum standards and promoting key principles of non-discrimination. Some of the principles proclaimed by liberal egalitarians are more demanding than those included in the major human rights documents. For example, Rawls's principle of fair equal opportunity and his difference principle are both stronger than anything found in the Universal Declaration or the European Convention. But liberal egalitarians and human rights activists have broadly similar aims. This fact alone should remind us of the strength of the case for liberal egalitarianism and the degree to which its principles have achieved widespread support.

## Equality of condition

Liberal egalitarianism is based on the assumption that many major inequalities are inevitable and that our task is to make them fair. The idea of equality of condition sets out a much more ambitious aim: to eliminate major inequalities altogether, or at least massively to reduce the current scale of inequality.[16] The key to this much more ambitious agenda is to recognize that inequality is rooted in changing and changeable social structures, and particularly in structures of domination and oppression. These structures create, and continually reproduce, the inequalities that liberal egalitarians see as inevitable. But since social structures have changed in the past, it is at least conceivable that they could be deliberately changed in the future. Exactly how to name and analyse these structures and their interaction is a matter of continuing debate, but one way or another they clearly include capitalism (a predominantly market-based economy in which the means of production are privately owned and controlled), patriarchy (systems of gender relationships that privilege men over women), racism (social systems that divide people into 'races' and privilege some 'races' over others) and other systems of oppression.[17]

This emphasis on social structures in explaining inequality affects the way equality of condition should be understood. In contrast to the tendency of liberal egalitarians to focus on the rights and advantages of individuals, equality of condition also pays attention to the rights and advantages of groups. In contrast to liberal egalitarians' tendency to concentrate on how things are distributed, equality of condition pays more attention to how people are related, particularly through power relations. In contrast to the tendency of liberal egalitarians to treat individuals as responsible for their successes and failures, equality of condition emphasizes the influence of social factors on people's choices and actions. These contrasts should not be overstated, but they do affect how equality of condition is defined, as will become clearer by looking at its central ideas.

Discussions of equality sometimes contrast the liberal idea of equality of opportunity with the idea of 'equality of outcome'. Although the distinction is a good shorthand account of the difference between liberal egalitarianism and equality of condition, it can be misleading, since equality of condition is also concerned with people having a wide range of choices, not with their all ending up the same. The difference is in how equal opportunity is understood. Liberal equal opportunity is about fairness in the competition for advantage. It implies that there will be winners and losers, people who do well and people who do badly. An 'opportunity' in this context is the right to compete, not the right to choose among alternatives of similar worth. So two people can have equal opportunities in this sense even if one of them has no real prospect of achieving anything of value. For example, a society that allows only 15 per cent of the population to attend third-level education could in this liberal sense give everyone an equal opportunity to do so, even though in a stronger sense it would clearly be denying the opportunity for third-level education to 85 per cent of the population.

Equality of condition is about opportunities in this stronger sense, about enabling and empowering people to exercise what might be called real choices among real options. In the dimension of respect and recognition, it is about the freedom to live one's life without the burden of contempt and enmity from the dominant culture. In the dimension of resources, it is about having a range of resource-dependent options that is of roughly the same value as those of others. In the dimension of love, care and solidarity, it means promoting circumstances in which everyone has ample scope for forming valuable human attachments. In the dimension of power, it means the roughly equal enabling of each person to influence the decisions that affect their lives. In the dimension of working and learning, it means ensuring that everyone is enabled to develop their talents and abilities, and that everyone has a real choice among occupations that they find satisfying or fulfilling. Inevitably equality in these fields of choice would lead to different outcomes, which could have profound effects on people's lives: wasting money on useless things, falling in love with the wrong person, choosing an occupation that doesn't suit. But these outcomes, precisely because they would take place in a context of continuing equality in the overall conditions of people's lives, would not undermine people's roughly similar prospects for making further choices. To make these ideas more precise, we return to the five dimensions of equality.[18]

### 1. Equal respect and recognition

Like liberal egalitarianism, equality of condition includes the principle of universal citizenship as an expression of the equal status of all citizens. Where it differs from liberalism is in relation to the ideas of toleration and the public/private distinction. The liberal tradition's commitment to respecting and tolerating differences is one of its great strengths. However, critics of liberalism have pointed out that toleration is not always quite what it seems, since it is perfectly possible to tolerate someone while retaining a sense of one's own superiority. Thus, dominant cultures can 'tolerate' subordinate ones, but not vice versa. The dominant view is still seen as the normal one, while the tolerated view is seen as deviant. There is no suggestion that the dominant view may itself be questionable, or that an appreciation of and interaction with subordinate views could be valuable for both sides.

For these reasons, supporters of equality of condition tend to talk about the appreciation or celebration of diversity and to say that differences from the norm are to be welcomed and learned from rather than simply permitted. They urge us to be glad to live in a multicultural society, to live among people with different sexual orientations and so on. While this shift from 'tolerate' to 'celebrate' is of real value, it can mislead us into thinking that it is wrong to criticize beliefs we disagree with, that the politically correct view is to cherish all difference. That could not possibly be a coherent position, if for no other reason than that not every group is prepared to celebrate – or even to tolerate – others. In fact, one of the common themes of writers who want to celebrate difference is that the dominant culture itself needs to be critically assessed, particularly if its sense of identity depends on belittling others. And since it seems to be the case that all cultures include oppressive traditions, none can be considered to be above criticism.

This conclusion is strengthened by a significant difference between liberal egalitarianism and equality of condition concerning the definition of the 'private' sphere, the area of life that ought to be protected from regulation by either law or social convention. Equality of condition accepts that some aspects of life should be protected from public scrutiny, but it rejects the idea that whole spheres of life should be largely exempt from principles of justice. In particular, it highlights the oppression of women and children inside both families and religions (Cohen 2000; Kymlicka 2002, ch. 9; Nussbaum 2000; Okin 1989). If we are truly committed to equality of recognition, we cannot cordon off these important spheres of life from critical scrutiny. By redefining the contrast between public and private, equality of condition widens the scope for criticizing and transforming both dominant and subordinate cultures.

In the end, we show more respect for others by engaging critically with their beliefs than by adopting a laissez-faire attitude. The real task is to engage in such criticism in an open and dialogical spirit, recognizing the real effort that the privileged must make to understand the voices of members of subordinate groups and to open their own ideas to critical interrogation. Such a dialogue often reveals that there is more common ground between apparently divergent views than meets the eye, and that there are centres of resistance within even the most oppressive cultures. We have adopted the label 'critical interculturalism' for this relation of mutually supportive and critical dialogue between members of different social groups. A commitment to such a dialogue does not of itself resolve all the difficult issues raised by cultural conflict, but it creates a space in which they can be addressed.[19]

We noted above that liberal egalitarians are generally quite comfortable with inequality of social esteem based on personal achievement. Perhaps this is because most liberal egalitarian theorists are members of high-status professions. The world looks very different from the point of view of those with low social status, who are in a position to recognize more clearly the contribution of accident, indoctrination and fashion in deciding who is due high esteem and who is not. For as long as human beings exist, there will always be attitudes of admiration and disdain, and these can play an important role in recognizing and encouraging valued behaviour. But the idea of equality of condition calls on us to limit their range. Without such limits, inequality of esteem is all too easily translated into all of the other dimensions of inequality.

## 2.   Equality of resources

In contrast to liberal egalitarianism, equality of condition aims at what can best be described as equality of resources. Like liberal egalitarianism, it recognizes income and wealth as key resources. But the idea of resources naturally includes a number of other goods that people find useful in achieving their aims in life. For example, Bourdieu (1986) has emphasized the importance to people's prospects of what he calls social and cultural capital. Social capital consists of the durable networks of social relationships to which people have access, while cultural capital includes both people's embodied knowledge and abilities and their educational credentials. People's resources also include non-financial conditions for their access to goods and services, such as their right to public services and their right not to be excluded from privately provided goods and services by discriminatory treatment, as well as environmental factors such as a safe and healthy environment, the geographical arrangement of cities, the accessibility of buildings and so on. Time, particularly leisure time, is another important resource in people's lives.[20]

Equality of condition accepts the urgency of satisfying basic needs and providing a safety net against poverty. But its wider understanding of resources helps us to recognize a wider range of needs than some liberal egalitarians are inclined to attend to and to take a less market-oriented view of how these needs should be satisfied. For example, people with physical impairments not only need higher incomes than those without these impairments, but also changes in the physical environment that promote their inclusion into the activities that others take for granted. Because of its commitment to equal recognition and power, equality of condition also rejects definitions of need imposed by experts and other dominant groups and endorses a process of democratic dialogue over needs (Fraser 1989, ch. 8).

Beyond the level of need, equality of condition aims for a world in which people's overall resources are much more equal than they are now, so that people's prospects for a good life are roughly similar. Because of the multifaceted and disputable nature of well-being and the complicated relationship between resources and prospects for well-being, one cannot hope to provide a precise account of equality of resources. It certainly cannot be equated with the idea that everyone should have the same income and wealth, because people have different needs and because there are so many other important resources to consider. There is also an egalitarian case for permitting modest inequalities in income to offset inequalities in the burdens of work. Otherwise people who worked hard would be worse off than those who didn't.[21] But if these are the only kinds of reason that would justify inequality of income and wealth, it follows that people who have similar needs and who work in similarly demanding occupations for similar amounts of time should have similar income and wealth. This implies, for example, that there should be no significant differences in income and wealth between manual workers and office workers, women and men or people of colour and whites, and that public services should serve these different groups equally well. So equality of condition would certainly involve a dramatic change in the distribution of income and wealth and in access to public services. In adopting this view, we reject the liberal belief that substantial inequalities of resources are inevitable.[22]

## 3. Equality of love, care and solidarity

As we have noted, human beings typically have both a need and a capacity for intimacy, attachment and caring relationships. The ability to recognize and feel some sense of affiliation and concern for others is a typical human trait, and everyone needs, at least sometimes, to be cared for. People generally value the various forms of social engagement that emanate from such relations and define themselves in terms of them. Solidary bonds of friendship or kinship are frequently what brings meaning, warmth and joy to life. Being deprived of the capacity to develop such supportive affective relations, or of the experience of engaging in them when one has the capacity, is therefore a serious human deprivation for most people.

Being cared for is also a fundamental prerequisite for human development. All of us have urgent needs for care at various stages in our lives, as a consequence of infancy, illness, impairment or other vulnerabilities. In addition, relations of love, care and solidarity help to establish a basic sense of importance, value and belonging, a sense of being appreciated, wanted and cared about. They are both a vital component of what enables people to lead successful lives and an expression of our fundamental interdependence. Love, care and solidarity therefore constitute a family of distinct but similar relationships that are important for their own sake and for achieving a wide range of other goals.

Tronto (1993), Bubeck (1995), Kittay (1999) and others have pointed out that caring is both an activity and an attitude. In caring for others, we act to meet their needs in a way that involves an attitude of concern or even love. This duality is characteristic of the wider field of relationships of love, care and solidarity. Love involves acting for those we love, not just feeling for them. Solidarity involves active support for others, not just passive empathy. So our needs for loving, caring and solidary relationships are needs to be enabled to do something for others as well as to feel attached to them.

These facts show that, at the very least, an adequate conception of equality must involve a commitment to satisfying basic needs for love, care and solidarity. But as with other dimensions of equality, the question arises of whether securing a basic minimum is enough to aim for. Equality of condition surely involves a more ambitious goal, a society in which people are confident of having, if not equal, then at least ample prospects for loving, caring and solidary relationships. To achieve this goal, it is necessary to change structures and institutions that systematically impede people's opportunities to develop such relationships, including the organization of paid work, processes of gender-stereotyping and the gendered division of labour, attitudes and institutional arrangements concerning disability, and of course the burdens of poverty and deprivation. Societies cannot *make* anyone love anyone else, and to this extent the right to have loving, caring and solidary relations is not directly enforceable. (Parents can be legally required to care *for* their children, but they cannot be forced to care *about* them.) But societies can work to establish the conditions in which these relationships can thrive. As noted below, a key element in this task is to make sure that the work involved in providing love and care is properly recognized, supported and shared. The quality of people's relations of love, care and solidarity is also affected by the other dimensions of equality: equal respect, equal access to resources and equal power. Equality in these other dimensions is important in protecting people involved in relations of love and care from domination and exploitation (Bubeck 1995).

## 4.   Equality of power

A central obstacle to equality of condition is the pervasive network of power relations in all societies. In recognition of the dangers of state power, equality of condition retains the liberal commitment to basic civil and personal rights, including the right to personal private property. But since the general right to private property enshrined in some declarations of rights, including the Irish Constitution (Articles 40.3.2 and 43), can be used to protect the economic power of the privileged, equality of condition has to involve a more limited definition of what this right involves. And because social structures often involve the systematic oppression of social groups, equality of condition may entail creating certain group-related rights, for example the right of members of a linguistic minority to educate their children in their first language or the right of an ethnic minority to political representation. This is not a blanket endorsement of the right of social groups to behave in any way they choose towards their members, which would go beyond even liberal forms of the public/private distinction. It is a recognition that specific group-based rights may sometimes promote equality of power.

As discussed earlier, liberal democracies have had a strictly limited impact on power inequalities, leaving dominant groups largely unchallenged in the political sphere and neglecting many other types of power and associated forms of violence. Yet it is precisely these power relations that sustain inequality between privileged and oppressed groups. Equality of condition responds to these limitations on two fronts. First of all, it supports a stronger, more participatory form of politics in which ordinary citizens, and particularly groups who have been excluded from power altogether, can have more control over decision-making. Strengthened local government, closer accountability for elected representatives, procedures to ensure the participation of marginalized groups, and wider access to information and technical expertise are some of the elements of this radical democratic programme (see Chapter 6).

The second aspect of equality of power is to challenge power in other areas, such as the economy, the family, education and religion. The agenda here includes democratic management of individual firms and democratic control over key planning issues for the local, national and global economy. It involves rejecting the power of husbands over wives and questioning the power relations between parents and children. It means a democratic, cooperative model of education. It implies that the power structures of religious organizations are just as open to question as those of the secular world.

In both cases, the aim is to promote equality of power rather than to contain inequalities of power, recognizing that power takes many forms, is often diffuse and has to be challenged in many different ways.

## 5. Working and learning as equals

As mentioned earlier, work is in some respects a burden, in others a benefit. In contemporary societies, both the burdens and benefits of work are unequally distributed, and those who shoulder the greatest burdens often receive the least benefit. The burden of menial work is generally accompanied by the lowest possible wages and working conditions. The burdens of caring in individual households are typically unpaid, unrecognized and carried out with little support (Daly 2001; Kittay 1999). Equality of condition involves reversing these inequalities, requiring that both the burdens and the benefits of work are much more equally shared and that the conditions under which people work are much more equal in character. As we have suggested, where some people continue to take on greater burdens, it is consistent with the idea of equality of condition for them to receive greater benefits. But the central aim of equality of condition should be to ensure that everyone has the prospect of satisfying work. This would affect both the benefits and burdens of work, since tedious, unsatisfying work can be a crushing burden and satisfying work has intrinsic benefits.

The most fundamental change involved in equality of condition would be in the division of labour. The current division of labour is not sacrosanct. It is the result of economic structures that function primarily for the purpose of maximizing profits in a deeply unequal world. To be sure, human life depends on the completion of many tedious and disagreeable tasks and will continue to do so. But it is a matter of social organization whether these tasks are concentrated in particular occupations or fairly shared among the population as a whole. In particular, the division of society into those who define tasks and those who merely execute them is unjust and needs to be radically reconceived (Young 1990, ch. 7).

One of the forms of work that has been most neglected by liberal egalitarians is the work of loving and caring: work that is done primarily by women and is usually unpaid. Caring for others and forming and maintaining solidary relations takes time, energy and commitment. It is emotionally laden work, especially in the developmental stages of life, but also in adulthood (Bubeck 1995; Daly 2001; Delphy and Leonard 1992; Kittay 1999). It takes an intense and prolonged engagement with others to be responsive to their needs, to establish and maintain relations of solidarity and bonds of affection, to provide moral support, to maintain friendships, to give people a sense of belonging and to make them feel good. Caring labour and love labour are demanding on our energies and resources (Lynch 1989; Lynch and McLaughlin 1995). Equality of condition requires that this work should be recognized, supported and shared. In particular, it entails a commitment to meeting the needs of those who provide care work to dependants (Kittay 1999). It also implies a rebalancing of other work so that everyone is able to engage in the work of love and care.

Work is an important part of life, but it is not its be-all and end-all. Whether people should have the right to opt out of work altogether is a contentious issue that partly depends on the range of work options open to them and on the degree to which society has enabled them to take on this work. We do not take a position on this here. But egalitarians must clearly be against social arrangements that impose such a burden of work on people that they have little space in their lives for pursuing other worthwhile ends. Working as equals must involve a limit to the demands of work.

Equality of condition does not entail the right of every person to the job of their choice. That would clearly be unrealistic. So who does what remains an important issue and equality of condition has to incorporate fair principles of occupational equal opportunity. There are other issues about work that are harder to think through, for example the role and distribution of voluntary and unpaid work in an egalitarian society. But the guiding principle is that the overall benefits and burdens of work should be as equal as possible.

These principles about work have important implications for learning because they require systems of learning that give everyone worthwhile occupational choices. But there are many other aspects of learning, including learning to develop personal relationships, to engage in literature and the arts, to participate in politics and so on. If equality of condition is about enabling people to exercise real choices, then equality in learning is about self-development in its broadest sense. And since learning is itself an activity that takes up a great deal of each person's life, we need to think of how to make it more satisfying in its own right (see Chapter 8).

### Challenge to existing structures

It seems clear enough that equality of condition challenges the basic structures of contemporary societies. As we discuss in more detail in Chapter 4, these structures work systematically to generate and reinforce inequality. A predominantly capitalist economy continually creates and reproduces inequalities in people's resources, work and learning; it relies on and perpetuates inequalities of power and status; it places tremendous strains on relations of love, care and solidarity. The cultural system embodies and reinforces inequalities based on gender, class, disability, ethnicity, 'race' and sexual orientation. Networks of care and solidarity – what we call the affective system – work together to the advantage of privileged groups while denying support to the most vulnerable. The political system reinforces the privileges of dominant groups throughout society. All of these systems pervade the social institutions that shape our lives.

Equality of condition would require very different institutions and structures, developing participatory, inclusive, enabling and empowering ways of cooperating in all areas of life. Although these structural changes are not strictly speaking dimensions of equality, they have an important role to play in helping to ensure that everyone has roughly equal prospects for a good life, largely through promoting greater equality in each of the five dimensions we have set out.[23] The central aim of Parts II and III of this book is to contribute to the task of imagining and bringing about these changes.

### Justifying equality of condition

Equality of condition presents a radical challenge to existing attitudes and structures, but many of the arguments in its favour come from basic and liberal egalitarianism. The most general way of putting the case is that the aims of both basic and liberal egalitarians are thwarted by inequalities of wealth, status and power that they refuse to challenge. On the face of it, it seems a simple enough task to ensure that everyone in the world has access to clean water and decent food, but layers of entrenched inequality make even these minimal goals unattainable. On the face of it, it seems easy enough to ensure that everyone's basic rights are protected, but in practice the rights of powerless and marginalized people are easily violated. Liberal egalitarians are eloquent proponents of equal opportunity, but equal opportunity is impossible so long as privileged people can deploy their economic and cultural advantages on behalf of themselves and their families – as they will surely continue to do, so long as the consequences of success and failure are so spectacularly different (Baker 2003).

Other arguments for equality of condition arise out of the internal tensions and contradictions of liberal egalitarianism. We have seen how the idea of toleration can involve the very inequality of respect it purports to reject. There is a similar contradiction in the 'incentive' argument for inequality, namely that when privileged people demand an incentive for helping the worst off, they are taking resources away from the very people they pretend to be concerned about (Cohen 1991). Another tension arises in arguments for the liberal ideal of occupational equality of opportunity. This principle is often justified by appealing to the interest each person has in 'experiencing the realization of self which comes from a skilful and devoted exercise of social duties' (Rawls 1971, p. 84). Yet it is clear enough that an unequal society provides precious few people with this experience.

Additional arguments for equality of condition come from reflections on the limited assumptions of liberal egalitarianism. In a curious way, liberal egalitarians seem to ignore the structured nature of inequality, the ways in which inequality is generated and sustained by dominant social institutions and the influence of these institutions on people's attitudes, preferences and prospects. Thus when Rawls, for example, explains fair equal opportunity by saying that people's prospects 'should not be affected by their social class' (1971, p. 73; cf. 2001, p. 44), he seems to be accepting the idea of a class-divided society at the very same time as he is endorsing a principle that implies the elimination of class altogether. His work is also notorious for its neglect of gender.[24] A related problem is the liberal egalitarian emphasis on choice and personal responsibility, which plays an important role in supporting the idea of equal opportunity but tends to ignore the extent to which people's choices are influenced by their social positions.

These, then, are some of the key arguments for equality of condition.[25] If they are sound, they show that although most of the principles of liberal egalitarianism are worth defending, they do not go far enough. Western societies in particular, and the world more generally, are deeply unjust and need to be radically rebuilt.

## Applying the framework to social groups

We have identified five key dimensions of equality and have contrasted the ways these dimensions are treated by liberal egalitarianism and equality of condition (see Table 2.1). In applying these ideas, it is often useful to focus on particular disadvantaged and privileged social groups because individuals usually experience inequality as a consequence of their membership of these groups. Although group inequalities vary across the five dimensions, inequality in one dimension is often accompanied by

*Table 2.1*  Basic equality, liberal egalitarianism and equality of condition

| Dimensions of equality | Basic equality | Liberal egalitarianism | Equality of condition |
| --- | --- | --- | --- |
| *Respect and recognition* | Basic respect | Universal citizenship<br>Toleration of differences<br>Public/private distinction | Universal citizenship<br>'Critical interculturalism': acceptance of diversity; redefined public/private distinction; critical dialogue over cultural differences<br>Limits to unequal esteem |
| *Resources* | Subsistence needs | Anti-poverty focus<br>Rawls's 'difference principle' (maximize the prospects of the worst off) | Substantial equality of resources broadly defined, aimed at satisfying needs and enabling roughly equal prospects of well-being |
| *Love, care and solidarity* | | A private matter?<br>Adequate care? | Ample prospects for relations of love, care and solidarity |
| *Power relations* | Protection against inhuman and degrading treatment | Classic civil and personal rights<br><br>Liberal democracy | Liberal rights *but* limited property rights; group-related rights<br>Stronger, more participatory politics<br>Extension of democracy to other areas of life |
| *Working and learning* | | Occupational and educational equal opportunity<br>Decent work?<br>Basic education | Educational and occupational options that give everyone the prospect of self-development and satisfying work |

inequalities in the others. We can see this clearly by looking at some examples.

Disabled people are a diverse group whose experiences are shaped in many ways by different impairments. What they have in common is their experience of exclusion from activities that other people take for granted. This exclusion results to a large extent from a social environment that is designed to suit people without impairments. So a key inequality here is inequality of appropriate environmental resources. This inequality has the further effect of excluding disabled people from mainstream education and the labour force, affecting both their learning and work opportunities and their incomes. But disabled people are also strongly affected by a culturally constructed image of disability that marks disabled people as strange, as 'other': an image that is easily sustained on account of their exclusion from everyday social activities. All of these factors interact with the way that disabled people are subjected to the power of non-disabled people, not just in the political system but most clearly in such institutions as special schools and hospitals. Because these institutions have traditionally treated disabled people as helpless, they have reinforced their isolation and exclusion. Residential institutions for disabled people have also often contributed to depriving them of relations of love and care, either through overt abuse or through discouraging disabled people from forming loving relations with each other. At the same time, the exclusion of disabled people from activities that other people take for granted and the stereotyping of disabled people as asexual have limited their opportunities for developing relations of love, care and solidarity with others. Thus, disabled people are typically worse off than non-disabled people in every one of the five dimensions of equality.[26]

Gender relations are in some ways similar to those of disability and in other ways different. A central feature of sexual inequality is the gendered division of labour, which assigns some roles primarily to men and others primarily to women. Early childhood learning and the educational system teach boys and girls to accept these roles and to acquire appropriate skills and dispositions for performing them. The gendered roles are associated with differences in income: women earn on average significantly less than men and of course receive no income at all for the unpaid work they are traditionally expected to do in the household. Women carry the lion's share of the work required for sustaining love and care, while men have greater opportunities for finding satisfying work outside the household and for achieving positions of power. A further dimension of gender inequality is a set of norms and prejudices that systematically belittles women and reinforces the gendered division of labour. The resources and economic power held by men, together with their higher social status, contribute to their near-monopoly of political power, power that is put to use in maintaining their economic advantages and protecting their power and use of violence in the household. In the dimension of love, care and solidarity, the situation of women is more favourable because the gendered division of labour provides women with the opportunity and indeed the duty to love and care for others. But this does not always give them the love and care they need themselves, and the other conditions of their lives sometimes leave them little space for relationships of love and care. So women are in general worse off than men in four of the dimensions of equality, and sometimes in the fifth.[27]

A third example of the intersection of the dimensions of inequality is social class. Here again the division of labour plays a key role, subjecting working class people to the power of employers, depriving them of opportunities for satisfying and fulfilling work, consigning them to a lower standard of living and providing their children with worse opportunities for learning. Cultural norms that treat working class customs, accents and activities as inferior interact with these economic factors to reinforce the unequal status of working class people and to exclude them from political power. By contrast, people in dominant social classes enjoy high income, status and economic power. They have extensive opportunities for engaging and rewarding work and learning, and can provide similar opportunities for their children. Their social, economic and educational advantages give them political influence as well.

How class affects people's opportunities for relations of love, care and solidarity is not well researched. Some evidence from Scandinavian countries indicates that companionship and solidarity are independent of material well-being, but of course the level of material well-being enjoyed in these societies is very high by international standards (Allardt 1993). We do know that severe material deprivation can lead to emotional deprivation. For example, poor people are more likely to become homeless or to go to prison, and thus to suffer the deprivation of love, care and solidarity these experiences involve (Focus Point 1993; O'Mahony 1997). So class inequality has at least four clear dimensions and has shown some evidence of this fifth one.[28]

These examples could be multiplied by looking at relationships of 'race', ethnicity, sexuality, age and so on. The general point is that the ways societies are structured around differences of impairment, sex and class generate inequalities across all five of the dimensions we have identified for the groups they systematically privilege and disadvantage. Of course, some groups may be more disadvantaged in one dimension than in others. For example, older people in some societies may suffer more seriously from a lack of love and care than from poverty or powerlessness. But the general tendency is for social structures to work in a way that generates inequality between groups in all or most of the five dimensions.

The fact that inequalities are typically interrelated is relevant to questions that face any multi-dimensional account of equality. Are some dimensions more important than others? What should we do if equality in one dimension conflicts with equality in another? It would be rash to insist that equalities in the different dimensions are always compatible: egalitarians may well have to decide in particular cases how to balance off conflicting demands. But the tendency of the dimensions to reinforce each other shows that there is often no such conflict, and that progress in each dimension is likely to require progress in the others.[29]

## Conclusion

In this chapter we have set out a framework for thinking about equality, distinguishing the basic egalitarianism that is the common assumption of nearly all modern political thinking from what we have called liberal egalitarianism and equality of condition. We have outlined and contrasted the main ideas of liberal egalitarianism and equality of condition by identifying five key dimensions of equality – respect and recognition, resources, love, care and solidarity, power and working and learning – and by commenting on their relation to social structures. These are, of course, broadly drawn positions, and we do not pretend to have presented a comprehensive survey of egalitarian views. We have also sketched the reasons why a person who takes basic equality seriously is obliged to move on to the beliefs of liberal egalitarians, and how the difficulties involved in holding those beliefs provide grounds for equality of condition. But these arguments are far from complete. In particular, we recognize that someone could support equality of condition in some dimensions but not others. Finally, we went on to illustrate the relations between the different dimensions by applying the framework to different social groups.

In contemporary western societies, basic egalitarianism is taken for granted at the level of moral and political rhetoric. The dominant parties of the left are primarily concerned with what we have called liberal egalitarian objectives. It is not our aim to disparage these goals: they represent a major challenge to existing inequalities. But we have tried to show that equality of condition is a natural extension of the concerns and difficulties involved in the liberal egalitarian outlook. If we are right in recommending equality of condition, this only emphasizes the scale of the tasks ahead of us. We face the challenge not only of constructing plausible models of an egalitarian society, but of developing a political movement for radical change. The central aim of Parts II and III of this book is to contribute to these tasks.

# 3
# The Centrality of Equality: Equality and Other Values

The idea of equality has always belonged to the ideals of the left. Nor could anyone deny its relevance in today's world, given the widespread and savage inequalities illustrated in Chapter 1. What is more controversial is to claim that equality has a special status among progressive ideals and that it should be the defining concept in our thinking about social institutions and how they should be changed. In this chapter we support this claim by briefly discussing the relationship between equality and some other human values. We start with ideas that are sometimes contrasted with equality but in our view are simply part of what egalitarians believe. We then move on to what we call 'human goods', namely those things and relationships that generally enhance the value of people's lives. We argue that far from conflicting with these values, equality demands that their benefits should be justly shared. We go on to discuss the connection between equality and some key political values, namely freedom, solidarity and the protection of the environment. We finish by identifying some genuine conflicts between equality and other values, where we are happy to endorse the egalitarian alternative.

We argued in Chapter 2 that equality is a complex idea, with five key dimensions, and we distinguished between basic equality, liberal egalitarianism and equality of condition. So right away it should be clear that the relationship between equality and other values has got to be complicated, depending on which elements of equality are being looked at. But this complexity also allows us to see that many of the traditional contrasts between equality and other values depend on a simplistic account of equality, and that a more realistic account leads to a different view of how these ideas fit together.

## Aspects of equality

It is partly because equality itself has a complex range of meanings that a number of important values can be seen as aspects or elements of an egalitarian outlook. For example, we have seen that protecting against inhuman and degrading treatment, providing for people's most basic needs and according them basic respect are endorsed by all egalitarians. These values are built into the very foundation of egalitarian ideals.

Other values, such as a commitment to civil and political rights, the relief of poverty and non-discrimination – values enshrined in charters of human rights – are embedded in both liberal egalitarianism and equality of condition, as are beliefs in (at least) the toleration of differences and (at least) liberal democracy. Many of these ideas are reflected in the attention that has recently been given to 'social inclusion' and to extending the idea of citizenship to encompass social and economic rights.[1] This overlap between equality and many of the dominant values of contemporary liberal democracies is unsurprising, since both liberal egalitarianism and equality of condition are built on these values.

Because the conceptions of equality that have been most prominent in liberal democracies have been concerned with non-discrimination and the distribution of resources, there has been a tendency for radical critics of liberalism to contrast equality with other ideas. For example, some authors have posed the question of 'equality versus difference' (cf. Bock and James 1992; Phillips 1987; Rhode 1990), while others have contrasted equality with the idea of liberation (e.g. Jaggar 1998). It should be clear from Chapter 2 that in our view these oppositions are misguided. Certainly, resource distribution plays a central role in equality of condition, but it is only one of its dimensions, while non-discrimination is only one of its minimal elements. Our discussion of equality of respect and recognition makes it clear that equality of condition involves accepting and valuing diversity. As Part II of this book shows, quite how to put this recognition of difference into practice is a question that has no simple answer, but the idea that equality is in principle opposed to ignoring differences between people is completely mistaken.

Nor should liberation be contrasted with equality, because liberation consists in the removal of unequal relationships of domination and oppression. Like the idea of equality itself, liberation is open to different interpretations. Liberals are apt to see it as consisting in the establishment of basic minimum standards and fair equal opportunity, while believers in equality of condition are likely to understand it as a more extensive and deeper challenge to all relations of power and dominance – a contrast found, for instance, in different versions of feminism. But in either case liberation is an essentially egalitarian ideal.

Something similar can be said about the idea of social justice. The views outlined in Chapter 2 represent three broad conceptions of social justice, all of which can claim to be called egalitarian. In the everyday politics of liberal democracies, the call for social justice typically refers to those ideas, particularly in the dimension of resources. But social justice is a flexible concept: the idea of an anti-egalitarian theory of social justice may sound strange, but it is not a contradiction in terms (cf. Miller 1976, 1997). Social justice has a range of interpretations: egalitarianism covers most, but not all, of that range.

## Human goods

In the case of some other values, the connection to equality is more complicated but still important. It arises out of the fact that any equality is an equality *of something* – income, wealth, power, respect, status and so on. We care about these equalities and their corresponding inequalities because the things or relationships they refer to matter to us: they are themselves of value. Thus, for virtually anything of value, whether it is freedom, love or a decent environment, it is possible to ask whether these goods should be available to everyone equally or just to a privileged few. Will we have equal freedom or will some people have much more freedom than others? Will everyone have prospects of love and care or will some be excluded? Will we work to conserve and improve the environment for everyone or only the well-off? Because these values are important, egalitarians have always asked these questions and must continue to do so. It follows that any simple contrast between equality and these other values fails to think through the basic logic of the idea of equality. On the contrary, because principles of equality are always about other values, we must assert them at the same time as we assert the claims of equality.

Looked at in this way, what the account of equality of condition in Chapter 2 attempts to do is to identify things and relationships that are important for nearly everyone's well-being or quality of life and to try to say something about what equality amounts to in each of these dimensions. Respect and recognition, resources of many kinds (including environmental resources), prospects for relations of love, care and solidarity, power relations and opportunities for and conditions of working and learning are of practically universal importance, and therefore equality in each of these dimensions is an important aim. There is no conflict between these values and equality: they are themselves components of equality.

Of course, opponents of equality may not care whether people are equally prosperous or have equal access to a healthy environment. What they cannot do is pretend that this isn't an issue, that the ideas of prosperity or the environment can be set out as social objectives without paying attention to how their benefits are distributed among the population.

Since questions of equality and inequality arise in principle for any human good, it might well be asked why there is not an indefinite number of dimensions of equality, each one concerned with something of value. For example, it might be said that all of the 'central human functional capabilities' listed by Nussbaum (2000, ch. 4), such as life, bodily health, bodily integrity and so on, are also important dimensions of equality. Our answer to this question is that the dimensions of equality we have focused on are meant to capture as well as possible the types of equality and inequality that affect most strongly people's prospects for achieving whatever it is that they value, rather than being a list of these valuable things themselves.[2] To the extent that they succeed in doing this, they offer a relatively complete account of equality of condition. But we do not claim that they are in principle complete, or that it does not make sense in specific contexts to focus on inequalities that are only implicit in our dimensions. So, for example, it is perfectly legitimate to study – and to deplore – inequalities in the health and mortality rates of different social classes. But the factors that cause these patterns are the inequalities of work, resources, power, status and care that arise in a class-divided society. It is because these inequalities play a pivotal role in shaping so many aspects of people's lives, including their health, that they are the focus of our framework.

## Freedom and equality

The classic principles of the French Revolution, which have resonated throughout progressive movements over the past two centuries, are liberty, equality and fraternity. But for nearly as long a time it has been asked how these principles relate to each other. Liberty (or freedom, which we treat as a synonym) is at least as complicated and disputable a concept as equality, and for that reason alone we could not possibly give a comprehensive account of the relationship between freedom and equality here. But it may be helpful to provide a brief account of our perspective on the issue.[3] What we would like to suggest is that there is a very intimate connection between these two ideas. It is not, as with other human goods, a question of freedom being one possible dimension of equality, but rather that each of the dimensions of equality is related to a particular set of freedoms. Yet, as with other goods, the idea of equality raises the question of whether these freedoms will be equally or unequally shared.

This point is particularly obvious in relation to equality of power. We have already seen how this dimension of equality is centrally concerned with the classic civil and political rights that constitute the fundamental freedoms of liberal democratic societies. There is obviously no question of a conflict between equality and these freedoms, as they are at the core of our account of liberal egalitarianism and equality of condition, both of which call for these freedoms to be held equally by all. Another aspect of equality of power is the idea of democracy. This connects to a rather different conception of freedom, namely self-rule or autonomy. The equal freedom of citizens to make their own collective decisions rather than to defer to the powerful is another way in which freedom and equality are two sides of the same coin. More generally, we have already commented on how the idea of equality of power is related to the idea of liberation, a third conception of freedom.

Turning to another dimension of equality, it is sometimes thought that the principle of equality of resources is directly contrary to freedom. Since everyone agrees that an unregulated ('laissez-faire') market economy will produce gross disparities of income and wealth, it appears that equality of resources requires constant interference with people's economic freedom. However, this appearance is deceptive. The first thing to notice is that a so-called 'unregulated' economy is itself a structure of limited freedom, because its central characteristic is private property. Private property only exists within a legal system that defines the rights of owners and restricts those of non-owners. It is the force of law, after all, that prevents a poor person from leaving a shop with the same goods as a rich person and excludes most employees from controlling the companies that employ them. Since such an economy does indeed generate gross inequalities of wealth and income, it follows that such an economy creates gross inequalities of freedom, and that anyone interested in equal freedom has to endorse a different kind of economy, with a different system of economic rights. Such an economy would give some people less freedom than they might have had as successes in a laissez-faire economy, but it would give more freedom to everyone else. How to construct economic institutions that promote equality of wealth and income is a difficult question for egalitarians, and we return to it in Chapter 5. The point here is that economic freedom and equality of resources go together.

The other dimensions of equality can also be easily construed in terms of freedom. Equality of respect and recognition is about the freedom of people to live their lives unimpeded by the depreciation and disdain that subordinate groups are burdened with in an unequal society. Equality of love, care and solidarity is about the freedom of everyone to give and receive care and to engage in relationships of love and solidarity, freedoms that are severely constricted for some people in unequal societies. Equality of working and learning is about enabling people to develop their capacities and to engage in satisfying and worthwhile occupations. This expansion of their real options clearly enhances their freedom to live a life of their own choosing.

As we have repeatedly emphasized, the point of equality of condition is not to prescribe a way of life for people but to open up to everyone the prospect of a good life by enabling them to make real choices among alternatives of similar worth. One might well call this equality of real freedom, but for the additional burden of having to distinguish this view from others that are similar (e.g. Sen 1992; Van Parijs 1995). Of course, freedom is a very open concept and for this reason equality is necessarily contrary to certain types of freedom, e.g. the freedom of the powerful to oppress the weak. But if we are interested in the idea of *equal* freedom, then there is a strong case for thinking that freedom and equality go hand in hand.

## Equality, solidarity and community

What about the third member of the classic triad, fraternity? That particular word has gone out of fashion because of its somewhat sexist connotations; it is more common nowadays for people to use the ideas of solidarity or community. In our account of equality of love, care and solidarity, we use the term 'solidarity' to express a relationship of mutual concern and support. Solidarity in this sense stands in strong contrast to the ideology of self-interest and individualism fostered by capitalist social relations. We take it as obvious that people in general have a basic need for solidary relationships and that these relationships help to enable them to live successful lives. That is why solidarity is included in the third dimension of equality. But we would also suggest that solidarity is an important support for the other dimensions of equality, because people who feel solidarity with each other are more likely to be willing to endorse egalitarian principles that give the same weight to the needs and interests of others as to their own. That kind of mutual concern makes it easier for people to be willing to accept their fair share of resources, to cooperate in developing egalitarian arrangements for working and learning and to renounce the opportunity to wield power over others. So we see a deep and natural connection between the ideas of solidarity and equality.

One of the most common complaints against egalitarianism has been that it implies a society in which everyone is the same and differences are suppressed. As discussed in Chapter 2, equality of condition involves a very different stance: neither a cultural imperialism that treats one set of values as the right ones nor a cultural relativism that treats all sets of values as equally valid. The question that this view raises is whether such an emphasis on diversity is compatible with the value of solidarity. Although it is easy enough to see that the acceptance of group difference allows for solidarity within groups, it is harder to see how we can establish and maintain solidarity between groups with very different cultures and interests. Surveying the bitter ethnic conflicts of the contemporary world, it seems hard to assert that differences between groups can be combined with solidarity among them.

Our response to this problem operates at three levels. First, it relies on recognizing the common humanity of members of every social group. As human beings, we do have the capacity to empathize with and care for other human beings, regardless of our differences (Jones 1999). Secondly, it notes that every society has many overlapping social groups with cross-cutting affiliations. People who are divided from each other by disability or sexuality may be united by class or gender. Thirdly, it stresses the ways in which different social groups can retain their distinctive commitments while endorsing a shared egalitarian conception of justice, a conception which itself recognizes and values diversity. Of course, developing such a consensus on egalitarian principles of justice faces the difficult practical challenge of achieving ideological change, but there is no reason to dismiss it as impossible. (We discuss that task further in Chapter 11.) Together, these points support the idea that solidarity is perfectly compatible with accepting diversity: that people can and often do form relationships of solidarity with others whom they recognize as different from themselves, and that equality of condition therefore neither implies nor presupposes assimilation and uniformity.

Community is a much broader and looser concept than solidarity. Its positive connotations make it attractive to a wide range of political programmes (Frazer 1999, ch. 2). Although communities are usually thought of as having a high degree of internal solidarity, the idea of community may also involve appeals to shared traditions, languages, cultures, localities and so on. Some 'communities' are hierarchical and oppressive, and all communities are to a certain extent exclusive. Our emphasis on solidarity has much in common with certain communitarian criticisms of both liberalism and contemporary societies. But rather than say that equality of condition supports the value of community, it would be more accurate to say that it is supportive of certain kinds of communities: those that are both internally egalitarian and relatively open for people who want to leave or join them.

### Equality and the environment

The environmental movement has posed one of the strongest contemporary challenges to the dominant values of western societies. Criticizing the idea of human beings as separate from nature and aspiring to be its masters, the movement has reasserted the view of many indigenous cultures that we are part of nature and need to act in harmony with the other inhabitants of our planet. Not only is it against the interests of our own species to pillage the earth's resources, but it fails to acknowledge that human interests are not the only interests concerned. The egalitarian tradition is not immune from these criticisms, since its proponents have often shared the dominant western belief in economic growth and in conquering the natural world. Is there, then, an intrinsic conflict between environmentalism and equality?

To answer this question, it helps to make use of the contrast drawn by Naess (1973) and other green political theorists between 'deep' and 'shallow' ecology (see Carter 1999, pp. 336–52; Devall and Sessions 1985). At one end of the scale, deep ecologists assert that 'all things in the biosphere have an equal right to live and blossom' (Devall and Sessions 1985, p. 67) and see the interests of human beings as a tiny fraction of the whole. At the other end, shallow or 'anthropocentric' ecologists base their defence of environmental values on the interests of human beings themselves: for humanity's own sake, rare species need to be preserved, resources conserved, pollution minimized and so on. Shallow ecologists also maintain that consumerism is a recipe for global disaster and that we need to re-examine our understanding of our own interests, challenging the dominant view of the good life as one of expanding consumption and pointing to other sources of fulfilment.

It seems clear enough that this shallow ecology is consistent with egalitarianism, and indeed that their insights need to be combined. One of the things egalitarians must take on board, as we have tried to do in our account of equal resources, is that environmental factors are themselves resources that have a major impact on people's well-being. Egalitarians also need to focus on the obvious truths that the earth's resources are limited and that, regardless of increases in productivity, we cannot reasonably expect an endless increase in consumption.[4] These truisms undermine one of the most persuasive objections to economic redistribution, namely that growth improves the living standards of the worst off anyway. If there are limits to growth, there are limits to the maxim that 'a rising tide lifts all boats' and equality of condition becomes all the more important (cf. Cohen 1995, pp. 9–12).

On the other side of the coin, environmentalists need to pay attention to how the costs and benefits of environmental policies are distributed. As the environmental justice movement has shown, the effects of environmental degradation are not equally felt (Dowie 1995; Guha 1997; Szasz 1994). Marginalized and subordinate groups are likely to be at the receiving end of pollution, hazardous production and global warming. Privileged groups are in a much better position to escape these effects. The policies necessary for reversing environmental damage also have their costs and benefits. The reduction in the use of fossil fuels, for example, has to be based on the principle of an equal entitlement to sources of energy.

It is less certain that egalitarianism is consistent with the various forms of deep ecology, because they involve such a radical redrawing of the moral universe. If egalitarians want to prioritize human needs, this must surely conflict in some cases with the needs of other living creatures, even if, as shallow ecologists maintain, the conflict is much less pervasive than is often assumed. An important issue here is the relationship between egalitarianism and the interests of non-human animals, sometimes captured by the idea of 'animal rights'. A number of arguments for human equality are relevant to other animals as well, whether these are posed in terms of concern for the well-being of other sentient creatures or more narrowly in terms of key capacities for choice and communication. To the extent that these arguments succeed, they represent an extension of egalitarianism rather than a conflict between it and environmental values. We do not take a stand on these arguments here. In the most prominent areas of environmental politics, such as opposition to motorways and large-scale dams, the preservation of wilderness and landscape, the protection of wild and domestic animals, the restriction of animal testing and the reduction of waste and pollution, there is a strong case to be made in purely human terms for environmentalist objectives. Some of the other concerns of environmentalists are best thought of as issues that should be settled through democratic political processes rather than bearing on the idea of equality itself (cf. Bell 2002). We therefore conclude that egalitarianism and environmentalism are essentially compatible outlooks, with the qualification that a conflict is more likely at the deep ecology end of the spectrum.[5] The affinity between them has a global expression in the increasing cooperation between social justice and environmental movements.

## Genuine conflicts between equality and other values

We have argued that equality is compatible with a wide range of values but we do not claim this for every possible value. In particular, egalitarian outlooks are clearly at odds with some widely held views about how income, wealth, power and status should be distributed in society. For example, there is a whole spectrum of views that state, one way or another, that some people are better than others and for that reason deserve to have superior rights, wider opportunities or more wealth and power. The crudest of these are the racist beliefs that have underpinned slavery, genocide and other forms of racist oppression. Although these anti-egalitarian attitudes are by no means extinct, a more prevalent view in our times is the meritocratic belief that people with superior talents and abilities deserve greater privileges and power than ordinary folk – a view that finds expression in our economies, our governments, our educational systems and elsewhere. Some liberal egalitarians are prepared to give qualified support to such doctrines; equality of condition confines their role to a very limited domain (such as limited inequalities of praise and public honours) or rejects them completely. We do not pursue these questions here, but note that this is one area in which equality and other values are in genuine conflict.

Another outlook that is clearly at odds with egalitarianism is the 'New Right' or 'libertarian' theory which states that within the broad legal limits defining a market economy, individuals should be free to use their ownership over themselves and their other property in whatever way they choose (e.g. Hayek 1976; Nozick 1974). If free, non-fraudulent trade leads to substantial inequality, so be it. And if the beneficiaries of this process choose to bestow some of their wealth on its victims, that is a matter of pure charity, not an obligation of justice. We have already commented on the way this perspective abuses the idea of freedom, but it remains a powerful ideology that is deeply opposed to equality and a core element of neoliberalism. Again, we will not pursue this debate here, but only register that we completely reject this view.

## Conclusion

In this chapter, we have argued that many important human values can be related to equality either as aspects of equality itself or as values to which the idea of equality can be applied. In particular, we have claimed that there are important connections between equality, freedom, solidarity and environmental values. We hope to have indicated how it is possible to have a consistent set of beliefs in which equality is the central and organizing principle.

In Chapter 1, when we set out the defining questions and methods of equality studies, we suggested that these presented a framework for approaching the central questions of our age. If different human values were constantly in conflict with equality and failed to combine into any kind of coherent egalitarian project, then the value of equality studies as a framework for integrating a variety of concerns would disappear. The fact that, on the contrary, the different values incorporated into egalitarian outlooks are mutually supportive and interdependent reinforces the argument for using equality in this way.

Equality is not the only value. As we have indicated, that does not even make sense. But it is more than just one value among many. It is a tool for making coherent connections between values and thereby constructing one or more coherent sets of principles for a good society. Such principles can be used to criticize existing social institutions and systems and to suggest ways to improve or replace them. That is the underlying premise of this book.

# 4
# Contexts of Egalitarian Change: Social Systems and Social Groups

The principle of equality of condition demands that the life prospects of every individual should be roughly equal to those of any other. What stands in the way of that principle are social structures that systematically produce worse life prospects for the members of some groups than for those of others. For example, the capitalist economic structures of our societies privilege certain social classes and reproduce those privileges across generations. Patriarchal structures throughout the world privilege men over women. Societies in which worth has been reduced to appearance and performance alienate and marginalize people with impairments by their very conception of what constitutes normality. And so on. Structurally-generated inequalities are reinforced, in turn, through the operation of institutional practices and procedures that frequently have hegemonic status and are therefore not subjected to scrutiny or debate.[1] The living out of inegalitarian relations in everyday practices further reinforces their powerful position, by making inequality appear natural and inevitable.

Social structures are embedded in and reproduced by social systems. The economic, political, cultural and affective systems are particularly important in generating equality and inequality, due to their core position within social life generally. Both Marx and Weber agreed that it was within the economy that basic material inequalities in wealth and income are generated (although they clearly differed in how they interpreted the operation of class relations within it and in the role they attributed to the economy in determining other inequalities). Weber further identified the ways in which political and cultural inequalities are independent of economic inequalities, treating the political and 'social' orders as discrete systems outside the economy.[2] Talcott Parsons (from a structural-functionalist perspective) also subscribed to the primacy of the economy, the polity and culture in explaining the dynamics of social systems.[3] Neither structural-functionalist, nor Marxist, nor Weberian social scientists identified any major role for the affective system of social relations independent of the economy, polity or status order. This neglect of the affective was not confined to sociologists: it also applied to philosophers, economists, social policy analysts and political theorists. The affective domain only began to be addressed as feminist scholarship highlighted the importance of care and love work within the lives of women particularly (Bubeck 1995; Hobson 2000; Nussbaum 1995b; Sevenhuijsen 1998).

In this chapter we start by outlining our understanding of the economic, political, cultural and affective systems and the relationship between these and the dimensions of equality set out in Chapter 2. We go on to illustrate the ways in which the systems interact to produce and reinforce inequality.[4] We suggest, however, that different systems play different roles in generating the inequalities experienced by different groups, and that this helps to explain why different groups have different political priorities. But because people often belong to more than one disadvantaged group, and because disadvantage is systematically reproduced across the whole range of systems, we argue that the members of different groups have a common interest in the development of a systematically different society, in which the institutions involved in sustaining all four systems are transformed. In Part II of this book, we set out some of the changes this transformation would involve.

## Social systems within which inequality is generated

A social system is a set of social relationships organized around a certain set of social processes and outcomes.[5] Analysing a society in terms of social systems is a way of trying to get a sense of the central sets of relationships that structure people's lives and in particular account for the inequalities between them.[6] As we shall see, the systems we distinguish here are not independent, but on the contrary are deeply intertwined, both conceptually and empirically.

An absolutely central system for generating inequality is of course the economy, the system concerned with the production, distribution and exchange of goods and services. As we think of it, the economic system refers not just to the set of institutions that operate in the market (what might be called the 'formal economy') but to the whole set of relationships, regulations, norms and values that govern the production, distribution, exchange and consumption of goods and services. There is therefore an economic aspect to virtually every social institution. As the defining system of capitalist social relations, the economy is at the centre of the processes through which capitalism generates inequality. So it is particularly important in relation to sustaining the inequalities imposed on working class people, the unemployed and other economically marginalized groups. It also plays an important role in sustaining and reproducing patriarchy, racism and other structures of oppression. Some of the key institutions that are important for the economic system are firms, trade unions and states, although practically every social institution in a capitalist society has an economic role.

A second important system of equality and inequality is a society's cultural system, which is concerned with the production, transmission and legitimation of cultural practices and products, including various forms of symbolic representation and communication. This system is especially important in generating and reinforcing social structures that are built around differences of appearance, values and preferences, such as racism, disablism, religious oppression and homophobia, teaching people to have different cultural and occupational expectations. The educational system, the mass media and religions all play important roles in the cultural system, as do such cultural institutions as museums, libraries, theatres and concert halls. The educational system passes the dominant ideas of society from one generation to the next, in ways that help to legitimate and reinforce inequalities, while at the same time it is a place where those ideas can be criticized and resisted. The mass media serve mainly to express and reinforce dominant ideas while again offering some opportunities for challenging them. Religions teach moral codes that tend to privilege certain groups and castigate others, although they, too, are a potential site of resistance. Other culturally important institutions, including art, literature, film and music are also involved in reinforcing, and occasionally challenging, dominant social norms. But practically every social institution has a cultural role.

The political system is the set of relationships involved in making and enforcing collectively binding decisions. Power relations are at the centre of the political system, although collective decisions do not always arise from exercises of power (Mansbridge 1999). As with the economy, we can distinguish between the formal political system – the set of institutions involved in making binding, coercively enforced decisions embodied in law – and this wider conception of the political system under which every social institution has a political aspect. In the political system, power is typically employed to back up, and occasionally to challenge, unequal social structures. Dominant groups use their power to pursue their own interests, while subordinate groups exercise whatever power or influence they can muster to resist this domination. The most prominent institution affecting the political system is the state, within which we can make a broad distinction between the set of institutions charged with determining public policy and legislation, the bureaucracy which puts these policies into practice and the legal system which enforces these laws through the courts. Other institutions that play an important political role include political parties, pressure groups, campaigning groups and the wider range of organizations in civil society. But collectively binding decisions occur throughout society: every social institution has a politics.

A fourth system of equality and inequality can be called the 'affective system', which is concerned with providing and sustaining relationships of love, care and solidarity. Inequality in the affective domain takes two primary forms: when people have unequal access to meaningful loving and caring relationships, and when there is inequality in the distribution of the emotional and other work that produces and sustains such relationships. The types of people who are likely to be deprived of love and care (for example, children who are left without a primary carer due to war, famine, AIDS, displacement, etc.) are generally very different from those who experience affective inequality due to undertaking a disproportionately high level of care work (women compared with men). The key institutions in contemporary societies for providing love and care are families, although these relationships are also sustained by networks of friendship and by public and commercial institutions such as schools and children's and old people's homes. The affective system plays a central role in generating and reproducing patriarchy, for example by socializing children into a gendered division of care labour that the adult members of kinship and friendship networks adhere to on a day-to-day basis. It also helps to reinforce links within dominant groups and to separate them from subordinate groups, although it is a source of solidarity for members of these groups, too. As before, it is important to emphasize that practically every social institution has an affective aspect in the ways that it generates and makes use of emotional bonds among its participants.

Although the distinction between the four systems is useful analytically, it should be clear from what we have said that they are completely inter-woven. The economic relationship between an employer and employee, for example, is also a relation of political power, as is the cultural relationship between a teacher and pupil. The relationships between a parent and a child are economic, cultural, political and affective. Similarly, social institutions typically play a role in all four systems. Mass media corporations, for example, are major economic actors, play a central role in cultural production, exercise political power both within and outside their organizations and shape the emotional relationships of their employees and their audiences. Governments wield political power, of course, but they use this power to influence the economic, cultural and affective systems as well as engaging directly in economic, cultural and affective activities. Just as every individual person is involved in economic, cultural, political and affective relationships, so it is typical of social institutions to be involved in all four systems, even if they play a more prominent role in some systems than others. Table 4.1 summarizes these points.

The distinction between these systems of equality and inequality and the dimensions of equality we set out in Chapter 2 creates a certain amount of terminological ambiguity. For example, the idea of 'economic inequality' can be used to refer to inequality of resources (and particularly of wealth and income). Similarly, 'political inequality' can be used to refer to inequalities of power. This is understandable since the economic system is important in

*Table 4.1*    Key contexts of equality and inequality

| *Key social systems* | *Central functions of each system* | *Systems and institutions with prominent roles in each key system* |
|---|---|---|
| Economic | Production, distribution and exchange of goods and services | Private sector producers and service providers<br>State economic activity (transfers, public services, etc.)<br>Voluntary sector service providers<br>Cooperatives<br>Trade unions |
| Cultural | Production, transmission and legitimation of cultural practices and products | Educational system<br>Mass media<br>Religions<br>Other cultural institutions (museums, theatres, galleries, concert halls, etc.) |
| Political | Making and enforcing collectively binding decisions | Legislation/policy-making system<br>Legal system<br>Administrative bureaucracies<br>Political parties<br>Campaigning organizations<br>Civil society organizations |
| Affective | Providing and sustaining relationships of love and care | Families<br>Friendship networks<br>Care-giving institutions (children's homes, old people's homes, etc.) |

determining the distribution of resources and the political system in determining power relations. But because economic relations almost always involve power relations, interpersonal relations, work and opportunities for learning, the expressions 'economic equality' and 'economic inequality' can also be used in a wider sense to refer to all of the equalities and inequalities that are endemic to these relations, including economic status, economic power, inequalities in economically relevant networks of friendship and kinship and inequalities of work and training. On this wider understanding of economic inequality, it is partly *constituted* by political, cultural and affective inequalities rather than having a causal relation to them. We adopt this wider understanding in this book. So cultural inequality includes not just inequalities of respect and recognition, but also inequalities of cultural resources like educational credentials, of the power to define what matters culturally, of love, care and solidarity within the cultural system and of access to culturally significant work and learning. Political inequality includes not just inequalities of power but also those inequalities of respect and recognition, resources, solidarity, work and learning that occur within the political system. And affective inequality includes not just inequalities of love, care and solidarity, but also inequality in the work that sustains these relationships, as well as the inequalities of status, resources, power and learning that our current arrangements for providing love and care involve.

A similar point applies to more specific contexts. Educational equality is primarily concerned with promoting a culture of equal respect and recognition and with providing each person with ample opportunities for satisfying learning, but it also refers to the other dimensions of equality that we would like to see in the educational system: that it should maintain an egalitarian distribution of educational resources, that it should foster and embody relationships of love, care and solidarity, that there should be a democratization of power within it and that the work within it should be satisfying and fulfilling. Legal equality is primarily concerned with reducing inequalities of power and of access to resources within the legal system, but it also involves fostering relations of equal respect and recognition, encouraging relations of solidarity and mutual aid, restructuring jobs and providing opportunities for learning.

## Interactions between the key systems

The economic, cultural, affective and political systems can be separately analysed, but that does not mean that they are independent. We have already seen that each of these systems is partly constituted by the others. To the extent that they are distinct systems, they also interact. What makes structural inequalities so persistent is that inequalities related to class, gender, disability, ethnicity, sexuality and so on are reinforced in all of the key social systems. In this section we illustrate some of the ways these systems interact.

### Interface between economic and political inequality

Economic inequalities have an obvious effect on political inequalities. The people who occupy positions of low income and power in the economy, such as those in poorly paid jobs or dependent on welfare payments, frequently have little say over collective decisions in other contexts as well, because of lack of time, energy and financial resources. Cultural aspects of their economic position, such as the low social status of their occupation, may also be reasons why they are regarded as unsuitable for powerful offices or positions of influence (Phillips 1999).

At the other end of the economic spectrum, the economically privileged are advantaged politically through their ability to fund political parties and causes and through their control of important economic decisions. Their access to privileged social networks in expensive schools, colleges, clubs or societies is an additional resource, a form of social capital that arises from their economic privilege and can heighten their influence with other powerful people (Bourdieu 1986). In addition, they are generally holders of valued educational credentials, occupational positions and roles that develop the skills and experiences deemed necessary for other powerful offices and positions.

## Interface between economic and cultural inequality

Economic inequality also affects the cultural system. This is most obvious in the relative exclusion of working class people from education, the mass media and the prestigious cultural institutions of society. Their accents, tastes, lifestyles, music, etc. are often defined as socially inferior (Bourdieu 1984), a factor that further exacerbates their cultural exclusion.

The interface between economic and cultural inequality is not one-way however. The way groups are treated in the cultural system can have profound implications for economic well-being. This can occur in different ways. The stereotyping and depreciation of Travellers has made it seem legitimate to refuse to meet their needs for decent halting sites and to force them into types of accommodation that are not of their own choosing.[7] The cultural definition of homosexual activity as sinful has made it seem legitimate to discriminate against gays and lesbians in the economy and in the welfare and taxation codes and to bully them in the workplace.

## Interface between cultural and political inequality

Cultural marginalization can also exacerbate political marginalization. Groups that are ignored, misrepresented, trivialized or otherwise negatively portrayed culturally are generally not granted credence in the political system. Consequently, they may be excluded from consultative arrangements, decision-making processes or other relevant political engagements. The exclusion of the unemployed for many years from certain Irish social partnerships, and of gay and lesbian organizations from Irish partnership bodies, are each examples of how cultural inequality can generate political inequality for a particular group (Mee and Ronayne 2000). Another example is the case of those who use Sign Language; they are not culturally recognized as a linguistic minority in most countries. Consequently it is difficult for them to influence language policy, a factor that further reinforces their cultural subordination.

Political inequality can, in turn, exacerbate cultural marginalization. Groups that have little influence over the operation of major cultural institutions are unlikely to have an equal status in the cultural system. In the Irish context, Travellers have traditionally had no influence in the educational system. They have not been defined as 'educational partners'; consequently, much of the education provided for Traveller children failed to take sufficient account of their culture and lifestyles (Government of Ireland 1995). Their lack of power to influence education policy added to their experience of cultural imperialism in education. The sense of alienation that ensued from such cultural imperialism precipitated Travellers' early departure from education, further reinforcing their marginalized status in society.

## Interface between affective and other inequalities

The impact of affective inequality on other inequalities is most clearly seen in the way in which the unequal role of women in the affective system serves as a basis for their subordinate position in the economic, cultural and political systems. Within the affective system, there is a gendered division of labour through which women are expected to provide most of the work involved in caring and in supporting personal relationships, although their resources to do so are limited and their care work is often controlled by others (Daly 2001; Delphy and Leonard 1992; McLaughlin 1991; Ungerson 2000). Although this division of labour may in general provide women with opportunities for loving relationships – a generalization to which there are many obvious exceptions – it has had the effect of excluding women from full participation in the economic, political and cultural systems. It has also had important effects on the position of women within these systems. For example, as a result of the way families, and sometimes schools, socialize girls into care-related work preferences, women are disproportionately involved in paid care work and disproportionately excluded from positions of economic power. The gendered division of labour has also reinforced male power and sidelined 'women's issues' in politics: the types of work that women tend to specialize in, particularly care work, are low on the political agenda. Those who do the care and love work are not present to name its importance in policy contexts. In the cultural system, the gendered division of care work has allowed for the cultural dominance of men and 'male' concerns and the relative subordination of women and of 'women's' concerns. Of course, all of these relationships work in both directions. The unequal position of women in the economic, political and cultural systems has operated to perpetuate their unequal position in the affective system by, for example, failing to provide resources to support women as carers and portraying caring as a low-status, unskilled occupation.

People who are homeless or people who are in prison suffer an extreme form of affective inequality through the severe disruption of their ties of love and care; in the case of prisoners, these affective relationships are typically replaced by their antithesis in the prison regime. We know from extensive empirical research that it is those who are economically marginalized who are most likely also to become homeless or to go to prison (Focus Point 1993; O'Mahony 1997; Stern 1998). Their protracted removal from affective relationships of all kinds has an impact on the self-esteem and self-confidence of homeless people and prisoners that makes it extremely difficult for them to participate fully in economic, cultural and political life even after their period of homelessness or imprisonment has come to an end.

The interaction of affective and other inequalities is also visible in the lives of refugees, asylum seekers, displaced persons and many economic migrants who are often cut off from family and friends. Those who are seeking asylum may have experienced brutal treatment before escaping from oppressive conditions. These affective burdens can make it very difficult for refugees and asylum seekers to establish a place in the economic, political and cultural systems of the countries in which they seek refuge. At the same time, the conditions in which they may be required to live can severely disrupt their affective relationships (Fanning, Veale and O'Connor 2001).

## Locating the generative causes of inequality across social groups

Although economic, political, cultural and affective inequalities are interrelated, different social systems may be more or less important in generating inequalities for different groups. In Table 4.2, we try to identify what, from a sociological perspective, could be defined as generative causes of inequality for some social groups. We realize that this is a highly simplified framework because social systems operate in complicated ways, and that it is open to empirical investigation. It is presented as a heuristic device to help identify the social systems that seem to contribute most fundamentally to creating and reproducing the inequalities experienced by different social groups. Identifying these systems can also help to locate the sites of social practice that are most important for each group in achieving social change.

*Table 4.2*   Key systems generating inequality for specific social groups

| *These* **Systems** | *play a primary role in generating the inequalities affecting these* **Groups** | | | | | | |
|---|---|---|---|---|---|---|---|
| | People dependent on welfare payments | Working class people | Disabled people | Travellers | Lesbians, gays, bisexuals | Women | Children |
| Economic | • | • | | | | | |
| Cultural | | | • | • | • | | |
| Affective | | | | | | • | |
| Political | | | | | | | • |

We acknowledge that research in partnership with different groups, especially research that takes account of the heterogeneity within groups, may arrive at a different understanding of these sources. The perspective of 'experts', even those who are committed to equality, is often different from that of people for whom inequality is a lived reality (Lynch and O'Neill 1994; see Chapter 9). At the same time, what may be identified from a sociological perspective as a generative force in the creation or perpetuation of inequality may not be what a given group sees as an immediate priority in terms of alleviating the inequality. One of the issues is that what may matter in the longer term may not be visible in the short term, or if visible may not be seen as important. In addition, those who have long been accustomed to hunger, poor health or discrimination may come to see their deprivation as natural (Sen 1985). Very oppressed people may have such low expectations that they accept unjust systems and institutions as unchangeable.

It is also the case that the ability to name the causes of inequality requires time, opportunity and in some cases education. There is a language to be learned, and those who are poor or marginalized are frequently deprived of that language by lack of education and information. This is an important consideration when analysing inequality as groups vary considerably in their level of education, politicization and awareness of their own inequalities. Lesbian, gay and bisexual groups, for example, have in recent times become more politicized and well-informed about the causes of their own oppression. By contrast, the learning disabled generally do not have a self-advocacy movement behind them to research, name and support their resistance to inequality. Thus, even if one engages in empirical research about the causes of inequality with the full participation of disadvantaged groups, this process will be affected by the different resources, abilities and experience of different groups.

The relationship between affective inequality and inequality in other systems is particularly difficult to map. It seems clear enough that the affective system plays a crucial role in generating the inequalities experienced by women. But while care-giving structures may work to the disadvantage of some older people and disabled people, this does not apply to all disabled or older persons in the way that economic structures affect all working class people or cultural structures have traditionally affected all Travellers. In identifying the political system as a primary cause of the inequalities experienced by children, we have in mind the subjection of children to the power of adults throughout society, and not just (or especially) in the formal political system. We do not identify the political system as the primary cause of inequality for other groups, but of course political relations have a very important role in reinforcing inequality for all groups. More generally, we hypothesize that every system has a role in sustaining inequality for every group, although this is open to empirical confirmation.

If Table 4.2 is at all accurate, then the systems that are most important in generating inequality vary for different groups. While the economic system may be primary in generating inequality among those groups whose most defining status is economic (working class people or those who are dependent on welfare payments such as the long-term unemployed), the economic inequality experienced by other groups may be an effect of either cultural, affective or political relations. Consequently, the political priorities of groups will vary in terms of mobilizing for change. While opposition to the capitalist institutions and norms that institutionalize inequality is vital for those struggling to break class inequality, it is obviously not as great a priority for lesbians, gays or bisexuals whose well-being, lifestyles and identities are more visibly threatened by homophobic laws and practices than by capitalism *per se.*

It should also be noted that because groups overlap, the causes of the inequalities experienced by members of two or more groups, for example working class women, are likely to be based in two or more social systems. We give particular attention below to the case of women to demonstrate that the inequalities experienced by women with different statuses or identities are generated in complex ways.

### Examples of the causation of inequalities for selected groups

For working class people and welfare claimants the key factor generating inequality is clearly the way that the economy creates and reproduces economic inequality, and the key issue for change is to restructure the economy to achieve greater equality of income and wealth, the democratization of economic relationships and the deconstruction of hierarchies of occupational status. Political or cultural inequalities for these groups are resistant to change so long as their economic position remains the same, because the greater economic resources and power of the economically privileged give them access to resources and power more generally, including cultural resources and power.

To say that economic change is a priority for those who are badly off for class reasons is to look at them from a particular perspective, namely their role in the economic system. It is *as workers* that the economy is particularly important for working class people. But people are not singular in their social identity. They have multiple identities: at any given time, a person is a member of several social groups. So the systems that are important for any particular working class person may include the cultural, affective or political as well as the economic.

Analysing the generative causes of inequality for disabled people is a difficult task. Early proponents of the social model of disability, who were influenced by Marxism, placed a strong emphasis on the role of the economic system in marginalizing people with impairments because they did not fit well into either the structures or ideologies of capitalist production (e.g. Barnes 1996, 2000; Finkelstein 1980; Oliver 1990). Other authors, influenced by postmodernism, have given greater emphasis to the role of the cultural system in generating and reinforcing stereotypes of helplessness and otherness that are often internalized by disabled people themselves (e.g. Shakespeare 1994). It is of course possible that these two processes work relatively independently in ways that reinforce each other, but for the sake of this discussion we hypothesize that cultural factors are primary.[8]

Travellers are much more clearly a group for whom the generative cause of inequality has been a prolonged history of cultural exclusion, marginalization and depreciation. While they also experience economic and political marginalization, these seem to originate in prior exclusions that are cultural in origin, including the lack of a culturally-sensitive education, exclusion from mainstream schooling and prejudicial attitudes fostered by the educational system, the mass media and other culturally important institutions.

The generative causes of inequality for lesbians, gays and bisexuals are also generally recognized as located in the cultural system, in which 'sexual deviance' has been portrayed in many cultures as disgusting and immoral. The implications of this cultural inequality extend beyond the cultural system to the economic, political and affective. For example, lesbians, gays and bisexuals are exposed to discrimination and bullying in the workplace (GLEN and Nexus 1995). They may feel especially vulnerable working in educational, health and other caring establishments in the context of a culture that regards same-sex orientations as immoral. The lack of recognition originating in the cultural system also affects such issues as pension entitlements, taxation issues, property rights and adoption (Mee and Ronayne 2000). In addition, cultural condemnation generally inhibits the participation of openly gay and lesbian people in politics and limits their opportunities for emotionally and sexually satisfying relationships.

In every society, children are subject to the power and control of adults (Archard 1993, 2003). In most legal systems, children are defined structurally as subordinate to the power of adults, especially their parents (see Duncan 1996; Government of Ireland 1996). In Ireland, as in many other countries, children are treated in many respects as the legal property of their parents; the family has inalienable and imprescriptible rights while children are subject to parents within this family context (Duncan 1996). The key system generating inequality for children is thus the political system in the broad sense defined above, backed up by the force of law and by a cultural code governing adult–child relations that is strongly protectionist and hierarchical (Devine 2000; Epp and Watkinson 1996). If children experience economic disadvantage, it is a derived state, arising from their position as subordinate to adults.

The fact that children occupy a different social status to adults illustrates the complex nature of inequality and how inequalities can change over the life course of a single person. As well as having relatively fixed identities, such as those based on gender and ethnicity, people also have transitory identities that change with age, marital status and other life course events. Their susceptibility to different forms of inequality varies therefore with time and experience.

## The particularities of different identities: the case of women

Women are a particularly important group to analyse, not only because they comprise half the population, but also because the problems of inequality faced by women are complex, given the high level of diversity among them. We have already discussed how the position of women in the affective system generates gender inequalities in the economic, cultural and political systems. But focusing on women highlights the problem of diversity within all groups. Women are not just women; they may also be advantaged or disadvantaged by their class, age, ethnic origin, sexual orientation, disability, etc. This is seen most clearly in the fact that certain women are subordinated to other women: working class to middle class, those with disabilities to those without disabilities, those who are lesbian to those who are heterosexual. In other words, gender-based inequalities interact with other inequalities.

To illustrate how multiple identities create inequalities in a given case, we focus here on how gender-based inequalities interact with other inequalities to determine women's incomes. Multiple identities mean that on some occasions it may be a woman's social class that is principally responsible for her relatively low income; in other cases, it may be her age, marital status or disability. Thus, while women *as* women tend to have lower incomes than men, quite how this affects individual women is mediated by their other socially important characteristics.

Women who are married and are dependent on a husband's income are typically financially disadvantaged by the patriarchal structure of the family and the power it gives to husbands to control the distribution of household income. But if the husband himself receives low wages or a low social-welfare income, the woman's relatively low income may be more strongly determined by her (derived) class position than by her gender.

A somewhat different analysis applies to the inequalities experienced by women employed in low-paid, often temporary, work. While their low income is directly related to their social class, it is compounded by a segregation of the labour market along gender lines that has its roots in the gendered division of labour in the affective system. As a result, working class women are disproportionately socialized, educated and guided into low-status, stereotypically feminine service occupations (cleaning, catering, assisting, etc.) with low pay and little security.

As most adult disabled women are not in employment, their low income is the effect of their dependence on disability-related welfare payments. Yet the poverty of disabled women may be exacerbated by the way in which disability interacts with femininity. Given the importance of appearance and the 'beauty culture' that underpins conventional definitions of femininity in our society, together with the cultural codes that assume that women will care for others rather than require care themselves (O'Connor 1998), women with physical impairments are especially vulnerable to stereotyping or prejudice (Hughes 2002; Morris 1991; Wendell 1996). This is the case not only in intimate relationships where their physical impairments are presented as making them less desirable as partners, but also in employments where appearance is highly valued and where bodily perfection is an unwritten normative code. Thus their financial prospects may be worse than those of disabled men because of these gender-related factors.

What the foregoing analysis suggests is that we should be careful not to assume that any group is homogeneous when addressing inequalities. All groups need to be disaggregated. The injustices experienced by a particular group may be rooted in cultural, economic, affective or political structures. But because all human beings operate with multiple and overlapping identities, there is no person whose social position, and correlatively whose experience of injustice, takes a singular form.

## Implications for policy and politics

The fact that inequality is generated and reproduced in the economic, cultural, political and affective systems means that these systems are of central importance in developing and maintaining an egalitarian society. How well people are doing in each of these four systems and in the institutions and practices that sustain them largely determines how well the ideals of equality set out in Chapter 2 are being met.

Since inequality is generated by social systems, the task of achieving greater equality depends on reforming these systems, while a programme for equality of condition must include proposals for systematically restructuring them. The problems of institutional design involved in such a task are enormous. For one thing, every society starts off with a somewhat different history, culture and institutional set-up, so institutional reform and restructuring must inevitably take a rather different shape in different societies (Goodin 1996; Offe 1995). For another, the sheer complexity of social change means that things never turn out quite as predicted, and sometimes turn out disastrously wrong. One classic response to this fact is to insist that any attempt to rethink systems and institutions holistically is fundamentally misguided and that the only reasonable approach is to engage in 'piecemeal engineering' by which small, incremental changes are made over an indefinite time span (Popper 1966, pp. 158–9). But if we believe that existing systems and institutions operate systematically to reproduce gross injustice, we have a duty to imagine structures that would work in a very different way: to imagine another world. How we achieve those changes is a further question; a vision of a radically different society does not necessarily justify a policy of trying to change things all at once. But if we have no conception of even the general shape of an egalitarian society, our belief in such a society is bound to seem unrealistic.

In Part II of this book, we engage constructively in the effort to imagine a different world. At some points we attempt to envisage radically different social structures. At others we are more concerned with some ways that present systems can be reformed for the better. We address only a fraction of the institutional changes that would be necessary to produce and sustain egalitarian societies in an egalitarian world, but we hope that by placing these analyses within the context of this book we can indicate the value of a coherent framework for thinking about egalitarian change. Our contribution to this task is unavoidably limited by our own experience, knowledge, interests and perspectives, and is informed particularly by our knowledge of and engagement in the social institutions of the Irish republic. But we are confident that our proposals for institutional change will strike a chord with many readers both inside and outside Ireland and will help them to formulate their own programmes for an egalitarian future.

In Part III, we turn to the question of how to strengthen the egalitarian movement for change. In that connection, it is important to remember the point made in this chapter that different groups are likely to prioritize different systems in their programmes for egalitarian change. If our analysis here is correct, this is a perfectly rational response to the ways that different social systems generate inequality for different groups. One of the major challenges for egalitarian activists therefore is to establish how to engage politically with the different priorities of different groups. As the labour–capital nexus is but one (albeit major) context of injustice, political mobilization for equality cannot be based solely on class politics. This is especially vital for such very large groups as women or ethnic groups whose experience of inequality is not generated in the first instance by social class relations. What Table 4.2 suggests is that sociologically speaking (and by extension politically speaking), mobilization around equality issues must extend across all four systems. This conclusion is reinforced by the fact that everyone belongs to a number of social groups, that the contexts that generate inequality for a given person change over their life course and that the different systems of inequality interact to deepen the inequalities experienced by any one group. Thus the programme of institutional change set out in Part II is not a piecemeal programme in which each context is of exclusive interest to a single set of groups. It is a coherent programme in which each element is relevant to constructing the kind of world in which everyone can live as equals.

## Conclusion

In this chapter we have given a broad overview of the ways that economic, cultural, political and affective systems work together to produce and reinforce inequality. We have suggested that different systems play different roles in generating the inequalities experienced by different groups and that this helps to explain why different groups have different political priorities. But we have emphasized that people often belong to more than one disadvantaged group, that the contexts that generate inequality for a given person change over their life course and that inequality is systematically reproduced across the whole range of systems. The practical point of this analysis is to show that an egalitarian programme has to take up the challenge of reforming and restructuring the systems that generate inequality and of developing inclusive strategies for bringing about change. It is to these tasks that we now turn.

# Part II
# Putting Equality into Practice

# 5
# Towards Economic Equality

The economy is a central context for the achievement of a more egalitarian society. So it is important to understand the ways in which economists have approached the idea of equality and particularly the issue of a more equal distribution of income. Issues of equality and efficiency are central aspects of most economic problems, yet within the discipline of economics itself, both the theoretical literature and empirical analysis have concentrated on issues of efficiency. Our response to this imbalance is to focus on the different explanations of inequality proffered by economists, the claims they have made about the relationships between equality, efficiency and growth, and the implications for identifying paths towards a more egalitarian economy.

The first section gives a brief sketch of the pervasiveness of economic inequality and the extent of the material divide between North and South. The second section addresses the question of equality within the discipline of economics by looking at the views of equality taken by different schools of thought including the classic liberal perspective, modern liberal schools (including post-Keynesianism and neocorporatism) and more radical views including institutional economics, social economics, feminist economics and the post-Marxists. We focus in particular on neoclassical economics because it has a dominant status among the competing views in political economy. It embodies the mainstream of economic theory, thought and practice. Its theoretical assumptions are often translated into economic policy prescriptions accepted and utilized by government, business, the media and the public. Thus rather than operating as a neutral science it has served instead as an ideology of the free market and the maximization of economic growth. Furthermore the possibilities for economic change within the more radical perspectives have been so strongly influenced by neoclassical economics that visions of an egalitarian society no longer necessarily preclude significant private (productive) ownership and a reliance on markets. An understanding of its approach to economic inequality is therefore essential.

The third and fourth sections address a core area of economic theory and empirical research concerned with equality, namely the relationship between equality and efficiency. We begin by reviewing the evolving literature at the macroeconomic level on the relationship between equality and growth. We go on to explore at the microeconomic level the policy implications of the equality/growth relationship and to review the continuing debate on the equality–efficiency trade-off and the issue of distortionary effects. The final section of the chapter explores alternative routes to greater economic equality and concludes by suggesting that more attention should be given to ways of reducing the disparity in primary incomes rather than focusing entirely on mechanisms for correcting that disparity through taxation and transfers.

The chapter is primarily concerned with examining two widely held views in economics – that inequality is necessary for economic success and that equality compromises efficiency. It therefore does not discuss other important literatures within economics that are also important for equality, for example the development literature and most notably the work of Sen (1988, 1999). While the emphasis in this chapter is on income, since that is the dominant indicator used for both growth (as in GDP or GNP) and inequality (income distribution), it is recognized that economic inequality is also concerned with inequalities of status, power and work and has important effects on love, care and solidarity. While traditionally these issues have not been widely debated within economics as a discipline, they do feature in feminist economics, an important contribution of which has been to explore the interface between feminist theory and political economy with particular emphasis on caring labour and other forms of non-market work (Folbre 1996; Nelson 1996).

## Economic inequality: a glance

As we pointed out in Chapter 1, the existence of economic inequality is indisputable. Economic inequalities, which are embedded in the economic structures of society, include various forms of exclusion, deprivation and exploitation of a material kind. Significant levels of inequality exist across many areas of the economy, for example ownership, wealth, disposable income, wages, taxation, employment, health, housing and education.[1] Here we focus on inequalities of income.

According to the Luxembourg Income Study, which used data from the mid-1980s, the only country in the OECD with a more unequal distribution of income than Ireland was the US (Atkinson, Rainwater and Smeeding 1995). A later study showed Ireland having the same level of income inequality in the mid-1990s as the UK, Greece and Italy but higher levels of inequality than Australia and Canada (Forster 2000). In Ireland, the poorest 10 per cent of the population receive about 2 per cent of total disposable income whereas the richest 10 per cent receive about 27 per cent of total disposable income. Indeed, much of the inequality in disposable income in Ireland is due to the relatively elevated position, by international standards, of the rich. Wage dispersion in Ireland is very high by international standards and the evidence suggests that there has been a consistent widening in dispersion at the top of the wage distribution and a marked increase in the ratio of the top to the bottom decile in the 1990s despite the existence of centralized wage setting in social partnership programmes from 1987 onwards (Nolan *et al.* 2000). The Irish Household Budget Survey demonstrates a widening gap between the disposable incomes of the highest income households and those of the lowest, with the ratio between them increasing from 11:1 to 13:1 between 1996 and 2001 (CSO 2002). Such evidence of economic inequality is not confined to Ireland; the evidence suggests that inequality in the distribution of earnings and of household income increased very sharply during the 1980s and 1990s in a number of industrialized countries and most dramatically in the UK and the US. There has been some levelling off of the increase in the US since the mid 1990s but no reversal of the trend.

In addition to paid employment, income is generated through the ownership of wealth. A key factor therefore in addressing inequality of income is inequality of wealth. The most common difficulty in examining the distribution of wealth both in Ireland and elsewhere is the lack of reliable comprehensive data. The available data for Ireland suggest that the richest 10 per cent of the population own about half of total household wealth while the top 1 per cent owns about a fifth (Nolan 1991). In the US the share of the top 20 per cent is about 80 per cent of total wealth while the share for the top 1 per cent is about 38 per cent (Boshara 2003). The distribution of wealth is unlikely to be very different in most other industrialized countries.

The issue of income inequality also arises between nations and especially between developing and developed countries. Indeed the most extreme income inequalities at present exist between countries, and especially between North and South. The World Bank's Development Indicators in 2003 recorded a range of per capita income from $490 in Sierra Leone to $34 142 in the US.[2] One conventional measure of inequality, the Gini co-efficient, indicates a level of global inequality in excess of 0.6, a figure significantly higher than within even the most unequal of the developed countries (in the US the Gini co-efficient is 0.4).[3] On a global level, over half of the world's population has access to only 12 per cent of total income. At the other extreme, about 15 per cent of the world's population commands around three quarters of world income; the three richest people in the world have assets that exceed the combined GDP of the 48 least developed countries. In the second half of the 1990s, 1.3 billion people in developing countries were living on less than a dollar a day, 32 per cent of those in the transition economies on less than four dollars a day and 11 per cent in industrial countries on less than $14.40 a day (UNDP 1998). Thus, any attempt to develop a more egalitarian economic system cannot limit itself to a particular country, or group of countries, but must take account of both the extent of world-wide inequalities and the context of globalization.[4] With over 70 per cent of global income inequality accounted for by across-countries income inequalities, a reduction in global income inequality is impossible without serious attention being directed to the issue of the North/South divide.

These are some of the central facts of income inequality. But our main concern is with how economists explain this inequality and with the insights they can provide into how it can be reduced.

## Economic perspectives on equality

### Neoclassical economics: market allocation and equality

The government and the market represent two possible structures for organizing the distribution of a society's resources. The market allocates resources and arrives at a particular income distribution against the backdrop of a particular set of property rights. To the extent that they engage with the normative concept of 'fairness', extreme proponents of the market system maintain that this distribution of income will be fair if the background property rights are themselves fair. In contrast, government allocates resources according to conscious policy decisions. Proponents of government allocation maintain that it allows for a broader conception of fairness that includes economic, political and social rights, for example the homeless person's need for, and right to, housing; the disabled person's need for, and right to, access to public spaces; or the right of each person to have a (single) vote in elections. The differences between these two approaches to achieving fairness or 'equity' can be overstated, as, for example, few people think that every allocation of goods to people should be made by the state, while few would argue that votes or people should be marketable. Hence, in practice, most people – including economists – accept that equity, however defined, relies on both the market and the state.

The perspective on equality found in the work of many neoclassical economists, however, is heavily influenced by the narrower approach to equity or fairness associated with allocation by the market. They justify this restriction by their commitment to a rather narrow scientific method (non-holistic modelling) that is taken to require the avoidance of variables, relationships or connections that are difficult or impossible to measure, such as those involved in comparing the welfare of different individuals or in expressing the broader ideas of justice associated with government allocation. The shaping of individual preferences by social factors or even social conditioning has also been neglected in the standard neoclassical literature. Even efficiency in neoclassical economics is defined narrowly, as Pareto-efficiency, which stipulates that a particular allocation of resources is efficient so long as no change would make someone better off without making someone else worse off. This definition fits very neatly into allocation by the market because it can be shown that, given certain conditions, Pareto-efficiency occurs whenever all mutually beneficial market-based exchanges have been exhausted. Thus many neoclassical economists avoid choosing between the various Pareto-efficient (or Pareto-optimal) allocations on egalitarian or any other grounds, as they argue that such a choice would require a moral judgement that goes beyond the boundaries of economic science. This reasoning inevitably gives prominence to the status quo as almost any proposed policy change (e.g. redistribution) involves losers as well as winners and so cannot be justified as a Pareto improvement. Thus, in general, neoclassical economists tend not to address the concept of equality from a theoretical perspective. Although they often present themselves as concerned only with explanations about what happens and what causes it, they implicitly endorse the fairness of the market by ruling out other evaluations.

Varian (1975) offers a challenge to this perspective from within neoclassical economics itself, by developing an account of equity and fairness that discriminates among Pareto-efficient allocations without violating the central assumptions of the discipline. Varian defines an equitable (or envy-free) allocation as any allocation in which every person prefers her or his own share to anyone else's share. A fair allocation is then defined as an allocation that is both equitable and Pareto-efficient. Varian makes a significant contribution to the theoretical literature by incorporating production, as well as exchange, within this neoclassical framework; he includes in an allocation the labour or production input, as well as the consumption bundle, associated with each individual. But despite the attempts of Varian and others (e.g. Harsanyi 1976) at founding what might loosely be termed a neoclassical economic moral theory, the neoclassical economics approach has been criticized as being rather sterile and abstract as it 'starts with the notion of exchange of material things as the self-evident beginning and end of human behavior, and attempts no construction of a deeper foundation for the theoretical edifice that follows' (Zajac 1995).

Thus, notwithstanding the refusal of many neoclassical economists to attempt moral judgements, it is clear that in practice they tend to evaluate market outcomes in terms of efficiency, thereby rejecting any attempt to achieve equality by interfering with the market. Given their dominance in contemporary economics, this position has a powerful influence on how different schools of thought approach equality.

## Contrasting perspectives on equality

The perspectives on equality of the various schools of economic thought show up most clearly in their attitude towards the role of government in the allocation of resources.[5] The classical political economists' doctrine of laissez-faire was supported by the neoclassical economists' later discovery of the efficiency attributes of markets. This classical liberal perspective is also reflected in the Austrian School's rejection of government involvement in the economy. By contrast, what can be called the modern liberal perspective is more supportive of the need for government involvement. 'Although Modern Liberals recognize potential conflict between the values of individualism and equality, they remain confident that the two values can reinforce each other when the powers of government and the market are appropriately balanced' (Clark 1998, p. 36). This view is today associated with new Keynesian and post-Keynesian economics. Finally, institutional economics (e.g. Veblen) and post-Marxian theory represent two descendants of the Marxist perspective, which supported government control of productive resources.

These differences between the various schools of economic thought with respect to government involvement in the economy are reflected in their approaches to the distribution and redistribution of income. Two distinct explanations for differences in income – the human capital (or achievement) model and the exploitation model – tend to dominate the analysis of economic inequality in market economies. These models are primarily concerned with employment rather than investment income and sidestep the issue of inherited wealth. In essence, the human capital model views income as a return on people's productive capacity – their 'human capital' – which is a function of their natural capacities and the efforts 'invested' in them by themselves and their parents; the focus is on individual choice. Different degrees of economic success between people with similar natural endowments simply reflect different choices to invest in education and training, and these investments determine people's later earning capacity (i.e. current earnings are exchanged for future earnings). The exploitation model, on the other hand, views income distribution as a result of economic and social relations. Income is determined by where one fits into the processes that determine income rather than individual achievement based on individual attributes. This model concentrates on the distribution and control of those assets (physical and financial capital, skills, technological knowledge) that put one in a position to appropriate a disproportionate share of output (Clark 1998).

The human capital model accords neatly with the classical liberal belief that all should have the same formal opportunities to engage in economic activity and the same civil rights. Within this framework, together with the theory that factors of production are paid according to their marginal productivity, inequality is seen as resulting from, and justified by, different levels of human capital or other resources. Inequality is explained by individual preferences (e.g. via compensating wage differentials) and changing technology as well as by inappropriate government intervention; it is seen as arising from 'capitalist acts between consenting adults' (Nozick 1974). In addition, inequality is seen as providing the essential incentives and motivations for the saving and investments that drive the economic growth necessary for eliminating poverty.

In the modern liberal framework, in contrast, inequality is explained by past injustices, cycles of poverty and discrimination as well as by imperfect competition. This explanation draws on both the human capital model and the exploitation model. Using some of the principles associated with liberal egalitarianism, modern liberals claim that fair equality of opportunity is jeopardized by large inequalities in income and wealth and hence accept the need for limits to inequality of income, especially at the bottom of the distribution. In addition, they recognize that the market fails to protect some human rights such as the right to an adequate standard of living. Both of these considerations justify a significant economic role for government. Modern liberals also maintain, from a utilitarian perspective, that the maximization of societal welfare requires redistribution and, more generally, that the market will lead to an inefficient allocation of resources, i.e. that government involvement in redistribution is justified on efficiency as well as equity grounds (Hochman and Rodgers 1969). Given that inequality may also undermine support for capitalism and democracy, more equality is seen as a prerequisite for economic growth. However, modern liberals also highlight the potential trade-off between redistribution (i.e. the pursuit of equality) and the pursuit of efficiency, a claim to which we return below.

The radical perspective on inequality found in the Marxist tradition initially focused on the concentration of property ownership that underpinned capitalism. The presence of a reserve army of workers allowed capitalists to reward themselves with the surplus produced by workers who were paid subsistence wages. More recently, radicals have pointed to the existence of dual labour markets, with workers in the secondary sector in effect subsidizing the high wages of workers in the primary sector. Low productivity in the secondary sector is seen as the effect, as opposed to the cause, of low wages and meagre job prospects. Equality, while viewed as valuable in itself and as a prerequisite for social order, is also seen as providing the self-esteem and motivation necessary for economic growth. This commitment to equality is taken to justify such government policies as high levels of taxation and the confiscation of private property. Although some radicals demand a major restructuring of the economy and an alternative to the market system (e.g. Albert 2003; Devine 1988), most appear to accept that a more egalitarian society is achievable through a market economy with a more equal distribution of property ownership and/or substantial government involvement (e.g. Bowles and Gintis 1998; Roemer 1994, 1996; Schweickart 1994). Some of these approaches are briefly discussed in the final section of this chapter.

In summary, classical liberal economists view inequality as a legitimate feature of the market order and a prerequisite for long-run economic growth, whereas modern liberals as well as some radicals view equality of some form as morally desirable as well as necessary for growth. Thus part of the disagreement is normative and relates to the issues we have discussed in Chapters 2 and 3. But part of it is about the relationships between equality, growth and efficiency: does equality have to be traded off against growth and efficiency or not?

## Economic inequality and economic growth: theory and evidence

There is a large and rapidly expanding literature in economics on the nature of the relationship between income inequality and economic growth.[6] Kuznets (1955) hypothesized that income inequality in developed countries, after an initial increase, would decrease with economic growth; indeed, Kuznets thought that the data available in the 1950s showed a trend towards greater equality in the US and the UK. As illustrated above, data for both the US and the UK in the 1980s and 1990s, as well as for other countries, undermine this simple yet still influential theory. The Kuznets hypothesis was overtaken on both the theoretical and empirical sides of the economic literature during the 1990s by an emerging consensus that income inequality adversely affects economic growth. However, the exact nature of the negative link between income inequality and economic growth, and hence the appropriate policy responses, remain extremely contentious issues.

On the theoretical side of the literature, there are several competing explanations that focus on human capital. Some authors argue that inevitable capital market imperfections hinder investment by poor households in education and hence the development of human capital, leading to greater income inequality and lower-than-potential economic growth. Hence, they argue, the appropriate policy response is to decrease income inequality, perhaps most directly by higher levels of redistribution, in order to increase economic growth (Aghion and Bolton 1997; Chiu 1998). A more psychologically based theory, associated with Knell (1999), suggests that higher levels of income inequality lead poor households to over-consume and hence under-invest in an attempt to match rich households' consumption in the short run. In this framework, high levels of income inequality again lead to low levels of economic growth through the channel of under-investment in human capital. An increasingly influential strand of the economics literature focuses attention on households' decisions with respect to fertility as well as investments in human capital. High levels of income inequality are associated with decisions to invest in the quantity of children, as opposed to greater human capital investments in a smaller number of children. This high fertility rate, through low levels of investment in human capital, gives rise to low levels of economic growth.

Two other influential explanations focus on the social effects of inequality. Some political economy models suggest that increased income inequality inevitably gives rise to attempts (at least in democracies) at more redistribution, which, in turn, lowers incentives to invest and reduces economic growth.[7] Hence, it is argued, the appropriate policy response is to commit to lower levels of redistribution, for example lower levels of capital taxation, in order to encourage investment and increase economic growth. Another socio-political explanation is that high levels of income inequality cause political, economic and social instability, which reduces economic growth.

The empirical evidence goes only some way towards clarifying matters. The negative correlation between income inequality and economic growth appears to be a fairly stable feature of the literature, as it holds across many different sets of countries and for many different time periods. The negative relationship also appears to be statistically robust, that is, it does not appear to be caused by such issues as the presence of outliers or measurement errors. However, the existence of a negative relationship does not imply cause and effect, nor does it imply the necessary success of a policy of redistribution. Indeed, a part of the literature that focuses on the evolution of the relationship between income inequality and economic growth within individual countries suggests that a decrease in income inequality within a country has no relation, positive or negative, to economic growth. This appears to suggest that income inequality is akin to an original sin – its presence is associated with lower levels of economic growth but its removal would make no difference. In addition, it appears that a significant part of the negative relationship between income inequality and economic growth stems from regional differences between Latin America (mainly a region of high income inequality and low economic growth) and South East Asia (mainly a region of low income inequality and high economic growth). It is possible that cultural differences between these (and other) regions may lie beneath at least part of the negative relationship between income inequality and economic growth.

Notwithstanding all of these problems, the empirical evidence appears to offer little support for the political economy models that claim that inequality generates a politics of redistribution that reduces economic growth. For example, there does not appear to be a positive relationship between income inequality and redistribution nor does there appear to be a negative relationship between redistribution and economic growth, both of which are envisaged in the basic political economy model. Support is lacking even when attention is restricted to democracies, where the linkages should be particularly clear.

The vehicle for redistribution is usually the taxation and social expenditure system, via higher rates of taxation on labour and capital income in combination with increased expenditures, including both direct transfers and spending on education and training. It is here that the second line of defence of inequality is erected, based on the issue of the effects of redistribution on economic efficiency.

## The equality–efficiency trade-off: theory and evidence

The central claim of this second line of defence is that there is a fundamental conflict between the objectives of equality and efficiency. Any review of this hypothesis has to begin with Okun's famous and influential book, *Equality and Efficiency: The Big Tradeoff* (1975). Okun's starting point is that capitalist democracies adopt what he calls a double standard when they try to pursue both efficiency and equality, that is, when they try both to maximize the output from a given set of inputs and to honour their commitment to treat citizens equally. He argues that attempts to equalize the distribution of the output of any given economy will reduce efficiency because inequalities reflect incentives that are essential for efficient productive activity. Inequalities in material wealth 'reflect a system of rewards and penalties that is intended to encourage efficiency and channel it into socially productive activity. To the extent that the system succeeds, it generates an efficient economy. But that pursuit of efficiency necessarily creates inequalities. And hence society faces a tradeoff between inequality and inefficiency' (Okun 1975, p. 1). Like a 'leaky bucket', redistribution always involves some loss. Much of the theoretical and empirical research in this area concerns the existence and size of this alleged trade-off. This section gives a brief synopsis of the trade-off argument and assesses the empirical evidence.

At the centre of the argument are a number of suggested effects on work, saving and investment. First, the direct impact of transfers is to reduce their recipients' incentive to work. Secondly, the taxation of income and capital holdings required to fund these transfers further distorts incentives to work, save and invest. Both of these affect behaviour more broadly, for example child rearing, household formation, etc. A third aspect of the trade-off is the administrative cost of taxation and transfer payments. There has been some research questioning the validity of these assumptions but most of the empirical work undertaken in this area has attempted to estimate the size of the disincentive effects of both taxation and social welfare transfers on employment and unemployment (Atkinson and Micklewright 1989; Dilnot 1992).

### Social welfare transfers

As McLaughlin (1994, p. 145) remarks, 'it is difficult to overstate the political and associated policy influence of the idea that the provision of out of work income constitutes an inherent disincentive to find, take or keep employment'. The common-sense appeal of this idea finds voice in public rhetoric where it has often been asserted that paying the unemployed discourages them from really looking for a job. In Ireland, for example, concern about disincentive effects resulted in the phasing out of the earnings-related supplement to unemployment benefit that operated in the 1970s and 1980s. Yet the empirical evidence for the argument is, at best, inconclusive. The disincentive to work rests on the existence of an 'unemployment trap', which refers to a situation where people are better off financially by remaining unemployed than by taking up work, that is, their unemployment compensation is higher than the net take-home pay they could earn from employment.[8] The disincentive is usually represented and measured in terms of the 'replacement ratio', the ratio of unemployment compensation to net take-home pay. Analysis based on various hypothetical situations in Ireland and the UK suggests that for some types of welfare recipients the replacement ratio is very high, i.e. they could receive 80 per cent (or in rare cases over 100 per cent) of what they would get if they were working. These accounts are invariably based on particular categories of welfare recipients – for example, the disincentive facing a couple with four children, living in public housing and in receipt of long-term unemployment assistance. Analysis based on actual samples indicates that only a very small proportion of those currently employed face a high replacement ratio, and further, that there are people currently working who would be better off in cash terms if they were unemployed, but this receives a lot less attention (Callan and Nolan 1992; Glyn and Miliband 1994). Friedman's assertion that there is no such thing as a purely economic issue seems pertinent here as we can see that a non-holistic approach based on a narrow conceptualization and measurement of what constitutes disincentives, limiting itself to cash income, underplays the institutional and sociocultural context. The most important influences on people's incentives to work are institutional factors such as the way benefit is administered, the constraints imposed (e.g. whether it is means tested or universal) and the nature of labour markets, as well as cultural factors such as the fact that individuals work for a variety of other reasons including social norms, satisfaction, status and power. Claims about the incentive effects of transfer payments are therefore based on a fundamental misconception of human motivation and circumstance (McLaughlin 1994).

### Taxation

Taxation is the most direct mechanism available to a government to alter the degree of income inequality produced by the market. Taxation policy therefore requires explicit equity decisions and yet nowhere is the inability to make those decisions more evident (Thurow 1980). Contradictions abound within any given tax regime, with the progressive effects of cash transfers and non-cash benefits often offset by regressive indirect taxes. In Ireland, analysis of the redistributive effects of state taxes and benefits indicates that the modest progressivity of the income tax system is significantly offset by tax expenditures (tax deductions), which can be claimed on a wide range of items including private health insurance and pension contributions (Cantillon and O'Shea 2001). In the UK the evidence suggests that the tax system (combining direct and indirect taxes) is actually regressive to the extent that it widens the income distribution from a ratio of seven to one between the top and bottom quintiles for gross income (including benefits) to almost eight to one after tax (Johnson 1994, p. 162).

Economic theory suggests that taxation affects incentives to work, save and spend, creating distortions and inefficiencies. The main issue is direct taxation, with the assumption that high rates of income tax encourage avoidance, destroy enterprise and reduce work effort. However, just as the evidence of the impact of income support on incentives is inconclusive, so too is the evidence of the impact of tax on work. This is because the evidence on what are called the *income* and *substitution effects* of taxation is very difficult to disentangle. An increase in the rate of income tax will affect an individual's desire to work in two ways. First, it will reduce the amount of income received from working an extra hour and hence make it less attractive to work relative to pursuing leisure activities. Accordingly people might reduce the number of hours worked. This *substitution effect* means that an individual substitutes hours spent in leisure activities for hours spent working. Alternatively, the reduction in an individual's income due to the tax increase may make the person want to work more hours in order to regain the income level enjoyed prior to taxation. This is the *income effect* whereby the person increases the hours spent working to come out with the same income. These income and substitution effects underlie neoclassical economics' theories of labour supply. Because the effects generally work in opposite directions and the impact of the increase in taxation is the net effect of the two, it is very difficult to predict the overall effect on work effort. It is widely assumed that increases in taxes always deter individuals from working harder. But if the income effect is greater than the substitution effect then an increase in taxation will increase willingness to work, not reduce it. While repeated studies have shown that highly progressive tax systems do not reduce work effort because income effects tend to dominate substitution effects (see Putterman, Roemer and Silvestre 1998, pp. 876–7), it is still widely believed that raising tax rates has such strong disincentive effects that total tax revenue is reduced and vice versa. This view, summarized by what is known as the Laffer curve, was used to justify recent cuts in capital gains tax in Ireland.[9]

Although the view that taxation reduces work incentives is questionable, there is another sense in which taxation is said to have an effect on efficiency. In the neoclassical theory of taxation, taxes on labour are considered distortionary because they change the relative prices of work and leisure. The theory compares the effect of labour taxes with lump-sum taxes based on unalterable personal characteristics. It goes on to show that such lump-sum taxes, because they are non-distortionary, could raise more revenue with the same inputs (or, equivalently, could raise the same revenue at a lower cost to the welfare of individuals) (Stiglitz 1988, p. 392). The difference between the lump-sum tax and a tax on labour is called the 'deadweight loss' of the labour tax and is taken to show that redistribution makes the average person worse off than if the lump-sum tax had been levied (Heady 1993, pp. 22–3). Estimates of the size of the deadweight loss vary widely but there is general agreement that higher tax rates generate much higher losses (e.g. that the deadweight loss of a 40 per cent tax rate is four (not two) times that of a 20 per cent tax rate). None of this shows that redistributive taxation is wrong: after all, the point of redistribution is to promote equality, and it is perfectly reasonable to be willing to pay for it. But, if valid, it does reveal a sense in which we face a trade-off between equality and efficiency.

Is the theory valid? Putterman, Roemer and Silvestre (1998, pp. 877–80) point out two central problems. First, the claim that income taxation is inefficient in the standard, Pareto-efficiency sense presupposes that the lump-sum-tax alternative is feasible and not just imaginable. But lump-sum taxes are not feasible because they depend on information that it would be impossible or extremely costly for governments to obtain. Secondly, the idea of deadweight loss relies on the methodological assumption that there would be an efficient market equilibrium in the absence of taxation. Since this assumption is highly questionable in relation to the labour market, it is not at all clear that labour taxation decreases rather than increases efficiency. Both objections cast doubt not just on the theory of deadweight loss but on the neoclassical analysis that underpins it.

In summary, although the 'big trade-off' between equality and efficiency sounds plausible, it is far from proven. Neither welfare payments nor redistributive taxation appear to have significant effects on people's motivation to work. The theory that redistributive taxation generates deadweight losses is also questionable. But even if it were to turn out that redistribution reduced efficiency, that would not show that redistribution is wrong. It would simply challenge us to find paths to greater equality that are as efficient as possible.

## Routes to greater economic equality

The first part of this chapter showed that both the relationship between inequality and economic performance and the causes of income inequality are complex. In the paid labour market, investment in human capital, the differential marketability of different skills, various market failures (including restricted entry into certain occupations, inequalities of opportunity, etc.) are all factors. The distribution of income is also affected by the type and level of state transfer payments and, as stated earlier, by the distribution of wealth. However, while ownership of wealth is one of the key factors generating inequalities in economic resources, it is hard to get reliable data on its distribution.

The second part of the chapter showed that greater equality is compatible with economic growth. It also argued that neither the theory nor the evidence demonstrates that a redistributive tax and social welfare system has a significant effect on willingness to work. Finally, it raised doubts about the theory that redistributive taxes and transfers involve substantial deadweight losses. But because the evidence on motivation comes from economies with relatively modest schemes of redistribution and because there is a continuing debate on deadweight loss, one cannot conclusively reject the claim that a much more radical use of tax and social welfare systems with very high tax rates or social welfare benefits would have a negative effect on efficiency. Such a regime might also incur significant administrative costs. If these costs are the unavoidable price of achieving economic equality, it may well be right to accept them. But it would clearly be better to find more efficient ways of achieving the same aims.

What does all this suggest in terms of routes to greater equality of income? Generally speaking, most economists concerned with developing a more egalitarian economy seek ways of working with the market rather than constructing a non-market economy that would organize economic relationships in a completely different way. The central questions relate to changes in the structure of market economies that would bring about greater equality of income and of wealth in the most efficient manner. While we wish to concentrate on one particular suggestion, based on directly influencing primary incomes, it is useful to put this approach in context by providing a brief overview of some proposals that attempt a more radical restructuring of the economy.

## Market socialism

Since one of the key factors generating income inequality is inequality in the distribution of wealth, a number of economists have continued to be interested in ways of reducing inequality of wealth and of the income (and power) that arises from it. The most radical proposals are in the socialist tradition and call for the collective ownership of wealth but in ways that are amenable to markets.

Roemer's model of market socialism is perhaps the most detailed work by an economist in this area (Roemer 1994, 1996). Roemer defines market socialism as 'any of a variety of economic arrangements in which most goods, including labour, are distributed through the price system and the profits of firms, perhaps managed by workers or not, are distributed quite equally among the population' (1996, p. 13). The central problem, he says, is to find a mechanism for distributing these profits without unacceptable costs in efficiency. Roemer's mechanism is to give every citizen an equal share of 'coupons', which are the only currency in which company shares are traded. This has the effect of giving each person a roughly equal share of the ownership of all the major companies in the economy and therefore a roughly equal share of their profits. Such an economy would not only eliminate the impact of dividends on inequality of income; it would also eliminate a small, powerful class of wealthy people who benefit from and perpetuate some enormous 'public bads' such as pollution, noxious advertising, poor health and safety standards and low levels of education and training for many workers. The impact of market socialism on inequality of wealth would therefore have further effects on unequal political power that would in turn create greater equality of resources, working and learning. Roemer allows for the retention of some standard features of the welfare state, such as income tax and unemployment benefit, but accepts that there are limits to the degree to which earned incomes can be redistributed: 'considerations of efficiency pretty much determine the distribution of wages among workers' (Roemer 1994, p. 120).

A key feature of some other proposals for market socialism is a reliance on worker-managed firms, where the 'capital' invested in the firm is either owned by the workers themselves (as in present-day cooperative enterprises) or leased to the firm by publicly owned banks.[10] Democratic control of the firm would have the potential to reduce income differentials, particularly between workers and managers, while income from profits would accrue either to each firm's workforce as a whole or to the public through the banking system rather than to shareholders. Democratizing the firm would also deal directly with the question of inequality of power in the economy, with knock-on effects on status differentials. In addition, it would open up the prospect of restructuring jobs to promote greater equality of work.

### The primary income approach

The above models call for very fundamental changes in the structure of capitalist economies. Since these changes, however desirable, are currently remote, we concentrate on some other changes in economic institutions that could be pursued more immediately. The 'traditional' social-democratic approach to inequality of income is through progressive income taxes and transfers, and as we have seen there is little substance in the standard objections to this strategy. This is essentially the approach taken by Glyn and Miliband (1994, p. 10), whose 'purpose is to show that the economic justification for current levels of inequality is spurious'. However, in the context of the discussion so far in this chapter, one might cast some doubt on the degree to which traditional redistribution can achieve substantial equality. The problems we have already mentioned are that the empirical evidence deals only with rather modest redistribution and that taxation and redistribution may involve significant administrative and efficiency costs. A further problem is that the central explanations for inequality of earned income, whether based on the human capital or exploitation model, suggest that attempts to use taxation to redistribute primary incomes will, to some extent, be counteracted by changes in gross incomes that preserve inequalities in net income. The tax-and-transfer approach also faces a challenge raised by public choice theorists, who point out that governments are far from perfect in carrying out economic policies, because they seldom face a hard budget constraint. The failures of bureaucrats operating under incomplete information should therefore be compared with the standard market failures. State failures and the intrinsic and practical limitations to government intervention in relation to poverty alleviation and income security also feature in the work of egalitarian economists (Bardhan, Gintis and Bowles 2000). All of these reasons provide arguments for accepting the costs involved in altering the distribution of primary incomes, thereby reducing those associated with redistributive tax and social welfare policies. If we had a relatively equal distribution of primary incomes we would not need to rely so much on taxes and redistribution; there would be less risk of throwing away some of our ability to increase the size of the pie before we share it. In what follows, we explore one approach to focusing on gross market income rather than taxation and transfers, employing existing institutional structures (corporatist/partnership models using collective wage bargaining arrangements) to regulate the disparity in primary incomes.

Our proposed route to greater economic equality is prompted by the rather paradoxical example of Japan, which, along with the Nordic countries, has one of the most equal income distributions in the OECD.[11] Unlike the Nordic countries, however, this is not achieved through progressive taxation and extensive social welfare programmes as redistribution via government transfers is minimal in Japan.[12] Rather the approach adopted has been a type of 'corporate welfarism'. From the 1960s onwards, against a background of high economic growth and labour shortage, public policy has been directed at closing two gaps – 'the gap between high and low wages in different firms and industries and the gap between economic growth and wage growth, i.e., between national economic prosperity and individual well-being' (Sheridan 1998, p. 25). This socio-industrial approach where greater economic equality is generated from within economic growth is very different from the welfare economy approach of the West and the antithesis of 'trickle down' economics. Rather than viewing the growth of the economy and greater equality as distinct social objectives, they are promoted equally by both the state and private sector. Public policy for industrial and economic development is supported by a corporate welfare system within the economy that promotes equity in terms of wage and working conditions both within firms and between larger firms and their smaller counterparts across industries. The primary mechanism employed in relation to equity in the wage structure is the flattening of payment scales within and across firms so that the variation in pre-tax income is relatively low. The outcome of the compression of wage differentials is evident in international comparisons. As we noted in Chapter 1, high-level executives in Japan receive about 15 times the income of a typical production worker, far less than in Germany (20), Ireland (23), the UK (25) or the US (50) (Cantillon *et al.* 2001, p. 14; Kenworthy 1995). Although the Japanese economy has recently faced some severe problems, unlike other countries (e.g. Sweden) no one suggests that these are due to its relatively egalitarian distribution of income.

While the experience of Japan and other Asian countries suggests that greater equalization in primary incomes may be the most efficient and effective path to income equality, it is an open question whether their model could be successfully implemented in other industrial economies. Each economy operates in a particular institutional context with particular co-ordinating mechanisms, ownership patterns, legislative provisions and social norms that limit transferability. At a more general level, however, their experience seems to show that three main conditions are necessary for compressing primary incomes:

- some principles of wage relativity
- an institutional framework and mechanisms of delivery
- a broad consensus on reducing income inequality.

If we consider these conditions in relation to the Irish economy, the first two are relatively straightforward and as argued below both relativities principles and a mechanism for introducing wage compression already exist in Ireland. The third is more difficult because the partnership model in Ireland over the past 15 years has never specifically aimed at, or had the effect of, reducing income inequality.

Principles governing wage relativities have been applied in Ireland on both a horizontal and vertical basis. In relation to the former, there has been a desire to maintain roughly similar wages for different categories of workers across the public sector, for example, for teachers, nurses and the police force. The main principle governing wage relativities on a vertical basis has been to maintain existing wage differentials between grades of worker by granting percentage increases so that, in theory, differentials present at the outset remain unchanged, that is, to retain the status quo rather than change it. However, wage increases under separate processes (such as the Buckley Report or the Benchmarking Body) have departed from this principle and have usually given higher percentage increases to the already higher paid. For example, the percentage increases for higher

categories of workers in the public sector (heads of government departments, university professors, etc.) have been much higher than the percentage increases given to lower grades. This has had the effect of widening
further the ratio between the higher and lower paid workers within any
given category. The combined effect of these processes has been that
increases for particular categories have had knock-on effects for the other
groups to which they are tied but that increases in salaries for those on the
highest scales within any category have not necessarily implied similar
increases for those on the lowest salary scales. So over time there has been
increasing wage divergence and hence increasing income inequality,
reflected in the figures cited at the beginning of this chapter. Nevertheless,
the system has involved relatively clear principles of relativities and so
meets the first condition for institutionalizing greater equality of primary
incomes.

The second condition, an institutional mechanism for applying wage
compression, is available in Ireland in the context of the social partnership
agreements in operation since 1987. The social partnership process is
typical of the neocorporatist arrangements found in many European countries. The agreements include government, employers, farmers' organizations, trade unions and, since 1996, the community and voluntary sector.[13]
While the agreements have been primarily concerned with harmonizing
wage increases across the economy for successive periods of about three
years each, they have extended beyond the centralized wage agreements of
the 1970s and already involve macroeconomic, social and public policy
aims. These objectives have included 'social inclusion' but not greater
equality of income. Indeed, unlike other countries where the evidence
indicates a tendency for centralized wage bargaining to be associated with
lower levels of wage inequality, the partnership agreements in Ireland have
done little to counteract the increase in income inequality. While a
number of explanations can be offered for this including coverage (where
some groups, e.g. the self-employed, fall outside the institutions of social
partnership or where a high percentage of professional and managerial staff
have their wages determined individually rather than through collective
bargains) and adherence (where, especially in the second half of the 1990s,
a substantial proportion of firms gave pay increases to skilled workers in
excess of the terms of the agreement), the underlying formula of wage
moderation in exchange for tax cuts has benefited the higher paid. While
the formula meant that employees saw their real income rise well in excess
of their wage increase because of tax cuts, the overall effect was to give
more benefit to those with average and above average incomes than to
those with lower incomes. Furthermore, the formula of wage moderation in
exchange for tax cuts has resulted in a fall in both tax revenue and welfare
expenditures as a proportion of national income, meaning that it has
become more and more difficult to address either the gaps between

national income and individual well-being or the gap between rich and poor through the more traditional route of social welfare transfers and programmes.

Were the partnership model to be used to achieve greater equality of income, it could be applied in a relatively straightforward way to employment incomes and welfare transfers, but would be difficult to apply to income from self-employment and investments. For employment incomes, it would involve compressing differentials by granting greater percentage increases to low-paid workers than to high-paid workers. A particularly important element of any such system would be agreements on the level of executive pay, that is, it would have to cover the pay of all grades of employee in all firms. In relation to welfare transfers, the ideal solution would be an explicit linking of the level of payment to average earnings so that, for example, welfare payments equalled 50 per cent of average income.[14] The conversion of the traditional social welfare system into a basic income system might also be considered, particularly as a way of promoting greater equality of income between those inside and outside the formal labour market. Whether this could be achieved consistently with a reduced reliance on traditional forms of taxation and redistribution is a question we do not pursue here.[15]

It is difficult to see how the institutional arrangements of partnership could be adapted to include the incomes of the self-employed, since these are outside the control of the parties to the agreements. The market itself does constrain self-employment incomes to some extent on the basis of supply and demand and through competition, but even if combined with measures to reduce entry barriers to various professions, it could not be relied on to achieve the levels of primary income equality we might desire. Another important source of inequality that does not lend itself to compression through the partnership model is investment income. We would therefore expect there to be a continuing role for the tax system in redistributing both of these forms of income. The fact that the great majority of people would be involved in a centralized system aimed at reducing inequality would presumably strengthen public support for taxing these other types of income.

As to the possible disincentive effects of such a model, the discussion earlier in this chapter provides some reassurances. As we noted, the empirical evidence, based on comparisons between countries and within particular countries over long periods of time, suggests that equality and economic performance may well be complementary rather than in conflict. The synergy between equality and performance casts doubt on some basic economic assumptions at the micro-level and especially in relation to the human capital model. In contrast to the implication of that model that a compression of wages would lead to an under-investment in human capital, recent research in economic theory indicates that it is inequality itself that has adverse incentive effects leading to lower levels of work effort, less on-the-job training and restricted opportunities to undertake investments both in human capital and at an entrepreneurial level. Furthermore the research suggests that inequalities in wealth and in pay impede the effective functioning of organizations and firms and in particular limit the scope of co-operative problem solving in the workplace and in other spheres (Baland and Platteau 1998; Moene and Wallerstein 1997). These considerations suggest that the efficiency effects of a partnership model may well be positive rather than negative, in spite of the fact that it involves a deliberate constraint on the use of markets for setting wages. But a full analysis of the efficiency effects of the model is beyond the scope of this chapter.

While principles of wage relativity and the institutional apparatus of the partnership model are necessary conditions for implementing a compression of wage differentials, there is a third condition we have yet to consider. It is that any attempt to reduce inequality of income across a whole economy would depend on a broad consensus in favour of this goal. Social norms in relation to inequality, both in terms of its generation and its level, are crucial to any attempts to ameliorate it.

Recent studies of industrialized countries have demonstrated international differences in social norms relating to wage inequality (Austen 1999; Fortin and Lemieux 1997). While there is broad agreement on both the legitimacy of pay inequality and on significant differences in pay between high status and low status jobs, there is no agreement on the legitimate scale of these differences. Country-specific factors were found to be the most important sources of variation in attitudes to legitimate pay differences, with individual experience of income inequality having a major effect. Unsurprisingly, therefore, the US was at the extreme end of the spectrum in having a high level of tolerance for unequal pay and approving the greatest ratio between the two categories of high and low status jobs. On the other hand, the fact that the research demonstrates that these attitudes are influenced by existing levels of inequality, and thus that changes in inequality would be likely to have ongoing effects on people's beliefs, illustrates Lindblom's (1988, p.81) remark that 'much of politics is economics and most of economics is politics'.

In that context, and reviewing the experience of the Irish partnership model to date, we can see how a lack of consensus in relation to income inequality has prevented it from having any egalitarian objectives. While it has been asserted that 'there are strong egalitarian tendencies in popular debate on economic issues in Ireland' and that 'Irish policy objectives have a Rawlsian flavour' (McAleese and Burke 2000, p. 63), the evidence would suggest otherwise and it seems more accurate to describe the results of the partnership process to date as 'solidarity without equality' (Ó Riain and O'Connell 2000, p. 339). What all this indicates is that although national agreements do have the potential to be used to promote greater equality of income, they can do so only against the backdrop of a strong commitment to equality by the parties involved. In a more egalitarian society, with a consensus on the importance of greater equality, institutions of social partnership could play an important role in putting that commitment into practice. But we cannot expect these institutions to create more equality unless the people involved in them want that to happen.

We have concentrated in this chapter on one institutional mechanism for bringing about greater equality of income in countries with an experience of 'social partnership', drawing on existing practices. In other countries, different institutional approaches may be appropriate, relying on their own experience. At the international level, there are already some institutions in place that could be used to promote economic equality, tempering globalization's short-sighted drive for efficiency by guaranteeing greater economic security. These institutions, which include the World Trade Organization, the International Monetary Fund and the World Bank, could in principle adopt rules and policies that promoted equality, for example by establishing a global minimum wage and global health and safety regulations. While the prospect for such changes currently seems remote, the point here is simply that all economic activity takes place within sets of rules that are open to change. Once we have rid ourselves of the myth that equality is inimical to efficiency and growth, we can get down to the difficult business of establishing support for egalitarian ideals and constructing institutions to put those principles into practice.

## Conclusion

The evidence of widening gaps between rich and poor within most industrialized countries and especially between countries has generated renewed interest in economic inequality and especially inequality of wealth and income. There has also been an increased questioning of the validity of the neoclassical approach for understanding how the economy might better serve human, social and environmental needs. Combined, they suggest that the future of heterodox economics looks brighter and that the prospect of returning economics to the much wider canvass of enquiry that engaged Adam Smith and his contemporaries is greater. The possibilities for the adoption of a more equal income distribution through wage compression seem more promising when it is recognized that what is considered a quintessentially Japanese economic and social structure based on homogeneity, trust and cooperation was only introduced in the inter-war period. Before that the Japanese economy operated much as the UK or American economy does today. The proposed changes were hugely controversial and fiercely resisted, with the expected predictions of perdition. In Ireland and elsewhere, the apparatus for promoting equality is in place. What is lacking is the political will to use it.

# 6
# The Challenge of Participatory Democracy

To achieve and sustain a more equal society, we need to act collectively as citizens. That project of collective action is what politics, in the best sense of the word, is all about. In modern societies the most prominent and visible institutions for political action are governments, but collective action can also be taken by non-governmental organizations such as local development partnerships, trade unions, residents' associations, churches and other voluntary groups, by international organizations such as the European Union and the United Nations and of course by corporations and other businesses. In western societies, most of these organizations subscribe to the idea of democracy, which as we have already seen is an essentially egalitarian idea. But the quality of these democracies, and in particular the degree to which they promote genuinely equal power, varies widely and almost always leaves room for improvement. There is widespread cynicism about and disengagement from politics, reflecting a sense of powerlessness. Many people feel that it is pointless to engage in political activities.

In this chapter we argue that egalitarians should try to construct participatory forms of democracy, and we try to address some of the key questions involved in designing such political systems. Because the range of issues involved is vast, the discussion here is limited to a few central problems, mostly related to how collective decisions should be made at national and local rather than transnational levels. Most of the specific proposals we make could be implemented in many societies, although some are more applicable to some countries than to others.

## Basic principles

Drawing on the framework set out in Chapter 2, we see all five dimensions of equality as relevant to democratic politics. As we noted, the standard approach of liberal democracies is to accord every citizen equal recognition as an individual member of the political system. The extension of the status of citizen from a narrow, propertied, male elite to nearly all adults was a tremendous victory for equality won over centuries of struggle. It has in turn served as the cornerstone for many other egalitarian claims (Phillips 1992, 1993). But it is not enough. For one thing, there are remaining issues about who is entitled to citizenship in both its legal sense and the more theoretical sense in which we use the term here, meaning a person fully entitled to participate in the political system. The idea of equal respect entails extending this status to all long-term residents and is therefore incompatible with the prolonged exclusion from political participation of asylum seekers and other immigrants or the disenfranchisement of people with criminal records. Moreover, the status of citizenship is not enough to guarantee that democratic institutions operate in ways that respect differences among individuals and groups. For example, institutions usually operate in a way that implicitly shows more regard for the typical language, behaviour and attitudes of dominant groups (Young 1989). Since politics is among other things a highly symbolic expression of the status of citizens, these implicit endorsements of some citizens' ways of life and the corresponding diminishment of others' is a key problem in modern democracies.

The other dimension of equality most closely related to democracy is power. It is widely acknowledged that democracy presupposes basic civil and political rights, and indeed all contemporary liberal democracies are committed to their protection. Yet the basic rights of poor and marginalized citizens are less secure than those of the privileged because of overt discrimination, unintended bias, financial barriers to proper legal representation and other causes. We discuss some of these issues in Chapter 7; here, we simply note that a truly egalitarian political system requires not just formal equality in citizens' rights but their equal protection in practice. But basic rights are only a minimal protection against the powerful. Dominant economic and cultural groups exercise power over disadvantaged groups not only within the sphere of government but in many other areas of society. Moreover, citizens in general exercise relatively little control over government, their role being more concerned with electing their rulers than with governing themselves. The politics of equality of condition must therefore put equality of power at the top of its agenda, and look at how liberal democracies can be reformed and restructured to this end.[1]

Although recognition and power are the central dimensions of political equality, politics also involves equalities and inequalities of resources, of love, care and solidarity and of working and learning. In relation to resources, it is clear that the only way to remove persistent inequalities of recognition and power is to foster much greater equality of resources among citizens, where resources include not just income and wealth but also access to information, social networks and cultural credentials. We argue below that the political system cannot be fully insulated from wider inequalities of resources.

In the dimension of love, care and solidarity, we reject the common assumption that politics is a form of warfare (see Bresnihan 1997), since at its best it is an activity in which citizens can show concern for each other's welfare and develop bonds of solidarity (Mackay 2001; Sevenhuijsen 1998; Taylor 1995). Egalitarian political structures have to recognize our interdependence and foster these relations of care and solidarity. Politics is also an area of life in which people do valuable work and develop new capabilities. So egalitarian political practices need to give every citizen opportunities for meaningful participation and self-development.

In sum, an egalitarian political system must strive for a form of democracy that shows equal respect and recognition, guarantees basic rights and promotes equal power, facilitates equality of resources and mutual care and solidarity, and equally enables people to learn and participate, while also being efficient, competent and consistent. To achieve these aims, we need to develop a participatory democracy.

## Participatory democracy

The ideal of a participatory democracy has been discussed and debated for centuries, with many different variations and emphases.[2] The model of participatory democracy put forward here has six interrelated features. First of all, it involves *widespread participation* of ordinary citizens in political decision-making. Unlike existing systems of liberal democracy, in which only a small proportion of the population are actively involved in any form of collective decision-making (Parry, Moyser and Day 1992; Verba, Schlozman and Brady 1995), a participatory democracy would involve the vast majority of citizens in full, effective control over at least some of the collective decisions that affect their lives. Many of the consultative mechanisms in liberal democracies offer partial participation, such as the extensive processes of consultation that took place in Ireland to develop its National Anti-Poverty Strategy (Government of Ireland 1997, p. 2).[3] We do not mean to disparage these processes, and see them as a step in the right direction, but the idea of participatory democracy represents a decisive shift of power into the hands of ordinary citizens, moving as closely to the position of full participation as is feasible in a large, complex society.

Secondly, participatory democracy involves a thorough *democratization of society*, extending beyond what is now considered politics to the practice and ethos of all major social institutions, particularly businesses, schools, churches and families. In contrast to the view that these are 'private' bodies that are free to be as authoritarian as they like, participatory democracy recognizes that building a democratic society involves the wide-ranging practice of democratic activities. We are not claiming that all of these bodies should be under state control, or even that they should all be legally required to adopt democratic forms of governance, and we are certainly not claiming that there is one blueprint for democracy that applies to all these different forms of human interaction. Democratizing local government, for example, is clearly a different process from democratizing the family, where no one pretends that children should have exactly the same rights and privileges as adults. Our claim is simply that egalitarians should try to extend democratic relationships throughout society rather than to confine them to formal government. This second feature is closely tied to a third, namely that a participatory democracy must be rooted in a *democratic social ethos*. A proper democracy cannot be a question of institutions alone, but depends on the attitudes and values of its members. In particular, it requires a commitment to democratic and egalitarian values, including a willingness to give equal weight to the rights and interests of minorities.

Unlike some participatory models, we do not envisage a society in which every citizen chooses to be deeply involved in every type of political affairs, particularly in light of the wide range of 'political' activities in such a society. Our vision is, instead, of a society in which all collective decisions involve active participation by some of the people they affect and nearly everyone participates in some of the decisions that affect them. For this reason, a fourth key feature of a participatory democracy is that participation at all levels should be *representatively diverse*. In particular, in contrast to existing liberal democracies, where participation is dominated by members of powerful and privileged groups (Conover, Searing and Crewe 2002; Parry, Moyser and Day 1992; Verba, Schlozman and Brady 1995), participatory democracy seeks to ensure effective and roughly proportionate participation by members of social groups that have traditionally been marginalized (Williams 1998, pp. 27–30).

A related difference between this model and some others is its acceptance of the extensive use of elected representatives. What matters are the details of how representatives are chosen, how accountable they are to their constituents, how well resourced their constituents are for advising and controlling their representatives and so on. Indeed, one of the most important types of political participation is action taken to inform and influence one's representatives. We see participatory democracy as an *accountable* form of representative democracy, not an alternative to it.

The final feature we attribute to participatory democracy relates to the way that democratic citizens should communicate with each other in the course of their varied democratic activities. It is hard to find the best label for this, but an appropriate description might be that participatory democracy is *communicatively rich* in a number of different ways.[4] Democratic communication should be varied in form, from closely argued policy documents to vivid campaigning images. It should include personal testimony, passionate rhetoric, detached analysis, song, debate, poetry: the whole gamut of human communicative forms. These reflect the rich content of democratic communication, which consists not simply of the expression of self-interest but also of social and political values and of beliefs about the social and natural world. This rich democratic communication needs to be supported by diverse channels of communication that themselves take democracy seriously rather than reducing it to sound bites, personalities and the vocabulary of sports commentators. It also requires high levels of informational transparency, so that citizens know how decisions have been made, by whom and for what reasons.[5] In describing participatory democracy as communicatively rich, we draw on recent work on 'deliberative democracy'. Deliberative democrats emphasize the value of an inclusive discussion in which people put forward reasons that everyone can recognize as relevant and decisions are made through the free exchange of arguments rather than by bargaining and power plays.[6] We agree that deliberation should play an important role in democratic practices and that democracy requires a vibrant 'public sphere' of democratic communication and debate concerning not just the activities of government but those of a wide range of other collective actors. But we think that deliberation is only one aspect of rich democratic communication. It should be a central part of decision-making but it is not what typically mobilizes political action or develops bonds of care and solidarity.[7] We see the fifth and sixth features of participatory democracy as implied by the other four, because only accountable representation and a communicatively rich democracy can serve to inform, motivate and empower a wide and representative range of citizens.

Although participatory democracy can be contrasted with liberal democracy in several respects, it is important to note that they share some key characteristics. In particular, participatory democrats can freely endorse constitutional safeguards, the rule of law, the separation of powers between legislative, judicial and executive branches of government and the division of powers between local, regional, national and supra-national bodies. As with the general contrast between liberal egalitarianism and equality of condition, participatory democracy should be seen as an extension of liberal democracy rather than as a completely different system.

### Arguments for participatory democracy

It need hardly be argued that widespread and representatively diverse democratic participation that extends throughout society's institutions and ethos is the only way of achieving or even approximating equality of power, since the opposite is to give some individuals and groups power over others. These central components of participatory democracy are also the best way to show equal respect to all citizens, not just because they express a mutual recognition of each other's right and competence to contribute to collective decisions, but because widespread and representatively diverse participation is the most effective way to ensure that the political system shows equal regard for cultural and symbolic differences related to class, gender, sexuality, ethnicity, disability, age and so on. Another argument for participatory democracy is that a genuinely equal opportunity to learn about and participate in the work of politics can best be fostered through the practice of widespread actual participation in a variety of settings. Conversely, any political system in which participation is concentrated and unrepresentative of the society as a whole is evidence of restricted and unequal opportunities. The process of political participation and engagement can also provide a way of developing and strengthening bonds of care and solidarity with other citizens, as they interact to solve common problems and to find fair resolutions to political conflicts. In addition, the increased political participation of women can help to raise the priority of issues of care and interdependence. Finally, it is only through widespread and representatively diverse participation in a wide range of settings that citizens, and particularly minorities, can help to ensure that democracies serve their needs and interests in practice and not just in name. Even if groups could rely on the goodwill of others to take their needs seriously – and to some degree this is a necessary assumption in any working democracy – no one is better placed to articulate their needs effectively and accurately than the people who have them (Phillips 1995; Williams 1998; Young 2000, ch. 3).

## Obstacles to participatory democracy

To see how this ideal of an egalitarian, participatory democracy can be realized in practice, it is useful to start by considering a number of difficulties we need to overcome to make it a reality. Three of these can be thought of as intrinsic problems of participatory democracy. The other two obstacles are more concerned with the transition to an egalitarian society.[8]

The first set of problems with participatory democracy concerns the characteristics of citizens. Could ordinary citizens really know enough to be trusted with making important collective decisions? Would enough of them really want to be involved? And even if they did, would they participate on the basis of mutual respect and concern and with a commitment to fair solutions to political disagreements? A second problem is that participatory democracy seems to be simply impractical. Is it too time-consuming? Can it cope with the sheer scale of modern government? And even if these basic problems could be solved, wouldn't participatory democracy be wildly inefficient? A third set of intrinsic problems is related to the idea of majority rule. Surely there is no equality of power in any meaningful sense in a system in which some groups – perhaps Travellers, disabled people or lesbians and gays – are present but almost always find themselves on the losing side of the vote?

The three problems just mentioned seem to be intrinsic to participatory democracy, although they are particularly striking when set against the conditions of existing unequal societies. By contrast, the other two problems are more concerned with the transition to an egalitarian society. In unequal societies, subordinate groups are typically under-represented in or excluded from elected decision-making bodies. Is it really possible to achieve representative participation for these social groups at all political levels? More generally, economically, culturally and affectively privileged groups have more resources than marginalized groups and define the language and style of politics. Would increased participation perpetuate or even exacerbate these inequalities?

By working through these difficulties we can begin to clarify some of the main features of an egalitarian democracy, bearing in mind that solutions need to be tailored to particular political settings.

## Overcoming the intrinsic obstacles

### Good citizens

We take it for granted that problems about citizens are no excuse for less democracy, since rule by 'elites' has always had the fundamental drawback of reinforcing and perpetuating inequality (Dahl 1989). It is also important to note that the most careful research about the capacities of ordinary citizens in established democracies has confirmed that they have a reasonably good basic grasp of political events and processes and reasonably strong and consistent democratic values.[9] But the fact that these competencies are fairly basic, and that they vary significantly with social status (Delli Carpini and Keeter 1996), does raise the challenge of how to improve the capacities of citizens in the long run, and more immediately of how to raise the knowledge and understanding of the less powerful.

The first point to consider is that participation and competence are mutually reinforcing. All of the evidence confirms that actual, effective participation in political processes increases people's knowledge, understanding and commitment (Delli Carpini and Keeter 1996; Parry, Moyser and Day 1992; Verba, Schlozman and Brady 1995). It is also to be expected that the experience of participation, involving the need to engage with others in a collective process and therefore to see issues from a variety of perspectives, encourages at least some degree of civic virtue and fair-mindedness, although in the nature of things it is harder to find clear evidence for this (Mansbridge 1995b). Participation that brings together people from different backgrounds can strengthen mutual understanding and concern (Baiochhi 2003, p. 61; Fishkin and Luskin 1999, p. 7). Finally, participatory democracy radically extends the knowledge available for decision-making because it taps into the practical, everyday knowledge of citizens (Wainwright 2003). There is nothing very surprising in the idea that people learn by doing: that is how most knowledge develops. But these changes in competence do not have to be left to chance. Case studies of 'empowered participatory governance' in Porto Alegre in Brazil, Kerala in India and Chicago, Illinois all show that intensive training for participation can enable ordinary citizens to engage in participatory, deliberative decision-making (Abers 1998, pp. 526–9; Baiochhi 2003; Fung 2003; Thomas Isaac and Heller 2003). So rather than worrying about citizens' limitations, we should be demanding more opportunities for participation supported by appropriate training. In the meantime, one of the best ways of closing the knowledge gap between the best- and worst-informed sections of the population would be for organizations like trade unions, political parties of the left, women's and community groups and local campaigning groups to do more to mobilize and train their members.

Communications media are an important source of political information. We have already mentioned the need for rich, varied forms of political communication through diverse networks that engage with political issues and not just personalities. The proliferation of broadcasting channels and the growth of the internet create opportunities for diversity, but these can only be realized by positive state action that encourages diverse ownership and control of broadcasters and information-providers, strengthens public broadcasting and requires mainstream providers to carry diverse messages (Keane 1993; McChesney and Nichols 2002). The mass media can play an important role in encouraging citizens' engagement with issues and disseminating its results, as the experience with deliberative polls demonstrates (Fishkin 1995, pp. 154–76). Political broadcasting in a participatory democracy would need to broaden its focus from day-to-day reporting to deeper issues about basic political choices and values, with special responsibility to give voice to a diverse range of groups (McCaffery 1992). Institutionalizing this aim seems to require both legislation and changes of priorities and habits. The growth of the internet offers the potential for considerably easier access by citizens to politically relevant information. Independent reporting and perspectives have become available via web sites like Indymedia (www.indymedia.org) and Znet (www.zmag.org) and the wealth of online news and analysis means that no one with access to the internet is completely reliant on media empires for information. However, the egalitarian value of these developments depends on establishing universal internet access and computer literacy and on making public information easily retrievable.

A participatory society would not limit democratic participation to formal politics, but would encourage it throughout society. In education this would mean not just a curriculum that prepared students for political participation but also a democratic pedagogy and the involvement of students in the decision-making processes of educational institutions (Apple and Beane 1999; Coleman 1998; Gutmann 1987; see also Chapter 8). Democratic participation in families, residents' associations, trade unions, sports clubs, charitable organizations, campaigning groups and religious bodies would play an important role both in establishing a strong democratic ethos in society and in developing people's democratic capabilities. A particularly important setting for increased democratic control is in the workplace (Archer 1995; Bachrach and Botwinick 1992; Bowles and Gintis 1987; Dahl 1985; Pateman 1970). A democratic transformation of the welfare state involving the full participation of clients in the definition of needs and the planning and delivery of services would also be welcome both for its own sake and for the sake of providing experience in democracy (Fraser 1989; Wainwright 2003; Watt 1997a).

Participatory democracy does not require all citizens to be experts on every question of collective decision. It does require widespread and socially representative publics to be able to assess policy issues intelligently, drawing on their own wealth of experience and using information provided by experts with differing points of view. In this respect, citizens are expected to have the same limited capacities as many other people who need to assess expert opinions on a regular basis, from householders and consumers to corporate executives and political leaders. Like those others, citizens need access to expert opinion, provided through appropriate channels including the mass media, the internet and publicly funded consultants for community organizations. The experience of Porto Alegre provides a good example of how technical information can be both provided to and mastered by ordinary citizens (De Sousa Santos 1998).

Once we recognize that the very process of developing a participatory society would itself improve our knowledge, skills and commitments as citizens, we can see that concerns in this area are misguided. On the contrary, a participatory society would tap into and make use of a wealth of potential skills that are now squandered under the assumption that only a few people know the answers. We are not suggesting here that every citizen would know and care about every political issue, but we are confident that a deepening and widening of political competence would both accompany and facilitate the widespread and representatively diverse participation that defines participatory democracy.

### The practicalities of participatory democracy

Our first response to the practical problems of size and time is to point out that a great many collective decisions occur in small groups dealing with reasonably straightforward issues. There is not always a problem of scale. At this level, the key issue is probably learning better ways of managing collective decision-making, so that democratic control can be maintained with shorter, more efficient and more enjoyable meetings, the delegation of routine tasks, better channels of communication outside of meetings and so on. There is very relevant experience in this area within the community development sector, experience that was put to use, for example, in the way participatory planning has been structured in Porto Alegre and Kerala.[10] Developing democratic skills is a key challenge for a participatory society, and when one reflects on the very limited attention this currently receives in education and training, one can understand why people are not at the moment very proficient at democratic decision-making.

But although we envisage a society in which ordinary citizens are directly involved in decisions from which they are now excluded, we accept that there will be many more areas and levels in which the main business of decision-making will be in the hands of elected officials or representatives. Here the key task is to develop representative democracy in a participatory manner, involving better channels of consultation and clearer lines of accountability.

To clarify these issues, it is helpful to start by contrasting two traditional models of the role of the representative (Pennock 1979, ch. 8; Pitkin 1967, esp. chs 7–10). According to what has been called the 'trustee' model, representatives should be relatively free in the exercise of their duties to make judgements on behalf of their constituents, using their specialized knowledge and ideally their superior wisdom. Constituents entrust them with this power and use periodic elections either to confirm that trust or to select another person for the job. According to the 'delegate' model, representatives should be tightly controlled by instructions from their constituents. Initially, these take the form of a mandate to carry out the programme set out in the candidate's election manifesto. Should circumstances require representatives to go beyond their mandate, they should consult with and take instructions from their constituents. For fairly obvious reasons, the trustee model has been associated with conservative attitudes towards democracy and the delegate model with the radical democratic tradition.

In existing liberal democracies, the behaviour of representatives has tended towards the trustee model. Although elected on the basis of more or less explicit political platforms and principles, representatives have considerable freedom to follow their own judgement (or that of their party leaders) without interference from the public. Of course, the expressed views of voters sometimes influence their decisions, particularly when considered relevant to the prospect of re-election. But what is much more common is for policies to be shaped by the interests of powerful and well-resourced groups. No one pretends that representatives are closely controlled by their constituents.

Our vision of accountable representation is closer to the delegate model, but contains some important revisions and clarifications. First, we agree that most citizens, most of the time, really should trust their representatives. This does not cease to make representatives agents of their constituents, any more than trusting architects undercuts their role as agents of their clients. In both cases, what matters is that the agents have clear guidelines within which to work and are able to consult with their clients or constituents about details when necessary. Throughout our lives, we need to be able to trust others to make decisions we broadly agree with: politics is no different. We can hold representatives accountable for their use or abuse of our trust, but we cannot expect to control their every move (Williams 1998, pp. 30–3 and ch. 5). A second clarification concerns when consultation really is necessary. In many cases, representatives may have perfectly adequate evidence of their constituents' views without consulting them directly. The key point is that it is the constituents' views – what they actually want, or at least would want after careful consideration – that are decisive. Thirdly, and following that phrase 'would want', we recognize that representatives are not just political messengers but political leaders, whose role includes inspiring, informing and persuading their constituents. Democracy relies on political leadership, and in particular on the role of those who are able to bring various publics to a clearer recognition of both their own interests and the good of the whole (cf. Rawls 1999, sec. 14.2). But accountable democracy requires that the powers of these leaders are limited by what their constituents are willing to endorse. A fourth clarification relates to the importance of political parties. The classic models of representation are typically constructed in terms of single representatives and single-seat constituencies. In modern democracies, representatives are typically members of parties and as such often represent unidentifiable groups of supporters in multi-seat constituencies as well as groups of supporters who lie outside their electoral areas. In many contexts, then, we need to think of representation as relating groups of representatives to vaguely defined groups of supporters, with whom they should engage in a continuing dialogue. Party organizations clearly have an important part to play in this process.

Thus our model of accountable representation differs from the classic delegate model by relaxing the requirement for explicit instructions on every issue and by recognizing the need to adapt to changing circumstances. But it retains its spirit by insisting that representatives remain agents of their constituents and are subject to their control. For in our view it is not enough for a representative to come to the conclusion that such-and-such a policy is the best on offer. Her constituents must also be able properly to assess that judgement and to reject it if they see fit. If she believes in the policy in question, she should of course try to persuade her constituents of its value, but in the end it is their decision, not hers. There may indeed be occasions when representatives have to make a choice based on their best judgement of what their constituents *would* want, if fully informed. But the test of that judgement lies in a political process of democratic information-sharing, consultation, dialogue and popular endorsement, within the rich context of political communication already described. And because policies do need to adapt to changing circumstances, this consultative process has to be continuous, with widespread and socially representative participation.[11] Accounts of the participatory budget process in Porto Alegre suggest that the relationship between its elected delegates and their communities is very much of this form and that the process of communication and reporting back has been a consistent focus of attention (Baiocchi 2003; De Sousa Santos 1998, pp. 487-91; Wainwright 2003, pp. 42–69).

A final aspect of the issues of size and time is the possibility for greater devolution of authority and the principle, incorporated in the European Union's 1992 Maastricht Treaty, of subsidiarity: that decisions should be taken at the most local level possible (see Duff 1993). There are many potential opportunities for devolution, including the revitalization of local government, the creation or strengthening of regional governments, the devolution of authority over specific issue areas to empowered participatory local units (Fung and Wright 2003), the delegation of certain powers and responsibilities to democratically accountable non-governmental organizations (Cohen and Rogers 1995; Hirst 1994; Mansbridge 1995a), the granting of autonomous decision-making in some areas to well-defined indigenous peoples (Kymlicka 1995; Young 1990) and the creation of local or regional partnerships between government, business, trade unions and community groups, with specified roles and powers (Lynam 1997). This programme of greater local autonomy is central to many contemporary social movements (Kingsnorth 2003; Wainwright 2003). Combining respect for diversity with greater equality of power, it constitutes an agenda that is too wide and varied to be pursued here. There are, however, some key issues of principle that are worth addressing. One is that such devolved authorities ought themselves to be democratically organized and accountable to the citizens affected by their decisions, either through their direct participation or through accountable representation. If their members are not directly elected but, for example, consist of nominees of relevant organizations and groups, these nominees need to have clear lines of communication with and responsibility to their constituents. Another key principle is that devolution should not be a way of insulating privileged communities from their obligations towards disadvantaged ones. In the US, for example, residential segregation combined with decentralized authority has allowed suburban populations to avoid responsibilities for the urban areas that provide them with numerous benefits (Young 2000, ch. 6). A third principle is that devolved authority must operate within a framework that guarantees the equal rights and interests of women and minorities. The history of civil rights in the US, for example, demonstrates the importance of national action to enforce racial equality in the face of local intransigence, just as the treatment of Catholics in Northern Ireland from 1922 to 1969 showed the danger of unchecked devolution. Similarly, a chronic issue in Canadian politics has been the tension between cultural autonomy and equality (Phillips 1995, ch. 5). These principles imply that devolved local units should operate within a framework set by higher levels of government that monitor, supervise, support and coordinate local decision-making and help to disseminate good practice (a feature emphasized by Fung and Wright (2003) in their model of empowered participatory governance).

We have argued that participatory democracy is a practical proposition, but we recognize that it calls for significant resources. First of all, if people are to participate more, they need the time to do this. Some people will freely give up their leisure time for participation, attracted by its intrinsic satisfactions, but others may find that the pressures of life are not so accommodating. In western democracies, the obligation of employers to facilitate people's participation in jury service and in formal political office-holding is widely recognized. If we are to take participation seriously, we need to extend this support to other forms of involvement, most obviously participation in trade unions, works councils and other employment-related democratic practices, but also in the wider society. For non-employees and for participation outside of working hours, we need to develop ways to facilitate and support participation, both by ensuring that it is recognized as consistent with receiving welfare payments (e.g. does not violate availability-for-work rules) and by subsidizing transportation and child care. Such resources as meeting rooms, computer equipment, office supplies, printing, photocopying and postage are also vital to successful participation, and a society that depends entirely on private support for these will inevitably advantage the participation of the privileged. Hence, we need public support for these costs, particularly in an unequal society. Ultimately, a participatory democracy depends on the willingness of citizens to pay the costs of participation, one way or another. If we are right about the interrelations between political and economic inequality, and more generally among the four main contexts of equality, it is a cost they will gladly pay for a more equal society.

We conclude that participatory democracy is a practical option for modern societies. The development of small-group decision-making, accountable representation and coordinated devolution would all contribute to making effective participation a feasible goal. Participation does have its costs, but they are costs worth paying.

### The dangers of majority rule

The danger of tyranny of the majority has been a persistent theme in thinking about democracy. For many authors, the main worry was that the propertyless majority might oppress the privileged minority by confiscating its assets (cf. Madison 1787–88; Mill 1861). Some of the institutional features designed to deal with this threat, including the constitutional protection of property rights, remain important in many legal systems. But what matters to egalitarians are institutional devices for protecting vulnerable minorities from powerful majorities and for promoting equality of power.

Broadly speaking, these can be divided into two types: entrenched rights and non-majoritarian decision rules.[12]

The first type of device, entrenched rights, involves setting constitutional limits to the power of governments. These rights are sometimes found in constitutional bills of rights, such as the first ten amendments to the US Constitution or Articles 40–44 of the Irish Constitution. They also appear in supra-national conventions like the European Convention on Human Rights. They have typically been accorded to individuals, but there can also be group rights, such as the right of groups to control their own educational institutions or to take steps to protect their languages.

Constitutional rights provide some safeguards for minorities against reckless legislative majorities. Where these rights have the status of international obligations overriding local law, the obstacles facing a tyrannical majority, though not insuperable, are increased. It remains the case that constitutional rights are established, sustained and interpreted through democratic processes and are therefore vulnerable to revision by either a majority (as in Ireland) or a super-majority (as in the United States). It is thus important for minorities to be fully involved in these processes and not just to rely on the majority's goodwill (Phillips 1995, p. 140).

Following this cue, the second type of constitutional device for protecting and empowering minorities operates at the level of decision-making itself, by instituting rules that one way or another strengthen their influence. There is a wide range of possibilities here; we will survey a few representative examples.

One of the strongest devices for empowering minorities is for decisions to be made by consensus, following a thorough, deliberative discussion that allows everyone's views to be taken into account in a spirit of co-operation and mutual respect (Williams 1998). This type of decision-making seems to be particularly appropriate in relatively small groups that broadly agree on overall aims and objectives, bodies that Mansbridge (1983) calls 'unitary democracies'. A great deal of cooperative, democratic decision-making takes this form, in such diverse settings as workplace groups, committees, neighbourhood groups and classrooms, where the task is to find solutions to common problems. As Mansbridge points out, however, this kind of setting is not all that relevant to protecting minorities, since it presupposes common interests. On the contrary, the very presumption of common interests can sometimes marginalize 'outsiders'.

Deliberative consensus has also been recommended as the solution to issues of moral disagreement. Since each side expresses its views in terms of values and principles, it is possible that an attempt to resolve moral conflicts through discussion will lead, if not to agreement, then at least to a resolution that everyone can understand and accept (Gutmann and Thompson 1996). The deliberative process of trying to find a consensus can help citizens to take a wider view of the issues, deepening their understanding and respect for other positions.

Deliberative consensus faces its hardest challenge in dealing with serious conflicts of interest. In principle, it should be possible to work out fair solutions to conflict through a deliberative process drawing on ideas that everyone can recognize as relevant. If we imagine this process occurring in the context of a broadly egalitarian society in which participants relate to each other with respect and concern and have roughly equal resources and power, we can recognize its potential for ensuring that everyone's interests are given equal weight and thus for protecting minorities. What is more problematic is how feasible it is in existing unequal societies, where it is hard to expect the privileged and powerful to yield to the force of argument when their interests are at stake. We return to this problem below.

In larger groups, and in cases where the search for consensus breaks down, some of the benefits of consensus may still be achieved by using non-majoritarian forms of voting. A widely employed rule is to require a super-majority for deciding certain issues. For example, amendments to the US Constitution need to be approved by three-quarters of the states (Article V) and many areas of EU decision-making are subject to qualified majority voting. In the Belfast Agreement of 1998, there is a provision to require a 60 per cent majority for some issues, with at least 40 per cent support from each of the two main political groups (Strand 1, clause 5(d)(ii)). Such rules are designed to ensure wider support for decisions than a simple majority would require, but they seem inapplicable to small minorities such as disabled people, ethnic minorities or gays and lesbians.

Under both simple and super-majority rule, the votes of the minority are in a certain sense empty: they have no effect on the outcome. One plausible way of achieving a more consensual decision is to use a voting procedure in which every vote has an equal influence on the outcome, effectively dragging the outcome in the direction of the aims of the minority. The outcome would then be 'proportionate' (Hyland 1995) rather than biased towards the majority. The difficulties with this suggestion are both technical and political. On the technical side, the problem is to construct a reliable proportionate voting procedure. There are some well-established candidates, all of which involve asking voters to rank a range of alternatives rather than simply voting for or against a single proposal. But there is no consensus over which works best (Baker and Sinnott 2000; Dummett 1984, 1997; Emerson 1994; McLean 1987, ch. 8). A more political difficulty with proportionate decision-making is that by its very design it reflects group size. Large minorities will have a large impact on decisions, but the effect of small minorities may be negligible.

A more direct way to protect minority groups is to shift decision-making from individual voting to inter-group agreement. For example, another provision of the Belfast Agreement is to require certain decisions to have the support of both unionists and nationalists (Strand 1, clause 5(d)(i)). The most thorough expressions of this principle of concurrent or parallel support are the 'consociational' constitutional structures of Belgium and Switzerland, which combine a requirement for inter-group agreement at national level with a high degree of autonomy for the major linguistic/cultural segments of the population on internal issues.[13] Like super-majorities, consociational arrangements are most applicable to cases where there are only two or three large groups.

A different form of inter-group agreement is the use made in many European countries of 'neocorporatist' national economic agreements between major 'social partners'. In Ireland, national agreements between government, business, farming and labour are a longstanding institution.[14] Recent negotiations have also included representatives of the community sector, organized as the Community and Voluntary Pillar, although this group has had much less influence in the process (Community Platform 1997; Watt 1997b). At local level there has been a growth of development partnerships along similar lines (Lynam 1997). A variant of inter-group agreement can occur when the subordinate group is a small minority, such as gays and lesbians, disabled people or Travellers, and group-relevant policy is negotiated between the group's representatives and state officials (Young 1995). Inter-group agreement in all these cases provides one way in which the interests of minorities can achieve some protection.

This brief survey shows that democracy does not need to be defined in terms of unrestricted majority rule and that there are several ways to protect minorities in a participatory democracy. Each of these proposals could find a role in the democratic practice of a society committed to equality of condition and determined to ensure that the interests of minorities are properly protected and their voices heard. What is less certain is how well these devices can work to protect vulnerable minorities in an unequal society. For example, entrenched rights and non-majoritarian voting procedures can work just as much to protect privileged minorities as vulnerable ones. But the problem is particularly acute when it comes to consensual forms of decision-making.

We have already noted the difficulty of relying on deliberative consensus in cases of conflicts of interest between unequal participants. Powerful groups are more likely to protect their interests, even under consensual procedures, by bargaining rather than pursuing a deliberative agreement. The results of bargaining typically reflect the unequal positions of the participants, indicated by the relative costs to each party of a breakdown in negotiations (Barry 1989). So in unequal societies, consensual procedures protect privileged groups more than vulnerable ones. This logic is particularly clear at the level of inter-group agreement. Consociationalist and neocorporatist processes are typically concerned with conflicts of interest, and the consensus they seek usually occurs through bargaining rather than deliberation.

Their results therefore typically benefit their strongest participants (cf. Hardiman 1998).

It is for this reason that progressive change in unequal societies has often occurred when legislative majorities have overruled the privileged. Theoretically this may seem paradoxical, since it appears to use anti-egalitarian procedures to promote equality. It would be more accurate to say that it reveals the need to take a wider perspective in looking at power, and to assess decision-making procedures in terms of how far they reinforce or counteract broader inequalities of power. By this criterion, consensual decision-making is not always superior to majority rule in an unequal society.[15]

Consociationalist and neocorporatist structures have some other typical drawbacks in unequal societies. Since they involve bargaining between representatives of selected groups, those who are left out of the process are likely to be ignored, as has indeed been the case in Irish national agreements (Immergut 1995). In addition, it is widely recognized that both consociationalist and neocorporatist institutions work best when group leaders have a substantial degree of autonomy from and authority over their members, so that they are free to shift their demands to the point of agreement and capable of delivering the compliance of their constituents (Immergut 1995; Lijphart 1977, pp. 49–50). This is hardly encouraging news for participatory democrats. More generally, such institutions may lack adequate structures of accountability between representatives and their constituents, for instance when 'community' representatives are chosen from above or have too few resources to communicate effectively with the groups they represent. In Ireland, some of the constituent groups of the Community and Voluntary Pillar are committed to 'mechanisms of accountability', but it is not clear from their own description of the processes of consultation over *Partnership 2000* how deeply these extended into the communities they represented (Community Platform 1997, p. 19; Watt 1997b, p. 68). Analyses of the role of the community sector in Local Area Partnerships also note the obstacles involved in achieving real accountability for community representatives (as well as for the representatives of other sectors), for reasons to do with weak formal structures and lack of resources (Community Workers Co-operative 1997; Lynam 1997). Another widely recognized tendency is for neocorporatist structures to co-opt trade union and community group leaders into unjust arrangements or at least to create an atmosphere of compromise and collective responsibility that weakens movements for radical change and undermines effective opposition to government policies (Dryzek 1996; Levine 1995; Shapiro 1996; Szasz 1995). These problems are mainly a reflection of the difficulty of achieving political equality in the context of broader social and economic inequality, a topic to which we return below. Meanwhile, it seems clear enough that one way to minimize some of these dangers is to strengthen the accountability of the participants to their base constituents, by requiring and resourcing democratic arrangements within each constituent group (Cohen and Rogers 1995; Schmitter 1995). A more difficult task is for the members of subordinate groups to develop a dual strategy of working effectively within neocorporatist structures while maintaining a vibrant campaign for change outside them, a strategic issue discussed further in Chapter 12.

If there is a general theme that has emerged from this discussion of the dangers of majority rule, it is that institutional solutions to the problem are heavily dependent on context. In an egalitarian society, any of the devices mentioned could play a part in protecting vulnerable minorities. In an unequal one, they could reinforce inequality and impede progressive change. This is not really surprising, once we recognize that every social institution reflects the values and interests of the society in which it operates. We need to think of participatory democracy as a tool devised by egalitarian populations to sustain their own democratic and egalitarian values rather than as a constraint that is somehow imposed on them against their basic inclinations. Our primary task in this chapter is to think about the design of institutions for a society that already has (or is developing) an egalitarian ethos and practice, not for a society that strains against them. In that context, the dangers of majority rule would be less daunting than they are now.

## Overcoming the transitional obstacles

### The representation of subordinate groups

By definition, a participatory democracy would involve representatively diverse participation at all levels. That would mark a dramatic contrast with existing democracies, in which privileged groups participate more at every level of decision-making. But since the main causes of this inequality are other inequalities of respect, resources and power, it is likely that participation in an egalitarian society would be much more representative of its constituent groups. The issue we discuss here is whether there are shortcuts to that goal, in the form of arrangements for making elected bodies more representative in unequal societies.[16]

The most common institutional device for representing political diversity is the use of proportional representation (PR) electoral systems. There are many PR systems, making varying use of such devices as multi-seat constituencies, party lists and the single transferable vote (Farrell 2000). PR systems are fairly effective in representing diverse political outlooks. They have been less successful at ensuring the election of members of subordinate groups, though better than non-PR systems. For example, PR systems on average elect higher proportions of women to national legislatures, with pure list systems (in which voters vote for party-designated lists) ranking highest. Within PR systems, the evidence tends to show that women and minorities do better in systems with more seats per constituency (Rule and Zimmerman 1994, esp. chs 2, 3, 21). But no PR system has succeeded in securing fully proportionate representation for these groups.

How, then, can the representation of subordinate groups be improved? Two widely suggested models are quotas and separate representation (Kymlicka 1995, ch. 7; Phillips 1995; Williams 1998, ch. 7; Young 2000, ch. 4). A commonly used quota policy is for parties to nominate a given percentage of women candidates. In both PR and non-PR systems, this device has raised the proportion of women elected to national legislatures (Norris 1993). Establishing nomination quotas or targets for other subordinate groups is possible but more complicated, largely because of the indeterminacy and fluidity of group membership (Phillips 1995, ch. 7).

The central challenge for the use of nomination quotas is that at the end of the day elected representatives do have to be elected, and so have to win votes from an electorate that (by definition) is on the whole biased against excluded, subordinate groups. To put it bluntly, if a substantial number of voters will not vote for a woman, then parties that nominate women (or in list systems, nominate 'too many' women) will not only fail to get them into the legislature but will lose otherwise winnable seats. This point is reflected in evidence showing that electoral systems, though important, are less significant for the representation of women than such 'contextual' factors as dominant attitudes, the position of women in the workforce, women's educational attainment and the extent to which women have actively campaigned to increase the number of women nominated and elected (Rule and Zimmerman 1994, chs 2, 3, 5, 10). It is also illustrated by American politics, where racially polarized voting in single-member constituencies means that black congressional candidates rarely get elected in majority-white districts and reform has focused (and stalled) on creating 'majority-minority' districts (Grofman and Handley 1992; Phillips 1995, ch. 4; Williams 1998). Our analysis here is not at all a comment on the quality of women and minority candidates but arises from the truism that members of dominant groups are held in higher esteem by most citizens than members of subordinate groups.

A striking variant of the use of quotas is the system for electing the lower house (Lok Sabha) in India, under which 79 of the 543 single-member-district seats are reserved for members of the scheduled castes (former 'Untouchables') and 41 for the scheduled tribes (Electoral Commission of India 1999; Joshi 1982; Tewari 2001). Such a system could in principle be introduced to reserve seats for women (it already exists for Indian local government), ethnic minorities, disabled people or gays and lesbians. But as before, the key question is whether a public strongly prejudiced against certain groups could accept being required to vote for them. The upshot is that although quotas can be helpful, particularly when used in conjunction with a PR system with large constituencies, the best guarantee of representatively diverse participation in elected bodies is the development of an egalitarian ethos in which citizens respect and appreciate diversity and are therefore happy to vote for parties with socially representative candidates. Quite a different model for minority representation is to establish separate representation for specific groups through the use of separate electoral rolls. In New Zealand/Aotearea, seven of the 120 seats in Parliament are currently elected from a separate electoral roll on which Māori may choose to register (Electoral Commission 2003). An advantage of this model as compared to quotas is that representatives have clear constituencies to whom they can be made accountable. A corresponding disadvantage is that the model seems to entail a relatively clear division of the electorate into distinct groups. This is difficult enough with two groups – Māori and non-Māori – but apparently insoluble when it comes to cross-cutting distinctions of class, ethnicity, gender, disability and sexuality (Phillips 1992). Here again, the real solution is an egalitarian society in which members of all social groups are well-placed to be elected.

Legislatures, however, are not the only bodies where the representation of subordinate groups is desirable. The national neocorporatist structures already referred to are convened by governments and can be more or less representative according to how they are constructed. So too can advisory bodies such as Ireland's National Economic and Social Forum, which includes representatives of political parties, business, labour, farmers and the community and voluntary sector (Crowley 1997; O'Donnell and Thomas 1998). Similar arrangements can exist at local levels (Lynam 1997). We have already discussed some of the dangers of neocorporatist institutions, but it is one of their strengths that they are able to ensure the representation of groups that may lack a voice in the normal electoral process.

### Economic, cultural and affective inequality

The problem of economic, cultural and affective inequality is, again, a problem about democracy in an unequal society. Are there ways of preventing more participatory processes from working systematically in favour of the privileged, or is the only solution one that attacks privilege itself? We will briefly consider two responses to this challenge: reform of political finance and reform of political communication.

The most familiar area of reform concerns political finance. This is a major issue in many democracies and it is beyond our scope to pursue its details here. Some of the typical provisions concern limits on the size of political contributions, public financing of parties and campaigns and public disclosure of donations (Alexander and Rei 1994). Despite such legislation, parties and candidates representing the privileged are significantly better resourced than those representing poorer sections of the population.

Thus in American elections, Republican candidates outspend Democratic candidates; in Irish elections, Fianna Fáil outspends all other parties.[17] In any case, election spending is only one aspect of the role of money in politics, which includes financing lobbyists, think-tanks and so on (Callahan 1999; Covington 1997). Funding legislation is important, but it has not been, and does not seem capable of being, fully effective in insulating politics from economic inequality.

A more proactive policy is public funding for the political activity of relatively powerless groups. Such funding can help vulnerable groups to organize, to develop their own analysis and policies and to campaign for their views once developed (Fraser 1989, 1997a; Knight and Johnson 1997; Mansbridge 1996; Shapiro 1996; Young 1995). But this is hardly a substitute for a wider egalitarianism, since it relies on the dominant group's willingness to fund its own critics and carries corresponding risks. For example, in 2002 the Irish Minister for Justice, Equality and Law Reform cut off funding for the public relations campaign Citizen Traveller after it criticized legislation on criminal trespass.[18]

Finding ways to counteract cultural and affective inequality is another challenging problem. Part of the aim must be the reform of the mass media to include a wider range of voices, an issue already raised in connection with citizen competence. But such alternative voices and concerns will only be effective counterpoints to dominant perspectives if subordinate groups have already found their voices and named their own priorities (Przeworski 1998), and these voices and concerns will only be heard and taken seriously by an audience that is ready to question dominant views. It is perhaps for these reasons that a recent study found that women, older people and poor people were less likely to engage in public political discussions, even though they were just as willing to talk politically in more private settings (Conover, Searing and Crewe 2002). These considerations point to limits in the ability of a participatory democracy to avoid reproducing inequalities in an unequal society.

Despite these limits, some of the experience of local participatory governance is encouraging. Studies of participatory planning in Porto Alegre and Kerala indicate that a system that encourages and supports participation from marginalized communities can do a lot to erode the general advantages of privileged groups (Abers 1998; Baiocchi 2003; Cohen and Rogers 2003; Thomas Isaac and Heller 2003; Wainwright 2003, pp. 42–69). It is significant that both of these cases were initiated by governments of the left that were determined to empower ordinary people as part of a broader egalitarian political project.

We conclude that there are limits to the degree to which political processes can really be insulated from economic, cultural and affective inequality. The only reliable and enduring strategy is to tackle these inequalities head-on. This is simply another indication of the interrelations of egalitarian aims. We need political equality partly for the sake of economic, cultural and affective equality. But we also need equality in the economic, cultural and affective systems for the sake of achieving it in politics.

## Conclusion

In this chapter, we have argued that an egalitarian society requires a participatory democracy, characterized by six key features: the widespread participation of ordinary citizens, a thorough democratization of society, a democratic social ethos, representatively diverse participation at all levels, accountable representation and rich, varied forms of political communication. Such a democracy is necessary for promoting and sustaining the egalitarian principles identified in Chapter 2.

We have discussed some of the central obstacles to participatory democracy. We have argued that participation itself is the best way to improve citizen competence and that the practicality of participatory democracy rests on a strong but realistic model of accountable representation. We have reviewed some of the ways that a participatory democracy could protect minorities within the context of a broadly egalitarian society. We have also argued that the best guarantee of representative participation in elected bodies is the development of an egalitarian ethos in which citizens respect and appreciate difference, and that the only reliable and enduring response to the challenge of economic, cultural and affective inequalities is to tackle these inequalities head-on.

These conclusions indicate two important points. First, that participatory democracy is a self-reinforcing system that to a large extent supplies its own solutions to its alleged problems. Secondly, that the development of a participatory democracy depends on a wider egalitarian project that attacks economic, cultural, affective and political inequalities together.

At the policy and institutional level, we have made a number of recommendations that call for major institutional change, but we do not pretend that they represent a comprehensive agenda for the development of egalitarian political institutions. We have only touched upon some key issues, and there are a number of other important questions that we have hardly mentioned, including transnational democracy, the relationship between governments and legislatures, the role and structure of political parties and the structures and functions of bureaucracies, the courts and police. Nevertheless, the topics we have discussed provide an idea of the direction and scope of necessary change. They show that there is an alternative to the politics of the present: the alternative of a participatory democracy.

# 7
# Equality, the Legal System and Employment Law

The legal system is an important context for equality because it regulates all other social institutions and is located at the intersection of state and civil society. While law helps to legitimate state authority, it also purports to serve civil society by providing a framework that secures public accountability and facilitates transactions between private parties. This chapter examines the potential role of the legal system in promoting equality of condition, in light of the complex and often contradictory functions it fulfils in society. We begin by reviewing some of the ways that the legal doctrines and institutions of liberal democracies currently serve to resist egalitarian change, going on to set out some ways that they could be reformed. We then examine anti-discrimination law as one of the major areas in which the legal system has been used to promote equality of opportunity, and analyse its shortcomings. This analysis forms the basis for exploring some of the ways that legislation could be used to promote equality of condition in the workplace, drawing on and developing some existing legal instruments.

There are of course many other areas of substantive law that currently create or reinforce inequalities, including those pertaining to crime, families and property; each of these raises specific challenges for achieving greater equality. But we hope that discussing one area of law in some depth will indicate the kinds of change necessary for promoting equality within the legal system.

## How the legal system reinforces inequality

Law often supplies the language and location for egalitarian strategies. Encouraged by episodic legal victories, such as those enjoyed by the civil rights and feminist movements, activists may resort to litigation in the hope that favourable judgments will trigger changes in other contexts (Eskridge 2002; Harlow and Rawlings 1992). In Ireland minority groups including Travellers and disabled people increasingly appeal to courts' supposed ability to correct flaws in representative systems of government

(Whyte 2002). 'Rights' discourse, in particular, has come to occupy a dominant role in engagements with the state (Brigham 1987) and of course has a resonance outside legal forums as a political resource to be mobilized by the oppressed. In this section, we concentrate on how the operation of the legal system itself serves to reinforce inequality, using elements of public law as an exemplar. Of particular concern is how courts, while ostensibly providing one place to challenge relations of power, curtail the demands of social movements. Later on in the chapter, we turn more specifically to the limitations of anti-discrimination litigation.

Feminist and other commentators have highlighted the problems inherent in pursuing reform within established frames of reference (Bottomley and Conaghan 1993; Kairys 1998; Lacey 1998; Smart 1989). Liberal legal doctrine, precisely because it acknowledges rights claims and expresses a commitment to equality of opportunity, can curb our ability not only to pursue more ambitious forms of equality, but even to imagine these alternatives. By appealing to law for solutions, egalitarians may be overlooking the inequalities embedded in the internal workings of the legal field and reinforcing the primacy of law over politics associated with 'liberal legalism' (Loughlin 2000; Ward 2001; West 1990). Liberal legalism combines the ideology of liberalism with a commitment to governance through law (Klare 1979, p.132; Quinn 1989; Radin 1989). Its central premise is that political power can be effectively checked by such legal doctrines as are typically expressed in the human rights guarantees and the provisions on the separation of governmental functions that are found in constitutional texts (Lane 1996, p. 19). In liberal democracies the operation of these doctrines is steered by adjudicative bodies, primarily the constitutional courts at the apex of their legal systems.

Under this vision, courts are capable of standing apart from the partiality of politics and ensuring that the state does not encroach unduly upon the domain characterized as 'private' (Abraham 1996; Bandes 1990; Quinn 2000). A sharp distinction must therefore be maintained between law and politics, both as fields of knowledge and activity and at the level of institutional design. For instance, while partiality is considered a legitimate feature of the political context, in that elected officials will represent particular constituencies, those charged with steering the legal context are meant to be neutral arbiters who are barred from promoting particular interests.

This view misrepresents the relationship between law and politics. In fact, these contexts are similar in two important ways, in that courts play a political role that tends to reinforce the position of dominant groups, while at the same time they generally exclude citizens from participating effectively in key decisions affecting their lives.

### The political role of the legal system

Law is shaped by other social contexts but it is not dominated by them and so may be considered relatively autonomous (Bourdieu 1987; Collins 1982, pp. 47–52). With respect to the economic context, for example, the evolution of laws governing businesses is more contingent and particular than a classical Marxist model would suppose, and judges have preferred the interests of labour over capital on occasion (Harris 2000). Law's apparent independence from external determinations does not, however, stem from adherence to a set of neutral principles that stand apart from the fabric of social relations. Rather it consists in forms of closure that define the legal field as a domain of expert knowledge and practice controlled by an interpretive community of lawyers and judges (Bourdieu 1987; Cotterrell 1992, pp. 195–200; Smart 1989). Operation of the legal field is guided by a set of internal protocols, assumptions and self-sustaining values that tend to obscure its complicity in sustaining relations of domination and oppression (Terdiman 1987, p. 806).

Law's claim to enunciate truths in the form of detached and objective judgments and its construction as a closed knowledge system mean that the political aspects of legal decision-making are continually masked. Adjudication, the decision-making process at the heart of the legal field, is presented as a neutral exercise in rule application that assures law's coherence by following principles elaborated in prior cases. The doctrine of precedent suggests that judges simply unfold and then apply the rules in a disinterested manner (Mossman 1986). Judgments are presented as the inevitable result of principled deliberation and interpretation, thereby distinguishing court decisions from the blatant exercises of power often associated with the political context (Bourdieu 1987, p. 818).

As critical scholars have illustrated, however, the rationalizations advanced to justify legal opinions conceal the considerable latitude afforded to legal actors by the elasticity of texts. For example, the open-textured nature of the human rights provisions found in most western constitutions allows judges to elaborate upon the meaning of broad statements of principle with reference to self-selected canons of interpretation (Davis, Chaskalson and De Waal 1996; Kavanagh 1997; West 1990).[1] Equality guarantees often baldly assert that everyone is entitled to equal treatment but fail to specify the conditions under which differential treatment may be considered justified, whether equality of form or substance is mandated and so on. Abstract concepts such as 'reasonableness' are indeterminate and so invite value judgements (Bartlett 1990; O'Donovan 1989), and the manipulability of precedent means that it is possible to appeal to competing and contradictory rules to decide any contested case (Altman 1986, p. 209; Bourdieu 1987, p. 833; Llewellyn 1960, p. 74).

This is not meant to suggest that judicial decisions are reducible to the conscious imposition of individual judges' personal values. Judgments are constrained by several factors that relate to safeguarding law's legitimacy both as an institution and a sphere of professional activity (Cross and Nelson 2001; Loughlin 2000, pp. 92–3). Judges may strive to tie the proposed result to existing practice and may work from the premise that there is a sharp distinction between the adjudicative function and the roles entrusted to other state bodies. Legal education imbues practitioners with a belief in the coherence of legal rules (Kennedy 1998). But all of this is consistent with the claim that the courts are constantly engaged in political rather than purely technical judgements. Law's 'truth' is continually constructed from a limited point of view, the normative universe of dominant groups within its interpretive community (Cover 1983; Lacey 1998, ch. 1). Consistency is assured not through the application of determinate laws but by the 'immersion of the judiciary in a shared culture' (Loughlin 2000, p. 93).

The legitimacy and authority that attach to legal institutions mean that law can have a robust political impact not only through the material effects of its official orders but also through the ideological or symbolic effects of its language and form. Legal language abstracts from 'the contingency and historicity of particular situations to establish a general and universal norm which is designed as a model for later decisions' (Bourdieu 1987, pp. 846–7). Through such processes of normalization, law disqualifies other forms of knowledge, including claimants' understandings of their own identities and interests (Gilkerson 1992; Schepple 1992; White 1990). Ideologies embedded in the legal process can prove particularly resistant to change, not least because law periodically makes concessions to competing visions (Ewick and Silbey 1998).

The political role of the courts is seen most clearly when courts challenge existing power relations, for example in the Canadian Supreme Court's development of the equality guarantee in the Charter of Rights and Freedoms (Grabham 2002). But because legal doctrines and processes favour preservation of the status quo, the general tendency of the courts is to reinforce inequality. In Ireland, for example, the robust protection that judges have afforded to the right to private property has stymied proposed legislation aimed at advancing social justice (Morgan 2001, pp. 45–6). Experience before the US courts with affirmative action demonstrates that reforms generated in the political sphere can be rolled back by courts with relative ease (McCrudden 1996; Nice 2000; Post and Siegel 2000). More generally, entrenched inequalities are treated in constitutional law and litigation as facts of nature. For example, the civil and political rights, including the right to private property, enumerated in most western constitutions are depicted as fundamental and 'natural'; their protection cannot be left to the vagaries of politics but must be safeguarded by courts. Social and economic rights are conspicuous by their absence and so apparently do not share the same inherent qualities (Murphy 1998). Courts need not unearth the historical and social contingencies that gave rise to this division, such as the liberal assumption that social and economic rights are incompatible with market economies or the influence of post Cold War geo-politics

(Craven 1995). Similarly, constitutional arrangements for the allocation of power are considered inevitable and necessary, as following a neutral course, with the result that few people ask whose interests they might serve (Lobel 1998). In general, then, courts play a political role on behalf of inequality.

### Participation in legal decision-making

Courts also reinforce inequality by exercising power over citizens in a way that is almost entirely exempt from democratic control and thus contrary to the principle of equality of power set out in Chapter 2. It might be objected that the right to assert one's rights before the courts is the legal counterpart to the right to vote in the political context, and it is true that each of these rights allows for some influence over the decision-making processes occurring in these fields. But just as voting is not enough to establish equal participation in politics, litigation on its own does not amount to an equal opportunity to participate in the legal system. A necessary condition for equal participation is a legal process that allows for the effective articulation of competing perspectives (Bryden 1987; Fredman 2000, p. 105).

Young's (2000) distinction between two forms of political exclusion can be usefully applied here. What she calls 'external exclusion' occurs when certain individuals or groups are either absent from decision-making forums or are dominated by others. However, even when these individuals or groups are nominally included, their participation may be rendered ineffective or meaningless owing to what she calls 'internal exclusion'. This arises when 'the terms of discourse make assumptions some do not share, the interaction privileges specific styles of expression, the participation of some people is dismissed as out of order' (Young 2000, p. 53).

In the legal field, external exclusion occurs in states, such as Ireland, where legal services are essentially privatized, so that access to courts is severely compromised and effectively guaranteed only to those with sufficient resources to meet the extraordinary costs involved (Whyte 2002, ch. 9). Legal aid schemes are classified as a form of welfare provision (Harlow 1999) and so tend to be subject to qualifying restrictions that exclude large segments of the population. While a wide range of rights is conferred on people, many are excluded from exercising these rights because they lack the resources necessary to do so (Galanter 1974; Rhode 2001; Zuckerman 1999).

Moreover, where legal aid is available, what is offered is simply access to a professional versed in a legal language that is so complex and intricate that years of training and practical experience are required for basic literacy. Court processes place a premium on legal knowledge and so the ability to participate in and influence decisions is effectively confined to lawyers and judges (Penman 1987). This creates a form of enforced dependency on middle class 'experts' (Gilkerson 1992). So even in the absence of external exclusion, most people are internally excluded from effective participation in legal processes. Both forms of exclusion generate inequalities of power.

## Making the system more egalitarian

In emphasizing political aspects of the legal system, and particularly of constitutional litigation, we do not mean to imply that there is no difference in the functions of the legislature and judiciary and that the doctrine of the separation of powers should be abandoned. What we do maintain is that the legal system should operate in an open manner, so that there is greater equality of participation and its political role is more transparent and open to debate. We consider direct judicial involvement in central policy choices to be symptomatic of an unhealthy underlying democratic system. Rule-making in a participatory democracy would occur outside of the court system to a far greater extent than at present. Under current conditions, however, activist courts form part of the political process, and adjudication should therefore be acknowledged as a political act. Although we reject the idea that courts should supplant democratic decision-making processes, we do suggest that they could play an important role in advancing political debate, prompting rather than inhibiting change. Any such role would involve abandoning the notion that the application of legal methods to social problems necessarily arrives at the 'correct' result. As Klare (1998, p. 187) remarks, lawyers 'can best address problems concerning the democratic legitimacy of judicial power by honesty about and critical understanding of the plasticity of legal interpretation and of how interpretive practices are a medium for articulating social visions'. With respect to public law this would entail re-working judicial review procedures and resultant remedies so that the separation of governmental powers is respected and attuned to participatory democratic principles (Scott and Macklem 1992, pp. 134–48).

Within most legal systems inter-group relations are reduced to interpersonal contests, in which a winner and loser must be identified (Menkel-Meadow 1996) and courts are not obligated to illustrate the overall impact of their decisions. Although 'public interest law' in some jurisdictions permits the judicial review of institutional practices that affect given social groups (Chayes 1976; Dasgupta 2002), many of these models simply augment the power of courts without securing an effective voice for subordinate people.

Participation by third parties in legal proceedings can assist in moving legal decision-making away from this individualist orientation towards one that takes account of the structural inequalities that shape relationships between groups. Interest groups can make submissions on matters before the courts of some legal systems in the form of *amicus curiae* briefs.[2] These interventions are a valuable mechanism for bringing external perspectives to the attention of adjudicators (Bryden 1987). Significantly, they may also differ qualitatively from the technical expert evidence usually drawn upon by courts and enable the presentation of issues in a form that emphasizes their relational and affective dimensions.[3] Unlike individual litigant narratives, briefs can have an application wider than the facts of the case at hand.

However, the production and reception of this information does not itself expose or challenge the political role of the courts and may even serve to reinforce it by asking the courts to make a judgement that should belong within the legislative process. In any case, the capacity to participate in legal proceedings as an *amicus curiae* is contingent on the existence of formally constituted and representative organizations with adequate resources, including access to legal expertise, an issue that is of particular importance for subordinate social groups.[4] We suggest below how the production of such material could be institutionally supported.

Using the courts as a forum for promoting equality of condition requires paying attention to how legal doctrines structure and define relationships between people. These issues can only be addressed by using data produced outside law's interpretive community, ideally through the application of emancipatory research principles (see Chapter 9). Under existing systems, sociological and other contextual information can be introduced by the parties to a case via *Brandeis* briefs (Harlow and Rawlings 1992, pp. 76–8; Sherlock 1991) or oral expert testimony. It may also be deemed relevant on the initiative of judges through the doctrine of judicial notice[5] or through legislative provisions. So there are already mechanisms for bringing this kind of material into the courtroom. But although the placement of social context evidence before US and Canadian courts in particular is a long-standing and commonplace practice, the manner in which such evidence is distilled by judges, the weight to be attributed to it and the criteria for assessing its relevance are far from clear (Boyle and MacCrimmon 2001; MacCrimmon 1998; Nowlin 2001). The tendency has been to treat knowledge from other sources merely as a factor to be considered in revealing the meaning of legal texts, rather than as a means of questioning core ideological assumptions (Cotterrell 1995, pp. 65–6). For social research to play a truly transformative role in the courtroom, it needs to be treated as evidence for the best decision, not just as evidence for interpreting what the law means.

If restructured, the doctrine of judicial notice, in particular, could function as a vehicle for employing evidence that situates legal rules in their overall political, social and economic climate, that is, for referring to what Davis (1955) calls 'legislative facts'.[6] Instead of uncritically accepting the 'truths' enshrined in traditional practice, judges would be required to bring these assumptions to the foreground of their deliberations. Exploring competing perspectives, such as those offered by minority groups and critical theorists, could also challenge and refine individual judicial predispositions (Matsuda 1987). Judges should be required to address contextual evidence and explain how their decisions affect relationships between groups in addition to individual litigants. In essence, this would require judgments to include an equality impact assessment and not just a ruling on the particular case at hand.

For this kind of process to become a permanent feature of the legal system, relevant research, including *amicus curiae* briefs produced by interest groups, should be resourced, and if necessary commissioned, by a dedicated state-funded agency. As suggested above, this research should be conducted in accordance with the principles of emancipatory research, a factor that should be taken into account in assessing its value as evidence. A court officer, similar to the advocates general who provide preliminary opinions for the European Court of Justice, could be tasked with gathering and presenting material to be used in specific cases.

The question of judicial training and appointments is beyond the scope of this chapter, but is clearly relevant. We agree with Freire's (1998) observation to the effect that social change requires personal transformation, not just of the disadvantaged, but of the privileged. Canadian judges now undertake social context education, a development that ought to be mirrored in other jurisdictions (Devlin 2001).

Reforms of this kind would help to address both the political role of the courts and inequalities of participation. They are by no means a complete solution to these problems, but they could play an important role in promoting equality of condition.

## Workplace anti-discrimination laws

As outlined in Chapter 2, a key assumption of liberal egalitarians is that there will always be major inequalities in people's status, resources, work and power. Proponents of equality of condition instead recognize that inequality stems from changeable social structures. These perspectives generate distinct legal strategies. Within liberal egalitarianism, the role of equality law is to achieve fairness in the competition for a more favourable place in unequal structures, whereas laws premised on equality of condition would be committed to altering those structures.

Particular legal rights are not properly understood until viewed as part of a larger systemic whole. In this section we argue that contemporary anti-discrimination laws cannot effect radical change in the workplace because they operate within a 'limited institutional, imaginative universe' (Rhode 1991, p. 343). By adopting equality of opportunity as their primary theoretical base, legislatures set an immediate ceiling on what can be achieved.[7] This perspective is typically reinforced by judicial interpretations of the equality provisions in constitutional texts. The more robust forms of equal opportunity legislated for in some jurisdictions are therefore dependent on a favourable judicial climate.

Contemporary anti-discrimination laws tend to exhibit several inter-related features. First, they are subordinate to the operation of market-based economies and reinforce a public/private dichotomy to the detriment of particular groups. Secondly, they focus on individual justice rather than group relations. Thirdly, their reliance on the idea of a comparator limits their relevance to many disadvantaged groups. Because, fourthly, they are based on the assumption that justice requires ignoring certain socially prominent differences, they treat positive action as exceptional and open to challenge. Finally, even when they do require positive action, anti-discrimination laws have a severely limited impact on inequality.

## Market relations and the public/private distinction

Liberal legal doctrines assume that certain 'private' matters should remain outside the preserve of governmental regulation. According to this perspective, the patterns of distribution and power relations at play in given contexts arise naturally and independently of state action; as a result, 'intervention' in arenas such as the economy and family should occur only within prescribed limits. Because the state does not itself cause poverty and interpersonal oppression, its role should be confined to alleviating the outcomes generated by market forces and family arrangements, through for example labour law and welfare provision.

This approach ignores the manner in which state institutions create and shelter particular forms of oppression. The market is not a naturally occurring phenomenon but an amalgam of the rules of property and contract that constitute it, including those of international trade and investment. Economic activities take place within a framework that is produced by political choices, is continually shaped by the state and is dependent on its enforcement agencies. Courts in particular play a significant role in protecting economic power. For example, a primary concern of the US Constitution's framers was how to protect property from potential redistribution by legislative majorities (Lobel 1998, p. 592; Nedelsky 1991, p. 16). Constitutionally entrenched rights were the favoured mechanism, a policy that has worked especially well during certain periods (Abraham 1996; Michelman 1987, p. 1327; Sunstein 1987). Active judicial promotion of particular economic policies is more apparent in the field of European Community law: as Ball (1996, p. 308) notes, the court's jurisprudence 'elevates to the normative status of fundamental rights, capitalist principles that promote free trade and movement across national borders'. State neutrality is therefore an illusion and 'intervention' a misrepresentation of the role of government.

Anti-discrimination laws are a quintessential example of this model of the relation between 'public' and 'private'. Although they 'intervene' in the market, they do not question the ownership of the means of production and they confine themselves to paid work, excluding the unpaid labour undertaken, primarily by women, in the home. In fact this job-related paradigm underscores the entire corpus of EU social policy (More 1996; Scheiwe 1994). Rights in the field of free movement and social security also attach only to 'workers', defined as individuals who are engaged in or seeking paid employment. The principle of equal treatment between men and women in statutory social security does not extend to a person who cares for a family member, unless they have abandoned market-based work in order to do so.[8] Likewise, freedom of movement within the EU is confined to persons engaged in economic activity, defined by the European Court of Justice to exclude employment that has a rehabilitative element.[9] Caring, love labour and certain forms of social employment do not, according to the Court, constitute an occupational activity and so do not attract the benefits of European citizenship (More 1996, pp. 271–5).[10]

### Individual justice versus group relations

Anti-discrimination statutes conceptualize the harm to be addressed as that of differentiation based on identity. Identity is codified in the form of protected grounds, and then used either as the basis for forbidding discrimination against members of target groups or for redistributing employment or educational opportunities in their direction. These two forms of provision could be called 'negative' and 'positive' respectively. Neither type exists in pure form in any jurisdiction.[11] However, positive measures are for the most part simply grafted onto a negative framework and are therefore conceived of by courts as exceptional, suspect and open to review.

The first and most common type of negative anti-discrimination law embodies formal equality of opportunity by banning direct discrimination on any prohibited ground. A fair employment practice is thus taken to be one that *abstracts* the individual from her group identity and considers ethnicity, gender, etc. to be irrelevant. However, as feminist commentators and critical race theorists have shown, this kind of neutrality does not produce just outcomes, because it masks adherence to a particular set of norms, based on those of dominant groups (Conaghan 1986; Crenshaw 1988; MacKinnon 1987; Young 1990, p. 25).

To succeed in an anti-discrimination case of this kind, claimants must fit within a delineated group, establish that they have been treated less favourably than a comparator and establish a connection between group membership and the conduct concerned. The use of identity categories as bases of comparison is problematic on several fronts. First, the contours of group membership are not shaped by those affected but by persons who enjoy significant social and political power, that is, legislators and members of the judiciary. As a result, statutes with an apparently benign motive can import identity categories that contribute to perpetuating the inequalities that generated the need for anti-discrimination law in the first place (Iyer 1993). Minow (1992, p. 79) explains that using identity as the sole basis for adjudicating may drag people into inappropriate categories, while treating the categories themselves as immutable. Reliance on medical rather than social models of disability by national legislatures constitutes one striking example (Hendriks 2000).[12] Essentialist assumptions about the roles of men and women with respect to caring for children underpinned the European Court of Justice's decision to uphold the exclusion of fathers from adoptive leave entitlements under Italian law[13] and continue to inform the court's decisions in the arena of pregnancy and maternity discrimination (Di Torella, Caracciolo and Masselot 2001; McGlynn 2000).

Identity classifications also cling to an understanding of difference as inherent and binary rather than viewing it as multiple and relational (Crenshaw 1989; A. Harris 1990). Thus even though some statutes may admit claims involving multiple grounds of discrimination, the treatment in question may have resulted from the *conjunction* of, say, racism and disablism; these practices are not captured by a categorical-comparative framework. In the EU context these difficulties are compounded by the emergence of a hierarchy in the various grounds of discrimination (Flynn 1999; Fredman 2001, p. 159). The subjects of US equal protection doctrine are also stratified according to identity category; certain groups are said not to warrant 'protection' while rules affecting those covered are subject to differing levels of scrutiny (Dorf 2002; Eskridge 2002).

The second principal type of negative provision moves beyond formal equality of opportunity to embrace a more substantive approach to employment matters by prohibiting indirect discrimination. Indirect discrimination or disparate impact liability occurs where there is an apparently neutral job requirement with which fewer members of a protected group can in fact comply, and where that requirement turns out not to be relevant to the performance of the job in question.[14] While this concept can be used to remove unnecessary job performance criteria, these are only unearthed in cases concerned with what employers have done, not with what they have failed to do, and so cannot capture all of the ways in which rules and practices adversely affect minorities. For instance, a failure to provide 'family-friendly' work arrangements will clearly have particular implications for women, given the gendered division of labour, yet this is immune from challenge as a form of discrimination.

The egalitarian potential of laws against indirect discrimination is also weakened by the defences available to employers, arguments based on market forces being especially pernicious in relation to pay.[15] When combined with bona fide occupational requirements and general derogations, such defences can end up preserving the status quo (cf. Bolger and Kimber 2000, ch. 11; Thornton 1991). One recent example stems from the Preamble to the EC's Framework Directive 2000/78, which stipulates that it applies 'without prejudice to national laws on marital status and the benefits dependent thereon'. This means that an employer may refuse to confer rights on an employee's partner because they are not married, irrespective of the fact that such a policy amounts to indirect discrimination on the grounds of sexual orientation. Exclusion of employees with same-sex partners from family-based benefits not only constitutes a material deprivation but expresses unequal recognition and jeopardizes equality of love and care.

Negative anti-discrimination laws operate in a reactive manner. They rely on finding an objectionable practice to kick-start the process. Even blatant discrimination goes unchallenged unless an aggrieved individual is in a position to take a case, and generally the remedy is that of compensation. These laws rarely require restructuring to prevent such patterns arising time and again. At both a conceptual and practical level, therefore, the generative causes of inequality in employment go unchecked and tend to be translated into problems about discrete acts of individual injustice. As a practical matter, individuals who belong to well-resourced groups, typically those in a dominant position, have the best chance of pursuing claims effectively. While pursuing a claim is formally open to everyone, in substance the individual grievance approach is limited by disparities in power, status and money among potential claimants (Kilpatrick 2002, pp. 505–6).

As argued above, law produces cultural meanings as an aspect of its power and therefore is a key site of ideological activity. By zoning in on individual agency, discriminatory practices are presented to the wider public as an aberration (Lacey 1998, p. 23). Sexism, racism, homophobia and so on are misrepresented as the unreasonable attitudes of individual employers, so nothing stands in need of systematic transformation. Liberal equality regimes thereby endorse the continuation of what is in essence a positive action system that operates in favour of dominant groups (Armor 1997). They adopt what Freeman (1978, pp. 1053–4) describes as 'the perpetrator perspective'.

### The comparative approach

Another problem with negative anti-discrimination legislation is that it typically relies, either tacitly or explicitly, on the notion of comparators.[16] So in an equal pay claim based on gender, for example, the most crucial task facing an applicant is to find a man with whom she can compare her work. In predominantly female workforces, there may simply be no relevant male employee. Hierarchical and occupational segregation are frequently immune from challenge, and consequently the legislation is irrelevant for a large proportion of workers, arguably those most in need of improved working conditions. Pay equity is narrowly construed and does not demand any reconsideration of how certain forms of work are devalued while others bring enormous financial reward; it is concerned only with correcting the wages of individual employees.

The rights of atypical workers within the EU are severely curtailed by the comparative approach, which ensures that a ceiling is set on the permissible types of change that can occur (Jeffrey 1998). The Part-time Workers Directive 97/81/EC does not attempt to remedy the ills of casual labour by granting appropriate substantive rights but has the more limited ambition of ensuring that part-time workers are not treated less favourably than their full-time counterparts (Barnard and Hepple 2000, pp. 579–83). Even directly discriminatory measures can be objectively justified and no right to access to part-time work is conferred. By taking full-time, permanent work as the norm, the directive ignores the specific needs of temporary workers for transferable rights that acknowledge accumulated experience and bridge gaps in market employment (Murray 1999).

The comparative approach to anti-discrimination law therefore implicitly endorses a conception of equality as sameness (MacKinnon 1990, p. 219). By ignoring relevant differences it typically works to the disadvantage of subordinate groups. But its final flaw is rather different. Because it lacks any overarching criterion of distributive justice, the principle of treating like cases in the same way can be satisfied either by levelling up or levelling down. As European Court of Justice decisions in the area of pensions demonstrate, anti-discrimination legislation can in practice end up reducing the level of protection afforded to the majority of workers (Fredman 1996).[17]

## The problem of symmetry

The failure of negative anti-discrimination legislation to take account of the contexts of inequality within which it operates is evident in the 'symmetry' of its equality guarantees, which consider *all* classifications based on impugned criteria to be inherently questionable. Because formal equality construes the harm to be addressed as one of differentiation rather than subordination it does not distinguish between using a classification to shore up privilege or challenge it (Vojdik 2002).[18] By contrast, positive forms of anti-discrimination law have more substantive aims. Regarding the under-representation of disadvantaged groups in given occupations as symptoms of inequality of opportunity, they work from the premise that employment practices may need to take account of workers' differences in order to promote equality of opportunity overall.[19] However, these provisions, whether in the form of accommodation-type policies or positive action measures, are usually grafted onto the negative model discussed above. As a result, most jurisdictions categorize positive provisions as an exception to the wider non-discrimination principle (Barnard and Hepple 2000, pp. 576–9; Jolls 2001). When constitutional texts do not embrace substantive equality goals, the asymmetrical and group-based approach involved in positive legislation remains in fundamental tension with the underlying vision of equality as an individual right to formally equal treatment. Upon judicial review, courts are then free to set rule neutrality as the baseline and to assess 'deviations' through the application of proportionality tests.[20]

Several ideological and practical problems flow from the designation of such measures as exceptional. Fundamentally it reinforces a vision of the ideal worker as one who does not demand 'special' treatment; he does not become pregnant, have domestic responsibilities or a disability. Departures from this norm should be catered for only within prescribed, 'reasonable' limits, if at all, and the functioning of the market economy should not be disrupted to any great extent. Positive measures are often construed as unfair attempts at transferring the costs of social 'problems' onto employers, or in the case of affirmative action onto 'innocent' actual or prospective employees (Harris 1993). That reasoning underpinned the decision in *Re Article 26 and the Employment Equality Bill 1996* [1997] 2 IR 321, where the Irish Supreme Court found that a provision obliging employers to make reasonable accommodation for disabled employees constituted an unjust attack on the property rights of employers, specifically the right to carry on a business and earn a livelihood.

The implication here is that the difficulties encountered by various groups in meeting market expectations are traceable to their own problematic attributes rather than to the unequal structures bolstered by the operation of capitalist economies. The alternative to sharing or transferring costs is of course to leave things exactly as they are, which is to say that the costs of structural inequalities, both fiscal and personal, should continue to be borne solely by members of disadvantaged groups, a fact that was acknowledged by the Canadian Supreme Court in *Brooks* v. *Canada Safeway* [1989] 1 S.C.R. 1219. We return to the concept of reasonable accommodation as developed by that court below.

### The limits of positive action

Positive action legislation is routinely subject to successful litigation-based challenges (Yount 1993).[21] That courts are receptive to these challenges is unsurprising because the very principle that is meant to justify positive action, namely equal opportunity, gives primacy to protecting individuals against unfair practices. Judges are therefore inclined to see workforce quotas or even tie-break clauses as penalizing employees who do not belong to the 'protected' group (Fredman 2000). Furthermore, the equal opportunities approach tends to accept or gloss over prevalent notions of merit (Armor 1997; Thornton 1985), despite the fact that the concept is socially constructed and capable of encompassing myriad values (McCrudden 1998; Parekh 1993, pp. 273–6; Rhode 1989, p. 186). In fact, conceptions of merit that are not strictly aligned to job performance do not always attract judicial opprobrium: the US civil service policy of giving preference to veterans is legally secure despite adverse affects on female candidates.[22] What seems to matter legally is not merit narrowly defined, but whether a wider definition of merit fits in with the aims and values of dominant groups.

Even where positive action legislation survives judicial scrutiny, it has clear limits (Fraser 1997a; Young 1990, p. 193). First of all, increased representation of women or other groups in targeted sectors does little to alter underlying unequal patterns. While positive action schemes may insert some individuals into higher positions, the vast majority of people from subordinate groups continue to be deprived of the opportunity to acquire 'merit' and so are confined to low status, underpaid jobs (Hepple 1990, p. 411). Affirmative action therefore tends to favour the more privileged members of disadvantaged groups (Kymlicka 2000, p. 198; Parekh 1993, p. 278). At the same time, precisely because it has not dealt with the structures generating inequality, positive action legislation entails continuous remedial activity. The result, as Fraser (1997a, p. 25) notes, is to 'mark the most disadvantaged class as inherently deficient and insatiable, as always needing more and more'. In addition, positive action measures tend to capture only certain dimensions of workplace inequality. They may reduce inequalities of income and of employment opportunities, but may not address inequalities of power or recognition. For instance, persons from a minority culture may be forced to assimilate to the dominant one, and as Malamud (1997, p. 1709) observes, 'the diverse candidates must do their jobs, be role models, and teach the rest of the workforce how the world looks from their diverse perspectives. They can never be at peace in the same way as those whose right to be on the job is socially constructed as based on their pure individual merit.' Finally, as discussed earlier, programmes that address only the market are inherently limited and can create new pockets of inequality. Labour undertaken in the home may result in a double shift for women in employment or be delegated to a new primarily female underclass, whose own caring tasks are not part of the equal opportunities equation.

To sum up, workplace anti-discrimination laws suffer from a number of interrelated limitations: the priority they give to market outcomes; their focus on individual rights rather than group relations; their reliance on comparators; their tendency to treat both dominant and subordinate groups symmetrically; and the limited impact of their provisions for positive action. They do not constitute an appropriate legal framework for promoting equality of condition.

## Towards equality of condition in employment

As we pointed out in Chapter 2, the concept of equality is open to many interpretations, as are such related concepts as rights and the public/private distinction. Critical legal scholars and social movements have shown that rights can be understood in wider and more progressive ways than those found in conventional legal analysis (CCPI 2001; Crenshaw 1988; Jackman and Porter 1999; Minow 1987; Nedelsky 1993b; Williams 1987; Women's Economic Equality Project 2000). But as Williams (1987, p. 433) argues, these understandings will only emerge if courts and the legal profession are prevented from monopolizing the interpretation and articulation of rights. This point is borne out by the dynamic character of international norms in the area of social, economic and cultural rights (Craven 1995; Hunt 1996; Scott and Macklem 1992), where developments have been fuelled by NGO participation in the UN's human rights machinery (Porter 2000; Winter 2002). In this section, we focus on the kinds of legal understandings that would help to promote the aim of equality of condition. We continue to concentrate on employment law.

Laws based on equality of condition would encompass both procedural rights to participate in various spheres of life and substantive rights designed to enable people to choose among real options of similar worth. Such rights would clearly be concerned with the relative positions of people within society and could not be construed as objects possessed by individuals in isolation (Minow 1987; Nedelsky 1993a, p. 1289, 1993b; Young 1990, p. 25). Equality law would continue to refer to social groups, but groups would be conceived of in structural rather than purely cultural/identity terms (Young 2000, p. 82). In other words, the focus would not be on identity *per se* but on the relative detriment or benefit that attaches to membership of particular groups (Colker 1986; Vojdik 2002). This approach would avoid symmetrical applications that permit dominant groups to appropriate equality and rights discourse in order to secure their privilege.

Some recent developments contain the seeds of an approach that moves towards embedding equality of condition in legal doctrine. Two examples of these developments are requirements to provide reasonable accommodation and positive duties to promote equality in the workplace.

### Reasonable accommodation

Laws aimed at accommodating 'difference' currently take a variety of forms. Those pertaining to disabled people usually require adjustments in workplace practices and environments to enable them to participate in the labour market.[23] Similar provisions operate to facilitate workers with family responsibilities but these are generally confined to statutory leave entitlements.[24] Thus while an employee may take time off work for maternity, parental or care-taking purposes, employers are not required to restructure workplaces so that love and care labour can be undertaken without a resultant loss in status or opportunity in market terms. In most jurisdictions so-called 'family friendly' work arrangements are instigated at the discretion of employers and thus are contingent on the bargaining power of employees and on wider labour market considerations. In any case, as Day and Brodsky (1996, p. 435) note, the traditional conception of reasonable accommodation is flawed since it accepts that social norms can be set by powerful groups 'with manageable concessions being made to those who are "different"'. Furthermore, associated costs can be largely externalized through the operation of 'undue hardship' defences or the absence of an obligation to provide paid leave for all categories of worker (Barnard 2000, pp. 266–80; Colker 1986).

Equality of condition requires transformation rather than adjustment of the factors that give rise to and exacerbate inequalities in work settings. An expansive formulation of accommodation requirements has the capacity to deliver some degree of change. The Supreme Court of Canada's decision in *Meiorin*[25] seeks to adopt a structural approach to discrimination analysis by recognizing a positive right to be accommodated, extending beyond the individual complainant to all workers potentially affected by the impugned rule. Whereas the conventional approach emphasized an individual applicant's difference from the norm and required adjustments to allow that person to reach the standard set for others, the Court held that the validity of the standard itself must be scrutinized in detail. Its decision requires employers to identify and implement alternative approaches that do not have discriminatory effects. The question of individual accommodation arises only where a general policy change cannot be effected for reasons of health and safety, business necessity or undue hardship (Sheppard 2001, pp. 552–3).

These developments, while significant in directly challenging institutional practices, are limited in several important respects. Orders of this type are deployed only as a remedy following successful employment-related litigation (Leposky 1998, p. 168) and so cannot produce widespread effects. To have a systematic impact, the duty to accommodate must apply at the stage at which policy and practice are designed and must involve the input of individuals from groups that are ordinarily excluded from these processes. We suggest that a right to be accommodated, exercisable by all employees, could form a central component of the proposed statutory duty to promote equality of condition considered below.

## Positive duties to promote equality of condition in employment

One of the central flaws we have identified in anti-discrimination laws is their potential to legitimate and naturalize inequalities, by focusing on the individual claimant, clothed in her group traits, and neglecting to highlight the oppressive practices of the powerful. By contrast, laws based on equality of condition would not entail assimilation to or comparison with existing norms and standards but would seek to change the practices that perpetuate unequal relations between groups. They would aim to transform systems of oppression such as racism, patriarchy, disablism and the operation of capitalist economies with a view to promoting equality.

With respect to positive action for example, instead of focusing on the under-representation of given groups in occupational sectors, laws based on equality of condition would start from the opposite premise and regard the disproportionate numerical presence of white males as evidence of institutional bias in favour of one gender and ethnic group. This change of lens would mean, for example, that concepts such as 'merit' would no longer be allowed to slip under the radar but would become a central object of inquiry (Thornton 1991). Rules or practices that were originally constructed in ways that favoured particular groups would be reassessed. Structuring of work and state holidays around a given religious creed, or preferential rates of pay for male-dominated occupations, could be considered directly anti-egalitarian, in that they single out one group and accord its members special treatment. If this type of evaluation were undertaken, it might well emerge that although the original connection between privileged groups and particular practices is now hidden from view, their members continue to benefit from a positive action system designed with their interests and preferences in mind. When viewed from this perspective, the correlation between certain educational credentials or length of service and the merit standard applicable for a given job is also not as neutral as it may first appear. Some jurisdictions already require employers to probe qualification requirements for potentially exclusionary effects. Under section 20 of the South African Employment Equity Act 1998, a person may be suitably qualified for a job as a result of a combination of factors including 'learning by doing and life learning' and the 'capacity to acquire, within a reasonable time, the ability to do the job'. This would be a standard provision in legislation promoting equality of condition.

At the level of individual employers, legislation to promote equality of condition could be developed out of existing models. Mandatory equality audits, pay equity schemes (NAWL 2002) and action plans already form part of the legislative package in some jurisdictions and are valuable devices in that they apply prospectively and potentially cover a wide range of employers, not just those found in default.[26] However, in common with other mainstreaming initiatives, most do not include in-built consultation mechanisms and simply transpose norms formulated elsewhere into workplaces (Mullally and Smith 2000). Under these 'expert-bureaucratic' models, the experiences and needs of affected groups are mediated by professionals located in statutory agencies (Nott 2000). A participative-democratic model, by contrast, would rely heavily on the secured involvement of relevant groups. One such system, which covers all public policies and practices including those pertaining to employment, is now operational in Northern Ireland (Beveridge, Nott and Stephen 2000; McCrudden 1999). Section 75 of the Northern Ireland Act 1998 imposes equality duties on designated public authorities and implementation is overseen by a statutory body, the Equality Commission. Compliance with these duties is secured through publication of 'equality schemes' which demonstrate to the Commission's satisfaction how the public authority will promote equality of opportunity between certain different individuals and groups. Schemes must state the agency's arrangements for consulting representatives of persons likely to be affected by its policies. Early indications are that the inclusion of these consultation mechanisms has contributed quite significantly to the formulation of policy but is hampered by a failure to sufficiently resource the relevant groups (Donaghy 2003).

Although it has been developed for the purpose of advancing equal opportunities, this model could be adapted to the aim of promoting equality of condition. To do so would require three central changes. First, the positive duties set out in legislation would have to be framed in terms of objectives that promote equality of condition. Secondly, the scheme would have to be extended to encompass private employers. And thirdly, provisions for consultation would have to be strengthened so that representatives of subordinate groups were both resourced and empowered to exercise real influence over relevant decisions.

Legal regulations framed in this manner would lay the basis for site-specific examination of institutional practices that hamper or promote equality of condition. The concern here is not with equalizing outcomes for groups as such but with enabling individuals to make real choices between real options. Equality schemes that prevented employers from imposing exploitative contracts or oppressive work environments could be justified as necessary to protect individuals' dignity. Likewise, it violates even the liberal commitment to personal autonomy to confine employees to a range of poor work options from which they can 'freely choose'. In addition, equality of condition emphasizes the influence of social factors on people's choices and actions and so implies that practices should be examined for how they systematically shape the choices of members of different social groups. For example, decisions on the part of employees not to seek promotion are generally considered reducible to personal preference and therefore as having no equality implications. However, on closer investigation several factors may be at play. The higher grade may not have in-built job-sharing possibilities. It may involve longer working hours or weekend work. The individual concerned may have been excluded from networks that produce and reproduce social and cultural capital enhancing one's prospects of success (Bourdieu 1986). There may be covertly homophobic practices, including signals that 'inappropriate' behaviours or conversations ought to be silenced among prominent members of the organization. As Bourdieu (2001, pp. 1–4) explains, masculine domination is constructed in both the material and symbolic world. So symbols, rituals and practices may mark senior jobs as appropriate for men and not women.

Another way equality of condition could be promoted through employment equality schemes is through job enrichment and greater opportunities for training and personal development. One aim of equality of condition is to ensure that everyone has the prospect of satisfying work, so that it not just seen as a means to an end but rather as an intrinsically worthwhile activity (cf. Sayer 2000). A legally instituted practice for promoting equality of condition would call into question existing divisions of labour and provide the basis for job redefinition and support for work-based learning.

For equality of condition to be fully realized in employment would require a re-examination of the rights and immunities that attach to ownership of the means of production. Changes effected in the field of labour law cannot be hived off from overarching rules, particularly those of property and contract. As discussed in Chapter 5, bringing about equality of condition could involve very fundamental changes in the structure of capitalist economies. But even within a capitalist framework, the kind of equality-promoting model we are talking about here could play a role in reducing inequalities of income, power and working and learning between workers and employers and among employees themselves.

Equality of condition also requires that caring labour and love labour be recognized, supported and shared. This requires an integrated conception of the work performed across all spheres, in recognition of the fact that unwaged workers currently subsidize employment in the market. Although the development of employment equality schemes could contribute to this aim by identifying and dealing with systematic biases against care work, its full realization implies legislation addressing the distribution of the benefits and burdens of work, irrespective of where or for whom it is carried out. The Supiot Report (European Commission 1999) provides a useful starting point for reforms along these lines. It advocates constructing social and economic rights around the concept of 'occupational status', which would reflect individuals' engagement in socially useful unwaged work in addition to their history of paid employment.

### Constitutional issues

Entrenchment of socio-economic and workplace rights implies constitutional change and attention to interactions between the formal political and legal contexts. As we have seen, the interpretive scope afforded to courts means that specific decisions can exert a heavy political influence. The plasticity of legal norms means that 'progressive' judgments on discrete issues are possible. But these do nothing to tackle, and may in fact mask, the inequalities of power inherent in adjudicative processes. Unless constitutions specifically endorse transformative objectives, through for example interpretive clauses and substantive equality guarantees (Grabham 2002; Klare 1998), the legal system can end up preserving the status quo and containing change within confines set by an unelected arm of the state.

An egalitarian constitutional order would generate institutions whose rationale is the active promotion of equality of condition across all the dimensions identified in Chapter 2. This would entail changes in the functions of courts, while maintaining the separation of powers between the legislature and judiciary. We are not suggesting that inequalities should be altered by judicial fiat, but we do think that judgments should critically engage with and highlight the underlying policy choices. As Millett (1970, p. 58) puts it, 'when a system of power is thoroughly in command, it has scarcely need to speak itself aloud; when its workings are exposed and questioned, it becomes not only subject to discussion, but even to change'.

We also suggest that courts in exercising their power of judicial review can adopt a context-sensitive approach to the separation of powers doctrine (Minow 1990, pp. 361–2). The nature of the interest at stake or the parties involved and the responsiveness of other branches of government should inform the appropriate balance to be struck (*ibid.*; Whyte 2002, ch. 1). Intervention on behalf of groups who have no access to effective political representation, such as children, should raise different considerations from those applicable to members of relatively powerful groups.

Creative use of public law remedies could strengthen democratic legitimacy by avoiding either/or dispositions of cases (cf. Scott and Macklem 1992). Courts could, for example, issue judicial decrees requiring a structured participatory process for resolving a particular problem, with a clear role for the groups it affects. To illustrate: recent Irish legislation, the Housing Miscellaneous Provisions Act 2002, criminalized trespass in order to ensure the effective removal of Travellers from unofficial halting sites. This statute was promulgated in a manner that bypassed established consultation mechanisms, yet it appears that under current interpretations of the separation of powers doctrine this deliberate omission would not be open to any constitutional challenge, as courts have continually refused to interfere in legislative processes (Casey 2000, pp. 348–50). This refusal is made more plausible by the assumption that the courts' only options are to uphold or strike down the law in question. Were they to have the additional option of requiring a participatory resolution of the issue, they could act to strengthen rather than undermine democratic procedures.[27]

With respect to the contested terrain of socio-economic rights, the problem is that these rights are generally considered to be programmatic in character and dependent on the prevailing economic climate (CESR 2000). It is concluded that courts can have no role in upholding these rights. A more expansive reading of the type of duty imposed on governments by socio-economic rights, such as that found in the South African Constitution, would suggest that a positive obligation is placed on the state to secure available resources, acknowledging that it is the state that dictates how material wealth is distributed in the first place (Heywood 2003; Trengrove 1999). Public law remedies could then be directed at ensuring that the problems underlying inadequate health care and housing provision, for example, are identified and named, and that the state is tasked with finding the resources to solve them. Judgments in such cases would not limit themselves to addressing the claims of those living in poverty (e.g. *O'Reilly* v. *Limerick Corporation* [1989] ILRM 181; *Gosselin* v. *Quebec* [2002] SCC 84). They might also explain that government policy permits privileged groups to derive large profits from other sources of unearned income, including the rewards that accrue to property developers as a result of state-funded infrastructure improvement (Bell and Parchomovsky 2001; Chomsky 2000, p. 194; Sayer 2000). This would not require the courts to legislate but would help to hold the state to account for its policies.

## Conclusion

In this chapter we have been concerned with the potential of the legal system to promote equality of condition. We have argued that the legal doctrines and institutions of liberal democracies currently act to resist egalitarian change, and that the system needs reform in a number of key respects. We have also argued that there are some serious flaws in current forms of anti-discrimination legislation, which is the most prominent use of the law for egalitarian ends. However, existing legislation does contain the seeds of an approach for using the law to promote equality of condition. We have set out a model of how this could be pursued in relation to equality in employment and have considered some of the constitutional issues this would raise.

The experiences of some transitional democracies suggest that profound shifts in legal systems only occur through an effective political mobilization that exposes the structural roots of inequality (Davis, Macklem and Mundlak 2002). Under the new South African Constitution and certain provisions of the Northern Ireland Act 1998, for example, transformation of society became an explicit goal. It was no longer possible to present widespread inequalities, patterned according to group membership, as natural or to reduce them to isolated acts of discrimination. Constitutional change was impelled when social relationships were understood to have outgrown their legal form. These examples suggest that the kinds of changes recommended in this chapter are contingent on the success of egalitarian social movements, a topic we return to in Part III. The legal system typically acts to reinforce inequality. But given enough political momentum, it has the potential to promote egalitarian change.

# 8
# Equality and Education

In a global society in which so many aspects of life are controlled by professional interests, it is important to remember that education is not confined to schools and other institutions of formal education. Human beings are creative agents and the learning they do outside of schools can be a liberating process (Freire 1998; Illich 1970; Postman and Weingartner 1969). While acknowledging the importance of such non-formal education, this chapter focuses on formal systems of education as these play a particularly important role in regulating access to a wide range of goods, as well as playing a major role in defining what is of cultural worth in most societies. Much of our attention is devoted to the compulsory sectors of education, as these are the most pervasive and formative in the lives of children and young adults.

Formal, publicly controlled education originated in the nineteenth century in most western countries. The motives for developing mass public education were manifold and by no means driven largely by egalitarian concerns. While liberals, socialists, Fabians and feminists fought for mass education on egalitarian grounds, public education was introduced primarily for the purposes of social control. Its principal remit was to develop a compliant and obedient workforce for the emerging factories of the new industrial age (Bowles and Gintis 1976; Katz 1971). It was also regarded as a useful mechanism for developing disciplined bodies and minds in the emerging nation states, and for proselytizing by religious bodies (Coolahan 1981; Foucault 1991; Inglis 1998). Schools and colleges were not principally designed therefore as institutions of liberation and enlightenment, although that was clearly one of their purposes from the perspective of egalitarian educators. They were primarily designed to be agents of social control, to regulate citizens, to socialize people into particular religious beliefs and into particular gendered, ethnic and sexual identities. They were also assigned the task of selecting, labelling and stratifying students by age and level of attainment.

This nineteenth-century inheritance still impacts on public schooling in the twenty-first century as schools continue to operate according to mutually contradictory principles in relation to equality. While they profess principles of basic equality of opportunity, and are bound to these by legislation in some countries (the Universities Act 1997 and the Education Act 1998 in Ireland being a case in point), at the same time schools and colleges select and stratify students in a manner that clearly defeats certain aspects of their equality remit. While they are expected to develop democratic attitudes and values, they are, for the greater part, profoundly undemocratic in their organization. While they propound the values of holistic education, much of their work is focused on developing linguistic and mathematical competencies.

If schools and colleges are to promote equality, they need to abandon their inegalitarian inheritance and adopt an inclusive and consistent approach to the realization of equality objectives. Drawing on the equality framework outlined in Chapter 2, this chapter presents a basic framework for the pursuit of a holistic and integrated approach to the achievement of equality in education. The discussion opens with a brief résumé of the reasons why equality in education matters. This is followed by an analysis of four major equality problematics that arise from the central role that education plays at the nexus of economic, cultural, political and affective relations. We examine the role of education as a site of equality practice that is simultaneously defining and defined in terms of economically generated goods and services, cultural practices, the exercise of power and authority, and the ordering of relations of care, love and solidarity. In each of these areas we analyse the problems and suggest some resolutions.

## Why equality in education matters

The right to education is articulated in several international legal instruments including Article 24 of the Universal Declaration of Human Rights (1948). Education is valued because of its intrinsic worth for all human beings and because it is indispensable in achieving other human rights, including the right to economic well-being and good health. Where the right to education is guaranteed, other rights are greatly enhanced (UNESCO 2002). The primary reason why equality in education matters therefore is because it is a fundamental human right, a right that has an enabling function in relation to the attainment of other rights.

In a global order where advanced skills in literacy and numeracy are required for economic, social and political participation, one is confined to a state of powerlessness, dependence and lack of control if one is deprived of education: education is essential for the exercise of global citizenship. Equality in education matters therefore because education is indispensable for the full exercise of people's capabilities, choices and freedoms in an information-driven age.

Education can and does play a major role in empowering those who experience multiple disadvantages in particular (be it because of gender, class, ethnicity, sexuality, disability, age, caste or a combination of these). It exercises a powerful emancipatory function for oppressed groups when allowed to do so (Freire 1998). Equality in education matters therefore because of the potential that education offers to counter inequalities in other social institutions and systems.

More generally, education has a powerful formative influence. Childhood is a crucial time for both personal and social identity formation. The influence that schooling exercises over children's sense of capability is often definitive, especially among those whose parents lack the education, power and resources to counter the school's definitions of the self (Reay 1998b; Walkerdine and Lucey 1989; Walkerdine, Lucey and Melody 2001). Equality in education matters, therefore, because of the impact of education on personal development.

Education is not simply a private resource, however: it is also a public good. It plays a foundational role in determining the character of any given society. It is above all a major site of cultural practice, playing a key role not only in distributing cultural heritage, but also in defining that heritage, in excluding as well as including. Schools and other educational institutions are recognized arbiters of what is culturally valuable, not only in terms of what is formally taught, but also in terms of the manner in which it is taught, to whom, when and where. By legitimating and ordering socio-cultural relations, educational institutions play a central role in defining what is and is not (and by implication who is and is not) of cultural worth. Equality in education matters therefore because of the central role that schools and colleges play in defining who and what is of cultural value in a particular society.

Education is also a deeply social and political force in the public life of societies. In a globalized order in which credentialized knowledge plays an increasingly powerful role in determining occupational opportunities, education is a central player in the distribution of privilege. Those who receive much formal education are considerably advantaged over those who receive little, and those who receive their education in elite institutions are privileged over those who do not (Bourdieu 1996). Equality in education matters therefore because of its public role in mediating access to a host of social, political and economic goods in society.

Even though millions of children throughout the world (especially girls) receive no formal education, one of the Millennium targets of the United Nations is that all children will receive a full course of primary education by 2015 (UN General Assembly Resolution, A/56/326 6th September 2001).[1] In most countries, particularly in economically developed countries, such participation in formal education is compulsory, with many states imposing strong sanctions on children who fail to attend (unless parents make approved alternative arrangements). This compulsion makes it all the more important for school to be an enabling and enriching experience for young people that not only develops their capabilities, but also reinforces their sense of well-being and self-esteem.

The mandatory and universal character of schooling is therefore another reason why equality in education matters. Education is not simply a 'preparation for life' as it is so commonly portrayed (Archard 1993). From a child's perspective, it is life itself, and as such needs to be egalitarian in both its processes and outcomes. An implication of what we are saying is that if educational practices, processes and outcomes operate systematically to disadvantage certain classes or groups, or to damage their sense of well-being and self-esteem (and there is plenty of evidence that this can and does happen), then it is morally questionable whether or not the state has a right to consign young people to such experiences (Epp and Watkinson 1996).

While schools do help to ensure widespread literacy and numeracy, they have not succeeded in promoting this basic form of equality among all social groups, even within some of the more economically advanced countries (OECD 1998). Given the very significant conservative opposition that has been developing internationally to the funding of state-supported universal education (Apple 2001; Brighouse 2000), it is vital for the case for universal public education to be morally unequivocal. The only way to ensure such unequivocal support in the long term is by demonstrating the equal benefits of education for children from all social groups. Equality in education matters therefore in protecting public interest values in education. If education is inegalitarian in its outcomes and processes, this undermines the worth of education generally and thereby facilitates challenges to the very existence of publicly funded mass education. This is especially the case when neoconservative interests exercise significant influence in public life.

## Four major equality problems in education

Equality in education has generally been viewed as a matter of dividing educational, and education-related, resources more equally or fairly. Inequalities of status and power have been defined as secondary, while issues of love, care and solidarity have been largely ignored. Consequently, the intrinsic importance of power and status relations for the pursuit of equality has been neglected, while the role of caring in education has been treated as a personal rather than policy matter (Connell 1993). In this chapter, we treat the subject of equality in education in a holistic manner. Drawing on the equality framework in Chapter 2 we examine four key dimensions: equality in educational and related resources (which is strongly connected to the interplay between education and the economic system); equality of respect and recognition; equality of power; and equality of love, care and solidarity. We indicate in each case some of the major changes that need to occur if we are to promote equality of condition in each of these dimensions of educational practice.

Education is intimately integrated into the economic systems of society in two distinct ways. On the one hand, access to, and successful participation in, education is generally dependent on having the economic resources to avail fully of the opportunities that education can offer. On the other hand, schools and colleges are major institutions of selection and stratification for the labour market; they mediate life chances within the economy. Because the distribution of economic resources plays such a key role in determining the quality of education one receives, and because education is such a powerful determinant of life chances, equality in education cannot be thought of separately from economic equality.

Education is also engaged in the definitively cultural task of legitimating and distributing various cultural forms and practices. It can either legitimate or devalue particular abilities, cultures or identities. Recognizing diversity in the abilities of students and appreciating the importance of cultural, religious, sexual, ethnic, gender or other differences is therefore a second key equality issue. Insofar as schools and colleges define what is valuable knowledge, and define how that knowledge should be interpreted and presented, education also plays a central role in educating people to deny, challenge or ignore local and global injustice.

While much of the general education we receive in life takes place outside of formal institutions, formal education is for the most part a publicly funded service. It is governed by regulations and procedures that are deeply political both in terms of how schools and colleges are governed and organized, how subjects are selected and taught, and how teaching and learning relations are ordered. As issues of power and control are endemic to the operation of education, how authority is exercised is a third key equality problematic.

Finally, because the business of teaching and learning is highly emotionally-engaged work, and because human beings are emotional and not simply rational-economic actors, emotional dimensions of education are of central importance both to the process of education itself and to our understanding of what it is to be educated. They have far-ranging effects, particularly on students' capacities to engage in relations of love, care and solidarity.

## Equality of resources and economically generated inequalities in education: the primacy of social class

While the formal purpose of education is to educate the whole person and develop people's capabilities, in a global market economy education has become a market commodity like many others. Although education does enable students to develop capabilities, competition for advantage (in terms of grades and credentials) is the governing cultural norm within the field (Bowles and Gintis 1976; Lynch 1989). The intensity of the competition has increased as the credentials one holds play an increasingly powerful role in determining life chances. The rise of the globalized knowledge economy has also exacerbated the intensity of the competition. Any analysis of inequality in education therefore has to take cognizance of the fact that education is a social good that is distributed within a system of competitive social relations.

Given the competitive context in which educational goods are distributed, and the feasibility of using economic capital to buy educationally relevant social and cultural capital, it is evident that those who are best resourced economically are best placed to succeed educationally.[2] The economically advantaged are best positioned to confer educational advantage on their children in an economically stratified society.

In capitalist societies, economically generated inequality manifests itself fundamentally as a social class problem in education, a problem of unequal access, participation and outcome arising from unequal access to resources.[3] It is visible in the way students from low income backgrounds are unable to access, participate and achieve in education on equal terms with other students (Ball 1997; Clancy 1995, 2001; Gambetta 1987; Gewirtz, Ball and Bowe 1995; Green 2003; Hatcher 1998; Lynch and O'Riordan 1998; Mortimore *et al.* 1995; Shavit and Blossfeld 1993; Teese and Polesel 2003). The generative cause of lower rates of attainment among students from low income (most often working class) backgrounds is their inability to compete on the same terms as other classes for educational advantages, and derivatively for the advantages and privileges that accrue from education. Their educational marginalization is economically generated even though it may subsequently take cultural and political manifestations.

Economic capital can be relatively easily converted into the kind of cultural capital that schools and colleges both require of their students and go on to value and accredit, by buying extra educational services and supports for one's children if one does not possess them oneself (Bourdieu 1973, 1986; Bourdieu and Passeron 1977). It is therefore inevitable that those who lack the cultural capital that schooling demands, and who lack the resources and social capital (networks) to acquire it, will experience relative educational failure. That this has happened across several countries is now well established. In many societies the correlation between social class background and highest level of education attained has become so strong that educational credentials are operating in practice, albeit not in principle, as a kind of state-supported system of inherited privilege (Bourdieu 1996). There is a 'State Nobility' being created through the educational system, whereby academic titles (one becomes a Doctor, Master, Bachelor,

'A' or 'D' grade person) are bestowed in a class- and family-differentiated way that is reminiscent of the way titles were and are bestowed by royalty on each other.

## The role of educational institutions in promoting social class inequality

To recognize that social class background, mediated through the 'habitus'[4] of family origin, plays such a major role in determining educational outcomes is not to deny the role that schools play in the process.[5] While economically advantaged households can and will advantage their offspring by buying privately marketed services to underwrite their children's advantage, very often schools and colleges are complicit in the class act because of the mechanisms through which they select, stratify and evaluate students.

Schools and colleges contribute to class-based inequalities of educational resources through a host of mechanisms and procedures that are too complex and diverse to document in one chapter. We confine ourselves to outlining a few key practices that exemplify their role, focusing on processes and procedures that are within the control of the educational system itself: the selection or admission procedures controlling school entry, the grouping procedures used within schools, and curriculum and syllabus design and assessment. While these practices and processes are particularly important for understanding how social class inequality is reproduced and challenged, they also have relevance for other social groups that are relatively marginalized educationally, especially students with disabilities, Travellers and other students from low status ethnic backgrounds.

### Selection and admission

One of the most important mechanisms for allocating educational resources by class is the practice of student selection. Although several countries seriously limit the choices available to schools in selecting students (and the choices available to parents in terms of where they can choose to send their child), the practice of many schools in market-driven systems is to try to enrol the most educationally attractive students. In so doing, they operate a host of mechanisms that are clearly class biased. Expectations regarding voluntary contributions, donations, costly extra-curricular activities and uniforms are all indirect mechanisms of exclusion. Admission procedures that favour past pupils' children, or those from particular catchment areas or preparatory schools, are also examples of practices that advantage the already privileged (Gewirtz, Ball and Bowe 1995; Lareau 1989; Lynch and Lodge 2002; Reay 1998b). While certain countries, such as the Netherlands, try to offset the negative effects of choice by targeting state resources towards more needy children, the available evidence would suggest that the more competitive and market-driven the education system, in terms of grading schools on the basis of student performance in particular, the stronger the incentive for schools to select to boost their own position in the 'league tables' or market.

The conception of education as a kind of market with different schooling options has been presented to parents as giving them real choices regarding their children's education. Contrary to popular belief, however, the development of a market in schools, based on examination performance, has made access to educational resources more difficult for particular classes of parents. As schools become assessed on the basis of students' attainments, they have little incentive to take students who will lower their performance profile. Students with disabilities that affect performance, and students from economic and cultural backgrounds linked to low grades, are liable to become excluded. What schools want are parents who will invest time and resources in their children thereby boosting performance, and correlatively the status of the school (Carroll and Walford 1996; Whitty and Power 2000). There is extensive empirical research confirming that middle class and upper class parents fit this profile more fully than those from working class households (Ball, Bowe and Gewirtz 1995; Bourdieu 1998; Hanley and McKeever 1997). Working class students are more likely to be perceived as a liability, a risk to the status of the school in a market-driven system (Reay and Ball 1997). In any case, professional parents in particular are more likely to operate as active consumers in an education market; they have the knowledge, contacts, confidence, time and money to exercise choice and promote high educational performance (Crozier 1997; Gewirtz, Ball and Bowe 1995; Lynch and Lodge 2002; Lyons et al. 2003). The ideology of school choice obscures the negative impact of market systems on less well-resourced students, especially in societies where the state fails to intervene to offset the adverse effects of choice (Cole and Hill 1995; Reay 1996; Teese and Polesel 2003). It conceals the practice whereby educationally disadvantaged students are systematically discouraged from entering schools with higher levels of attainment, thereby fostering ghettos of advantage and disadvantage within the school system itself.

### Grouping and tracking

Grouping students on the basis of prior attainment (so-called 'ability') is a standard practice in most educational systems.[6] The only significant differences concern the timing, procedures and scope of the stratification. While Northern European countries (including Finland, Norway and the Republic of Ireland), some East Asian countries (Korea, Japan and Taiwan) and Canada have relatively unselective admission systems for second-level education, some other European countries (including Germany, Switzerland and Luxembourg) have more selective systems, while others (Portugal, Spain) practise openness at entry but have relatively strong stratification via streaming within schools (Green 1997, 2003).

Although practices of streaming, tracking or banding are portrayed as social-class-neutral methods of organizing learning groups, this is not the case in practice. The social class and ethnic profile of students influences both the type of grouping system that prevails in the school and allocation across groups. Students from working class and lower socio-economic backgrounds, and those from subordinated ethnic minorities, are most likely to be allocated to the lower tracks, streams or bands (Ball 1981; Boaler 1997a, 1997b; Douglas 1964; Hannan and Boyle 1987; Jackson 1964; Lynch 1989; Lynch and Lodge 2002; Rees, Argys and Brewer 1996; Rist 1970; Taylor 1993). (We know little about how disability relates to grouping as the subject is not well researched. This is not unrelated to the fact that segregated schooling has been the norm for students with disabilities in several countries.)

Being placed in a lower track significantly disadvantages students in terms of attainment and self-esteem (Gamoran *et al.* 1995; Oakes 1985; Smyth 1999). Systematic grouping into streams or tracks also appears to have independent effects on educational expectations. Lower tracked students have lower expectations of educational outcomes and demonstrate less commitment to school both in terms of academic work and extra-curricular involvement (Berends 1991, 1995; Jenkins 1997). They are also more likely to drop out of school early (Berends 1995). Grouping also affects friendship patterns, with students tending to mix mostly with students in their own track or group thereby leading to social as well as academic segregation (Gamoran *et al.* 1995; Kubitschek and Hallinan 1998). Those in lower tracks are more negatively perceived by teachers and higher tracked peers, both in terms of their behaviour and expected academic attainment (Hallam and Toutounji 1996; Sørenson and Hallinan 1986; Taylor 1993; Wang and Haertel 1995). They are more likely to experience greater alienation from school and to have more negative relationships with teachers (Lynch and Lodge 2002; Murphy 2000).

The most common justification of grouping is that it is required by the stratification of subjects into different levels (higher/advanced, ordinary, foundation/basic). But if subject stratification explained grouping then all schools with similar intakes would adopt similar practices. This is not the case, as there is considerable variability in the level and extent of grouping according to school policy, size, gender composition, tradition and other variables (Hannan and Boyle 1987; Hannan *et al.* 1996; Smyth 1999). Even if there were a good case for tracking or streaming, it would not justify social class bias in the tracking system. It would not justify disproportionately allocating working class students (especially boys) and students from ethnic minority backgrounds to lower tracks.

Undoubtedly one of the reasons for grouping, a reason that is less politically palatable than the knowledge stratification argument, is that of pressure from advantaged parents. Once privileged parents have invested in a school, either through fees, voluntary contributions, fund-raising or signing the school charter, they can and do press schools into providing advance tracks or streams (Kariya and Rosenbaum 1999; McGrath and Kuriloff 1999; Wesselingh 1996). Economically advantaged parents know that they can opt out of schools that do not track to the advantage of their children, and this threat alone is sufficient to reinforce a tracking culture. Schools fear what is termed 'white flight' in the US (in effect, middle class flight) (Kariya and Rosenbaum 1999; Lyons *et al.* 2003). Within a tracking system, middle and upper class parents have a greater knowledge of how things work and a greater capacity to exert influence over, or manipulate, decisions on grouping (Brantlinger, Majd-Jabbari and Guskin 1996; Crozier 1997; McGrath and Kuriloff 1999; Oakes and Guiton 1995; Wesselingh 1996). This helps to explain both why they favour tracking systems in the first place and why these systems operate to the advantage of their children.

While the grouping of students by prior attainment is not solely a social class problem, it clearly works to the disadvantage of students from economically marginalized backgrounds, especially male working class students. It also impacts negatively on students with particular disabilities and ethnic backgrounds. Grouping typically provides these students with worse resources within the educational system and with less valuable knowledge and credentials when they leave it.

### Curriculum and assessment matters: bias towards linguistic intelligences

Educational institutions also facilitate the reproduction of class inequality through the design and assessment of curricula and syllabi. The curricula, syllabi and modes of assessment adopted in most formal educational systems are heavily biased towards students with (written) linguistic and logical-mathematical capabilities, with the priority being given to one or the other varying cross-culturally (Gardner 1983, 1993, 1999).

Linguistic capabilities in particular are differently developed across classes because of differences in culture, lifestyle, work and opportunity. The types of linguistic capabilities, especially oral capabilities, developed within different classes are not equally valued in schools, thereby advantaging those whose class codes have been made synonymous with schooling itself (Bernstein 1971; Labov 1972). This inevitably means that students who are not proficient in the linguistic skills required in schools and colleges (what Bernstein (1971) has termed the elaborated codes) are defined as failures or lacking in intelligence simply by virtue of the way they relate to and know the world. They are required to work through the linguistic (mostly written) modes of expression that schools and colleges require but generally do not teach in a systematic way (Bourdieu 1973). The problem is compounded by the fact that pen and paper tests dominate the assessment procedures and thereby the processes of education. These tests are often remote from the reality that they purport to examine. As Gardner (1991, p. 133) has observed, 'academic knowledge is typically assessed with arbitrary problems that a student has little intrinsic interest in or motivation to answer, and performances on such instruments have little predictive power for performances outside of a scholastic environment'.

Research on human intelligences has demonstrated how claims regarding the singular and hierarchical views of human ability are unfounded (Devlin *et al.* 1997; Gardner 1983, 1993, 1999; Simon 1978; Sternberg 1998). Yet schools and colleges give most credit to those forms of knowledge, capabilities and intelligences that are associated with occupations and statuses that are already privileged in society. Abilities and intelligences associated with subordinate statuses and class positions are either excluded, minimally assessed or accorded a lower status within a given subject when fully assessed. Subjects specifically associated with spatial, bodily-kinaesthetic and musical intelligences (see Gardner 1983 for a discussion of these) are included in the curriculum but are generally given limited space in terms of time allowed and course options. In Irish schools, for example, there is only one subject in each of the wide areas of art and design, technical graphics, construction studies, music and home economics. While physical education is included on the school syllabus, it is not assessed in any public examination (Hanafin, Shevlin and Flynn 2002).

The prioritization of the linguistic and mathematically based subjects is paralleled by class biases within the subject syllabi themselves. Within art, it is fine art and art history (the art and knowledge of the upper classes) that have highest status, with design work (the art traditionally associated with more working class occupations such as printing) being accorded a lower status on the syllabus and in assessment systems. Within English, it is the literature, poetry and plays written by the upper classes, especially the male upper classes, that have pride of place in the syllabus, especially in the syllabus for the higher level courses. While there is no doubt that the upper classes, especially men of that class, have traditionally had more time and education at their disposal to enable them to write, and in that sense their work is more extensive than that of women or economically oppressed groups (as Bourdieu (1984) noted, one needs freedom from necessity to write, to create art, etc.), this does not undermine the argument that it is the tastes and interests of the elite in society, especially the male elite, that are institutionalized as legitimate knowledge in every field including history, art, literature, science, mathematics and music. Whatever the reason may be for its lower status or exclusion from the syllabus, the fact that the life and culture of the economically subordinate are not studied in schools reinforces the sense of their subordination in society.

The net result of these features of curriculum, syllabus and assessment practices is that the resources available within schools are geared towards the experiences and life plans of students from middle and upper class backgrounds, so that these students emerge with the most valuable knowledge and credentials.

## Resolutions

While social class inequality in education manifests itself in terms of individual injustice, its origins lie in the institutionalized inequality of access to wealth and income that directly influences one's capacity to buy educational services on equal terms with others. Income differentials also impact indirectly on class inequality by determining how the cultural capital relevant for educational consumption is distributed across classes (Esping-Andersen n.d.). There is no easy answer to the issues we have raised about class-based inequalities of educational resources, because they are rooted in wider economically generated inequalities. There is evidence to show that where states are willing to tackle these inequalities directly, by investing in high quality child care and related educational and welfare supports for children, as well as by providing high quality universalized welfare provision for adults, they can offset negative class effects on educational attainment (Sweden being a case in point: see Shavit and Blossfeld 1993). By contrast, the overall evidence from many economically more unequal countries indicates that attempts by states to improve the educational prospects of disadvantaged groups are generally neutralized by the efforts of advantaged households to increase their private investment in their own children. In the US, the resources of private third-level colleges have continually risen to outstrip those available in most public (state) universities. In Japan and Ireland, privilege has been maintained through the proliferation of private tutoring and the development of grind schools and fee-paying schools.[7] Even where there is a comprehensively designed state sector, economically advantaged parents perpetuate privilege by sending their children to more selective schools, buying out-of-school tuition and increasing the resources of their children's schools through voluntary contributions, donations and fund-raising (Lynch and Lodge 2002; Teese and Polesel 2003). Upper class and middle class families also exercise more control over how schools operate, not least because their resources permit it (Archer 2001; Gewirtz, Ball and Bowe 1995; Hannan *et al.* 1996; Lareau 1989). Wealth and income inequalities are also translated into educational inequalities by engaging in such educationally relevant experiences as extracurricular activities and travel and by purchasing computers, musical instruments, books and other culturally valuable goods. In these ways, people with greater economic capital are able, in effect, to buy valued credentialized cultural capital that others cannot afford (Bourdieu 1986), thereby reinforcing cycles of relative privilege and class advantage.

There is no comprehensive 'internal settlement' therefore to the problem of class inequality in education, as the source of class inequality lies outside the educational system. Its solution is an issue of social and economic rather than of educational policy. The overall policy aim is must clearly be to reduce income and wealth inequalities outside of school so that excess resources cannot be used to undermine more egalitarian policies within schools. Directly resourcing children who are poor in the kind of cultural capital that school requires them to have is also crucial. Some further principles and mechanisms for dealing with these issues have been outlined in Chapter 5.

To say that educational resources can be bought to a considerable degree is not to deny that education contributes to class-based inequalities or that schools and colleges can help to challenge them. Selection and grouping procedures are very obvious areas where schools can cease to collaborate with, and even challenge, class inequality. In most school systems, school managers and teachers have considerable freedom in how they group students into classes and, albeit to a lesser degree, in how they select students at entry. If they are committed to more egalitarian principles, they can and do implement more egalitarian practices. For example, girls' single sex schools in Ireland stream and band far less rigidly than their male counterparts although in social class terms their schools are no more socially or academically selective than boys' schools. The net effects of the more inclusive policies adopted in girls' schools are higher retention rates, a more inclusive social climate and higher aggregate rates of attainment (Hannan and Boyle 1987; Hannan *et al.* 1996; Lynch 1989).

To confront the reality of class inequality in education, as it operates through selection and grouping, would also require the democratic institutions of the state, as well as schools and colleges, to confront organized upper and middle class interests. This is a difficult task and is certainly unlikely to succeed if initiated purely on an individual school basis, as research on how economically powerful parents exercise influence on schools has shown (Brantlinger, Majd-Jabbari and Guskin 1996; Crozier 1997; Oakes and Guiton 1995; McGrath and Kuriloff 1999; Wesselingh 1996). As a first step, it is necessary to make public not only school selection and admissions procedures but also their grouping procedures, opening up the inside life of schools to democratic scrutiny and public challenge.

Changing curricula and modes of assessment that are class biased is generally not possible at school level. This is a decision for the bodies controlling curriculum and syllabus design and assessment procedures, and these vary considerably across countries.[8] As we have seen, the division of subjects into higher, ordinary and foundation levels or into different tracks is a tool for stratifying students in social class, ethnic and/or disability terms. What must be ended therefore is the stratification of knowledge itself. We have also seen that the whole system of subject and syllabus definition is deeply class biased, as are the modes of assessment.

Forms of knowledge and understanding that have hitherto been defined as inferior and unworthy of study and investigation need to be recognized and accredited systematically. Recognition of bodily-kinaesthetic intelligences (those involved in physical skills) would seem especially crucial as these are especially closely linked to working class cultures and lifestyles, albeit not exclusively so (Gardner 1983, pp. 206–37). There is a need too for *intelligence-fair* testing, so that the multiple intelligences that people possess can gain recognition in schools and colleges and be awarded credentials on a par with the more traditionally recognized intelligences (Gardner 1993).[9] Although it might be suggested that giving schools the authority to develop and accredit all forms of intelligence would give them too much power to define human capabilities, the fact is that schools and colleges already exercise that authority, but within a very narrow frame. Accrediting other forms of human capability or intelligence would merely be levelling the playing field for those whose talents are not currently recognized and credentialized. There have been several initiatives across the US to devise alternative curricula and modes of assessment that are more sensitive to students' different capabilities. The portfolio approach in Central Park East Secondary School in New York City is one of the better known successful initiatives (Meier and Schwarz 1999). There has also been a body of schools in the US that has introduced a Multiple Intelligences approach to schooling based on the work of Howard Gardner and his associates in Harvard (Gardner 1983, 1993). In Ireland the introduction of the Leaving Certificate Applied has introduced more innovative and inclusive assessment procedures for final year second-level students. The Transition Year Programme is another innovative curriculum initiative now operating in a majority of Irish second-level schools, allowing students to develop a wide range of skills and competencies over a one-year period in which academic subjects constitute but one element (Jeffers 2002).

To be able to challenge social class inequality in education, there also needs to be a widening and deepening of education on social class issues. We discuss this subject in more depth when we outline the responses needed to overcome the silences and devaluations that are endemic to the more cultural aspects of class politics in the following section on respect and recognition.

To sum up, we have highlighted some of the key practices that need to change so that schooling can operate in a more egalitarian mode in terms of economically generated inequalities. We recognize that given the deep injustice in the constitution of economic relations, there is no long-term internal settlement to the problem of social class inequalities in education. These will only be eliminated in full when class systems themselves are eliminated. Yet, education does occupy a contradictory location in relation to class reproduction: while it is an agent of class inequality it is also a potential site for developing resistance to inequality. In its role as unquestioning selector and stratifier, it reinforces class inequality; however, as a site of learning and conscientization, education can and does challenge social class and other injustices.

## Equality of respect and recognition in education: recognizing diversity

One of the main inequalities that many groups experience in education is lack of respect and recognition. These status-related inequalities, relating to age, sexuality, religious beliefs, disability, language, gender, class, 'race' or ethnicity, need to begin to be resolved through status-related initiatives. They are important not just for their own sake, but also because a failure to accommodate differences in schools and colleges can generate inequalities of resources as well (Connell 1993). An egalitarian educational system would show equal respect and recognition for all, based on the principle of critical interculturalism set out in Chapter 2.

Inequalities of respect and recognition in education are rooted in the symbolic realm, in patterns of interpretation, definition and communication. Institutionally, they involve practices of denial and depreciation (Fraser 2000). They are expressed in the educational system in degrees of inclusion and exclusion, both within and between schools and within and between texts, syllabi and subjects. The culturally marginal are identified as 'other' and are treated as irrelevant and/or inferior as a status group. They are subjected to a kind of cultural imperialism that renders them either invisible or, if visible, subject to negative stereotyping or misrecognition (Said 1991; Smith 1987, 1998; Young 1990). Negative images portray subordinate groups variously as 'native', innocent, inferior, deviant, ugly or threatening. In so doing they legitimate acts of disrespect, disdain and violence (Harding 2003; Said 1991). Because the values, perspectives and life worlds of dominant groups permeate cultural and institutional norms, members of oppressed groups have their lives interpreted through the lens of the dominant, defined as 'common sense'. Furthermore, they often internalize the negative stereotypes to which their group is subjected (Bell 1997; Freire 1998).

In schools, cultural non-recognition or misrepresentation is grounded in the practices and processes of curriculum provision and assessment, pedagogical approaches, peer culture and organizational norms. Three educational practices are particularly important in sustaining inequality of respect and recognition: a general silence or invisibility that is often accompanied by devaluation or condemnation, a systematic bias in the syllabus and practices of schools, and segregation into different classes or schools. In this section, we illustrate some of the ways these practices affect different groups and suggest some remedies.

## Silence, invisibility and devaluation: sexuality and class

One of the most common forms of non-recognition in education is for a group to be generally left outside educational discourse by not being named or known. This form of non-recognition is often accompanied by an undercurrent of devaluation or condemnation, so that on the exceptional occasions on which the group is named, it is only for the sake of depreciation. Fraser (1997a) suggests that people who are gay, lesbian or bisexual experience this form of non-recognition in society generally, in that their sexuality is often not named, and if named is not accepted on equal terms with heterosexuality. Fraser's claim holds true for education. The presumption of heterosexuality underpins educational policy and practice in many countries (Cole 2000; Epstein and Johnson 1994; S. Harris 1990; Lynch and Lodge 2002; O'Connor and Szalacha 2000). While higher education programmes do provide space for gay and lesbian studies, either within existing programmes or as separate subjects, education generally proceeds as if gays, lesbians, bisexual and transgendered people are peripheral to its core business (Epstein, O'Flynn and Telford 2003).

The assumption of heterosexuality has a variety of manifestations and implications. It manifests itself most powerfully in the silence that surrounds the subject of sexual orientation. The silence pervades all aspects of school life: it is evident in the absence of engagement with the subject of sexual orientation within curriculum and syllabus design and in the assumption of heterosexuality in education programmes on relationships and sexuality. The silence denies lesbian, gay and bisexual young people a legitimated social space and language for reflecting upon a defining part of their personal and social identity. It limits their self-understanding and inhibits the development of supportive and satisfying personal and sexual relationships. The silence also diminishes the education of heterosexual students by maintaining their ignorance of sexual diversity. The general invisibility of lesbian, gay and bisexual orientations creates a climate where norms condemning homosexuality as immoral and deviant are legitimated: norms that the syllabus sometimes reinforces, particularly in religious education.

Because they have to 'pass' as heterosexuals, lesbian, gay and bisexual young people experience all the personal and social trauma that goes with living a lie (Goffman 1968). They are also frequently subjected to the taunts and homophobic bullying that result from denying the legitimacy of one's sexual identity (Epstein, O'Flynn and Telford 2003; GLEN and Nexus 1995; Mason and Palmer 1995; Rofes 1989). The silence and denial about sexual orientation also affects lesbian, gay or bisexual teachers, forcing them into deceptions and denials about their personal lives (Gowran 2000).

Another silence that is typical of many educational settings is their failure to advert to the reality of social class. In cultural terms, schools are fundamentally middle class institutions (Mahony and Zmroczek 1997; Reay 1998b; Walkerdine and Lucey 1989; Walkerdine, Lucey and Melody 2001).

Their organizational procedures and mores assume a lifestyle and set of resources that middle and upper class households are most likely to possess. Parents and children who are outside this frame are variously defined by middle class teachers as culturally deficient or deviant (Ball, Bowe and Gewirtz 1995; Lareau 1989; Lynch and O'Riordan 1998; Lyons *et al.* 2003; Reay 1998b). Students are expected to have class-specific skills that the schools themselves do not teach (Bourdieu and Passeron 1977). The failure of schools to acknowledge the cultural dissonance that exists between their mores and practices and those of students from diverse class (and ethnic) backgrounds exacerbates their educational failure and their sense of alienation from the education process itself (Archer *et al.* 2002; O'Neill 1992).

The deeply classed culture of schools, and in particular of universities, is exacerbated by a lack of systematic education about social class. In most countries, for example, there is no programme of education that deals directly with social class. Certain European countries do have formal education about social and political processes and institutions such as the human rights education programme in France and the relatively light-weight compulsory course on civil, social and political education (CSPE) in Ireland. However, neither of these has a specific remit to educate about social class. (The closest the CSPE programme gets to the subject of class is through the analysis of poverty, which is by no means focused on either the causes or outcomes of social class inequalities and is in any case entirely optional.)

The denial of class inequality in contemporary culture is as profound as it is problematic, and it is by no means confined to schools or colleges (Savage 2000). Schooling plays a part, however, in enabling the silence about class to continue. When class is spoken of in education, it is named in euphemistic terms (Lynch and Lodge 2002). People in low-income working class households are termed 'disadvantaged', 'socially excluded' or 'socio-economically marginalized'. The word 'class' is generally left out of the vocabulary of politics and education, both nationally and internationally (Pakulski and Waters 1996). Working class identity in particular has become, in several respects, a negative identity (Reay 1998b; Savage 2000; Skeggs 1997); it is increasingly one that can only be named or claimed indirectly.

The failure to name social class inequalities has several indirect effects on the process and procedures of schooling. It leaves the attitudes of students and teachers in relation to class inequality untouched. There is no non-stigmatized nomenclature for the injustices of class when issues arise. Both students and teachers resort to the stereotypes of so-called common sense, often individualizing responsibility for differences in performance that are largely structurally determined. They lack a vocabulary-of-analysis to name class-based inequalities, thereby allowing them to persist unchallenged over time (Lynch and Lodge 2002).

## Systematic bias: the subordination of the feminine

Schools, colleges and universities are not neutral institutions in terms of how they select what is to be taught, how it is to be taught and assessed or who will be engaged in these activities. While they generally tolerate differences, they often do so in a manner that defines particular gender, ethnic, religious or ability groups and their interests as subordinate. There is a very real sense in which formal educational institutions are designed to impose the 'cultural arbitraries'[10] of more powerful groups on those who are subordinate, be that in social class terms (Bourdieu and Passeron 1977), in colonial terms (Harding 2003; Said 1991) or in gender terms (Harding 1986, 1991; Smith 1987; Weiner 1994).

Because much of formal education strongly prizes written linguistic and logical-mathematical intelligences, in particular, it marginalizes those capabilities and intelligences that either are not linguistically or mathematically encoded or cannot be mediated through linguistic and mathematical notational systems (Gardner 1983). As noted above, those who excel in bodily-kinaesthetic fields are generally quite marginalized in formal educational systems because of the mistaken belief that what we do with our bodies is somehow less important than problem-solving routines carried out chiefly through the use of language or mathematical reasoning.

Those who have developed strong interpersonal and intrapersonal intelligences experience a similar form of exclusion albeit for somewhat different reasons. The low status accorded to the personal intelligences (and to what Goleman (1995) calls emotional intelligence)[11] is undoubtedly related to the gendered nature of much human service work.[12] For it is women who do most of the caring and love labouring in societies throughout the world (see Daly 2001; Delphy and Leonard 1992; Finch 1983; Hochschild 1983, 1989; Sevenhuijsen 1998; Ungerson 1990; Waerness 1984). The lower status accorded to women generally has inevitably contributed to a lowering of the status accorded to the work that women do, to the interests that women pursue. Thus, the intelligences that are developed around human service work, especially care and love work, are subordinated by their association with the feminine itself, and with the subordinated contexts of the privatized family and household where so much care work takes place.[13] The fact that human service work often involves physical work also contributes to its low status.

The lowly status accorded to care and love work has meant that there is no room in mainstream education for students to learn about this work in a systematic way. Those who are interested in developing their personal intelligences (be they for care work or human service work generally) have no opportunity to excel in this field. Although care work is sometimes given attention in subjects like home economics or religious education, it is not the primary focus of these subjects. Even when it is accorded a space in the curriculum, such as in personal development programmes or relationships and sexuality education, such programmes are generally quite peripheral to the main business of schooling.

While the neglect of the personal may represent a very profound form of cultural imperialism in gender terms, it also impoverishes education for men. It means that all young people, male and female, are deprived of a real opportunity to develop an understanding of care, love and solidarity work, work that is as central to the business of human well-being as materially productive work (Kittay 1999; Nussbaum 1995a, 1995b). The neglect of personal intelligences is not solely a gender matter, therefore. It is indicative of a wider problem in society whereby the emotional and affective world generally has been defined as separate from the rational world, and even a threat to it (*ibid.*). A false dichotomy has been created between the rational and emotional, leading to a serious neglect of education about the emotions generally, and in relation to care and love work in particular. (See the discussion below on the emotional dimensions of education for further analysis of this issue.)

While the indifference towards the personal may be the clearest expression of the subordination of the feminine, there are numerous other ways in which patriarchal norms and interests are embedded in educational thought and practice. The lack of attention given to women's work in literature, art, science, history, etc.; the subordination of girls' extracurricular activities to those of boys; the fact that girls get less attention in class; the fact that positions of authority and power are disproportionately held by men; these are all indicative of the subordinate status of women in education (Harding 1991; Kelly 1985; Paechter 1998; Spender and Spender 1988; Walkerdine 1989). A similar case could be made about the status of other social groups including ethnic, religious and linguistic minorities and disabled people.

The systematic bias against different groups has multiple and long-term implications, not only socio-culturally, but also in terms of resources. When differences in students' abilities, cultures or languages are not recognized as deserving full accommodation, resources are not put in place to meet their needs. This disadvantages students and lowers their attainments. Lower attainments reinforce the image, in turn, that certain groups are ineducable, of low status and unworthy of educational investment.

## Segregation and disability

Segregation has been a common institutional response to the management of differences in education. The degree of segregation varies historically and cross-culturally for different social groups; it often occurs invisibly through broader patterns of residential segregation, selection procedures and parental choice. However, almost all societies practise some forms of overt educational segregation, especially for children and adults with disabilities (Ballard 1999; Vlachou 1997). The segregation of people with disabilities into separate schools has frequently resulted in their receiving non-standard, poorer quality education. The long-term effects have been overwhelmingly negative, resulting in lower educational qualifications, fewer job opportunities, lack of job choice, lower pay and higher unemployment (Conroy 2003; EIM Business and Policy Research 2001).

Although segregated education arguably benefits certain groups at certain times (it has been sought by deaf students in particular to enable them to work through the medium of sign or bilingually), it seems undesirable that anyone's education should take place entirely in a segregated setting. What is particularly relevant to equality of respect and recognition is that the practice of segregation prevents people with different cultures, religious beliefs, abilities or genders from learning about each other's differences on an informal day-to-day basis. Insofar as it deepens ignorance of differences, segregation is anti-educational in and of itself.

### Resolutions

In contrast to the problem of unequal resources, the task of resolving inequalities of respect and recognition within schools and colleges is much more amenable to action within education itself. This is not to deny the role played by the media and other cultural institutions (such as the arts, music, literature and religion) in framing our understanding of other lifestyles, abilities, languages and values. Rather it is to assert the central role that education itself plays in the cultural system in framing our understanding of and respect for differences. Research on effective pedagogical practices has shown how education can play a major role in developing the kind of critical thinking and inclusive ethical perspective that underpins respect for differences (Adams, Bell and Griffin 1997, pp. 30–43).

Educating people to respect the values, beliefs and lifestyles of others is not a simple matter for which one can provide a blueprint in one chapter. There are already several examples available of the kind of pedagogical principles that should underpin such programmes at both curriculum and school level.[14] It is possible, however, to outline one of the key principles that would guide such education, the principle of inclusion.

If students and teachers are to learn to respect and recognize diversity, they need to experience it; they need to live with differences, rather than merely learning about them in the abstract. Respect is internalized not only through the development of a critical and empathetic perspective, but also through the experience of dealing with diversity on a daily basis. And in many societies, schools are the only places where such learning can safely take place, although this is sometimes impossible due to severe hostility, conflict or separation between groups. The first principle that must guide us in respecting difference in education, therefore, is that of inclusion.

Developing a fully inclusive educational environment is a challenging task as the experience in Northern Ireland and other polarized societies has shown. It involves setting up procedures for respecting differences not only in the organizational culture of the school or college, but also in its curriculum, pedagogy and assessment systems. It involves adopting, and acting upon, a critical, interactive approach to other people's beliefs, lifestyles, values and institutionalized practices – to their cultures in the broadest sense of the term – rather than simply allowing differences to coexist or merely tolerating them (examples of how such an approach can be developed are outlined in Freire 1998, King and Kitchener 1994 and Shor 1987, 1992). To develop a critical intercultural perspective, education about cultural difference needs to be integrated into the curriculum itself. There needs to be a subject, or at the very least a defined space on the curriculum timetable, devoted to the study of cultural differences from an egalitarian perspective. Such a development needs to be complemented by introducing a critical cultural studies and equality studies perspective across all subjects. Inclusive education also means educating teachers and lecturers about diversity, as well as ensuring that the teaching body itself is characterized by diversity.

In effect, to promote egalitarian ways of seeing the world, students must be educated about the subject of equality itself. In particular, schools and colleges need to educate their staff and students about the equality-specific issues that arise in relations of social class, gender, colour, nationality, ethnicity, ability, religion and other differences. Syllabi should be social-class-proofed, gender-proofed, abilities-proofed, etc., so that the lives of all people are allowed to be read, recognized and critiqued in a critical intercultural manner. Education in equality studies could become part of the formal curriculum of subjects dealing specifically with social issues (such as civics, geography, history, politics and home economics) as well as being mainstreamed into other subjects including literature, art, music, engineering, mathematics and science. Education about differences and how to eliminate inequalities arising from the non-recognition or misrecognition of differences could also be made a core part of education courses for teachers, lecturers, educational decision-makers and managers, including the civil service and curriculum and assessment bodies.

An essential part of any initiative to educate people about inequality is to include members of oppressed groups in the design of educational programmes. Without such engagement there is a danger of privileged experts colonizing the experience of subordinate groups, with all the dangers this presents (Lynch and O'Neill 1994). On the positive side, a cooperative practice of educating about inequality can help create alliances for social change between those with experiential knowledge of inequality and those with professional knowledge. Such alliances would also be mutually beneficial educationally.

By promoting the principle of inclusion through formal study and the practice of inclusion through the adoption of difference-respectful procedures and processes, schools and colleges can help challenge inequalities of respect and recognition. However, just as it is not possible to eliminate resource inequalities in education without eliminating them in the economic system, so too does equality of respect and recognition in education depend on the wider cultural system. If segregation, depreciation or subordination are the guiding principles governing general social and cultural relations between groups differing in ethnic origin, religion, sexual orientation, gender or intellectual or physical capabilities, it is not possible for education alone to overcome such forces. Education is a very powerful cultural institution but by no means the only one and its work needs to be complemented by wider cultural initiatives in the media, workplaces, law and politics if it is to be fully effective.

## Equality of power: democratizing education

Inequalities of power occur in educational decision-making and in the exercise of educational authority. Power inequalities take many forms, and include processes of exclusion, marginalization, trivialization and misrepresentation when people are engaged in decision-making or policy-making in schools and other educational institutions. Power relations exist not just in the exercise of organizational authority, but also in aspects of curricula, pedagogy and assessment. Across the world, schools and colleges select, classify and stratify students in a hierarchically ordered way. In so doing, they not only exercise power over students but also assign them to positions of relative power and powerlessness. Educational institutions also accord power to certain forms of knowledge (and ways of teaching and learning) while disregarding or subordinating others. Unequal power relations between subjects are institutionalized through systems of curriculum design and assessment. The business of education is never neutral politically, therefore, either in terms of what it teaches, to whom, how and when, or in terms of how it assesses attainment in particular fields (Bourdieu and Passeron 1977; Freire 1998). Arising from the work of Foucault (1977, 1980, 1991) in particular, there is a growing realization among educators of the importance of power as a focus for research (Francis 1998). Power is increasingly regarded as a series of relations that may not be readily observable, but are of profound egalitarian importance nonetheless.

The rise of intellectual interest in power has been paralleled among educators by new 'voice' and 'rights' discourses around relations between students and teachers in particular (Archard 1993; Archard and MacLeod 2002; Epp and Watkinson 1996). On the one hand, schooling practices that fail to respect the autonomy and individuality of the student and fail to manage power relations between students and teachers in a respectful manner have been found to have quite negative educational consequences

(Collins 2000; Fagan 1995; Herr and Anderson 1997; John 1996; Pomeroy 1999; Yoneyama 2000). On the other hand, power inequalities are not simply a problem for students. Teachers experience power differentials in relation to both school management and colleagues (Ball 1987, 1989). They are subject to control by external bodies and by the authority of those in superordinate positions within their own institutions. They are simultaneously both powerful and powerless (Davies 1996).

There are therefore two reasonably distinct levels at which equality of power is an issue in education. At the macro level, it concerns the institutionalized procedures for making decisions about school management, educational and curriculum planning and policy development and implementation. At the micro level, it concerns the internal life of schools and colleges, in terms of relations between staff and students and among the staff themselves.

### The need to democratize educational relations

When educators have addressed the issue of power and authority, it has frequently been from a managerial perspective: how to manage schools more effectively, how to 'keep discipline'. The power relations between students and teachers especially have been taken as a given, and the analyses have been undertaken from a 'top-down' perspective (Ball 1989). Young people's concerns regarding the exercise of power have been named as the predictable complaints of disgruntled teenagers. Yet research suggests that all types of students are increasingly opposed to hierarchical forms of control and authority, rejecting the assumption that a teacher is to be obeyed because of the authority vested in her or his role (Devine 2000; Humphreys and Jeffers 1999; Lynch and Lodge 1999; Yoneyama 2000). They seek a greater democratization of schooling, both at the organizational and at the classroom levels. The first reason why teacher–student relations need to be democratized therefore is because students are beginning to expect it and want it.

There is a second reason to promote the democratization of schooling relations and this has to do with education itself. If we are to educate students to engage in public life as democratic citizens, it is essential that they learn how to participate democratically in the public domain. The first public forum where that opportunity arises for all members of society is in schools, where students can learn about democracy by practising it (Dewey 1916, 1950; Mulligan and Griffin 1992).

The democratization of school relations is not only a challenge to teachers, it is also a challenge to school managers and school owners. In New Right discourse schools have been increasingly defined, within a management science framework, as hierarchical bureaucracies (Bennett Demarrais and Lecompte 1999; Packwood 1988). Hierarchy itself has been routinized and made unproblematic. In the educational literature it has become increasingly accepted that power is exercised vertically downwards for staff as well as for students. Such hierarchical relations are fundamentally inegalitarian as well as organizationally dysfunctional, not least because educational institutions of all kinds are highly complex organizations requiring careful management of both internal and external social relations (Ball 1987, 1989; Phelan 2001; Ritchie, Rigano and Lowry 2000; Westoby 1988). Schools and colleges need to democratize their relations with staff, parents and their constituent communities, not only to preclude conflict but also to understand differences and facilitate the education process itself. There is also a need to democratize research, a topic we pursue in Chapter 9.

## Resolutions

Resolving inequalities of power in schools involves democratizing the pedagogical and organizational relations of schooling. At the level of teacher–student relationships, it involves substituting dialogue for dominance, cooperation and collegiality for hierarchy, and active learning and problem solving for passivity (Freire 1998). At the level of school and college organization, it involves institutionalizing and resourcing democratic structures such as student and parent/community councils that exercise real authority and responsibility. It also requires initiating new systems of dialogue with students, teachers, parents and local communities. The latter can be advanced though the use of new and old technologies, including the internet, systematic surveying of opinion and open discussion forums. Creating curriculum-specific experiences that are democratic in practice as well as in theory is also a fundamental part of the democratizing project of education. In effect, it involves devolved governance requiring trust and education of all parties to the education process (Apple and Beane 1999; Bastian *et al.* 1986; Wood 1988).

Democratizing education is not simply about democratizing schools and colleges. It also involves democratizing the wider set of relations within which schools and colleges operate, including relations between the state and service providers and between the state and educational participants. It is about developing a participatory politics in which those who are affected by policy decisions have a say in all levels of educational planning and decision-making. It is not just about having a consultative role, consultations that can be easily ignored when the relevant party leaves the table. It is about listening, engagement and accountability in a participatory democratic context (see Chapter 6).

Unless educationally disadvantaged groups in particular are involved in the planning and development process in education, other inequalities cannot be meaningfully challenged. They are the people with the day-to-day experiential knowledge of injustice that is a necessary condition for informed decision-making. And they are the ones with the emotional and political will to pursue the changes required.

## Equality of love, care and solidarity: the emotional dimensions of education

The educational system is an important site for promoting equality of love, care and solidarity. Students are placed in the care of their teachers on a daily basis, and good teachers care about their students. Relations between students and their teachers, and among students themselves, are important in providing, or denying, the care that they need, as well as helping them to learn to care for and to develop bonds of solidarity with others. Education therefore has to take seriously the need to provide students and teachers with ample prospects for relations of love, care and solidarity. The biggest obstacle to this challenge is the way that education has neglected not just the emotions involved in love, care and solidarity but the emotions generally. This neglect has had profoundly negative effects.

### The importance of emotions and emotional work

Education is human service work. It is based on a dialogue between students and teachers and between students themselves. Like all human service work, education involves emotional work (Hochschild 1983, 1989). Good teachers engage the student in learning. They are inspired and enthusiastic about their subjects and communicate this inspiration to their students. Good teachers love their students, in the sense that they are deeply committed to their development in a way that enables them to be free (Freire 1998). Education is about liberation rather than domestication and in that sense is a profoundly emotional activity. Just as the best teaching occurs when the teacher engages with the subject and the students, so it is with students: students learn best when they are in a relationship of trust and care with the teacher. The teacher challenges them to learn but in an environment of trust and support (*ibid.*). So the first reason we must learn about the emotions and about the emotional work involved in education is because they are central to teaching and learning itself. Failure to recognize this results in a denial of the educational needs of both teachers and students as emotional beings.

Emotional work is not only central to the business of teaching and learning, it also plays a key role in human service work generally, especially in fields such as nursing and counselling, but also in human resource management and politics, and in developing and maintaining intimate personal relationships. To deprive students of learning about the emotional work involved in caring is to disempower them in terms of their future work and responsibilities.

Emotions also play a key role in developing a politics of solidarity and concern for others, something that is fundamental to the functioning of an inclusive democratic society. It is only by being in touch with one's own vulnerability that one can develop empathy and concern for others, while having an appreciation of one's own dependency needs enables one to be compassionate. Intellect without emotions is often harsh, because it is indifferent to the feelings and needs of others. Even when we do not recognize it, emotions therefore play a part in our judgements, and for this reason we need to learn about them. Educating people about their emotions, and about the role of caring and solidarity within the affective sphere of life, is necessary for enhancing our sense of other-centredness. Without such understanding, it is difficult to develop the empathy (and the sense of justified anger and urgency) that local, and particularly global, solidarity requires.

A final reason why we must focus on the emotions is because of the way they impact on young people's ability to realize their educational rights generally. Students do not simply engage with schooling intellectually, they also engage with it emotionally. The feelings of failure, purposelessness or isolation that many students experience in schools cannot be addressed unless the language of emotions is allowed to enter educational discourse in a legitimated way. Respecting the rights of the child means educating them holistically, including emotionally (Epp and Watkinson 1996).

## The neglect of the emotions

Despite the centrality of emotional work to teaching and learning, there has been relatively little attention paid to the issues of emotions *per se* in education. While there is much written about the issue of motivation, the profoundly emotional nature of teaching itself has been given less attention (Blackmore 1996; Hargreaves 2000, 2001). Moreover, there are few serious attempts to educate people about their emotions and affective relations.

Formal education has been premised on the assumption that the principal function of schooling is to develop intellect. Many of the most influential thinkers in education (Bruner 1963, 1966; Piaget 1950, 1970; Rousseau 1762), and indeed contemporary information-processing and cognitive science researchers, equate educational development with intellectual development. In recent times, the intellectual has become increasingly equated with the logical-mathematical so that 'in common with Piagetian psychology, nearly all the problems examined by information-processing psychologists prove to be of the logical-mathematical sort' (Gardner 1983, p. 23). Because reason has been defined as distinct from emotions, education about the emotions and about human service work that is heavily emotionally driven, particularly care and love work, has been seriously neglected. The neglect of the emotions has been paralleled by the neglect of education of the personal intelligences involved in emotional work.

The devaluing of the emotional realm as an area of legitimate concern for educators has its origins in the dualism of western thought that characterized the emotions as being in opposition to reason, and therefore subordinate and morally suspect (Bendelow and Williams 1998; Lupton 1998; Sevenhuijsen 1998; Williams and Bendelow 1998). The Platonic view of the philosopher as rational and detached, and the Cartesian assumption that the intellect is what defines our identity (*Cogito ergo sum*: I think therefore I am) has created a legacy in academic thought and in education that is deeply antithetical to the emotional, and by implication to the emotional work involved in loving and caring in particular.

Because care and love work have been undertaken in large part by women, especially in relation to their children's school work, the neglect of the affective domain in education is a profoundly gendered matter (Duncombe and Mardsen 1996, 1998; Reay 1998b, 2000; Smith 1998). If education about emotions in general or caring work in particular is included at all in schools, it is generally granted a subordinate position. It is included within other subjects, particularly home economics, or given a peripheral place on the timetable as part of occasional educational programmes on personal development or relationships.

Recent developments in education internationally that emphasize the outcomes of schooling in terms of grades and league tables rather than the process of learning also marginalize interest in the emotions. They focus attention on education as a product rather than as a process and in so doing disregard the fact that both teaching and learning are highly emotionally engaged activities. They distract attention from the ways in which learning is often seriously impaired because students lack emotional support and care in their personal lives, or because of their deeply negative emotional response to particular subjects (Boylan and Lawton 2000; Boylan, Lawton and Povey 2001). In some cases, such as in Japan in recent years, students even opt out of school for emotional reasons, despite being academically quite successful (Yoneyama 2000).

## The emotional turn

There is, however, an 'emotional turn' in education discourses in certain fields. Psychologists increasingly recognize the role that emotional intelligence or personal intelligences play in our work and personal lives (Gardner 1983, 1999; Goleman 1995, 1998). It is also increasingly recognized that emotional competencies are essential for good teaching (Hargreaves 2000, p. 814; Noddings 1992). In addition, feminist scholars have highlighted the centrality of the emotions to the care, love and solidarity work that is disproportionately undertaken by women (Bubeck 1995; Delphy and Leonard 1992; Sevenhuijsen 1998), a work for which people need education.

There is a growing realization therefore that the emotions are ways of perceiving and knowing the world; they are always attached to beliefs about their object and to at least that degree are rational. But it is also increasingly appreciated that a false dichotomy has been drawn between reason and emotion, a dichotomy that is highly gendered and disadvantageous to women in its portrayal both of the emotional world itself and of women in particular (Nussbaum 1995a, 1995b, 2000).

To know how to name one's feelings and to recognize and appreciate the feelings of others, to know how to care for others and to develop supportive relations, requires not only time and effort but also education. The life worlds associated with the emotional realm, and in particular the work within that realm, cannot be enhanced without education.

## Resolutions

There has been little research on issues such as personal or emotional intelligences and no major advance in devising methods for developing or assessing emotional capabilities. While Bloom's (1956) taxonomy of cognitive skills has gained global recognition, his taxonomy of emotional skills (Bloom 1964) has received little attention. It is difficult to define precisely what the goals and purposes of emotional education should be in the absence of a clearly defined framework.

What is clear is that to have education about emotional life generally and emotional work in particular, it is necessary to undertake research. Only after adequate research will it be possible to develop curricula, practices and assessment systems that are appropriate to the field. There is also a need to undertake research on the relationship between emotional and personal intelligences and other capabilities.

Despite the dearth of research on the development of emotional capabilities, it is possible to identify some of the issues pertaining to the promotion of equality of love, care and solidarity within education. And in that regard, developing an appreciation of the intrinsic role that emotions play in the process of teaching and learning is crucial. There is a need to name the emotions so that students and teachers have a language and a space to talk about their feelings and concerns. A conspicuous example of the need for education is evident in the field of mathematics, where research suggests that the prevailing emotional reaction of adults generally to mathematical tasks is one of panic: being asked to complete mathematical tasks evokes feelings of anxiety, fear and embarrassment as well (Buxton 1981, cited in McLeod 1992). Feelings of anxiety, vulnerability and insecurity are also prevalent among second-level mathematics students (Boylan and Lawton 2000; Boylan, Lawton and Povey 2001; Lyons *et al.* 2003). Yet students and teachers are rarely given the space to talk about their feelings about learning and teaching, nor do they always have the language to name what they feel (Lyons *et al.* 2003).

Because our emotions are as endemic to our humanity as is our rationality, it is necessary to develop educational experiences that will enable students to develop their emotional skills or personal intelligences *per se*, that is, as a discrete area of human capability. This area of education is particularly important in preparing students for care, love and solidarity work, given that all people live their lives in relations of dependency and interdependency, relations that are deeply emotional in character.

## Conclusion

In this chapter, we have examined some of the ways that education reinforces inequalities in the dimensions of resources, respect and recognition, power, and love, care and solidarity, and some of the ways this could be changed. We have indicated how education can be either an agent of oppression or emancipation in the ways it interfaces with and defines economic relations, political relations, cultural relations and affective relations. Throughout the chapter we have been implicitly concerned with the fifth dimension of equality, because all of issues we have discussed have powerful effects on students' learning and on the work of teaching. All five dimensions of equality are relevant within education, and all are mutually reinforcing.

Focusing on the formal educational system, we have argued for major changes in the way schools and colleges are run and in the structure and content of the curriculum. Current practices of selection and grouping need to be abandoned, while the syllabus design and assessment systems that facilitate them also need reappraisal. Approaches to curriculum and assessment need to be dramatically widened to embrace the full range of human intelligences and the full range of human achievements. Schools and colleges need to be inclusive institutions that teach students and teachers to engage critically with difference and to analyse and challenge inequality. Relations between teachers and students, as well as decision-making about education in general, need to be democratized in a participatory way. Education needs to take the emotional work involved in caring seriously, and to foster the emotional development of both students and teachers.

As we have emphasized, the educational system is strongly integrated into the society around it. We cannot expect equality in education without progress towards equality in the economic, cultural, political and affective systems in which it is embedded. But by the same token, changing education is a vital part of those transformations. It is a central part of the egalitarian agenda.

# 9
# Emancipatory Research as a Tool of Change

Research plays an important role not only in academic institutions but throughout society. It defines what counts as a legitimate intellectual or practical problem and it provides the grounds for a wide range of decisions. The questions that are chosen for research and the ways that research is conducted and used can have significant effects on inequality. This chapter is particularly concerned with debates about the role of academic research on issues of equality and inequality. It explores some of the limitations of positivist methodologies and examines the implications of adopting an emancipatory research perspective on equality issues. The chapter is based on the assumption that the purpose of academic discourse is not only to describe and explain the world, but also to change it. It shares its intellectual and epistemological origins with critical theory (as developed by Habermas (1971) in particular), Marxism and other interdisciplinary fields of investigation focused on transformative action including women's studies and disability studies. The basic questions it asks are therefore not only descriptive or explanatory; they are also visionary and utopian. It attempts to develop an alternative model of research to the model that dominates work in contemporary academic settings.

Research is inevitably politically engaged, be it by default, by design or by simple recognition. No matter how deep the commitment to value neutrality, decisions regarding choice of subject, paradigmatic frameworks and even methodological tools inevitably involve political choices, not only within the terms of the discipline, but even in terms of wider political purposes and goals. The academy and academic knowledge in particular are deeply implicated in the operations of power. To explore the business of power, this chapter examines the structural conditions under which researchers in equality studies (and in cognate disciplines focused on the study of inequality or injustice) conduct their work. They share these conditions with many other researchers in the human rights and social scientific fields, many of whom are motivated not simply by detached scholarship but by the unjust and evil outcomes that racism, sexism, homophobia, classism and disablism visit upon society (Siraj-Blatchford 1995, p. 209). Their work has its origin in the Enlightenment vision of education and research as tools for the development and improvement of society, even though such a vision may not always be explicitly articulated.

One might question whether the academy, which is so deeply implicated in the cultural reproduction of elites, can facilitate emancipatory change through research and education. Given the embeddedness of the academic world in the business of cultural production and reproduction, it is not at all self-evident how a given discipline or academic discourse can contribute to radical social change. Universities *qua* institutions are engaged in elite forms of cultural production. Moreover, they are heavily engaged in the practice of cultural monopoly, not only through their selection procedures for students and staff, but also through their rigorous boundary maintenance procedures within and between disciplines, and between what is defined as academic knowledge and what is not (Bourdieu 1984; Bourdieu and Passeron 1979). Yet, within all institutions there is scope for resistance; there are contradictions that can be exploited and utilized at all levels of education, including higher education (Giroux 1983). The obstacles to adopting a more emancipatory model of research are substantial, but they are not insurmountable.

## Positivist methodologies and equality

Much of the policy debate about poverty and inequality in society generally (especially in terms of social class/socio-economic groups) has been framed within the language-of-analysis of positivism, an approach to research that emphasizes the distinction between facts and values, the collection of independently verifiable and objective data and the use of scientific and particularly, though not exclusively, statistical methods to interpret this data.[1] A good example of this work is in the area of education, where research by what are sometimes called the 'equality empiricists' has been especially effective in documenting the persistence of social-class-related inequality in different states (Callan *et al.* 1996; Clancy 1988, 1995, 2001; Cormack and Osborne 1995; Dowling 1991; Erikson and Jonsson 1996; Green 2003; Hatcher 1998; Shavit and Blossfeld 1993; Teese and Polesel 2003; Thomas, Wang and Fan 2000). Within Ireland, work by Barry and O'Connor (1995), Drew (1999), Hannan *et al.* (1996), Mahon (1998) and Ruane and Sutherland (1999) has performed a similar function in the gender field. This type of 'political arithmetic' is crucially important for holding the state publicly accountable. It is a vital tool of democracy in a world where inegalitarian ideologies are gaining hold:

> At a time of increasing social inequalities and injustice, when the 'self-regulating' market threatens to undermine the foundations of social sol-

idarity ... and when the dominant ideology of meritocracy in liberal democratic societies has been seriously weakened at the same time that right wing politicians proclaim the 'classless society', a new political arithmetic must be asserted as a vital tool of democracy as well as of sociology. (Brown *et al.* 1997, p. 37)

When positivist research is sufficiently critical and independent, it also has the potential to facilitate social and individual reflexivity. It informs the general body politic, giving them access to knowledge that is detached from powerful corporate, government and media interests (Halsey 1994).

In the international arena the merits of traditional positivist methodologies for the understanding of social phenomena generally, and inequality in particular, have been debated intensely in recent years. While positivism has not been without its defenders, Hammersley (1992, 1995) being among the more vocal of these, postmodernists, critical theorists and feminist scholars have been the most ardent critics of positivist epistemologies and methodologies (Bernstein 1976, 1983; Harding 1987, 1991; Harré 1981; Humphries 1997; Lentin 1993; Reay 1996; Smith 1987; Stanley and Wise 1983). Their work demonstrates how, despite its visible benefit as a tool of political arithmetic, mainstream positivism is open to philosophical and moral criticism (Reason 1988; Reason and Rowan 1981) and is of limited value for understanding and challenging the oppressions it documents (Ahmed and Sheldon 1993; Brah 1996; Lewis 2000; Oakley 1981; Oliver 1992).

A common criticism is that positivism employs a model of the person that regards people as 'units of analysis', treating them as 'variables' whose attributes can be neatly reified into dependent and independent types. People are not defined therefore in a holistic way; their subjectivity and their relational conditions of structured inequality often become invisible. What Bourdieu (1973) once referred to as 'the substantialist atomism' of the social sciences conceals the structural and relational conditions that generate inequality, injustice and marginalization. The person is treated as a detached atom (undoubtedly with attributes of gender, class, ethnicity, etc.); the language-of-analysis does not identify the sets of relations through which particular attributes are translated into particular inequalities. The research focuses on how particular characteristics, such as colour, class or religion, are associated or correlated with particular outcomes, such as occupational status, education or legal provision. There is therefore a tendency to locate the causative factors contributing to particular inequalities in the attributes of disadvantaged people, in their gender, poverty or 'race', rather than in the structured relations, the planned and unplanned exclusionary systems, that transform individual attributes into inequalities.

Moreover, once the research has identified correlations and associations between individual attributes and unequal outcomes, this is generally regarded as sufficient for promoting an understanding of the underlying causes of inequality. This methodological individualism creates a silence around the social, economic, political, legal and cultural relations of inequality. There is no space in which to debate or frame radical structural critiques or alternative visions based on relational understanding.

While it could be argued that the failure to examine the relational character of inequality is a universal problem within the social sciences, rather than one that is tied to strong positivist methods, the culture of assumed objectivity that dominates positivist discourse lends itself to a lack of reflexivity about the philosophical and ethical limitations of the tradition. The role of the researcher is defined as that of a 'disinterested' observer and analyst; one is expected to discover 'truth' via the use of reliable research instruments and rational discussion; the goal is to represent reality accurately, no matter how limited that particular reality may be. The researcher is defined as being beyond politics: her knowledge is 'innocent', untainted by political agendas. Thus, a culture of objectivism prevails that precludes a debate about the politics of research production. It allows methodological individualism to persist as long as it operates according to the scientific canon of objectivity. There is no framework for analysing the epistemological and ethical limitations of one's own position; questions regarding the purposes and outcomes of research are defined as being the work of policy-makers rather than researchers.

The methodological individualism underpinning positivism also focuses attention on the powerless rather than the powerful, while failing to explore relations between the two. While there are some studies of the impact and influence of the powerful and wealthy in society (studies on white collar crime by McCullagh (1995) and Tomlinson, Varley and McCullagh (1988) being cases in point), there are proportionately many more studies on the vulnerable and subordinate (Chambers 1983). The lack of a substantial body of empirical data on the implications for equality and social justice of the operation of money markets or the ownership structures of equities and other forms of corporate and productive wealth indicates how biased the focus of analysis has been.[2] We are often presented with a detailed analysis of the lifestyle of those who are subordinate or poor, while little attention is devoted to the analysis of the generative forces and processes that maintain others in positions of dominance or affluence.[3]

The relative social scientific silence that exists around the systems governing relations between the powerful and powerless is no doubt related to the ability (sometimes legally protected) of particular groups to hide from the research gaze. The rich and powerful are in a position to refuse access to sensitive data about themselves; the poor are rarely in this position. The focus of research attention on the attributes of powerless people means that the causes of injustice are often sought in the lifestyle of the marginalized themselves, the most visible and measurable group. Poor people or ethnic minorities thus become associated with or even 'blamed' for crime, not the poverty-inducing and degrading structures that induced and facilitated crime in the first place; women are held individually and personally accountable for their marginalization rather than the patriarchal structures that oppress them in the first instance (Connell 1987).

The dichotomy that is drawn between fact and value in the positivist tradition also discourages analysis of the impact of funding bodies on the nature of the questions asked. When research on equality is funded by the state, for example, it is frequently undertaken for the purposes of controlling or containing the 'problem' of inequality.[4] Big research studies based on national data sets are big business. The research is designed to answer the questions of those who pay for it: it is undertaken in a managerial context.

Large-scale studies of poverty, such as those currently being undertaken across several countries in the EU, are prime examples of state-funded, top-down surveys.[5] They are designed and planned by 'experts' generally without systematic dialogue and collaboration with the subjects of the research. Such research often 'studies those at the bottom while holding up its hands for money to those at the top' (Reason and Rowan 1981, p. xv). The methodologies and interpretations employed are based on models and paradigms that have been derived from a conception of poverty developed by academics, and approved by senior policy analysts and policy-makers, without the consent of those who are the subject of the research.

While such research does enable policy-makers to plan programmes for poverty alleviation, of its very nature it cannot challenge the structures, institutions and hegemonic policy frameworks that perpetuate poverty over time, not least because the critical appraisal of the latter is not part of the research agenda. Despite the good intent of those engaged in it, much quantitative and qualitative research may therefore operate as a form of colonization. It creates public images about groups and contexts of inequality (in both the academic and the policy world) over which people participating in the pain and marginalization of injustice and inequality have little or no control. Poor people, Travellers, asylum seekers, disabled people and, increasingly, women become the subjects of books and papers in which their lives are recorded by professional experts who are frequently removed from their culture and lifestyle. This creates a context in which professional researchers, and the policy institutions and state departments that pay them, know and own a part of some people's world about which those people themselves know very little. By owning data about oppressed peoples, the 'experts' own part of them.[6] The very owning and controlling of the stories of oppression adds further to the oppression as it means that there are now people who can claim to know and understand you better than you understand yourself; there are experts there to interpret your world and to speak on your behalf. They take away your voice by speaking about you and for you. The abstractions of researchers are expressed in the language of 'expert opinions' that are superior to your own understanding.[7] This is sometimes referred to as the 'hit and run model of research' wherein the career advancement of researchers is built on their use of alienating and exploitative methods of inquiry.

Colonization by experts is especially acute for low-income working class communities and for ethnic minorities, such as Travellers, whose cultural traditions are strongly oral (Lynch and O'Neill 1994).[8] For 'Classes exist twice over, once objectively, and a second time in the more or less explicit social representation that agents form of them' (Bourdieu 1993, p. 37). While there are women, albeit upper middle class women, who can challenge, mediate and redefine the images of women in the policy and academic arena, and while the same holds true for many other groups such as disabled persons and religious or ethnic minorities, this cannot happen for working class people; by designation, working class people are not part of the defining classes in society.

Within traditional positivist research, reflexivity is not a requirement of the research task. The fact that the perspective of the expert is only one viewpoint, and one which is generally at least one step removed from that of the people being researched, is rarely discussed. But since all claims to knowledge reflect the perspective of the knower, academic knowledge reflects the theoretical and empirical assumptions of the researcher. Knowing poverty or racism through the medium of academic frameworks, and framing propositions about it empirically and theoretically, makes an important contribution to human understanding. However, it is but one window on reality; it can only offer a limited perspective. Experiential knowledge – 'knowing a person or thing through sustained acquaintance' (Heron 1981, p. 27) – provides quite a different perspective on the world. By virtue of their personal experience, those who carry the burden of inequality often have a better vantage point for understanding the social world that creates inequality than those who enjoy its advantages. They can have a much deeper understanding of how particular laws, policies and procedures operate to promote inequalities than those who are advantaged by them (Connell 1993, pp. 39–41; hooks 1994). What is at issue here is therefore the case for an extended epistemology within the academy (Heron 1981, pp. 27–31).

There is also a need to unravel the complex set of power relations that operate within research production. Too often academics and other researchers present what is a select viewpoint as one that is more comprehensive and epistemologically powerful than others. Even within the 'expert' tradition itself, 'hard data' in the form of quantitative evidence is often presented as being superior to 'soft' ethnographic evidence, while the accounts of people affected by inequality are defined as merely 'anecdotal'.

The net effect of interpreting the world from the perspective of the 'expert' is that the viewpoint of the outsider is privileged over that of the insider who has experienced the inequality. The privileging of the expert therefore produces perspectives on inequality and injustice that are not only politically and emotionally detached from the experiences that generated their articulation in the first place but dominate those experiences in public policy. The meaning of poverty or inequality as it is understood and acted upon at policy level is as researchers have defined it, not as poor people see it (O'Neill 1992). The need to democratize the creation of academic knowledge therefore arises from the simple fact that such knowledge is acted upon as the defining understanding of a situation.

We therefore need multiple perspectives on the nature and experience of injustice. Quantitative, qualitative and experiential perspectives complement one another intellectually. If each is in dialogue with the other, networks of understanding and avenues for social action can develop; these are precluded by a singular methodological approach.

## The conditions in which research is produced

The positivist tradition is not the only obstacle to egalitarian practices of research. Another major factor is the logic of the cultural relations within which academic knowledge is produced. Even those intellectuals who have rejected positivism 'tend to leave out of play their own game and their own stakes'. Yet 'the production of representations of the social world, which is a fundamental dimension of political struggles, is the virtual monopoly of intellectuals' (Bourdieu 1993, p. 37). Academics create virtual realities, textual realities, ethnographic and statistical realities. These overhang and frame the lived existence of those who cannot name their own world; it is frequently in the context of these detached and remoter realities that public policy is enacted. The frame becomes the picture in the public eye. Yet theoretical knowledge has serious limitations imposed upon it by the conditions of its own creation.

The relations of cultural production within which critical theory, feminist theory and egalitarian theory are produced are generally no different from those that operate for the study of nuclear physics, corporate law or business and finance. Although some academics may view themselves as radical, reforming, feminist or emancipatory, they occupy a particular location within the class system (Bourdieu 1993, pp. 36–48). They are part of the cultural elite of society. It is the designation of cultural elitism that provides them with the structural conditions to write; it gives them credibility over other voices and reinforces the perception of superiority that maintains the salary differentials between themselves and other workers. Being granted the freedom to write and discuss is a privilege that academics (be they liberal, radical or conservative) in well-funded universities are rarely asked to reflect upon, however.

Yet academics are also subordinate to powerful corporate interest groups in the business and industrial sector. In a sense therefore they occupy a contradictory class location (Davies 1995), being at once an elite in the cultural sphere and relatively subordinate in the economic sphere. Gender further compounds the relations of academics to the institution of the academy. While radical (and indeed conservative) women academics are part of the privileged class whose income and status differentials are maintained by well established practices of social closure (Collins 1979), women academics are simultaneously subordinated to men within this class. Not only do they tend to occupy subordinate positions to men in terms of seniority and security of tenure, they are also heavily concentrated in disciplinary and research fields that are subordinate in terms of status and resources (Acker 1990; O'Connor 2001). Thus, while the concept of the 'free-floating, disinterested intellectual' with no stake in hierarchies of wealth and status may be part of the ideology of academia, it is not grounded in any sociological reality. In class terms, radical intellectuals are culturally and financially privileged; in gender terms, women are subordinate members of that privileged class.

Operating within a contradictory state of being personally radical and publicly privileged makes it difficult for many politically left-wing and feminist academics to be progressive in cultural or university politics. It is much simpler to be progressive in general politics that do not touch the core values of one's own work. Bourdieu (1993, p. 45) suggests that there is no easy resolution to this dilemma for radical intellectuals. He proposes a radical, ongoing reflexivity wherein one prepares 'the conditions for a critical knowledge of the limits of knowledge which is the precondition for true knowledge' as the principal protection available. Lather (1991) suggests a similar option for feminists.

Even if academics do engage in ongoing reflexivity, this does not alter the structural conditions under which they work. The dilemma posed by unequal power between researcher and research subject is not readily resolved, even when the researcher works with emancipatory intent (Lentin 1993, p. 128; Martin 1996). It is generally the researchers who produce the final text, the written record of the research event. This gives them a power of definition that cannot be abrogated at will. Moreover, the very efforts of those interested in transforming the relations of research production from those of dominance to those of partnership or emancipation are deeply implicated in the exercise of power. One cannot escape the reality of power relations even within the language of emancipation.

In addition, intellectuals work in institutions that lay down working conditions based on the dominant meritocratic principles of our time – ostensibly at least, promotion is based on merit. Merit is measured in terms of conformity to the dominant norms of intellectual and academic discourse. This includes not only writing within the dominant paradigm

(Kuhn 1961) but writing about what is currently intellectually fashionable. Without at least a nodding recognition of the importance of the dominant discourses, one's work is unlikely to be published. And it is through their publications that intellectuals in universities are generally assessed. While 'there is something desperate in the docility with which "free intellectuals" rush to hand in their essays on the required subject of the moment' (Bourdieu 1993, p. 43) the fact remains that academics' jobs and incomes are often dependent on such conformity:

> The secret resistance to innovation and to intellectual creativity, the aversion to ideas and to a free and critical spirit, which so often orientate academic judgements, as much at the viva of a doctoral thesis or in critical book reviews as in well-balanced lectures setting off neatly against each other the latest avant-gardes, are no doubt the effect of the recognition granted to an institutionalized thought only on those who implicitly accept the limits assigned by the institution. (Bourdieu 1988, p. 95)

Freedom of expression is allowed, but the publication and dissemination of that expression is often dependent on working within the received wisdom. And this is even truer when trying to establish new forms of knowledge or understanding. While resistance to innovation may be concealed within established disciplines, more open resistance has confronted new disciplines such as women's studies and equality studies.

Thus, some of the strongest forces of conservatism arise from the simple organizational dynamics of academic work as a career. Although academics may have tenured posts, the freedom that flows from this does not always encourage people to think critically; rather people become beholden to the concept of the career – moving upwards promotionally within the system. All too frequently the line of least innovation is the line of ascent. While it is clear that people do innovate and resist the forces of conformity within the academy in many different ways, it is also evident that this often happens at considerable personal cost, especially when the innovations challenge traditional values and practices among dominant groups.

Not only does the academy generally only recognize those who conform to the intellectual norms of the day, it penalizes those who attempt to redefine the purpose of the academy in relation to the society around it. Lectures, consultations and involvements with non-academic bodies do not count in terms of the enumerations of one's work or achievements. This acts as a very effective control on academic work, limiting and containing interests within the safe confines of the university. It also works effectively to preclude intellectuals from involving themselves, and the university, in radicalizing initiatives. Yet public lectures and involvements with voluntary, statutory, community and other organizations are essential if research findings are to be circulated outside the narrow confines of the academy. Given that the production of scientific knowledge generally is often legitimated on the grounds that it will contribute to progress, and to the ultimate general good of humanity, it is difficult to see how this can happen without the dissemination of research findings outside the academy in accessible contexts and language.

What is interesting about the boundary-setting that goes on in universities is that it is not confined to any one field (Bernstein 1971). It occurs within and between disciplines; the marginalization of feminist research within male-dominated disciplines is an example of the former, while the control that medicine has traditionally exercised over nursing is an example of the latter. The narrow parameters within which academic dialogue takes place inhibit criticism of academic discourse itself and prohibit academics from understanding the world from the perspectives of the 'other' outside the academy. Academic knowledge is defined as 'superior' knowledge. The fact that the academic perspective is only one viewpoint, and that it may need to be complemented by other forms of understanding by non-academic research subjects is largely ignored (Lather 1986).

## Emancipatory methodology

Feminist scholars have been especially effective in challenging the core epistemological and methodological assumptions of mainstream social scientific practice. They have challenged patterns of bias in research design, including the absence of research on questions of central importance to women, the focus on elitist research topics, the naïve understanding of objectivity, inadequate data dissemination and the improper interpretation and over-generalization of findings (Jayaratne and Stewart 1995, p. 218). The challenges posed by feminist theories for research, in terms of reflexivity, dialogue and cooperation with marginalized people, are considerable.

Feminist theorists have also been leaders in developing a theory of emancipatory action through education and research (Bowles and Duelli Klein 1983; Harding 1987, 1991; Humphries and Truman 1994; Lather 1991; Lentin 1993; Mies 1983; Oakley 1981; Roberts 1981; Smith 1987; Stanley and Wise 1983; Weiler 1988). Together with progressive authors concerned with the social sciences more generally (Bernstein 1983; de Koning and Martin 1996; Oliver 1992; Reason 1988; Reason and Rowan 1981) they have attempted to document the type of procedures that must be followed in order to create an emancipatory research approach.

The aim of emancipatory research is to increase 'awareness of the contradictions hidden or distorted by everyday understandings' and in so doing to direct 'attention to the possibilities for social transformation inherent in the present configuration of social processes' (Lather 1986, p. 259). Lather claims that

> the development of emancipatory social theory requires an empirical stance which is open-ended, dialogically reciprocal, grounded in respect for human capacity, and yet profoundly sceptical of appearances and 'common sense'. Such an empirical stance is, furthermore, rooted in a commitment to the long-term, broad-based ideological struggle to transform structural inequalities. (Lather 1986, p. 269)

This approach is based on an ethics of human rights and equal power, involves reciprocal research relationships, builds theory through dialogue and proceeds reflexively.

## Ethical issues

Research is a massive industry across all fields and disciplines. It operates not only in universities or research institutes but also in government departments, private companies, local and national service agencies and voluntary bodies. Cultural capital, of which research is a fundamental part, parallels industrial, financial and agricultural capital as a source of wealth and power. Unless it is shared with those who are directly affected by it, research data can be used for manipulation, abuse and control. The importance of democratizing research arises therefore because knowledge is power.

Although human rights thinking has tended to focus on conventional political rights, there is also a need to recognize human rights in relation to the operation of public and private institutions and systems that exercise control over people's lives but are not democratically elected. Research-generating institutions and universities are such bodies, as they play a central role in validating and developing the cultural forms and scientific knowledge that underpin social, economic and political policies in society.

Emancipatory research involves a recognition therefore of the moral right of vulnerable, marginalized or oppressed research subjects to exercise ownership and control over the generation of knowledge produced about them and their world. As Heron (1981) observes this is a human rights issue. It constitutes part of people's right to political membership of their community. If people who are already relatively powerless are also structurally excluded from democratic engagement with research practice, they are precluded from assessing its validity in an informed manner. They are effectively disenfranchised from controlling the creation and dissemination of knowledge about themselves and about the institutions and systems within which they live and work.

> For persons, as autonomous beings, have a moral right to participate in decisions that claim to generate knowledge about them. Such a right

does many things: (1) it honours the fulfilment of their need for autonomously acquired knowledge; (2) it protects them from becoming unwitting accessories to knowledge-claims that may be false and may be inappropriately or harmfully applied to others; (3) it protects them from being excluded from the formation of knowledge that purports to be about them and so from being managed and manipulated, both in the acquisition and in the application of knowledge, in ways they do not understand and so cannot assent to or dissent from. (Heron 1981, p. 35)

Assessing the relations of research production and exchange in human rights terms raises questions not only about the rights of vulnerable or marginalized research subjects, but also about the rights of all research participants, whether vulnerable or not, to have democratic control over the research process. As this is an enormously complex question, it cannot be dealt with in depth here. What is evident, however, is that the relationship between 'experts' and 'lay' people is changing, and that the right to know who is collecting information on you and for what purpose is becoming increasingly protected, notably by freedom of information legislation. To what extent freedom of information legislation will eventually affect research is unclear. What is certain, however, is that democratizing ownership and control of research raises further issues about inequalities of power, such as the unequal capacities of different groups to participate effectively in any democratized research process. Moreover, powerful groups can and do resist research on themselves and often have the capacity to hide from research analysis when they see fit (Chambers 1983).[9] Democratizing research cannot mean that such individuals or groups should be able to exercise a veto on research, as this would mean that their role in the unequal relations that operate in society could never be examined. The human right to participate in the research process does not constitute a right to suppress research into the nature and causes of injustice. There is therefore an asymmetry between how egalitarian researchers should treat disadvantaged groups and how they should treat the privileged. In both cases there are basic human rights to information and consultation that need to be respected. But in the former case, equal power is promoted through a thorough democratization of the research process; in the latter case, it is precisely the principle of equal power that justifies limiting the ability of the privileged to control research about them.

Although the human right to know applies primarily to research on persons, it is also significant in other fields including research in the physical sciences. The most obvious example arises in relation to research involving experimentation within the natural environment (as in the case of the nuclear industry) or the development of genetically modified foods; these, and indeed many other forms of research that are not so high-profile, have serious health and environmental implications not only for the living generation but for future generations. Concealment of the scope and impact of research may add to the power and influence of the companies and states that produce it, but it also creates a world order where ordinary people are politically and informationally disenfranchised. Research and information enfranchisement must complement political enfranchisement.

Often a research information deficit can be the differentiating factor between having a meaningful or an alienating experience in an organization. An immediate and concrete example arises in the field of education. Parents who know the basic research findings regarding such practices as streaming and ability grouping can exercise control over schools and teachers in a way that other parents cannot. Knowledge about the effects of different forms of ability grouping enables them to act in a way that protects the interests of their own child; they can exercise strategic choices such as moving the child to a more supportive school if they find her or him in the 'wrong' class. No such possibility exists for those who do not even know the implications of different forms of grouping in the first place. Similar examples could be taken from the health services where, for example, most people are not aware of research findings regarding the long-term implications of taking different types of drugs and medication. Those who have access to (and can decode) the information are in control and can exercise choices in a way that those without it cannot.

While the problems associated with dialogue or partnerships in policy-making are not simply problems of information deficits (resources are crucial, too, as Phillips (1999, pp. 74–98) has argued so cogently), nevertheless, people who lack information are denied the opportunity to make informed decisions. Having the resources and capacity to name issues in an informed manner is therefore vital for effective participation in public debates or policy partnerships. If people lack the technical knowledge to participate effectively, they can be physically present but technically absent, living in fear of a professional put-down from those who are part of the research-informed. Thus, what is at issue is not only the exercise of democratic procedures in research production, but also the effective, democratic dissemination of research findings.

### Reciprocity in the research relationship

Emancipatory research also involves developing a reciprocal relationship between the researcher and the research subject. This requires a democratization of the research relationship so that the research process enables participants to understand and change their situation. This is especially important for research in the area of equality as research that is not oriented towards transformation effectively reinforces inequality by default. It allows inequality to persist by diverting intellectual and public attention elsewhere. The experience of women's studies has taught us that egalitarians are as likely as other academics to remain unknowingly complicit in reproducing the organizational power of the academy unless they work actively to challenge it.

Reciprocity involves engaging participants from the start in the research planning and design, as it is only through such participation that marginalized groups can begin to control the naming of their own world. If research participation is confined to the interpretation or theoretical elaboration stage, it may be too late; issues that are not central to the group or community may already have become the focus of attention. Involving research subjects in planning poses numerous challenges to researchers and theorists, not least of which is the information and expertise differential between the researcher and the subject. Mutual education is at least a partial solution to this dilemma; there is an especially strong onus on researchers to facilitate and promote education given the power differential between them and research subjects (Heron 1981). Integrating education with research imposes time and resource constraints on research, however, that cannot be easily set aside. And neither the funders nor the research subjects themselves may be interested in bearing the cost.

Reciprocity also demands that the research enables people to know and control their own world. This takes time, trust and negotiation; it is quite possible that the researcher and participants may not agree on the definition of the inequality, or indeed on how it should be addressed. Kelly's (1996) research shows how working class community groups themselves interpreted unemployment according to quite different sociopolitical frames – ranging from radical to reformist to localist – although the formal class identity of all 12 groups involved was the same.

Recognizing the very real practical difficulties posed by reciprocal research relations is not a sufficient reason to discount them. Operating out of principles of reciprocity, albeit imperfectly, would radically alter the way in which research is planned and conducted. Working reciprocally involves restructuring power relations; it would be an important movement towards the democratization of research.

### Dialogical theory building

Another feature of emancipatory research is building theory through dialogue rather than expert imposition (Lather 1991). Research respondents are not only involved therefore in the design of the research but also in the construction and validation of meaning. To undertake theory-construction in this manner represents an enormous challenge for researchers as it imposes a substantive educational commitment upon them (Heron 1981). A dialogical approach to theory building is even more demanding, in many respects, than partnership in empirical research, as it involves the accommodation of two very different epistemological standpoints on the world, the academic and the local or particular. It demands theoretical construction in a language that is recognizable and meaningful across disparate communities; the theorist can no longer construct a view of the world without knowing and recognizing the view of the 'other', howsoever the latter may be defined. What dialogical theory building involves therefore is the democratization of theoretical construction, a reordering of power relations between the academy and the named world. Yet theoretical imposition is the natural predisposition of most researchers. Given traditional academic training, the author assumes the superiority of her 'framework'. Grounding frameworks in the context of lived understandings challenges this tradition. It is a challenge that has a tangible dividend as it informs and enriches conceptualizations of the issues.

### Reflexivity

Systematic reflexivity is also a requirement for emancipatory research as it is only through the constant analysis of one's own theoretical and methodological presuppositions that one can retain an awareness of the importance of other people's definitions and understandings of theirs. But although reflexivity is necessary, it is not a sufficient condition for emancipatory research. An ethically disinterested reflexivity would not suggest any change in research practice. If reflexivity is to facilitate change it needs to be guided by principles of democratic engagement and a commitment to change.

## Emancipatory research in practice: research coalitions and learning partnerships

There are several practical problems posed by emancipatory methodology, including its fundamental challenge to the institutionalized power relations between researchers and research 'subjects', its intense and time-consuming character and the fact that it does increase the cost of research. Such work may not be supported by research funders, although this may change over time as the importance of dialogue and its educational outcomes becomes appreciated and as it becomes evident that emancipatory methods allow us to do better research by widening the lens through which we know the world.

A further task for emancipatory research is establishing procedures through which radical understandings can be developed into tools for challenging structural inequalities. Even if radical understandings emerge from research, which for example happened in Kelly's (1996) work, it may be difficult to move these understandings into discourses and political practices where they can contribute to the struggle for equality and social justice. Emancipation cannot be conferred by one group (academics) on another (oppressed or marginalized people) no matter how well intentioned the researchers might be (Martin 1994, 1996). While Mies (1983) shows how particular research led to important changes in Germany in relation to policies on women and violence, it is not clear what makes it possible for this to happen. Is egalitarian development contingent on a particular set of historical and political circumstances? One factor that does appear to be important is involving marginalized groups themselves at all stages of the research, including the policy-related implementation stage, if action is to be taken.

Within current discussions of emancipatory methods, the choice about whether or not to use emancipatory methods is left to the researcher; there has been no serious attempt to develop the structures necessary to ensure that emancipatory methods are implemented on an ongoing basis. To institutionalize a truly radical approach to research, however, would require the development in academic settings of new structures at both university and departmental level. Similar challenges would arise for institutes and bodies undertaking research elsewhere. Procedures would have to be put in place whereby those who are marginalized and oppressed in society can enter into dialogue about all research undertaken in their name. They would not simply be dependent on the goodwill of individual researchers who allow them to enter into dialogue on their own terms. Rather, community groups or other representatives of marginalized groups would be involved on an ongoing basis in planning, monitoring and commenting on research. They would play a very different and more powerful role than when their opportunity to participate in or engage in dialogue about research depends on the will of the researcher.

This would require a radical change in the structuring of departments in universities and in the management of research operations. It would involve the establishment of Research Coalitions with those marginalized groups and communities who are so often the objects of research. Such groups would move from being objects to subjects, from being respondents to being partners; they would have the opportunity to define research agendas relating to their own lives. No one would have the authority to name, codify and claim scholarly understanding and ownership of someone else's world without debate, negotiation and, ultimately, consent.

Under a Research Coalition arrangement, power would be shared. The researchers would have to explain and justify the nature of their proposed research and theory about marginalized groups to the groups themselves. This is not to deny the difficulties involved. Not all marginalized groups are coalitionable, be it because of their vulnerability (homeless people, asylum seekers, displaced persons, women and children who are being trafficked), their age (very young children), their invisibility (gays, lesbians and bisexuals who are afraid to be 'out' because of homophobia) or their institutional status (prisoners). A further problem is that the academic voice is validated by virtue of its scientific origin; it is structurally defined as superior to the local or community voice. Thus any research partnership between researchers and the community is not an equal one, in the sense that prior cultural relations define it otherwise. To say this is not to suggest that the power differential in Research Coalitions cannot be managed and controlled. It merely highlights the importance of enabling those who are not full-time researchers to have the capacity and skill to name their research agendas in the coalitions.

A further difficulty arises from the volatile character and composition of community groups themselves. Groups representing the marginalized or oppressed are not necessarily constituted in a democratic or representative manner; they often lack formal procedures of accountability and responsiveness to their own constituency. The complex ways in which they evolve and develop generally forestall such developments. Consequently there is always the danger that spokespersons within the non-governmental sector may only partially represent those for whom they speak (this is not to deny the fact that accountability and responsiveness is problematic even in formal representative systems of governance) (Papadopoulos 2003; Sabel 1996). The representativeness of community and related groups has to be constantly monitored therefore. While this is not essentially a research problem, it is nonetheless an issue that has to be addressed in partnership contexts.

If Research Coalitions are to be established, it is evident that the onus of responsibility for setting them up rests initially with those who exercise control over the research process. Negotiations and discussions need to be set in train to identify the needs and interests of both parties and to resolve the barriers that need to be overcome. These include barriers arising from differences in research expertise, language usage, life experiences and attitudes to, and experiences of, research.

The experience of Local Area Partnerships in Ireland has shown that community representatives cannot be fully effective participants without resourcing (Lynam 1997). If marginalized groups are to participate effectively in the research process, then training, resourcing and support will be essential, although the knowledge differential is not only confined to them. Academics also experience a (frequently unacknowledged) lack of knowledge about the daily, lived reality of the groups about whom they write. Such living knowledge represents an important resource that the community groups would bring to the research partnerships.

To be effective, Research Coalitions would need to be complemented therefore by Learning Partnerships. These would be mutual education forums for academics, researchers and community members, so that each could share their definitions and interpretations of issues and events. In this way research agendas could be assessed and prioritized. The Research Coalitions and Learning Partnerships would inevitably facilitate action for change, as the communities where action is required would be directly involved in defining and interpreting their own situations. The research understandings available to them would be a powerful tool in negotiations with politicians and policy-makers.

The importance of establishing Learning Partnerships between researchers and the community arises not only from the point of view of respecting the fundamental human rights of those about whom we write, but also as a means of realizing change. While critical theorists place considerable store on developing theories, including theories jointly created by researchers and participants, they do not make clear how such an understanding will lead to change. Most academic productions remain confined to a narrow community of readers and listeners. No matter how radical the knowledge may be, its transformative potential is far from evident unless it is available and disseminated in accessible form to those about whom it is written or whose lives are affected by it. Learning Partnerships arising from Research Coalitions would allow this to happen. They would ensure that an avenue of communication is established so that those who have most to gain from transformative action also have the knowledge to act. The Learning Partnerships would provide a forum for challenging biases and deceptions thereby reinforcing the incentive to act. Those who have experiential knowledge of inequality and injustice can ally this understanding with academic knowledge to create a new and deeper knowledge of their world. This deeper understanding can challenge established 'wisdoms' and 'ideologies' around inequality and injustice. Learning Partnerships would provide the opportunity to link analysis directly into a community of participants with the potential to act.[10]

But knowledge, no matter how radical in intent, is not inherently transformative. Even if critical intellectuals shift from being 'universalizing spokespersons' for marginalized groups to being 'cultural workers whose task is to take away barriers that prevent people from speaking for themselves' (Apple 1991, p. ix) this does not guarantee change. A deepening knowledge of injustices and inequalities, among marginalized people themselves, will not inevitably lead to transformative action outside of the research field; there is always an element of choice. Understandings need to be linked into a political forum so that knowledge does not become redundant and divorced from action. If Learning Partnerships are created between academics and community representatives, then it also seems necessary to develop Equality Action Plans on a collaborative basis. Action needs to be planned and implemented for changing structures at the political and related levels. Without integrating planning for change into the entire process there can be no guarantee that it will happen.

## Conclusion

Radical researchers occupy a contradictory location in relation to the academy. On the one hand, like all other academics, they are part of a cultural elite that receives salaries and work privileges in excess of many other occupational groups by virtue of their claim to expertise. On the other, they are working as agents for change and social transformation to create a more egalitarian society, one that may not endow their own groups with the same 'freedom from necessity' to research and to write.

A genuine and ongoing commitment to change cannot be guaranteed in this type of situation by simply relying on some form of subjective reflexivity. While reflexivity is essential, it is but one element in the process of developing an emancipatory research methodology. If the aim of critically inspired thought is to make theory, method and praxis inseparable from each other, then it is necessary to create structures that guarantee that this will happen rather than leave it to the goodwill or interest of individual researchers. Moreover, granting the researcher a veto on whether or not to utilize emancipatory methods on equality issues is to disempower the research participants in the very way that critical theorists have strongly criticized in other contexts. The only way in which people can exercise ongoing, systematic influence on naming their own world is by being centrally involved at all stages of the research process, including design, interpretation and outcome-implementation. For this to happen, procedures for Research Coalitions need to be developed between research bodies, universities (and their departments) and communities and groups who are being researched. In addition, Learning Partnerships need to be established to enable researchers to learn about the role of experiential knowledge in understanding and to enable marginalized people to exercise control over how they are identified and defined. Finally, if knowledge is to have transformative potential at a structural as well as an ideological level, then Equality Action Plans need to be developed from the research findings.[11]

For equality studies and other cognate fields to have moral, intellectual and political credibility it is incumbent upon researchers to implement the kinds of emancipatory research methods we have outlined. If they confine their emancipatory actions to the operational stage of the research and ignore the conceptualization, design, interpretation and action stage, then they are belying the notion of emancipation in its more substantive sense.

We are not suggesting that the emancipatory approach is a substitute for qualitative or quantitative analysis, rather that it should inform the design of equality research howsoever it is operationalized. The core issue is that experiential knowledge is an important complement to propositional knowledge especially where injustice is involved. Those who carry the burden of inequality often have a more refined and precise understanding of how inequality operates than those who are net beneficiaries of injustice. In addition, it is vital to link researchers with those experiencing injustice or inequality if the research is to be part of the capacity-building process for social change.

To operate a more radical form of emancipatory method does present many new and exciting challenges not only for research but for other work in the university as well. Clearly if emancipatory methods are being employed in research this also calls into question the authenticity and suitability of current pedagogical and assessment methods, most of which are based on a strongly hierarchical view of both teacher–student relationships and indeed of knowledge itself.

Many universities and colleges claim service to the community as one of their objectives. If this is the case, then there is a need to identify the many different communities with whom we are to work. Marginalized and excluded groups in our society are part of the community; indeed very often such communities comprise the subject matter of social scientific research, but rarely its designers or partners. It is time that Research Coalitions were established between the universities and socially excluded communities to enable the latter to control the naming of their own world.

# Part III
# Strategies for Change

# 10
## Class, Gender and the Equality Movement

How should we think about promoting egalitarian change? In this chapter, we argue for a social movement model in which change occurs through the loosely coordinated activities of a wide range of groups and organizations committed to egalitarian aims. We suggest that a social movement for equality already exists on a global scale. We examine some of the major structural changes that are occurring in the social class and gender orders of western societies and assess their significance for understanding the politics of change, concluding that a social movement seeking to mobilize opinions and resources for the sake of equality has to include movements that are separate from but interact with class politics. We focus in particular on the women's movement as an important source of discourses and projects that matter not just to women themselves, but to children and men as well.

### Two models of social change

The model of social change that has had the most influence on egalitarians comes from Marxism.[1] In its original formulation the model was relatively simple. The development of capitalism, and in particular its increasing dominance of the world economy and its intensifying exploitation of the working class, was seen as creating conditions under which workers would have both a compelling interest in social change and the capacity to bring it about. While Marx recognized some of the problems that arose within the working class from differences between women and men and between other social groups, the aims and interests of different sections of the working class were defined as relatively homogeneous. Skilled and unskilled workers, men and women, workers from different ethnic groups and so on had a common purpose in seeking social transformation. No explicit appeal needed to be made to moral considerations – to the claim that capitalism was unjust – because it was obvious that the working class had a compelling interest in ending exploitation and in bringing about radical social change. Furthermore, Marx regarded the moral codes of his time as essentially a cloak for class interests. Thus, to the extent that the socialist movement needed a morality of its own, it was to be a completely new set of principles based on the interests of the working class, who were projected to be the majority of the population when the polarization and pauperization generated by capitalism was complete. Nor was there a major problem about the organizational forms necessary for coordinating and directing social change. The task was to build a unified workers' movement with clear aims and goals.

Marx was correct in foreseeing the global expansion of capitalism and the deeply exploitative relations that are endemic to its untrammelled development, but in other respects this model of social change had serious weaknesses. In its broadest possible definition, the working class consists of everyone who relies on either employment or state transfers for their income. It is clear that this group is extremely varied, encompassing people with a huge range of incomes and personal assets, with major conflicts of interest over wealth, income, power and status (Crompton 1998; Offe 1985; Roemer 1994; Savage 2000). The working class, so defined, also encompasses important divisions based on gender, sexual orientation, nationality, ethnicity and disability. As numerous scholars have observed, an adequate model of social change needs to take these divisions and differences seriously, not least because social divisions of political import are generated outside the labour–capital relationship. Relations of production, distribution and consumption have been deeply inegalitarian, in gender and racial terms particularly, for extended periods of history quite independently of capitalism (Lerner 1986; Said 1993).

One phenomenon which Marx could not have foreseen, but which has had a profound effect on politics, is how the dynamism of the labour market backed up by the welfare state has diluted class politics. While patterns of class inequality have remained relatively stable in many Western countries since the end of the Second World War (Shavit and Blossfeld 1993), there have been very significant changes in the living conditions of the populations of these countries. These shifts in standards of living have contributed to a shift in class identities, so that class distinctions are more diversified and individualized, making mobilization around class identities more problematic (Beck 1992).

Another weakness in the original Marxist model was its reliance on self-interest. This overt dismissal of moral considerations was often accompanied even in Marx's own writings by strong if implicit references to the underlying injustice of capitalism.[2] In any case, an appeal to self-interest is unlikely to succeed in coordinating the efforts of a wide range of groups with a wide range of projects and preoccupations. If it is the sole mobilizing principle, it is likely to do as much to divide as to unite social movements. A more plausible model of change has to acknowledge the motivational importance of moral values, while recognizing that egalitarian movements are also driven by the interests of subordinate groups.

The organizational assumptions of the original Marxist model were also open to question. Only a movement in which there are no deep conflicts of interest or value could endorse the relatively monolithic organizations typical of Marxist and even social-democratic politics. Once we take on board the diverse aims and interests of different, sometimes overlapping, sections of the working class, however defined, we can see that the struggle for equality needs to reflect that diversity and in particular to protect and empower subordinate groups.

If we want to develop a model of egalitarian social change, then, we need to think of the ways in which a diverse population with a range of common and conflicting interests and values can nevertheless achieve progressive, egalitarian aims. Many writers and activists in the Marxist tradition have attempted to do this and have made important contributions to the theory and practice of social change. But in doing so, they can be seen as having moved progressively away from the core Marxist paradigm to a different model of change, based on the idea of an egalitarian social movement. This social movement model incorporates many elements of the classical Marxist model but differs in several key respects.

For the purposes of this discussion, a social movement can be defined as a sustained series of challenges by groups of people against those who have power over them, using a wide range of conventional and unconventional actions and of formal and informal organizations.[3] Social change does not take place on this model through the activities of a single, coherent organization but through the complementary actions of a large number of groups. Some of these groups are formally organized while others are not. Some work primarily 'within' the formal political and bureaucratic system using 'acceptable' methods while others work primarily 'outside' the system using radical, disruptive tactics, although even these tactics are rooted in existing political traditions. Their focus can vary from personal to local, national or transnational concerns, sometimes targeting and sometimes bypassing the state (Castells 1997). The motivations of activists are typically a mixture of self-interest and moral commitment, drawing on the existing ethical ideas of their societies but challenging hypocrisy and other value-contradictions within them. They achieve their aims not just by appealing to the interests of subordinate groups, but by emphasizing the injustice and immorality of existing social arrangements, as well as by pointing out ways that even members of dominant groups have something to gain from the changes they are seeking. The movements that have been studied in depth include labour movements, civil rights movements, peace movements, women's movements, gay and lesbian liberation movements and green movements. More recently, attention has been given to what has been called the 'anti-globalization' or 'anti-capitalist' movement.

If we apply the social movement model to the struggle for equality, we can see at least four ways in which that struggle differs from the classical Marxist picture. First of all, it has a more diverse social base because it is concerned with all relations of inequality and therefore with all subordinated and exploited social groups. Secondly, it employs a range of motives, because it recognizes that the opponents of inequality are moved not just by self-interest but by a sense of injustice. Thirdly, it faces a broader but perhaps more promising ideological task. It has both to convince subordinate groups that equality is in their own self-interest (something that cannot be taken for granted given the control of the means of understanding, particularly of the media, but also of education, by powerful interests: see Apple 2001; McChesney and Nichols 2002; Melucci 1996) and to make the moral case for equality, a case that can appeal to members of relatively privileged groups as well. This is particularly important because people belong to cross-cutting social groups and therefore may face both gains and losses from egalitarian change. Even as members of privileged groups, they may have something to gain: for example, men would lose power over women if there were greater equality in the sexual division of labour, but they would benefit from having more opportunities for love, care and solidarity and from being released from the cultural expectation that they are 'breadwinners' and women are dependants. Finally, the struggle for equality faces a different kind of organizational task: not to build one big organization but to strengthen the network of egalitarian groups and organizations in a way that advances their diverse but complementary aims. These differences are summarized in Table 10.1. Later in this chapter we discuss more thoroughly the implications of the diverse social and motivational base of the equality movement. Chapters 11 and 12 are devoted, respectively, to its ideological and organizational tasks.

## How the equality movement stands today

In our view, many contemporary social movements can be viewed as participants in a broader equality movement, because they are concerned with challenging inequalities in one or more of the dimensions set out in Chapter 2, focusing on one or more of the contexts, and often on one or more of the social groups, discussed in Chapter 4. The labour movement, which is at its heart a challenge by working class people against the power of capital, is structured around class divisions in accordance with the Marxist model of social change. But other movements, most clearly women's movements, disability rights movements, gay/lesbian/bisexual movements and anti-racist movements, arise out of and work against inequalities that are to varying degrees independent of class and may, at least in the first instance, focus more on inequalities of recognition and power than on inequalities of resources. In either case, the principles

*Table 10.1* Two models of social change

|  | *Marxist model* | *Social movement model* |
| --- | --- | --- |
| *Social basis* | Working class | All relations of exploitation/ subordination/inequality (including class) |
| *Motivation* | Self-interest | Self-interest and moral motivations |
| *Ideological task* | To *unmask* moral defences of the status quo; To show workers that their interest lies in change | To *challenge* moral defences of the status quo and to make the moral case for equality; To show subordinate groups that their interest lies in egalitarian change; To show relatively privileged groups that even they can gain in some ways from egalitarian change |
| *Organizational task* | To build a single, unified organization | To strengthen the network of groups and organizations with broadly egalitarian aims |

espoused by these movements are drawn from different points along the spectrum of egalitarian ideas, often appealing to basic human rights. Of course, not all social movements are egalitarian (e.g. reactionary nationalism and fundamentalism), but many of them are.[4]

We can think of the equality movement as, in effect, a network of related movements, encompassing women's movements, gay and lesbian liberation movements, human rights movements, anti-racism movements, disability rights movements, anti-poverty movements, global solidarity movements, anti-globalization movements and so on. Table 10.2 gives a partial list of the types of organizations and groups that might be included in this movement in Ireland, a list that is bound to have resonance for readers in other countries. The most recent of these movements, the 'anti-globalization' or 'anti-capitalist' movement, is popularly defined negatively, as being against capitalist globalization, transnational corporations and the international financial institutions of the World Bank, IMF and WTO.[5] If we look at its positive aims, however, egalitarian ideas are at the centre of the picture. For example, the Charter of Principles of the World Social Forum, first convened at Porto Alegre, Brazil in 2001, states:

> The alternatives proposed at the World Social Forum … are designed to ensure that globalization in solidarity will prevail as a new stage in world history. This will respect universal human rights, and those of all citizens – men and women – of all nations and the environment and

*Table 10.2*  Some participants in the equality movement in Ireland

| *Who belongs to the equality movement?* |
| --- |
| Anti-ageism and older people's rights organizations |
| Anti-globalization organizations |
| Anti-poverty and social justice organizations |
| Anti-racism organizations |
| Anti-sectarian organizations |
| Children's rights alliances and organizations |
| Community-based drug rehabilitation groups |
| Community-based women's educational groups |
| Community development organizations |
| Disability rights organizations |
| Environmental activism groups |
| Global solidarity organizations |
| Human rights organizations |
| Immigrants' rights groups |
| Lesbian, gay, bisexual and transgender rights organizations |
| Peace and anti-war groups |
| Refugee support groups |
| Reproductive rights organizations |
| Travellers' rights organizations |
| Trade unions and other workers' organizations |
| Women's rights organizations |
| Academic centres focusing on equality issues |
| Political groupings in the anarchist, socialist and feminist traditions |
| Political parties? – see Chapter 12. |

will rest on democratic international systems and institutions at the service of social justice, equality and the sovereignty of peoples. ... The World Social Forum ... upholds respect for Human Rights, the practices of real democracy, participatory democracy, peaceful relations, in equality and solidarity, among people, ethnicities, genders and peoples, and condemns all forms of domination and all subjection of one person by another. (World Social Forum 2001)

All of these principles, which recur again and again in the documents of the WSF, are closely related to egalitarian ideals.

The movements we have named appeal to egalitarian ideas and have shaped the egalitarian agenda. Their aims and principles are for the most part complementary and in many ways overlap. They draw on each other's experience, making use of parallel analyses, justifications, strategies and tactics. As each of these movements comes to recognize its own internal diversity, they become more and more intertwined. For example, the women's movement has come to recognize the importance of class, ethnicity, 'race', disability and sexual orientation.

Recognizing and naming an equality movement is not a way of minimizing the importance of the aims of more specific movements or subordinating them to a higher or more embracing set of ideals and aims, any more than talk about the women's movement, say, suggests a uniformity or hierarchy of aims among its various components or identifying the members of the anti-war movement implies that they have no other commitments than to peace. It is merely to suggest, as we pointed out in Chapter 1, that many of the principles and aims of these movements are recognizably egalitarian. Highlighting these connections is useful for each of the movements in question, because it supports the process of learning from each other's experience and because it draws attention to real or potential political alliances. But it is also useful from the point of view of equality, because it indicates how much is already being done to promote egalitarian aims and values, if not necessarily always in the name of equality itself. Instead of imagining that we need to construct a plan for achieving equality more or less from scratch, recognizing the existence of an equality movement allows us to see that there is already an implicit strategy in place, which we need to build on and strengthen. It is not the strategy of one big organization with a coherent set of goals and tactics, but of (largely) complementary actions by a diverse range of social actors, some more organized than others, some using more conventional and others more disruptive tactics, variously concentrating on personal, local, regional, national or transnational issues, and all of them drawing on such common egalitarian values as human dignity, liberation from oppression, democratic rights and the recognition of diversity.

There are of course heated debates and serious conflicts among these groups. Their different priorities are real political differences that have to be bridged in creating a coalition of social movements. Conflicts of purpose between groups, such as those currently articulated between branches of the women's reproductive rights movement and the disability movement over issues of abortion on the grounds of disability, can run very deep. What has to be achieved here, and what is extremely difficult to achieve, is continued collaboration on issues of common purpose, while also respecting differences.

Tensions frequently arise, too, about the moral status and the representativeness of social movements. There are fights for the moral high ground and divisions over the 'purity' of different groups' egalitarian credentials. All too often energies and time are diverted in maintaining relatively minor divisions between like-minded groups as each one claims to be the more authentic voice for the exploited and oppressed.

The problem of how representative a social movement can be is not easily resolved as groups and leaders originating in civil society are generated voluntarily, often without a representative structure. Recognizing the limitations of this position is as much as can be achieved, while instituting procedures to discourage organizations or groups from merely representing themselves rather than the communities on behalf of whom they claim to speak. Failure to face up to conflicts and differences between egalitarian groups consolidates the hegemony of elite groups as it fosters fragmentation among those sharing broadly egalitarian aims, a fragmentation that is further promoted by the elite themselves (Thompson 1984, 1990). Fragmentation, whatever its source, fosters a further perception that those who espouse egalitarian ideals are isolated factions, who are unwilling or incapable of cooperating even in their shared projects. This facilitates the demonizing and marginalizing of egalitarian movements in a way that lowers their status and sees them as unreliable and unrealistic political alternatives. The need to avoid fragmentation seems crucial therefore, especially when groups are diverse in their principles and preoccupations. We discuss some of the principles and procedures by which egalitarian movements need to be guided to help avoid such divisions in Chapter 12, while a framework for a more participatory and accountable democratic politics is presented in Chapter 6.

A further problem for egalitarian movements is that of funding. Nongovernmental organizations are institutions of civil society that generally work without core funding from state sources. If they rely on funding from private foundations and trusts, they are vulnerable to changes in policy and fashion. When they do receive government grants-in-aid for their services this, in turn, makes them vulnerable to state regulation and stymies their voice.[6] Even groups that rely heavily on voluntary donations to fund their work (such as many large development aid organizations) have to exercise care not to offend major donors. Lack of financial security also means that energies and time that would otherwise be spent on activism have to be used to seek short-term funding (McMinn 2000).

The role that egalitarian movements can play in promoting change is therefore not easily assessed, and we do not wish to present it simplistically here. What we do want to emphasize, however, is that such movements do exist on a wide scale and that the challenge is how to make them into a more effective political movement.

The groups and organizations that belong to the equality movement have a wide range of objectives. At the most general level, many of them aim at a transformation of existing social systems and social structures: the economy, the political system, the educational system, the legal system, the mass media, families, religious institutions and so on. We have outlined some of the ways in which some of these systems might change in Part II of this book. Groups within the equality movement also have more limited aims, including immediate changes in government policies and legislation as well as middle-range strategies for reducing poverty and homelessness, combating racism and sexual harassment and improving working conditions: issues of egalitarian public policy. Regardless of the character of the objective, it is clear that a major aim of the equality movement must be to influence the opinions and values of society as a whole – its general outlook or ethos. We discuss the importance of this aim, and some of the tasks it involves, in Chapter 11, and return to strategic issues for the movement in Chapter 12.

## The achievements and challenges of the equality movement

Within Ireland, egalitarian movements have affected public policy by engaging in grass-roots activism, targeted campaigning and representation on consultative bodies such as the National Economic and Social Forum.[7] In 1997, Ireland became the first EU country to adopt a national poverty reduction target through the National Anti-Poverty Strategy. A number of the targets set then have already been met, most especially those aimed at reducing the depth of poverty.[8] The Employment Equality Act 1998, the Disability Authority Act 1999, the Equal Status Act 2000 and the Human Rights Commission Act 2000 have already contributed to changing in-equalities of recognition and of opportunity. Groups that were hitherto subjected to discrimination without protection or contention, particularly Travellers and disabled people, have begun to use the law and the new enforcement institutions to assert their rights (Reid 2003). Other achieve-ments of the equality movement include the decriminalization of homo-sexuality, the enactment of legislation protecting women from violence in the home, the development of women's refuges, new approaches to dealing with drug use and AIDS, new legal obligations on local authorities to provide sites for Travellers and the establishment of a minimum wage.

Yet there have also been major set-backs. The reduction in consistent poverty has been accompanied by an increase in economic inequality (Cantillon *et al.* 2001; Combat Poverty 2003b; O'Hearn 2002).[9] Ireland has a very high proportion of low paid workers compared with most OECD countries (only the US has a higher proportion). Ireland also has a relat-ively low level of expenditure on public services which, in turn, impacts adversely on the most vulnerable people in society (Allen 2003; Combat Poverty Agency 2003b). Local authorities have been slow to create and improve accommodation for Travellers and unauthorized halting has been criminalized. Ireland has participated in a Europe-wide exclusion of asylum-seekers, while public discourse and policies on immigration are characterized by a mixture of institutionalized racism, exclusionary nationalism and growing xenophobia (Loyal 2003).

It would be wrong therefore to paint a rosy picture of what the equality movement has achieved in Ireland. However, it is equally mistaken to remain silent about the gains that have been made; to write them out of history. To do so is to induce a sense of hopelessness and fatalism for those actively engaged in promoting social change.

At the ideological level, egalitarian movements have kept equality issues on the public agenda in the face of a deeply inegalitarian politics and ideology promulgated nationally and internationally by neoliberal and neoconservative forces (Covington 1997; Ryan 2003). They have disrupted the consensus that emerged with the glorification of untrammelled capitalism emanating from the Celtic Tiger. They have helped to create a critical, counterfactual culture that challenges the dominant discourse of possessive individualism in particular. They disrupt not only the 'common sense' of everyday taken-for-granted injustice but also the structures that generate these injustices (Cox 1999). The ideals and principles that they have articulated have found expression and further articulation in populist debates about work–life balance and child care; in the assertion that housework and caring work are meaningful and productive forms of labour for both sexes; in challenges to the equation of consumerism with identity, the economy with society and well-being with a life confined to working, earning and spending (Ryan 2003). While many of them remain strongly focused on prohibiting discrimination rather than promoting equality of condition, they have also raised a wider set of issues, such as the need to institutionalize social and economic rights and not just civil and political rights (Irish Commission for Justice and Peace 1998; Human Rights Commission 2003, pp. 12–13).

The equality movement has played a major role in the politics of Northern Ireland as well. Equality is a core principle underpinning the Belfast Agreement of 1998 and the establishment of the Northern Ireland Human Rights Commission. The PAFT (Programme for Appraisal and Fair Treatment) guidelines have been given legislative effect, particularly under Section 75 of the Northern Ireland Act 1998 (McCrudden 1999). This requires all public authorities to submit an equality scheme to the Equality Commission. Equality schemes must follow very specific procedures in terms of consulting with people likely to be affected by them, assessing the impact of policies, monitoring, publishing data, training staff and so on (*ibid.*). In addition, equality proofing has become a key principle of organizational and policy appraisal in both parts of Ireland although it is arguably more institutionally embedded under the provisions of the Northern Ireland Act than under the Republic's Employment Equality and Equal Status Acts (Mullally 2001).

The rise of egalitarian movements within Ireland (Crotty 1998) is paralleled by comparable movements internationally (Bircham and Charlton 2001; Keck and Sikkink 1998; Melucci 1996). While such movements may not always have the capacity to radically alter patterns of distribution in the short term (Hardiman 1998, 2000), they do challenge dominant codes of meaning and interpretation and the rules of normality. They ask questions about who determines codes of interpretation. Their very existence weakens predominant power relations. In particular, new 'community' or 'grass-roots' movements signal a challenge to the dominant discourses of profit maximization, economic self-interest and environmental abuse. These movements are creating new political agendas and redefining the core from the periphery. They are in many respects prophetic, even though their political capacity is as yet unrealized in a clear systematic form.

## Class politics and egalitarian change

The social movement model of egalitarian change challenges the Marxist idea that progressive politics should be centred solely on class. But since this idea continues to have a strong influence on egalitarians, it is important to review the main factors that weaken social class as the primary force for political mobilization. These include the fact that many inequalities are rooted in international trade relations that are determined by nationalist as well as by capitalist interests, that the working class itself has changed dramatically, that large groups of people have little connection to paid work, that there are important divisions within classes, that many people have ceased to identify themselves as working class, that being working class is culturally depreciated, that class politics contains key internal contradictions and that class structures vary across times, cultures and countries. In listing these limiting forces on class mobilization, we are not suggesting that class politics is no longer relevant to equality. What they do show, however, is both that class politics needs to adapt to changes in the workings of capitalism (Lash and Urry 1987) and that it can no longer be seen as the defining element of the equality movement.

For a start, global politics and economics are clearly not governed by class relations alone, they are also governed by imperial relations between nation states, and by the fact that capital ownership and control is often bound up with national interests in militarily and politically powerful states such as the US. There is evidence, for example, that the General Agreement on Tariffs and Trade (GATT) (1993, the Uruguay Round) was influenced substantively by transnational corporations from both the US and the EU (Madeley 2000). Similarly, both the TRIPS agreement (governing intellectual property) and the Common Agricultural Policy of the EU are oriented to protecting the commercial interests of particular powerful western states at the expense of poorer states through the implementation of tariffs, quotas, regulations and conditions of trade that work to the advantage of the already advantaged (Correa 2000). 'The real problem is that some countries or regions have the power to make the world market work to their advantage, while others do not, and have to bear the costs' (Arrighi 2002, p. 34). Famine, forced migration and malnutrition are not simply the outcome of global capitalism working anonymously through its corporate agents; they are also the inevitable by-product of global and regional terms of trade that are designed to assist the wealthiest and most powerful nation states, either individually or collectively.

Within individual countries, focusing solely on capitalist relations ignores the reality of other social orders that generate deep inequalities. In particular it ignores the significance of the patriarchal order in generating inequality (Connell 1987, 1995; Walby 1990) as well as racial and ethnic orders (Crompton 1998; Said 1991) and disability orders (Barnes 1991; Barnes, Oliver and Barton 2002; Barton 1996). While economic inequality may be strongly correlated with social class inequality, the two are not identical (Savage 2000). In addition, social divisions outside of the economy arising from deep nationalist, religious and ethnic differences (such as those in Rwanda, Palestine, Sri Lanka, Northern Ireland, Croatia, Bosnia and Yugoslavia) are a significant determinant of political inequality. To ignore such differences is to ignore the complex character of inequality in many contemporary capitalist states.

The evolving character of the working class and class structures is a further challenge. The most rapidly growing areas of employment in Europe are in the services sector, and in many of these areas (e.g. retail, catering, cleaning, child care, gardening) work is often part-time or temporary (O'Hearn 2002). Workers in these areas are also overwhelmingly female and young, and increasingly belong to groups of ethnic minority migrant workers (Blackwell and Nolan 1990; CSO 2002, pp. 1–3; Lewis 2001; Ruane and Sutherland 1999).[10] It is difficult to integrate part-time and temporary workers into class politics, not only because of their vulnerability, but also because of their isolation and their differences in gender, age and citizenship status. Meanwhile, the decline of the manufacturing sector has decimated the political base of labour politics especially among working class men. This has been exacerbated in many countries (e.g. Germany, France, Ireland) by the ethnic diversification of lower paid workers particularly. There has been in effect 'a dissolution of the working class' as traditionally (and patriarchally) defined (Savage 2000, p. 162).

A further problem is that large sectors of the population are situationally disengaged from class politics because of their age or their dependent status. In the US alone (a country with a high female participation rate in paid employment, see Lewis 2001), 30 per cent of all women of employment age are home workers, making up 16 per cent of the total workforce (Folbre 2001, p. 181). (In Ireland, the proportions are 34 and 18 per cent respectively.) While 54 per cent of people over 15 years old are in employment in Ireland, there is a sizeable minority of adults who are not: 12 per cent are full-time students, 11 per cent are retired, disabled or ill while 4 per cent are unemployed (CSO 2002, Table 19). Retired people and disabled people are generally not active in labour politics. Those for whom the primary source of income is state transfers, an estimated 20 per cent of Irish adults (Fitzgerald 2001), live at a considerable distance from organized labour politics, both geographically and mentally. While they may be defined by middle class professionals and social scientists as working class, they often do not identify with class politics (Devine 1992a, 1992b).

The rise of the 'community sector' outside of the organized labour movement in Ireland and in several other countries (e.g. Britain, Brazil, Chile, India) is a further example of how the organizational basis of class politics is changing. Since the 1980s there has been a growth in community development groups in working class urban areas throughout Ireland. These have joined together to form the Community Workers Co-operative (CWC), speaking and negotiating at national level not only on behalf of working class communities, but also in the interests of other marginalized groups including immigrants, refugees, lone parents, disabled people, older people, low income women and disabled people. They work independently of organized labour and organized left-wing political parties. Other community-style groups emerged in the 1980s and early 1990s to represent the unemployed including the Irish National Organisation of the Unemployed (INOU) and similar organizations in France (Royall 2000). These operated relatively independently from the trade union movement in much of their work. While community groups have shared political agendas with political parties and the unions, they have also opposed them on issues such as reducing taxation.

Another problem for class politics is that of the deep divisions within classes, many of which are organizationally or categorically defined (Tilly 1998).[11] Workers differ considerably in terms of their ownership and control over cultural capital, especially credentialized cultural capital (educational credentials) but also skills acquired in work (Bourdieu 1986, 1996). They also have very different degrees of personal and professional organizational power (Wright 1985).[12] Those who hold valuable cultural capital and organizational power can command an income several times that of other workers. Moreover, these advantages can be used to access other forms of material capital, such as shares and partnerships. Owners of valued cultural capital can also use it to access social capital (see Bourdieu 1986) which in turn gives them access to networks of power and influence, reinforcing their relative labour market dominance. The market position of workers with high levels of cultural capital and organizational power (and consequently their lifestyle, values, patterns of consumption) is very different from that of workers who lack these advantages, although both may be formally defined as waged workers. Consequently their political interests are also different.

Another important factor impacting on the operation of class politics is the emergence of new forms of identity politics in contemporary capitalist societies riven by the politics of possessive individualism (Beck 1992). While many people can name and claim identity with a particular class, there are wide cultural variations in people's identification with their occupationally-linked social class cross-nationally (with Britain having the highest identification with the working class and Japan the lowest) (Marshall *et al.* 1988; see Savage 2000). Even in Britain, which is arguably one of the more class aware (if not class conscious) societies, manual workers tend to identify themselves as 'ordinary working people', neither better or worse than others, rather than as 'working class' (Devine 1992a, 1992b; Savage, Bagnall and Longhurst 2001). In our own research on class identification among second-level students in Ireland, we found that while most middle class students identified with their class, most working class students did not. They claimed to belong to the middle class although a number of indicators, including both parents' occupations and housing location, clearly identified their family of origin as working class (Lynch and Lodge 2002).[13] In addition, identifying with a class is not a strong signifier of political intent; it does not indicate a coherent social outlook or class consciousness in the Marxist sense. There is evidence that although certain attitudes and beliefs are linked to class (Wright 1997), many attitudes of political significance are not rigidly tied to class locations (Evans 1992; Scase 1992).

This lack of identification with class is linked to the distancing of social class, and class politics, that has occurred in popular culture (Pakulski and Waters 1996). Although the highly politicized may express pride in being working class, there is evidence that working class tastes, lifestyles, manners of speaking and so on are not celebrated in society generally. In the cultural sphere, working class manners, tastes, accents and other characteristics are defined as inferior (Bourdieu 1984), and working class people carry the anxiety of this judgement at the core of their being (Sennett and Cobb 1993). The work of Skeggs (1997) and Reay (1998a) suggests that working class women in particular do not want to identify with being 'working class'. Skeggs shows that 'respectability' is central to the formation of working class women's identity. Respectability is achieved by adopting many middle class cultural styles and dis-identifying with 'rough' working class culture. Reay (1998a) goes so far as to suggest that being working class is a 'spoilt identity' in Britain, something that people want to avoid, although Savage (2000, p. 116) suggests that this overstates the degree to which class identifications have been abandoned. What both Skeggs's and Reay's work suggests, however, is that working class identities are not highly regarded in a society that values social mobility and that sees education as the mechanism for leaving one's class if one is working class and for retaining one's class if one is middle class. These attitudes are reinforced in the education system by a meritocratic ideology that defines progress and success as moving on and up the higher education ladder, and by implication the social class ladder (Beck 1992; Lynch 1987). This fixation with social mobility as a measure of personal and public value is not just built into education and public consciousness, but also into the academic analysis of social stratification where researchers fail to reflect on the limited vision of equality underpinning the concept of class mobility itself (Lynch 2000; Swift 2000). The deep daily socialization that occurs in schools through streaming, tracking, grading and other meritocratic practices cannot be dismissed as insignificant in the formation of political identifications.[14] The role of the media in the formation of political identifications is also highly significant. From advertising to soap operas, the lifestyles that are most idealized in the popular media are not those of the working class as traditionally defined.

A related problem for class politics lies in the internal contradictions involved in being working class. Because being working class is a class position determined by exploitation and oppression, it is by its very nature a class position to be avoided (Lynch and O'Neill 1994). Noting the logical impossibility of celebrating one's class only with a view to terminating its very (exploitative) foundations is not new, as mobilizing around class issues has always been a problem for working class politics in particular. What is new, however, is that mobilizing around negative identities is more problematic in a period of history where politics is played out through media-driven images and discourses in a way that was not true when global information and communications systems played a lesser role in framing public opinion and popular perceptions. Identities arising from affiliations related to ethnicity, religion, gender, sexuality or disability are more positively defined in both intellectual analysis and popular perception, leaving them with greater possibilities for mobilizing for political action than is true of class. Class is a contentious and embarrassing subject around which people feel discomfort and unease (Sayer 2002). What seems to be happening is that the working class is being reconstituted through middle class identifications, yet it is far from clear how this will translate into political action. Although Allen (2000) believes that the 'discontented majority' can be mobilized along class lines in Ireland, and there have been 'middle class' strikes challenging downsizing, low wages and casualization (in the banks, in nursing, in the airlines), it is not at all clear how strikes by people who see themselves as separate from and superior to the working class will affect economic inequality.

Several of these problems are connected with a final issue for class politics, namely that class relationships and their political potential vary considerably across times, cultures and countries. For example, largely owing to its colonized status, Ireland did not experience the polarization of the class system that characterized many powerful capitalist states in the late nineteenth and early twentieth centuries. The largest single class in the formative years of the Irish republic was the self-employed, mostly agricultural, class (the petit bourgeoisie). The largest proletarian groups were agricultural labourers and domestic workers. The nationalism that heralded the new state in 1922 continues to affect the politics of today with the two largest political parties still being divided along popular nationalist lines rather than by class politics. Nationalist politics were prioritized over class politics for most of the twentieth century in the Republic of Ireland and are written into the very fabric of the political framework for the Northern Ireland Assembly through the Belfast Agreement of 1998.[15]

Over the last 40 years, the Irish class and occupational structure has changed dramatically with a rise in white collar employment and a massive decline in self-employment in the agricultural sector particularly.[16] Although Ireland became an employee society (and in a general sense became a society in which a majority of the population could be defined as working class in that they were dependent on the sale of their labour for survival), it has not become a propertyless society. There is a sense in which most people in Ireland have quite contradictory class locations: they are part of a small property-owning petit bourgeoisie through their investment in housing (and for a minority in other forms of capital) and part of a broad working class in their fields of employment. The impact of home ownership on the political landscape should not be underestimated. Home ownership in Ireland is higher than anywhere in the EU, with almost 80 per cent of householders owning their own homes. Buying a house is the biggest single investment most people make, while having one's own home is a symbol of status, of well-being and, in the case of large properties, of wealth and power. While homes for many people do not have productive or realizable commercial value during a given lifetime, they do have a serious inheritance value, especially in major urban centres. They can also be used as collateral for other forms of capital acquisition. The use of housing as a form of quasi-commercial investment has been exacerbated by a market-led, rather than a rights-based, approach to housing policy (Drudy and Punch 2001). The lack of regulation of the private rented sector and a steady decline in the provision of public housing at the end of the twentieth and into the twenty-first century, and the operation of a tax system that facilitated investment in housing, has further encouraged the commodification of housing. This has had a potentially conservatizing impact on politics, as the great majority of adults are at one time or another tied into a mortgage for 20 or 30 years of their lives, requiring them to devote a very high percentage of their income to housing. There is a strong fixation with having security of income and a fear of being left to the vagaries of an unregulated housing market and a poorly resourced state sector. There is no doubt but that this has precipitated a TINA ('there is no alternative') mentality in politics, although it has been counterbalanced in the early 2000s by 'creative alternatives' or 'limits' discourses (Ryan 2003).

Thus, in conclusion, there are several constraints on mobilizing around class politics in developed countries, particularly in countries that do not have the same economic history as the major industrialized economies where the classic forms of class division were so visible. This is not to say that class is unimportant in explaining inequality (Marshall, Swift and Roberts 1997; Savage 2000) or even to deny that class-based inequality can be an important source of an egalitarian politics. But it does show that class cannot be relied on as the sole foundation of the movement for equality.

## The gender order and the politics of change

Where, then, should we look for additional social bases of egalitarian change? As indicated above, our answer is that we should look to all of the different social groups that are in subordinate positions in our societies, each of which is the basis of a social movement with its own dynamics. While it would be ideal to spell out the scope and potential of all of the movements that comprise the equality movement, this in not possible in a single chapter. So to illustrate the potential of this approach, we focus here on the ways that the women's movement can be a source for egalitarian change.

The global order is deeply gender-stratified: women remain subordinate to men in terms of power, income and wealth and cultural influence (UNDP 2002). Ireland is no exception.[17] So any serious theory of egalitarian change must address the profound gender differentials in society and the implications of these for different classes and groups of women and men.[18]

To present a picture of gender politics as one in which women are entirely subordinated would be misleading. There have been several profound developments changing the status, and especially the incomes, of women in western societies through the latter part of the twentieth century in particular. Women are bearing fewer children, they are more actively engaged in paid employment, more involved in politics, especially at local level, and more public in their cultural engagements than they were in the first part of the twentieth century. While recognizing social divisions among women based on class, disability, ethnicity, sexuality and other factors, and the effect that these have on their emancipation in different areas of social life, it is also important to accept that major changes have occurred in the general status of women in western societies (Beck 1992; Castells 1997; O'Connor 1998).

Taking Ireland as an exemplary case, we can document clearly the depth of those changes. Women's labour force participation has risen dramatically since the 1980s, wage differentials have narrowed and women's participation in higher education exceeds that of men (Clancy 2001; Fahey, Russell and Smyth 2000). In addition, women bear only half the number of children that they did in the 1970s (Galligan 2000). Despite their relative subordination, women are a rising social group, although their ascent has been blocked at various stages and times, particularly for certain classes of women. The significance of the rise in women's status, and their contradictory location as a subordinate but emerging political force, is that women's groups have within them the sociological potential for generating change. Women are living in the border zones of political and economic life; they are inside and outside simultaneously (O'Connor 1998). They occupy a structural position that is particularly likely to facilitate change, a position where they have reasonable resources and capacities, including organizational skills, a will to change and a deep sense of frustration at the rate of change. They are engaged in struggles in the community sector over education, child care, paid work and unpaid work (McMinn 2000); in the political domain over their status in political parties and trade unions (Galligan 1998; Galligan and Wilford 1998); in higher education over the definition of scholarship at both the core and periphery (O'Connor 2000a); in Northern Ireland over the space that they won while involved in the peace process (Rooney 2002); in the cultural sphere over their place in literature (Bourke *et al.* 2002). Moreover, their resistance has a history in trade unionism (Jones 1988), in culture, in politics and in academia (Connolly 2002; Coulter 1993; Cullen and Luddy 1995; O'Connor 2000a, 2001).

Although women in Ireland do not constitute an organized mass movement in any clear sense (Connolly 2002; Rooney 2002), nonetheless they are at the heart of several egalitarian projects within and outside the institutions of the state.[19] They are a political force if not an organized political movement and they have the capacity to become the latter. The potential for social change that is possible through mobilizing around women's issues, not just reproductive rights but issues of care and related work, has not been fully tested. While there have been campaigns to promote women in politics, in trade unions and in public life, involving such radical groups as Irish Women United, the more mainstream Women's Political Association active in the 1970s and 1980s, and more recently the National Women's Council of Ireland and its affiliated organizations, women-generated issues have not been prioritized in national politics except in relation to reproductive rights when women opposed several attempts to further restrict their constitutional rights (during the abortion referenda in 1983, 1992 and 2002) and during the divorce referenda in 1986 and 1996. In Northern Ireland, the subordination of a women-specific politics has been greatly exacerbated by ethnic and sectarian tensions although there has been a long history of feminist resistance in the North, especially among nationalist women (Ward 1995). In recent years the formation of the Women's Coalition as a small political party has helped to redefine the culture of politics in Northern Ireland itself, although women's issues remain marginal to the largely male-defined peace agenda.

The women's movement offers a distinct possibility for mobilizing political dissent around which other egalitarian projects can coalesce. It has extensive networks and local infrastructures, as well as organizational capability. It has a core egalitarian ideology to unite other equality-focused movements, including older socialist-inspired labour movements.[20] It also has considerable experience in political campaigning from its leading role in the various constitutional campaigns. And, of course, it is rooted in a social group that constitutes half the population. While it shares some of the problems we identified with class politics, the changes experienced by women as a group seem to create more rather than less potential for political action. Although being a woman has been culturally depreciated, that negative evaluation is being powerfully challenged throughout society. The backlash against feminism in the late 1990s and early 2000s is itself an indication of the growing power of feminist perspectives in public life (Horgan 2001). Although feminists continue to challenge gender roles and stereotyping, women no longer feel that the only answer to their subordination would be to escape from being women, that is, to become more like men.

But there are two common objections to making women-generated political concerns the subject of mainstream politics. The first and most common claim parallels one of the central problems with class politics. It is that the deep structural divisions between women (of social class, 'race', age, nationality, ethnicity, disability, sexuality, etc.) make it impossible to mobilize dissent and political action; there is no universal woman (Lister 2000). The claim is made that women are too diverse as a social group, that they are more divided by their differences than united by their common projects (Rooney 2002). None of the aims women share is seen as sufficiently important to overcome these divisions and to mobilize women (or men) to action. The second objection is that any movement led by women would alienate men and thereby inhibit the growth of an egalitarian movement that needs the support of large numbers of women and men.

Despite the plausibility of these arguments, we believe that there are gender-related political projects that affect both women and men and that have mobilizing potential, particularly at the symbolic and ideological levels, for realizing egalitarian social change. In particular, the issue of affective equality is an equality theme that not only unites most women but also has political salience for men. All human beings benefit from relations of love, care and solidarity, and the relations of production governing emotional labour are of special but not exclusive concern to women. These relations are fundamental to the fabric not only of our personal relationships, but also of work relationships and our community and associational relationships. The work involved in building them is as important as the relations of material production and reproduction because all people are engaged in affective networks as well as in economic, political and cultural systems. So although women can be expected to play a leading role in the struggle for affective equality, it has the potential to attract the support of large numbers of men.

The problem is not that there are no gender-generated politics, but rather that the politics that women do generate have been privatized, and in being privatized have been silenced. What is at issue first is the gendered division of labour, not only in paid employment, but also within households in the doing and not doing of care work. Women undertake a disproportionately high level of care and love work throughout the world (Daly 2001). Such work takes place mostly, albeit not exclusively, in the sphere of familial relations (Delphy and Leonard 1992), a sphere that the patriarchal state has largely ignored. The silencing of the politics of care and love work stems in considerable part from the conception of the citizen that has informed contemporary politics. Citizens have been defined as warriors, as workers but never carers (Lister 2000; Sevenhuijsen 1998). Citizenship has been equated with one's public rather than personal obligations and commitments. At EU level, for example, most legal protections are for paid workers, those who contribute to the formal economy (see Chapter 7). Yet no economy or society can function effectively without care work.

Care work, the doing of it, the time and energy it requires, the cost emotionally, materially, socially and politically, is a profoundly important political matter, not just for women, but for caring men and for all who need care and love at different times in their lives. Care is not just an important political issue, it is also a narrative around which people can mobilize as there is an urgency and immediacy about it that does not pertain to other work forms. It is a subject matter that evokes strong emotions not least because the failure to do care work can have immediately harmful effects on those who are vulnerable (Bubeck 1995). In addition, there is no one who is not at some time completely dependent on others, if only in infancy. Most people experience intermittent states of dependence throughout their lives owing to illness or old age, while all of us live in varying degrees of interdependence on others. Thus the politics and economics of care and love work are as crucial to politics as formal employment. Yet its privatized character, and the masculinist codes that define what is a relevant public matter, have meant that it only enters public discourses in many countries when governments respond to labour shortages by offering incentives to entice women out of unpaid care work and into the formal economy.

Affective equality is therefore a core political project that is of major import politically and that could mobilize egalitarian action if it were allowed onto the political agenda. The task is to place affective equality on the political table, for it to gain legitimacy as an issue of political substance and significance in the first instance. To achieve this, the subject must first come to be named and known. These are essentially ideological challenges, and we return to them in Chapter 11.

To identify affective equality as a major theme is not to deny the importance of other egalitarian aims or to pretend that any egalitarian aim is so important that it can overcome all social divisions. But it does show that there is at least one source of egalitarian politics that originates outside the field of class relations and that has the potential for bringing new energy to the equality movement. The task of identifying other such themes, which surely include issues of globalization, human rights, environmental dangers, violence and war as well as issues more traditionally associated with egalitarianism, such as poverty, unemployment, working conditions, education, health care and other public services, is beyond the scope of this book. All of these themes are interconnected and are central to the concerns of various subordinate social groups. The potential strength of the movement for equality lies in the growing realization that its many aims can nevertheless be woven together into the fabric of a better world.

## Conclusion

In this chapter we have argued for a social movement model of egalitarian change as an alternative to the classical Marxist paradigm. We have suggested that there is already an equality movement, and that it has already achieved major social and political successes. To illustrate the potential of egalitarian social movements, we have analysed some of the characteristics and achievements of the women's movement, and have identified affective equality as an objective that the women's movement is well placed to promote. But as we have seen, the social movement model requires us to make significant departures from the Marxist model not just in its social bases but in its ideological and organizational tasks. We take up these tasks in the next two chapters.

# 11
## Ideology and Resistance

> We need to invent a new utopianism, rooted in contemporary social forces, for which – at the risk of seeming to encourage a return to antiquated political visions – it will be necessary to create new kinds of movement. ... Critical reflective social movements are, in my opinion, the future. (Pierre Bourdieu, in Grass and Bourdieu 2002, p. 77)

There has been a long and intense debate within the academic literature regarding the nature and impact of ideology, both as a theoretical construct and as a heuristic device for understanding the dynamics of social change (Abercrombie, Hill and Turner 1980, 1990; Barrett 1991; Eagleton 1994; Laclau and Mouffe 1985; Melucci 1996; Therborn 1980; Thompson 1984, 1990; Van Dijk 1998; Zizek 1994). Ideology has been interpreted in various ways. In orthodox Marxism, it is defined in pejorative terms as a form of false consciousness, while within the Mannheimian tradition it is treated as a social scientific category (Barrett 1991). In this chapter, we adopt a broadly Gramscian (1971) understanding of ideology, which, while recognizing the embeddedness of ideology in praxis, also regards it both as the means by which the powerful establish their hegemony and as an instrument of social transformation and counter-hegemony. We concentrate on the role of ideology in realizing change, with particular reference to the ideologies emanating from egalitarian social movements. We focus in particular on how the theory and practice of affective equality can be a mobilizing narrative given its generative basis in the women's movement and its wider appeal across other social movements.

### The role of ideology

The cultural sites of production where ideas are produced, assessed and promulgated are located both inside and outside the market system, in schools, colleges, community and adult education programmes, in the

212

media, in local and global networks and in religions. Although there is a clear interaction between the relations of economic production and those of cultural production, they are distinct and relatively independent systems (Bourdieu 1984, 1986). Ideologies are certainly affected, but not determined, by economic factors (Althusser 1971; Gramsci 1971). This relative autonomy means that the ideological field of any society is likely to contain contradictory ideas and interpretations, that these ideas will not always reinforce existing economic relations, and that, on the contrary, they can sometimes serve to mobilize changes and to present counterfactual perspectives and utopias that are themselves grounded in the social lives of the ordinary, everyday 'organic intellectual' (Gramsci 1971).

Ideology is a particularly important field for resistance in contemporary societies because of the changing institutional operation of power. Power is not confined to institutions such as the state or capitalist firms, important as these may be. It is also diffused throughout global networks and communication flows. It has both a material and a symbolic reality, each of which reinforces the other. The symbolic realm, the set of cultural codes though which the world is interpreted and defined, is of growing importance given the development of planet-wide systems of information and communication that can scope and map new intellectual and moral terrain outside the economy.

The capacity to collect, process and transfer information has developed, over the last 25 years, at an unprecedented pace. Knowledge and information flows constitute a core web of social practice in an information-driven age.[1] Throughout the world, people's understanding of social phenomena is increasingly mediated by print, audio and televisual media. Much of what people come to know is understood in terms of the frames and codes produced in global (and local) communications systems (Melucci 1985, 1996). In countries with high levels of literacy and extensive media usage, much of what is defined as political is dependent on what is named in media accounts of public debates. Other institutions of ideology, such as education, are often placed in a subordinated role. All too often, if issues are not named in the media, they are not recognized; if they are not discussed regularly in public they cannot become generative forces in social action (Gamson 1998).

Power and control is exercised, therefore, not only in the market or in control over the means of production, but also in the control of the means and codes of understanding. Those who control the dominant codes of information and communication networks exercise considerable influence over our thought processes, our tastes and our interpretations of events. They provide us with the operational codes, the formal rules and knowledge systems whereby we understand and evaluate the world. '*The new power lies in the codes of information and in the images of representation around which societies organize their institutions, the people build their lives, and decide their behaviour. The sites of this power are people's minds'* (Castells 1997, p. 359; italics in the original). To say this is not to deny the significance of social movements in generating change, it is merely to emphasize that in a globalized telecommunications and educational order, media movements and education movements are integral to the operation of social movements themselves.

Ideologies or systems of ideas, disseminated through global and local information systems and institutionalized in codes of practice and modes of organization, are therefore one of the primary engines of change (or of resistance to change) in contemporary societies. Thus, if we want to promote equality we must engage in the struggle to control both the means of understanding and the codes of understanding. That is to say, we must exercise influence on the technologies and institutions that disseminate ideas and on frames and codes of interpretation, if necessary by using alternative media outside the mainstream.

To create a public space for new egalitarian ideals is a major technical and political challenge, not least in a world where there is growing evidence of tiered communication systems, one for those with the income, education, technological equipment and expertise to access it, and one for those without the necessary resources, time, education and technology (UNDP 1999). The interaction between social movements and media organizations does provide access for some new ideas, depending on a variety of factors including the movements' media skills, the norms and practices of media organizations and the relation between new narratives and existing cultural assumptions (Gamson 1998; Gamson and Meyer 1996; see also Shaw 2001, ch. 5). But because so many of the media-based global communications networks are already connected with dominant sectors within the economy, forming a type of global corporate web (Castells 1996; Hamelink 1994; McChesney 1998), it would be naïve to assume that the communications industry is politically neutral. In the US alone, entertainment products are one of the largest exports, and both states and providers of communications services exercise censorship and control over communication. Ultimately, our aim must be to democratize mass communications – a major political challenge, but one that we do not have to reject as impossible (Hamelink 1995; McChesney and Nichols 2002). In the meantime, we must continue to make use of the opportunities offered by mainstream and alternative media to disseminate new ideas.

## Ideology and structure

One of the major objections to an emphasis on ideology is that the problem of inequality is structural rather than ideological. Inequality is institutionalized in relations of exploitation (Wright 1985) and in organizational and political categorizations (Tilly 1998). So surely, it is argued, we should concern ourselves with these relations of production, consumption and exchange rather than with their ideological reflection. This objection is right to emphasize social structures, as the rest of this book makes clear. Where it is mistaken is in claiming that they can be understood and changed independently of attention to ideology. While economic relations of production are profoundly influential in determining the course of history, they do not determine it. On the contrary, what is too often forgotten in debates about institutions and structures of exploitation is that they represent the realization of historically accepted inegalitarian principles and ideologies. Whether one is talking of the subordination of women, the stratification of the labour force or the practice of confining and incarcerating the poor and the mentally ill in workhouses, prisons or mental hospitals, one of the reasons why these relations of exclusion or subordination became embedded in social practice is because of the acceptance of ideologies regarding the subordination, control and ordering of particular classes of persons (Condren 1989; Foucault 1977; Lerner 1986; McDonnell 2003).

Yet there is always a struggle over cultural codes, a struggle that takes place in many sites that interface with politics and the economy, particularly within the informal networks and unregulated and decentred systems of civil society (Cohen and Arato 1992). There are cracks and contradictions that can be exploited for ideological challenge and resistance (Freire 1972, 1998; Gramsci 1971; Habermas 1970; hooks 1994; McAdam 1996; McLaren 1995; Tarrow 1998a, ch. 7; Zald 1996). Some of the very ideas that dominant groups use to justify their privileges are capable of being turned against them, and to this extent at least they never exercise complete ideological hegemony (Scott 1985). Those who challenge oppression do not have to invent entirely new systems of values and beliefs, because they can always find footholds in the belief structures of their own societies. If they could not, their efforts would be doomed from the start.

Technological changes can also facilitate the creation and dissemination of new ideologies with the use of satellite television, the internet and related communication technologies. Despite the development of powerful, centrally controlled communications networks, there are alternative networks and information flows that contest and challenge the dominant codes (Hamelink 1995). The anti-globalization movement, the environmental movement and the feminist movement have all used new communication technologies very effectively for the purpose of resistance (Castells 1997).

These 'new' social movements, built around complex and diverse identities resisting disenfranchisement and marginalization, have become one of the most important sources for resistance to the neoliberal project of building a global economy that ignores the interests of civil society. Such new movements 'anchor power in some areas of the social structure, and build from there their resistance or their offensives in the informational struggle about the cultural codes constructing new behaviour and, thus, new institutions' (Castells 1997, p. 360). The intensity and pervasiveness of ideological struggles, both within powerful groups themselves (such as that between the technically-oriented and the arts/humanities-oriented intelligentsia, or between neoconservatives and neoliberals) and between these and egalitarian social movements, indicate the importance of the ideological terrain and the role of frames of understanding in legitimating both power and resistance.[2]

Thus the relationship between structure and ideology is complex and interactive. We therefore agree with Harstock (1998, p. 25) when she says that 'we cannot work effectively for change without understanding the importance of ideas and recognizing the reciprocal effect of consciousness on actions and organizations'. It follows that 'the production of representations of the social world ... is a fundamental dimension of political struggles' (Bourdieu 1993, p. 37).

## The dynamics of resistance

Major structural inequalities will only be addressed when there is a public commitment to changing them. The political ideologies that define and defend unequal social structures must therefore be deconstructed and an alternative political understanding must be articulated and legitimated. While the success of Thatcherism, for example, was undoubtedly related to such material factors as the offer of individualized capital ownership on a mass scale, it was also related to the systematic way in which its ideas were articulated and sold as a vision of a new social order in which everyone would be a winner (preferably an entrepreneur) in the consumer game (Hall 1988). The time and effort put into developing a concept of the so-called 'Third Way' in Britain (Giddens 1998) is indicative of how New Labour learned from the Tories the object lesson of ideological diffusion and legitimation.[3]

For a social movement to name and frame the political agenda in a given society it must articulate a 'utopian' alternative in the sense of a picture of a better society. It must also develop an identifiable strategy for realizing these utopian goals, grounded in the materiality of existence. To mobilize for social change, it is vital to set out alternatives to the way things are. These political alternatives, emanating from the often unarticulated frustrations, concerns and anxieties of the body politic, need to engage the imagination of relevant publics before they can develop political momentum. This is especially true in most states in Western Europe, in which there are reasonably engaged democratic structures and institutions (Offe 1984).

Mobilizing narratives are necessary to unify movements and to give a sense of common purpose to those engaged in them (Lenin 1902; Lukács 1971; Melucci 1996, ch. 18). While 'resistance identities' – groups that reject dominant trends – may not develop 'project identities' – groups that seek to transform society – in any simple or straightforward manner, especially in highly fragmented societies where there is a plurality of interests at any given movement (Castells 1997, p. 357), a coherently articulated ideology is nevertheless central to transformative political action. It is a vital tool in any counter-hegemonic struggle (Gramsci 1971).

The first challenge that has to be met in developing a new political ideology is identifying core political concerns within a society around which it is possible to mobilize dissent against established ideologies. While it is possible to name certain issues on a cross-cultural basis, account must also be taken of the nuances of national politics and local circumstances.[4] In most European countries, the challenge is to identify the culturally specific sites and issues around which resistance can be mobilized against the ideologies of neoliberalism and, especially in terms of sexual morality, neo-conservativism. To be effective, an alternative ideology must have political resonance within the society; it must be readily recognizable and identifiable as bearing the concerns of a significant majority of people at that point in time. It must be framed in concepts and codes that are part of the everyday language of the society in question. The articulated utopianism must tap into unmet needs and desires as well as capitalizing on frustrations and anxieties. It has to tap into people's emotions as well as their beliefs (Tarrow 1998a, ch. 7; Taylor 1995):

> A true revolutionary project ... to which a utopian dimension is natural, is a process in which the people assume the role of subject in the precarious adventure of transforming and recreating the world. ... Revolutionary utopia tends to be dynamic rather than static; tends to life rather than death; to the future as a challenge to man's [*sic*] creativity rather than as a repetition of the present; to love as liberation of subjects rather than as pathological possessiveness; to the emotions of life rather than to cold abstractions.... . (Freire 1972, p. 72)

The symbolic representation of the interests of groups helps to transform them to a higher level of self-consciousness, a level that is vital for political mobilization. These symbolic expressions are not merely symptoms of the social relations that govern their emergence. By creating new meanings and understandings, ideologies become social forces in themselves, helping to shape social movements and determining the nature of the social relations that develop around them (Thompson 1990). Although there is unlikely to be a singular and universally agreed objective in any movement, it is possible to develop common ideological frames within which mobilization can occur. Even though we know from sociological analysis that there is great divergence in attitudes and values within classes (Evans 1992; Heath, Jowell and Curtice 1985) and in other social movements such as the women's movement (Connolly 2002; Rooney 2002) such diversity does not preclude the development of mobilizing narratives. The narratives may change over time; they may be partial rather than comprehensive and different group members may hold them with varying degrees of intensity. Nevertheless they can become part of what constitutes political reality through their framing and interpretations of social relations and events.[5] They can help to create unity in diversity, although such unity need not imply complete consensus or lack of conflict (McLaren 2000, p. 202).

## Egalitarianism as a mobilizing ideology

As explained in Chapter 10, we think that the project of the left needs to be built around a set of egalitarian movements that includes class-based struggles but is not confined to them. Such movements are rooted in a wide range of identities and projects. Some are built around simple resistance to established interpretations and structures, while others are more ambitious and are focused on creating new sets of meanings and institutions, enshrining alternative beliefs and principles in global and local practices. To strengthen this movement of movements it is necessary to articulate a set of mobilizing narratives, something that is already happening as emerging movements 'challenge and expand dominating codes and languages' (Feldman 2001, p. 148).[6] By so doing, they help reconfigure the social, political and economic relations underpinning the established orders (Melucci 1996).

In the contemporary age, the new narratives need, above all, to disestablish neoliberalism, given its hegemonic status as a discourse of public value (O'Neill 1999). They have to break the silence and fatalism that neoliberalism has engendered through the corrosive development of a TINA ('There Is No Alternative') and end-of-history mentality (Coulter and Coleman 2003). To accomplish these tasks, the equality movement needs to create a radical rupture from neoliberal principles, both in theory and practice. In particular, it needs to distance itself from anti-egalitarian ideologies and projects that emphasize property rights and 'deserved' inequalities, that pay no more than lip service to the idea of equal opportunity and that are used to justify capitalism, patriarchy and other oppressive structures.

We believe that an egalitarian perspective drawing on the ideas set out in Chapter 2, and especially the ideal of equality of condition, can play an important role in these projects. We regard this as a potential mobilizing discourse for a number of reasons. First of all, it creates a clear rupture with the dominant neoliberal justifications for inequality. Secondly, it integrates the project of socialism with cognate projects of feminism, disability rights, human rights, ethnic and minority rights and other equality-oriented movements. In this regard it creates a common bond across a diverse but deeply interdependent range of interests. The development of such a bond strengthens each separate egalitarian project by highlighting its universal status as part of a wider global project. It gives interrelated, but frequently unaligned, social movements a common language and set of projects, words and deeds that unify them in an intellectually cogent and logical manner. This common bond, grounded itself in a deep respect for differences in beliefs and priorities, allows groups to identify common concerns and to construct new codes of interpretation and understanding that can be used in turn to undermine anti-egalitarian ideologies and institutions. Thirdly, the discourse of equality defines these social movements as principled movements with a political purpose that goes beyond self-interest, rather than as sectional interest groups. Fourthly, egalitarianism provides an overarching framework whereby the pursuit of social, economic and cultural rights is naturally integrated with the promotion of civil and political rights. Fifthly, egalitarianism taps into a number of powerful emotions including love, solidarity, empathy, pride and indignation. Finally, egalitarianism is rooted in the political traditions and cultures of democratic countries and of wider regional and global contexts. At the European level, egalitarianism has deep historical roots within mainstream socialist, communist, feminist, anarchist and social democratic politics. This commitment to equality and social justice has been given renewed expression in legislative and social policy provisions in the last 20 years within the EU and in the growing number of signatories of the European Convention on Human Rights. At a global level, we have already remarked that both the Universal Declaration of Human Rights and the Charter of Principles adopted by the World Social Forum in Porto Allegre in 2001 are fundamentally egalitarian in character (see Chapters 2 and 10).

### Affective equality as a mobilizing narrative

In Chapters 2 and 4 we outlined the terms of an egalitarian framework that could form a basis for political mobilization. In Chapter 2 we pointed out that subordinate groups tend to be worse off in many dimensions of equality but not necessarily in all of them. In Chapter 4 we suggested that certain social systems are more important than others in generating inequality for specific groups. For both of these reasons, the equality priorities of groups can and do vary.

Given the range of equality concerns that exist in any society, it is not possible in one chapter to examine the role of ideology in challenging inequalities in each and every case. In this chapter we focus on the issue of affective inequality, that is, on the promotion of equality within the system concerned with providing and sustaining relationships of love, care and solidarity. We concentrate particularly on the mobilizing potential of the principles of equality of love, care and solidarity and of an egalitarian division of care work, for two main reasons. First, the ideas of solidarity and care play a central role within both old and new social movements. They draw on a tradition of solidarity that is deeply embedded in the 'old' labour, socialist and social democratic movements, as well as implicitly tapping into the wider principle of 'loving thy neighbour as thyself', which is central to most major religious traditions and permeates the secular culture of modern societies. But they also draw on the care narratives and practices of a number of 'new' social movements, including the human rights movement, the women's movement, the anti-globalization movement, the environmental movement and the animal rights movement, all of which are directly or indirectly concerned with issues of care and protection, be it for other persons, animals or the environment. Narratives of love, care and solidarity are therefore familiar, if latent, political narratives, a factor that greatly enhances their scope for facilitating political mobilization (Thompson 1990). The second reason for focusing on affective equality is that care has become a salient political issue at this juncture in history. The issues of caring and of the emotional work underpinning it are of increasing importance in the 'quality of life' debate internationally, where the intensification and casualization of so much of paid work has meant that personal time as well as care time is increasingly under threat (Daly 2001). The debate about love and care has therefore begun to move from being a personal problem to being a public issue. A hitherto politically unarticulated concern has been taken out of the private realms of discussion into public discourse.

## Love, care and solidarity as political themes

As we pointed out in Chapter 2, caring for others and being cared for and loved by them are integral to everyday existence. In cases of deep dependency, care is essential to basic survival, but more generally it is a central element in the mental and emotional well-being of most people. Human persons are not simply rational actors in social life, they are also emotional actors engaged with others at various levels of intimacy and care throughout their existence. Moreover, there is a wealth of psychological research demonstrating the central importance of social supports and care not only for mental well-being but also for physical health. Being supported and loved does not just free us from psychological distress; it enables us to live life more creatively, spiritually and socially.[7] Care is therefore a subject about which people feel very deeply. The depth of feeling that people have for those for whom they care, and for those who care about them, is in itself a generative source of political mobilization.

Although the issues of love, care and solidarity may have their roots in the political discourses of the women's movement, they are central to men as well as women, as dependence and interdependence are endemic to human relations regardless of gender (Fraser and Gordon 1997). Dependency is a defining feature of early childhood. It also arises when one is frail due to old age, severe impairment or illness. There is no person who is not at some time, to a greater or lesser degree, dependent on others. Interdependence is an inevitable correlate of normal human functioning. From the intimate to the most impersonal parts of our lives, we all live in varying states of interdependency (Nussbaum 1995a, 1995b).

Issues about caring are important not only to our family relationships but to our relations with everyone in need of care. Older people in many western societies may lack a care option outside of institutionalization, an option that is often seen as either emotionally or socially undesirable for cultural and personal reasons. People with impairments may require care on a regular or even full-time basis, yet they often lack opportunities for intimacy and solidarity. In many parts of the world people may have few options around love or care because of their forced migration across countries to find employment (the Philippines is a case in point, where the export of care workers, mostly women, is a huge growth industry: Daly 2001, p. 5). The millions who become refugees throughout the world each year because of war and political repression are also deprived in a most serious way of relations of love, care and solidarity; they have often been separated from their families and children. In many countries, particularly in Sub-Saharan Africa, the loss of life through HIV/AIDS has created a huge caring crisis for children (Arrighi 2002).

As we discussed in Chapter 4, affective relationships extend in many directions. The care and love relations involved in child-rearing are, arguably, the most defining of all affective relations. They are immeasurable in scope and intensity; they take multiple forms in both material and emotional terms and extend generally from childhood well into adulthood. When children are deprived of love and care, the harm that is endured is equally pervasive in its intensity and scope. Love, care and solidarity also play a key role in work relations, and not just because firms use these emotions to maximize customer relations and profits (Hochschild 1983). Where there is a lack of care for and among workers, where people have no time to listen to one another, to take account of personal needs or to modify work practices so that they are supportive of caring, there is an inevitable deterioration in the quality of work relations (Sayer 1995). Solidarity also plays a crucial role in voluntary and community associations from sports clubs to tenants' and residents' associations, both in their internal operations and in the bonds they establish among neighbours. Even though the extent of emotional engagement and interdependence varies greatly in scope and intensity across different spheres of life, there is an opportunity to show care and solidarity with others to a greater or lesser degree in every sphere. Bonds of solidarity and care are fundamental to the fabric of social life, and indeed of mental health.

Recognizing the significance of the solidarity narrative for contemporary politics is not to deny the persistence of contrary trends, especially in relation to the theme of love itself. While sentimental and romantic love remains a major theme in popular culture, people are sometimes very uncomfortable in speaking about intimacy and love. Even youth culture evinces cynicism about love, with popular songs often challenging the possibility of being loved in any trusting sense (hooks 2000). This growing cynicism about love among the young is coupled with a cultural silence about it among adults, even among those who privately know its significance:

> As a society we are embarrassed by love. We treat it as if it were an obscenity. We reluctantly admit to it. Even saying the word makes us stumble and blush... . Love is the most important thing in our lives, a passion for which we would fight or die, and yet we're reluctant to linger over its names. (hooks 2000, p. 2, quoting Diane Ackerman)

Resistance to narratives of love, care and solidarity comes not only from those who regard such issues as private, unnameable, non-political matters, but also from those who fear that such narratives would distract from a necessary materialist analysis of economic and political relations. What is all too often ignored is the materiality of love and care: the affective and the economic are deeply implicated with each other. Not only are many of the tasks of love and care deeply practical, but much of the work involved in love and care is increasingly commodified. Within the services sector, the counselling and therapy industries are growing at an accelerated pace, while the so-called 'sex industry' (organized prostitution in particular) is global in its scope and capacity.

Leaving aside the deeply inegalitarian relations upon which the prostitution industry is founded, not only between women and men, but also between richer and poorer peoples and between the old and the young (K. Barry 1995), there are other serious equality issues arising from the commercialization of different forms of intimacy. The commodification of intimacy and caring is problematic firstly because it involves the commercialization of a social good that develops naturally in intimate (and work and neighbourhood) relations of dependency and interdependency. Once it becomes commodified and marketed, there is a growing probability that access to love and care will depend on a given individual's market capacity to purchase intimacy and services, with all the attendant loss that this will bring for those who cannot buy 'good' care, or any care. The commodification of intimacy and care also facilitates a deskilling around care and love work in non-commercial zones, be these families, friendships, partnerships, workplaces or neighbourhoods, as outsourcing is an option, particularly for those who can pay. The deskilling around care work feeds back into capitalist interests in very direct ways: it creates a market for a social good that was and is a natural feature of the everyday interdependencies of human existence, and in so doing opens up new spaces for profit maximization. By making caring costly, both directly and in terms of opportunities lost, it also reduces the incentive to initiate relations that have care costs, including having children, taking responsibility for older persons or persons with impairments who are in need of care, or participating in employment-related and community activities that are solidaristic in nature. The bonus for capitalism is considerable when care is commodified, at least in the short term,[8] not just because of the new markets that it creates, but also because it precipitates the development of the 'unattached worker', the person with no ties who is free to migrate as capital requires, and who is not bound by the belongingness of family, friends, work colleagues or neighbours (Beck 1992).

We are not suggesting, therefore, that the solidarity narrative should replace the material, but that the two are complementary. A narrative of love, care and solidarity helps to create a space in public discourse where dissent from market-led ideologies and their effects on people's vital concerns can be articulated and mobilized. At a cultural level, it gives public recognition to feminist and socialist conceptions of the self as an inter-dependent and social being, while challenging the capitalist conception of the self as an economic maximizer, defined by what one can produce or buy on the market (Fitzsimons 2002).

Love, care and solidarity are not the only mobilizing themes in a wide and inclusive egalitarian project, but they have the potential to catch the public imagination, to unlock other debates about equality and to grant them political legitimacy. The ideology of inclusiveness that is at the heart of love, care and solidarity has the potential to cross borders, including those of nation states (hooks 1984, 2000). It focuses public concern on the needs of others, as opposed to one's self-interest as an economic actor. It challenges the public codes of 'carelessness' that have been institutional-ized and legitimated in public debate in the name of progress and develop-ment. It opens the way for feelings of substantive concern for others to become part of the public narrative for understanding the world, thereby challenging ritualized rationalizations of preventable human suffering, be it of famine, war or serious illness. By sensitizing the body politic to the pres-ence of others, it helps to undo the corruption of moral sentiment that has been the inevitable by-product of untrammelled and glorified capitalism. By defining the care of others both as a public value and ultimately as a political and economic necessity, it helps to alter our sense of what is valued, and consequently our political priorities.

The significance of bringing a discourse of care and solidarity into public debate cannot be underestimated. The articulation and legitimation of principles of love, care and solidarity in the public domain is crucial to cre-ating an empathetic public that will move politics from its overriding focus on self-interest to a politics of mutual concern. It will help to form a mob-ilizing narrative for the growing ethical concerns of contemporary publics (Ray and Sayer 1999).

## Caring work and the women's movement

The care-related narrative has the potential to build on one of the most significant social movements of modern times, namely the women's movement. Although the women's movement is often portrayed in the media as sectional and entirely self-serving for a feminist minority,[9] it has been very active at grass-roots level in the major social movements of the last 30 years (Castells 1983). Within Ireland alone, much of the work of the peace movement in Northern Ireland and of the community movements in the Republic has been undertaken by women (Connolly 2002; Rooney 2002).

The women's movement has played a central role in naming 'private' issues in the public domain and in a very real sense making the personal political. Much of the thrust of the movement has been devoted to articulating the negative implications both of the gendered division of labour and of power differentials within the privatized family. It has succeeded in making violence within the family domain a serious political issue within a relatively short period of time.

While issues of love, care and solidarity have been addressed at some length in feminist analysis (Bubeck 1995; Delphy and Leonard 1992; Sevenhuijsen 1998) they have not been articulated in the public discourse of feminism to the same degree as other issues. One obvious reason for this is the historical association of care and love work with the oppression of women, through the unequal, gendered division of care labour in the private domain and through the institutionalization of care work as low-paid women's work in the public domain. Although care work is not degrading in itself, the social conditions within which most care and love work is undertaken (of isolation, marginalization and subordination) have led inevitably to care-related work becoming devalued by association. There appeared to be a fear of being defined as conservative or reactionary if one took caring work seriously.

It was therefore more conservative women who first raised care as a public issue (O'Connor 1998). They articulated concerns voiced by lower paid workers, in particular, about the impossibility of caring for their families while being forced to take up paid work at low wages. They named the deep sense of frustration that many women, and some men, felt about the conflict between paid work and caring, a conflict that was named but not appreciated by the mainstream (and often middle class) women's movement and the male-dominated labour movement.[10] In an Irish context, the mainstream women's movement also largely ignored the political concerns of women working full-time at home, including their dependent status and their lack of any independent means of support.[11] The rise of new anti-feminist movements, including those of separated and divorced men, has taught us a vital lesson about the political importance of caring, especially in a society where there is no clearly defined status for carers or caring work.[12]

Recent feminist analyses of caring work, however, have begun to reclaim love work and care work as an appropriate theme of feminist concern (Kittay 1999; Nussbaum 1995a, 1995b, 2000; Sevenhuijsen 1998). These studies have demonstrated the significance of caring as an egalitarian ideological theme emanating from the women's movement, a powerful and inclusive theme that has a strong resonance in our political culture at this point in time. Feminist scholars have begun to recognize that the women's sector has generated a set of discourses and projects that have political salience for large numbers of people, well beyond the feminist movement itself (hooks 2000).

## The political significance of emotional work

Emotional work, particularly the emotional work involved in building relations of solidarity, caring and loving, is central to human existence. As Engels (1845) observed, the physical, social and emotional reproduction of the human species is one of its key projects. But while caring work has always been a major part of human work, it was not seen as such until it was politically problematized by feminists in the late twentieth century. A major reason for its politicization was the challenge by women to the expectation, not only that they should undertake a disproportionate share of care and love work, but that they were morally and socially obliged to do this work, usually without pay (Bubeck 1995; Delphy and Leonard 1992; Folbre 1994; Lynch and McLaughlin 1995). Women's growing economic independence, combined with their increasing control over sexual reproduction, enabled them to withdraw from economic dependency to a considerable degree. Like men, they developed options around care work. This has generated a debate about care work especially in societies where it has not been successfully commodified, which in reality are most societies (Daly 2001).

Of course, even in those societies where much of caring is commodified, the most intimate aspects of caring, love labour, cannot be commodified without undermining the very meaning of intimate relationships themselves (Lynch 1989). A clear example of this is engaging in an intimate event such as having a meal with a partner or friend. One cannot pay someone to go to the cinema or pub with one's partner and pretend it is oneself, to have dinner with a friend instead of oneself. The presence of the intimate other is what makes the meal or visit to the theatre special and important; the purpose of the meeting is to meet the other in an intimate context. There is no possible way of substituting or commodifying the intimate part of the relationship without changing the nature of the relationship itself. The essence of such relationships is the maintenance of the bond in itself, and this requires the time and presence of people involved.

Changing expectations about gender, including both the increased participation by women in paid work and an increased emphasis on the role of men in intimate relationships, have put increased pressure on love labour of this kind and have contributed to the emergence of emotional labour as a public issue.

Thus the work of love and care has become a potentially mobilizing narrative because of the growing tensions between care work and capitalism, and especially between care work and paid employment, in the context of the changing situation of women and changes in working patterns for both sexes. In much of the so-called developed world, women and men struggle with the conflict between paid work and unpaid care work as paid work has increased in intensity and flexibility. This conflict is exacerbated in certain societies by the time spent commuting to work, something that greatly lengthens the working day (Murphy-Lawless and Kennedy 2002). In Ireland the issues have been intensified by the changing economic status of women and the failure of the state to address the care needs that have arisen from this change.[13] Throughout Europe the crisis over the work involved in caring has become a political issue although it is not named in these terms. It is defined as a 'quality of life' issue, a problem of 'work–life balance' that demands 'family friendly' policies from employers and governments (EOC 2002).

Women's and men's lives are not as divorced from each other as they were before both the feminist and reproductive revolutions occurred. In western countries at least, there is an increasing overlap in the life experience of women and men, although men can and do resist the changing gender order when it diminishes their power (Connell 1995, 2000). Even though men may not expect to do as much care work as women do, women increasingly expect men to share this work. There is a growing resistance to the established gendered orders, in work, in power relations and in emotional relations (Connell 1987; Delphy and Leonard 1992; Hays 1996; Hochschild 1989). Women's ability to control their fertility has meant not only a decline in the birth rate, but also a very significant decline in the amount of time women spend in full-time childcare. While care work has to be done, the nature of the work has changed with a focus on the quality as well as the quantity of childcare, and with attention being given to the care of older dependent persons and not just young children. The gender of the carer is becoming visibly less significant than the quality and availability of care. So questions about care work, although first raised by the women's movement as a result of the traditional division of labour in the family and other affective contexts, have become questions for everyone.

## Conclusion

We have argued that the promotion and diffusion of egalitarian narratives, narratives that are emerging from within the various global and local movements for social justice, human rights and equality, are vital for promoting a political culture that moves us beyond a politics focused on narrow economic self-interest. The task of naming and claiming an intellectual space for new narratives in public discourse is an ideological task. It demands reflexivity, dialogue and debate among all those with an interest in equality-oriented change, while requiring that all involved remain rooted in the material reality of political practice. While it is essential that egalitarian ideas are grounded in the class, gender, ethnic, age, disability and other egalitarian movements of our time, it is also important that there are ideals or utopian alternatives with which people can identify. There is a need to have coherent egalitarian narratives that resonate with the daily concerns of all types of political actors, and that build on but go beyond sectional interests.

We have suggested that one of the major generative themes within contemporary egalitarian narratives is the theme of affective equality. The interest in affective equality has emerged with the systematic denial of the intrinsic interdependency of all human beings within neoliberal discourse and with capitalist interests in the commodification of care itself. The self has been defined as a self-inventing entrepreneur, for whom the rules of the market are the only appropriate ethic. Yet having the time to care and be cared for, in work, in one's personal life and in one's associational relations, is vital for the well-being of all human beings.

It is widely assumed that what motivates people to engage in politics is their self-interest, especially their economic self-interest. But while people clearly do care about their economic well-being, it is not the only concern that moves them politically. Political motivations are more complex. People are not simply economic maximizers, they are also emotional beings living in states of dependency and interdependency for their entire existence. Life is lived through the medium of relations with others, and through the varying attachments that we create. The domain of emotional work, and the love and care work that is central to this field, is therefore a political matter. Its political import arises not only because access to love and care affects the quality of our psychological well-being, but also because it affects our health and capacity to work in the material world itself. The unequal sexual division of labour that governs the doing of care and love work further reinforces the political salience of this work.

But humans are moral beings as well. They can be, and often are, deeply motivated by a desire to pursue the public good, particularly if they live in a civic culture that develops their moral sensibilities and their sense of fairness and justice. In any case, justice and self-interest are rarely in conflict, especially when people's non-economic interests are taken into account. For most people, a society dedicated to equality in all its dimensions would also be in their own best interests.

Without a discourse of care, solidarity and commitment to public welfare, at both local and global levels, egalitarian politics is less likely to flourish. Fostering human rights and egalitarian values demands not only a respect for civil, political, social and economic rights, but also for people's needs to care and be cared for as interdependent human beings. For all of these reasons, the promotion of affective equality is a key ideological task for the equality movement.

# 12
# Strategic Issues for the Equality Movement

What organizational forms, what methods of action should egalitarians adopt? In this chapter, we identify some key issues for the equality movement: the problem of coordination, the role of political parties, the tension between radicals and moderates and the interplay of means and ends. We argue for a 'strategic pluralism' that recognizes the diversity of the equality movement and makes a virtue out of the range of strategies pursued by different groups and organizations. By setting out in a dispassionate way the pros and cons of various strategies, we hope to convince activists to appreciate and support those who take different approaches to promoting equality.[1]

It is not our purpose here to discuss the specific tactics with which the various components of the equality movement can achieve their aims. These are matters on which many activists have a great deal of expertise, and although there is a need for more effective sharing of this knowledge, this is not the place to attempt that.[2] Nor is it the aim of this chapter to analyse the complete set of conditions under which the equality movement can hope to make progress. Those include events and institutional constraints that are largely beyond our control. What we are concerned with here are questions the movement has to answer for itself. As in the rest of this book, our focus is particularly on the questions confronting the equality movement in economically developed countries, because this is the part of the world we are most familiar with and because the strategic issues for such countries are rather different from those facing the movement elsewhere. We also want to emphasize what will be clear enough from our analysis, that we have no intention of laying down the law for other activists. We simply hope that our perspective and reflections will be of use to others in deliberating on their own part in the movement for equality.

## Coordinating action

The coordinated action of many individuals is clearly a necessary condition for egalitarian change. Other things equal, then, it seems obvious that the greater the coordination, the more powerful the equality movement and the stronger its results. A general strike makes more of an impact than a local strike. A demonstration of 200 000 makes more of an impact than a demonstration of 200. But coordination has its costs. At a basic technical level, it is more expensive to coordinate the actions of thousands of people than of hundreds, even if economies of scale reduce the cost per participant. Egalitarian movements inevitably have limited resources, so these costs will always be important. Coordinating big groups also has a political cost, because it becomes harder to ensure that decisions are fully supported by everyone involved. This is an issue for all social movements but it is particularly important for the equality movement because of its commitment to equal power. Most of the groups constituting the equality movement have emerged as a response to the experience of being subordinated and marginalized by powerful elites. It is not surprising that they do not want to be subordinated and marginalized within the equality movement itself.

For these reasons, the structure of the equality movement is less like an organization than a network. Even in a small country like Ireland, there are hundreds of groups working for equality but no national organization that brings all these groups together. Where national structures do exist, for example in the National Women's Council of Ireland, there is a strong commitment to consensual decision-making and a continuing challenge to ensure that everyone is included. Attempts at national organizing in other areas have often broken down in splits over principles and tactics. Despite this fragmentation, there have been a number of successful alliances among egalitarian groups for specific purposes, such as the defeat of the 2002 referendum to tighten restrictions on the availability of abortion.[3]

At an international level, the sheer diversity of groups dedicated to aspects of egalitarian change is staggering. For example, the 2002 World Social Forum included delegates from 4909 organizations world-wide (World Social Forum 2002). It is no wonder that one of its basic principles is that

> [n]o-one ... will be authorized, on behalf of any of the editions of the Forum, to express positions claiming to be those of all its participants. The participants in the Forum shall not be called on to take decisions as a body ... on declarations or proposals for action that would commit all, or the majority, of them and that propose to be taken as establishing positions of the Forum as a body.

Yet the Charter of Principles goes on to insist that

> organizations or groups of organizations that participate in the Forum's meetings must be assured the right, during such meetings, to deliberate on declarations or actions they may decide on, whether singly or in

coordination with other participants. The World Social Forum undertakes to circulate such decisions widely by the means at its disposal, without directing, hierarchizing, censuring or restricting them, but as deliberations of the organizations or groups of organizations that made the decisions. (World Social Forum 2001)

It is tempting to conclude that the equality movement has solved the problem of coordination by being a loose network of groupings that are always free to cooperate but never forced to do so. They can form ad hoc committees to run particular campaigns, organize demonstrations and hold conferences while retaining their independence to think and do as they see fit. And this is just what the idea of a social movement leads us to expect.

But we should not adopt too rosy a view of things. Coordination does not occur by accident. The World Social Forum has to be organized by somebody: in fact, an organizing committee drawn from a broad range of Brazilian organizations and supported by an International Council drawn from over a hundred trade union confederations, NGOs and other social movement organizations (World Social Forum 2003). The mobilizations against meetings of international financial institutions in Seattle, Prague, Genoa and elsewhere were extensively planned in advance. For example, local planning for the Prague mobilization in September 2000 began a year earlier and advanced through three international meetings and extensive email discussion. Working groups were set up for a number of tasks including accommodation, media relations, street action, medical care, cultural activities and training. Action Spokescouncils were held during the event, involving representatives from participating affinity groups, although it is not clear from reports how much of a coordinating role these councils performed (Abramsky 2001, ch. 75). Campaigns on equality issues need to have the organizational infrastructure to print leaflets, plan demonstrations and hold news conferences. So they, too, inevitably need to have umbrella organizations and specialized working groups, as instanced by the 2002 referendum campaigns in Ireland. These efforts at coordinating the activities of a large number of groups seem to work best when coordinating bodies and working committees are broadly based, respect diversity, operate by consensus and are accountable to their wider constituents. These are egalitarian virtues, but it is easy to ignore them in the effort to get things done and when people feel passionately about the issues.

The degree of coordination that the equality movement is capable of may well fall short of what some egalitarians desire. They may lament the fact that the aims of different groups and organizations are not wholly compatible, that the movement lacks the organizational capacity to respond to events at short notice, that it cannot impose any great discipline on mass actions and that it lacks a single voice with which to frame issues and defend its position. But are these really weaknesses? They all stem from the fact that the equality agenda is a complex mixture of aims that will inevitably be given different priorities by different groups and that political action is an uncertain process in which activists inevitably make different practical judgements. The loose structure of the equality movement reflects these differences: a single, disciplined organization would only repress them. So the loosely coordinated structure of the equality movement – one aspect of what we call its strategic pluralism – should be seen not as a weakness, but a strength.

## The role of political parties

The equality movement is a diverse, plural social movement pursuing related aspects of equality, but not necessarily with shared interpretations of the egalitarian ideal. It operates at many places simultaneously, without any central direction or coordination but with a potentially high degree of cooperation among various groups. As we pointed out in Chapter 10, this is a very different organizational model from the classical Marxist view that the natural vehicle for political change is a mass political party. It is therefore not surprising that there is a certain tension between many elements of the equality movement and political parties, since political parties are by their nature more or less centralized and coordinated organizations that require their members to support common policies and take a common line. They also have an essentially competitive stance towards other political parties. They compete with each other for members, supporters and voters and in doing so emphasize their distinct policies or other virtues, even if their activities also involve cooperation in the form of electoral pacts, coalition governments and so on. A person can easily belong to a wide range of social movement organizations, but it is typically difficult or impossible to be a member or supporter of more than one political party.

But if there is a tension between social movements and political parties, there is also an interdependence. How should we think about this interdependence and how to manage it? The most pressing problems arise when it comes to the relationship between the equality movement and what can be called 'mainstream parties', that is, parties that are potential members of government. There may be similar tensions in the relations between more marginal parties and other egalitarian groups, particularly if the parties hold a classically Marxist model of social change. But because these marginal parties do not have to face the problems involved in holding office within contemporary welfare capitalist states, they are more like the campaigning groups that are typical of the equality movement. So in this section we concentrate on the issue of mainstream parties.

It is easy to see why many sections of the equality movement have given up hope in relation to mainstream political parties. Before the advent of universal suffrage, political theorists of all complexions predicted that the right to vote would lead to radical policies of redistribution and expropriation. So socialists campaigned for it, conservatives opposed it and liberals sought some way of containing its effects. Yet after nearly a century of universal suffrage in many countries, with ample opportunities in government for parties of the left, inequality is still deeply entrenched. One way or another – but only occasionally at gunpoint – leftist parties seem to have all but abandoned whatever commitment to equality of condition they once had.

An additional reason for losing interest in mainstream political parties is the perception among egalitarians that what happens at the level of the nation state hardly matters any more in a period of globalization. The powerful world actors are transnational corporations and international financial institutions, both of which seem to have escaped control by national governments – with the possible but unencouraging exception of the US government. So why should egalitarians bother to engage with state-based political parties?

Neither of these reasons for ignoring mainstream parties is very convincing. Even if there is some truth to the thesis that capitalist globalization has limited the power of national states, it is clear that states still have important powers. There are significant variations among otherwise similar countries in their income inequality (Sutcliffe 2001, graph 10). States also have an important impact on dimensions of equality that are relatively independent of economic inequality, such as the protection of minority rights and the promotion of intercultural equality (e.g. Sutcliffe 2001, graph 113). And states are the organizations that have set up and continue to control international bodies like the WTO. Egalitarians are right to see that power is exercised in many contexts by many types of social actors and that it is therefore a mistake to concentrate entirely on the formal politics of the nation state. But states continue to play an important role in perpetuating or challenging inequalities.

There is plenty of evidence to show that parties are important in deciding what happens within states. Large-scale comparative research on economically developed countries shows that there are important differences between governments of the left and governments of the right, even if governments of the left continue to disappoint equality activists (Gallagher, Laver and Mair 2001, ch. 13; Korpi and Palme 2003; Minnich 2003; Muller 1989; Weede 1990). State policies matter, and the parties controlling state policies matter. So the idea that egalitarians should treat mainstream parties with indifference cannot be sustained.

But before concluding that the equality movement should throw its weight behind mainstream parties of the left, we need to consider some of the problems this raises. Perhaps the most basic difficulty is that mainstream political parties aim to win elections and not just to influence public opinion. In a two-party system, that means winning a majority of legislative seats; in a multi-party system, it means maximizing their representation in the legislature and being prepared to compromise their policies for the sake of entering coalition governments. In either case, it seems clear enough that the political circumstances of contemporary western democracies make it impossible for parties or coalitions to win power on the basis of robustly egalitarian policies. It follows that mainstream parties, that is, parties that aspire to government either on their own or in coalition, cannot currently be expected to adopt and implement strongly egalitarian programmes. So egalitarians face a dilemma. They cannot afford to act as though all parties are the same and that it hardly matters which is in office. But they cannot identify strongly with any mainstream party, because they are bound to have deep disagreements with some of its policies.

There are basically only three possible responses to this dilemma.[4] Although we see them as problems for collective action, for the purpose of exposition we call them the Tony Benn, Noam Chomsky and Ralph Nader options. The 'Benn' strategy is to work within a mainstream party to influence its programme in an egalitarian direction. This has been the typical strategy of the labour movement in relation to European social democratic parties and has also been significant in the history of the women's, peace and environmental movements (Hanagan 1998; Kriesi 1995a). The rationale of the strategy is that unless there are egalitarian voices within the party, it will become even more middle-of-the-road in its programmes and tactics than it needs to be to win electoral support. While it could be electorally disastrous for a radical grouping to win control over party policy prematurely (a scenario that some observers attribute to the British Labour Party in the early 1980s), it is important to draw policy in a leftward direction. The argument is that groups are better placed to do so by being within the party and having the party dependent on them for support than if they are outside the fold. The main drawback of this strategy is the difficulty of carrying it off effectively. A group that is seen as too deeply opposed to the party leadership risks expulsion or at least marginalization; alternatively, it may accommodate itself so closely to the logic of electoral success that it ceases to have a strongly egalitarian influence. We can see this dilemma being played out across Europe in the relationships between social democratic parties and both the labour and women's movements. These movements were very strongly integrated into social democratic parties in Europe in the 40 years following the First World War, but since the 1960s there has been considerable conflict within those parties in relation to both class and gender issues (Hanagan 1998). In the US, by contrast, there has been a strengthened relationship between the women's movement and the Democratic Party (Tarrow 1998a, pp. 171–4).

A second response – the 'Chomsky' strategy – is to remain resolutely outside any political party and to use this principled self-exclusion as a source of independent, external pressure. This is the strategy the British peace movement adopted after the rejection of nuclear disarmament at the 1960 Labour Party Conference (Hanagan 1998) and it is the explicit stance of the Zapatista movement in Mexico (Marcos 2001) and the Confédération Paysanne in France (Bové 2001). Under this strategy, social movements will be prepared to enter into dialogue with the leaders of mainstream parties, but any influence they have is just as likely to be through what Randy Shaw (2001, ch. 2) describes as a relationship of 'fear and loathing': politicians are not expected to be convinced by arguments or to share common values, but to fear political damage from embarrassing revelations, scandal, public indignation and so on. On this view, egalitarians should support mainstream parties only for specific and limited purposes, when there is a convergence of aims, and should just as regularly oppose them. Parties should be treated as 'brokers' who handle transactions between social movements and the state (Castells 1997, p. 358). The main disadvantage of this approach is that it seems irretrievably oppositionalist in character. It implicitly concedes that state power will always be wielded by supporters of inequality and that the highest aim of egalitarians is to find ways of opposing and limiting that power. This is certainly an understandable policy of resistance under present circumstances but seems to involve deep pessimism about radical change.

The third response to the dilemma – the 'Nader' strategy – is to try to set up a real party of the left that would stick to its egalitarian principles and build mass support for egalitarian change.[5] The great advantage of this approach is that you can maintain your principles while still engaging in the important business of party politics. Elections can be used to put a clear alternative before the voters; public offices can be won and their powers employed for egalitarian purposes. In its defence, one could point out that many mainstream parties, particularly parties of the left and nationalist parties, themselves emerged out of social movements and displaced parties that had become irrelevant to people's concerns. This was the original strategy of labour movements in Europe at the end of the nineteenth century when they established social democratic parties; more recent examples are Green and New Left parties in Europe and the US (Gallagher, Laver and Mair 2001, pp. 209–13; Wainwright 1994, ch. 7), the Women's Coalition in Northern Ireland and the Workers' Party (*Partido dos Trabalhadores* (PT)) in Brazil (Alvarez 1997). But this strategy also faces serious difficulties. The very problem it is meant to address is that there is currently no prospect of winning elections on the basis of radically egalitarian policies, with the result that mainstream parties must be far less egalitarian than we would hope. This third strategy is based on the presumption that a radically egalitarian party could become a major political force without compromising, or being seen to compromise, its principles. But that is an immensely difficult challenge. In political systems dominated by two parties, it faces all the well-known obstacles blocking the growth of third parties.[6] In multi-party systems, the acid test is the point of government formation, where a minority radical party has to choose between remaining in opposition and supporting a government programme that contradicts some of its most strongly held aims. A policy of perpetual opposition runs contrary to the arguments for taking parties seriously in the first place in view of their influence on policy outcomes. But participation in government inevitably involves compromises that can affect the party's integrity and popular support. It blurs, though it does not eliminate, the distinction between the 'Benn' and 'Nader' strategies: the 'Naders' become 'Benns' in an inter-party alliance, but the existence of a separate party provides a clearer platform for a distinct political perspective. Whether, even in a multi-party system, an egalitarian party is a feasible option is of course another question that depends on the resources available, the political context and other factors.

As many analysts of social movements have emphasized, strategies are always conditional on the political opportunities that movements face in particular contexts. It is perhaps not surprising that the Benn strategy has looked more plausible in the UK than in the US, where – except on gender issues – the differences between the Democratic and Republican parties are so hard to identify. Undoubtedly the relative merits of the three strategies will also be influenced by electoral systems. In a plurality ('first past the post') electoral system, a strong egalitarian party can have the effect of facilitating a right-wing victory, as the Nader candidacy in 2000 arguably favoured George W. Bush (but see Sifry 2002, pp. 224–5).[7] By contrast, list-based proportional representation systems allow voters to support more egalitarian parties without that risk. Electoral systems using the single transferable vote, such as PRSTV in Ireland and the instant run-off vote (IRV) system promoted by some US reformers, have an equivalent safe-guard since votes for an unsuccessful radical candidate can transfer to a more mainstream candidate.[8]

Perhaps the most that can be said at a general level is that there will often be a case for pursuing all three strategies at the same time, relying on the varying judgements of different equality activists to keep all three in play. It is easy to see how the 'Benn' and 'Chomsky' strategies can be com-plementary: the forcefulness of radical criticism from outside the party can help to strengthen the case of radicals within it, while the existence of a radical wing within a party can do something to translate external criticism into political policy. There is more of a tension between these two strat-egies and the 'Nader' approach, since a radically egalitarian party could use all the help it could get and so would clearly benefit from other egalitarians forswearing their previous perspectives and joining this party. But in the absence of such a development, an egalitarian party might still gain more than it loses from there being radical egalitarians both in mainstream parties and outside parties altogether. For these radicals will contribute to the general ideological change that is necessary for the growth of any egalitarian alternative. Conversely, the radical case within a mainstream party can be strengthened by the threat of a party to its left, while non-party egalitarians can hardly regret the growth of an egalitarian party, even if they are pessimistic about its success.

Quite how complementary these strategies might turn out to be will depend, among other things, on how their proponents relate to each other. If each group does nothing but disparage the others, that is likely to do their cause more harm than good. But if each group recognizes that the others are trying their best to make difficult judgements about the best way of promoting equality, and if each group sees that the three strategies can be mutually enforcing rather than mutually antagonistic, then the movement as a whole can gain. We need to remember the general insight that a social movement is strengthened by its diversity, and to recognize that there is a positive role to be played by those who operate within mainstream parties, those who belong to purer, more radical parties and those who want to work outside parties altogether.

Perhaps the most difficult task in achieving this mutual acceptance is to persuade party activists to adopt a less instrumental – one might even say less predatory – approach towards their relations to groups within the equality movement. Kriesi (1995a) describes how social movements have sometimes been exploited by parties to strengthen opposition against conservative governments only to be dropped when the parties gained power, a tactic that can win short-term electoral support but cannot build long-term alliances. Mainstream parties are necessarily preoccupied with winning votes: that is in their nature. But if they have no other aim than to maximize their votes, they are bound to find it difficult to communicate with a movement that is defined by its values. They need to approach the equality movement in a genuine spirit of dialogue, engaging in the arguments and not just calculating what has to be done to recruit people into the party or to win their support at the ballot box. This task will of course be much easier if the parties themselves are more open, more diverse in their membership and less bureaucratic and hierarchical.[9]

It is no good imagining that a dialogue between most major mainstream parties and groups within the equality movement will be anything other than strained. Egalitarian groups will continue to be seen by many mainstream politicians as demanding, unrealistic, obstinate and naïve while many politicians will be seen by egalitarians as compromised, cowardly, hypocritical and self-serving. But egalitarians have to face up to the fact that so long as they have failed to convince the majority of the population of the importance and feasibility of egalitarian aims, politicians will follow public opinion as much as lead it. And politicians have to recognize that a failure to engage with the equality movement can only fuel public disenchantment with politics in a way that is more useful to the right than to the left. In the political circumstances of contemporary western democracies, there is no prospect of a complete convergence between the equality movement and a major mainstream political party. But both sides would gain by developing an amicable relationship.

## Radicals and moderates

Like most social movements, the equality movement has both radical and moderate components, with a fair amount of tension between them. Radicals are likely to see moderates as too accommodating or even as having sold out the movement for their own personal advancement. Moderates can see radicals as utopian and their actions as counter-productive. In many countries, states have responded to pressure from egalitarian movements by setting up mechanisms for including their representatives in processes of consultation and, more rarely, decision-making. Moderates tend to welcome these changes as opportunities for influencing state policy. Radicals often see them as ways of co-opting leaders, weakening demands and taking the steam out of social protest. In this section, we argue that the equality movement needs both radicals and moderates, and that they should see each other, as far as possible, as allies in a cause.

To clarify the question, it is worth noting that activists can be radical in two different ways: by making more demanding claims or by using more disruptive tactics. The first kind of radicalism is ideological; it is about positions that risk being labelled as utopian or absurd by the opponents of change. One of the weapons used by the Conservative Party in Britain to discredit Labour in the late 1970s and 1980s was to brand its ideas as extreme, a tactic that has always been part of the ideological armoury of the right. It was the much more moderate programme of New Labour that won office in 1997. The benefit of 'extreme' views, however, is that they stretch the public imagination and the scope of what appears to be a 'reasonable' demand. If we look at the struggle for equality in historical perspective, it is clear enough that all its major advances – the abolition of slavery, the achievement of universal suffrage, the securing of the right to strike, the protection of civil rights, the establishment of the welfare state and many more achievements – were considered radical objectives when first put forward. Ideological radicalism plays an essential role in progressing the egalitarian agenda.

In any case, the equality movement can hardly control whether its component actors make radical demands: that is going to occur whether anyone likes it or not, because the world is so radically unjust. What matters more is whether the movement wastes its energies by engaging in bitter conflict over these issues. Radicals will *of course* see moderates as mistaken and vice versa: that follows from their having different political convictions in the first place. But it makes more sense for each of these flanks to use the existence of the other constructively than to try, vainly, to bury it. Ideological moderates can surely see the value of acknowledging the case for a more radical position, since this can help to make their own views look more acceptable. Ideological radicals can surely see that disparaging moderates only plays into the hands of anti-egalitarians, and that if they cannot convince moderates to strengthen their own egalitarianism they can hardly hope to win mass public support for radical change.

The second kind of radicalism concerns tactics. The use of disruptive action is one of the typical features of social movements, since they are usually composed of relatively powerless people who lack both material resources and access to state power. What they do have is a collective capacity to disrupt the ordinary workings of the systems that dominate them. In the modern period they have developed a 'repertoire' of disruptive actions including strikes, boycotts, rallies, demonstrations, occupations, barricades and so on. Disruptive action plays a role not just in forcing concessions but in communicating a perspective, establishing a sense of public urgency and drawing media attention to important issues.

A group that is completely excluded from formal systems of power has no choice but to engage in these tactics: they are the only means it has for making claims and establishing its status with those in power. But for many groups the question is more complex. Their organizations may have been recognized as legitimate players in the political system, with seats on committees and access to officials and politicians. Disruptive action is no longer their only option. The question is whether it should continue to be one of the tactics in their strategy. Here we are not talking about the violent overthrow of the state in liberal democracies: we take it for granted that this is neither a legitimate nor feasible egalitarian strategy. The question is the role of disruptive campaigns and protests as a way of strengthening the prospects for democratic egalitarian change.

The state, legal system and dominant ideas of any society are not neutral forces. They are always affected by the interests of the powerful and usually operate to reinforce inequality. As a result, in most political contexts some effective tactics will be widely perceived as illegitimate and may even be illegal. That in itself does not make them wrong: it simply shows that they are objectionable to the powers that be. But the success of the powerful in disparaging or banning particular forms of action is also important strategically, since it may make those actions counter-productive. First, it may make them more costly for activists to engage in, by risking a police reaction involving possible injury or arrest. The Irish National Organisation of the Unemployed (INOU) abandoned direct action in the 1990s because unemployed people were themselves reluctant to engage in it (Allen 1998, ch. 15; cf. Royall 2000). Secondly, it may divert attention away from the real issues to the question of whether the actions themselves were justified or the state's reaction excessive. It is a truism about the treatment of radical protest by the mass media that it often faces a no-win situation. Unless protest is accompanied by some form of serious conflict, such as destruction of property or violent confrontation between protesters and the police, it does not even warrant reporting. But when conflict does occur, it is the conflict itself that makes news and the original issues are eclipsed. Thirdly, disruptive action carries the ideological burden of being seen as illegitimate by a large proportion of the population, with the possibility of reducing support for the issue it propounds. Public reaction to violence was important in weakening support for the US Knights of Labor following the Haymarket bomb in 1886 (Voss 1996).

One of the ways tactical radicals can reduce these costs is by choosing forms of direct action that are particularly strong in their symbolism. Martin Luther King's use of direct action was effective not just in attracting media attention but in framing the issues in a way that it was hard to misinterpret (McAdam 1996). A more recent example is the 1999 raid led by José Bové on a McDonald's restaurant in France. Although the specific issue behind the protest was a US–EU trade dispute, the action symbolized the conflict between transnational corporations and small farmers (Bové 2001).

As a result of these considerations, there will inevitably be some disagreement among equality activists about tactics, ranging from moderates who insist on operating within the established rules of political engagement to radicals who regularly operate outside them. So, as before, the crucial question is not which of these positions is right but how these different activists should relate to each other. If they treat their disagreement as a source of conflict, they will expend vital energies and resources on combating each other instead of their common adversaries. The alternative is to accept that there are legitimate differences of opinion about tactics and to use these differences constructively.

In fact, the history of social movements suggests that a dual strategy of working both inside and outside the system is more effective than a concentration on either approach. One of the standard problems tactical moderates have to cope with is how to make access to powerful institutions a genuine tool for change rather than a way of co-opting and silencing the movement (Gamson 1990, ch. 3). Disruptive action serves their purposes by demonstrating the depth of the grievances and injustices they hope to redress. It unsettles the political landscape and creates opportunities for them to advance their agenda. Tarrow (1998b) shows how the events of May 1968 provided an opportunity for the French education minister, Edgar Faure, to introduce substantial reforms. Gamson (1990, pp. 157–60) describes how the actions of the radical Clamshell Alliance in the 1970s strengthened the position of the more respectable Union of Concerned Scientists. Piven and Cloward (1977) argue that it is only in response to disruption that poor people in the US have ever extracted concessions from the powerful. Klinker and Smith (1999) conclude that progress towards greater racial equality in the US has only occurred when protest movements brought pressure on national leaders. Szasz (1994) explains how toxic waste activists put environmental justice onto the American political agenda.[10] All of these examples confirm on a political level the fundamental assumption of trade unionism, that the power to disrupt, using industrial action, is an essential complement to negotiation and 'partnership'. So even egalitarians who prefer to work in conventional ways within established institutions have a reason to hope that there are others engaged in more radical forms of action.

But what these examples also show is the weakness of giving up on moderate tactics and engaging only in disruption. For they suggest that disruption succeeds best when it has allies operating within conventional structures of power. Indeed, in the absence of strong allies within the political system, the reforms prompted by disruptive action can be short-lived. Tarrow (1998b) explains that although May 1968 created the opportunity for educational reform in France, the reform process itself was vulnerable to shifts in power within the government and resistance to reform in the department of education. By contrast, Giugni and Passy (1998) describe how social movement organizations can have a major influence on policy outcomes when they engage in 'conflictual cooperation' with the state in the realms of decision-making, regulation and implementation (see also Allen 1998; Ward 1999). Egalitarians who support radical tactics may agree with Piven and Cloward's (1977) view that there is more to be gained by looking for opportunities to initiate and escalate disruptive action than by building organizations, but it is hard to deny that the presence of allies operating within the institutions of the state contributes to significant and lasting reforms.

Since tactical moderates and radicals have so much to gain from each other, it is perhaps unsurprising that a common strategy of the state is to drive a wedge between them by attempting to incorporate moderates and marginalize radicals. Kriesi (1995b) and Tarrow (1998a, ch. 9) trace a general pattern in protest waves in Europe and the US through which mass action with limited effects leads to a split between more moderate and more radical groups, as the state acts to integrate moderates into the system while repressing radicals. Quite how protest waves develop varies considerably according to the way they interact with different forms of state reaction, so it is pointless to suggest a general strategy for egalitarians. Nevertheless, it seems clear enough that tactical moderates can choose either to encourage or resist the repression of tactical radicals, and that their inclination to support the state's repression can work against their own prospects of success.

None of this implies that there are no limits to the types of action that the equality movement should engage in. The most important of these limits relates to the use of political violence, in the sense of 'the exercise of physical force so as to kill or injure, inflict direct harm or pain on, human beings' (Geras 1989, p. 186). As it happens, the use of violence is often counter-productive. In his study of challenging groups, Gamson (1990, ch. 6) found that groups advocating violence were much more likely to be arrested by the authorities and much less likely to succeed than other groups. Distinguishing between violence and 'feistiness' – the willingness to break rules and use non-institutionalized forms of action – he goes on to discuss how the explicitly non-violent but disruptive actions of the civil rights, anti-war and anti-nuclear movements drew attention and support to their causes (Gamson 1990, ch. 10). As Tarrow (1998a, p. 96) remarks, violence not only frightens sympathizers but provides authorities with a mandate for repression. The equality movement's commitment to equal respect and recognition, to human rights and to the importance of every human life also raises moral problems about political violence. This convergence between tactical and moral considerations probably explains why practically all of the egalitarian social movements in democratic states use non-violent forms of disruptive action. Where violence does develop, it is often a result of the state's repressive response to disruption rather than a deliberate strategy (Kriesi *et al.* 1995).

The distinction between ideological and tactical radicalism means that there are in principle four possible stances:

| Ideological and tactical moderate | Ideological radical, tactical moderate |
|---|---|
| Ideological moderate, tactical radical | Ideological and tactical radical |

Analysts have observed that there is a tendency for organizations that work within established structures to moderate their demands (e.g. Guigni and Plassy 1998, pp. 102–4; see also Dowie 1995 and Kriesi 1996). But this is an empirical generalization, not a necessary truth. The equality movement probably needs activists in all four corners of the grid to be maximally effective.

We have argued for a social movement model of egalitarian change involving the complementary activities of moderate and radical egalitarians, where this contrast refers to both ideology and tactics. If the equality movement were constituted by a single organization or party, this kind of plural strategy would face a serious problem, namely how a single organization could adopt contradictory beliefs and tactics at the same time. Its moderates could only be seen as deeply disingenuous, publicly rejecting principles and tactics that other members of their own organization persistently embraced. By contrast, the social movement model of change helps to minimize this problem. Being a loose network of groups and individuals, it can readily accept that some of its members are genuine moderates and others genuine radicals in either sense of the contrast. No one has to pretend that they believe something they do not, even if, as we have argued, they can recognize the benefits of being part of a movement that has all four types of activist. We do not want to pretend that the idea of a plural strategy is cost-free: we have already noted that it inevitably generates some conflict within the movement itself. But if we see it as a positive feature that emerges from the diversity of the equality movement rather than as the deliberate invention of a united organization, we can at least avoid the cost of appearing hypocritical.

## Ends and means

The issue of disruptive tactics and especially political violence raises a more general question about the relationship between egalitarian ends and means. The fact that anti-egalitarians tend to attack every effective political tactic as immoral can lead us to think that the only restraint on our means should be their political outcomes. Thus, Saul Alinsky has written that we cannot avoid 'corrupt' means if we want to achieve anything: 'He who sacrifices the mass good for his personal conscience ... doesn't care enough for people to be "corrupted" for them' (Alinsky 1971, p. 25). In our view, this approach is mistaken. It confuses the idea of challenging the moral rules laid down by one's opponents with the idea of rejecting moral principles altogether. The equality movement is defined by its principles: it cannot expect to achieve its aims by ignoring them. In particular, we need to bear in mind the central dimensions of equality in thinking about acceptable political strategies.

Equality of respect and recognition is, first of all, a principle that we have to apply to the other members of the equality movement. This means, among other things, respecting the diversity of the movement and its members, with special attention to ensuring that there is full and equal inclusion of people from subordinate social groups and that forms of communication and interaction within the movement do not work indirectly to exclude them. As we saw in Chapter 2, the idea of critical interculturalism involves a critical dialogue among people with different cultural commitments in which we try to engage constructively to challenge each other's prejudices and develop a truly egalitarian ethos. These ideas are already deeply embedded in various branches of the equality movement, although voices from the margins continue to point out differences between principle and practice (Abramsky 2001, ch. 76).

Equality of respect and recognition also involves self-imposed limits on unequal esteem, so that we do not create within our own movement the inequalities of status that we are concerned to criticize in society generally. And it sets the even harder task of maintaining an attitude of respect towards the opponents of equality in the face of their own intolerance and contempt for others. The idea of equal respect and recognition does not require us to tolerate their intolerance or to celebrate their culture of superiority, but it does call on us to engage with them as human beings and to remember that their lives matter as much as ours do.

The principle of equality of resources means that we need to look seriously at the distribution of resources within the equality movement itself. The most important resource available to any movement for change is the time and energy of the people willing to engage in it. But groups and organizations also need other resources, including money, know-how and social networks. Well-placed individuals and groups need to consider how to share these resources, not just through funding but also through strengthening capacities. Many NGOs already give money to locally-based organizations and help them develop their skills; some well-off individuals already contribute generously to the work of egalitarian groups. But although there are undoubtedly limits to the degree of sharing we can expect, it surely remains inadequate when measured against the principle of equality of condition.

As we pointed out in Chapter 10, a particularly difficult issue concerning resources is the degree to which egalitarian organizations can come to depend on state support. In Ireland, for example, a large number of the organizations within the equality movement are either directly or indirectly funded by government or EU grants. While it is unrealistic to expect every equality-related organization to emulate Amnesty International by refusing to accept any state funds at all, it is just as unrealistic to expect this not to affect their behaviour.[11] Thus as a movement it behoves egalitarians to think seriously about how we could establish more effective and reliable forms of funding that are as independent of the state as possible. In the absence of significantly greater economic equality, this will inevitably involve developing stronger systems for transferring resources from well-off egalitarians.

Another question we need to consider is how the equality movement affects its members' prospects for relationships of love, care and solidarity. As the examples discussed by Loeb (1999) illustrate, there is a world of difference between being involved in a group or organization that enhances the relationships among its members and one that subordinates these to political goals. A group that satisfies its members' needs for satisfying personal relationships will, other things equal, attract more members and more commitment than one that neglects these needs. But we should attend to relations within the group not just because it serves the group's purposes better, but because this is part of the egalitarian ideal (Taylor 1995). At the same time, we should not expect a level of commitment to the group that is incompatible with the relations of love and care that its members have with people outside it. To do so is not only self-defeating, when these ties draw people away from unrealistic demands, but also contrary to our commitment to satisfying these needs for their own sake.

Power inequalities are another key issue for the equality movement. It is taken for granted within the movement that groups should be organized democratically, but that does not avoid a widely-observed tendency towards becoming dominated by inner circles through perpetual office-holding or informal networking. In combating the large-scale power inequalities of the world around us, it is easy to ignore the small-scale inequalities in our own groups and organizations. These power relationships tend to mirror inequalities of status, resources and work role. To avoid them, then, we need not just participatory democratic structures within the movement but also equality in its other dimensions.

The equality movement faces similar issues in relation to working and learning. However efficient it may appear to be, it is no good reproducing within the movement a division of labour between people who do interesting, rewarding work and others who take on the drudgery. There are a lot of boring tasks involved in any activity or campaign, but there is no reason why these should be imposed on any particular group of people or why the allocation of responsibilities should exclude anyone from work that is personally satisfying. The idea that anyone should be happy to lick envelopes for the good of the movement contradicts the principles about work that the movement ought to be promoting.

The issue of the division of labour also raises questions about the work of caring and relationship maintenance. One question is how work within the equality movement relates to care work in households. If we reject the gendered division of labour that leaves men free to engage in paid work outside the home by requiring women to do unpaid work within it, we cannot accept the same dynamic operating within the equality movement itself. So it is essential to address questions about meeting times, venues, childcare facilities and the like. A related question is how the equality movement treats the work involved in maintaining its own relationships of care and solidarity. If, as have we argued, it is important to try to make the equality movement a space in which people can relate to each other with concern and solidarity, we need to put energy and resources into sustaining these relationships and into managing the positive and negative emotions involved in political engagement (Taylor 1995). If we do that in a haphazard way, it is all too likely that the burden of this work will fall disproportionately on women, again reproducing the gendered division of labour we find in the wider society. So the equality movement needs to think seriously about how to distribute this work in an egalitarian way.

Political involvement opens up a vast range of opportunities for learning. It is always tempting to make use of a person's existing capabilities in preference to training someone else, but that can reproduce within the movement the same cumulative inequalities of learning that exist in society generally. We need to recognize and share opportunities for learning so that everyone involved in the equality movement develops their own skills and personality in the process.

None of this is an argument against any division of labour whatsoever; it is against divisions of labour that systematically privilege some individuals and groups over others. We have to be sensitive to one another's needs for engaging work and self-development in our own movement if we believe in a society that satisfies these needs for everyone.

The principles of equality therefore generate their own set of constraints on the means acceptable to the equality movement. In most cases, as we have seen, neglecting these principles tends to weaken the movement as well. But it is not just their political effect that makes them important. If they are part of what we care about, then we should care about them in our practice and not just as a distant goal.

## Conclusion

In this chapter we have raised some key questions about the strategy of the equality movement. How coordinated should it be? What stance should it take towards mainstream political parties? How can it handle the tensions between radicals and moderates? How can it incorporate its principles into its own structures and processes? We do not pretend to have answered these questions, which will be addressed by each element of the movement in its own way. But we have tried to show that the diversity and plurality of the equality movement give rise to a fertile variety of activities that we have called strategic pluralism. Although we have argued for limits to this pluralism, arising from the principles of equality themselves, the central theme of this chapter has been that strategic pluralism is not a weakness but a strength.

This book is intended as our own contribution to the equality movement, recognizing that we, too, are only a part of a wide and diverse set of actors, each with their own priorities and perspectives. Against a backdrop of persistent and deep inequalities, we have argued that the idea of equality provides the basis for a coherent approach to social transformation. As an idea with several interpretations and five distinct dimensions, it has both the scope and the flexibility to bridge the concerns of a variety of social groups and to generate an agenda of change in a whole range of social contexts. We have set out our own views on what that agenda might include in relation to the economy, politics, law, education and research. Finally, we have set out a perspective on the equality movement, addressed some of the ideological issues it faces and explored some of its key strategic questions. From the very start, we have been inspired by countless activists who are working together to create another, more equal world. If this book helps them in their efforts, it will have achieved its purpose.

# Notes

## 1. New Challenges to an Unequal World

1. An excellent starting point is Sutcliffe 2001, which is the intermediate source of many of the statistics mentioned in this chapter.
2. Sub-Saharan Africa refers to the African countries south of the Sahara, which are generally among the poorest countries of the world. The thirty OECD countries (http://www.oecd.org) include those generally considered to be wealthy, 'developed' countries and are often used in statistics to represent the richest set of countries.
3. Unless otherwise indicated, we use 'Ireland' to refer to the Republic of Ireland.
4. Although greater flexibility in working hours is to be welcomed, part-time work has typically been associated with less security and worse conditions than full-time work.
5. Estimates for the percentage of disabled people in the population as a whole vary but are typically at least 10 per cent. For example, Burchardt (2000) estimates that disabled people make up 12 to 16 per cent of the UK working-age population. EIM Business and Policy Research (2001, p. 34) estimates that about 14 per cent of the EU working-age population were disabled in 1996.
6. In common with many authors, we use 'race' in quotation marks because this concept has no scientific basis.
7. For information about Irish Travellers see Government of Ireland 1995, McCann, Ó Síocháin and Ruane 1994, Murphy, McDonagh and Sheehan 2000 and Pavee Point (http://www.paveepoint.ie/).
8. A good explanation of the social model is Barnes 1996. As with all basic models, there are a number of variants and qualifications which we do not pursue here. For a recent review of the literature see Tregaskis 2002. We are indebted to our colleague Pat McDonnell for his advice, which has informed our treatment of disability throughout this book.
9. A very similar focus occurs in Adams, Bell and Griffin 1997.
10. *Lawrence* v. *Texas*, 539 U.S. ___ (2003).
11. The nine categories are gender, marital status, family status, sexual orientation, religion, age, disability, 'race' and membership of the Traveller community. The Equality Tribunal was originally called the Office of the Director of Equality Investigations (see Reid 2003, p. 4).
12. This section is based on a more detailed analysis by Lynch (1997).
13. For an account of how and why the Equality Studies Centre was set up, see Lynch 1999, ch. 3. Information about the Centre is available at http://www.ucd.ie/esc.
14. See the works cited in Chapter 2.
15. See in particular the works cited in Chapters 2 and 3.
16. Aspects of this task are taken up in Cohen 2000 and Swift 2003.

## 2. Dimensions of Equality: A Framework for Theory and Action

1. On the distinction between strict equality, sufficiency and priority, see Clayton and Williams 2002. In our view all three kinds of position can be considered broadly egalitarian.

2. It is sometimes objected that such a minimalist view is not a principle of equality at all. Our view is that its egalitarianism lies in its commitment to extending the basic minimum to all human beings, as opposed to considering some people to be beneath consideration.

3. A good survey of philosophical work on needs is Brock 1998. There is also a close connection between the idea of basic needs and the conditions necessary for achieving what Sen (1982, 1992) calls basic capabilities and Nussbaum (2000) calls threshold levels of central human capabilities.

4. The idea of liberal egalitarianism is therefore used by us to *stipulate* a certain family of views among all of those that might in one way or another be considered liberal and egalitarian. The paradigm case of a liberal egalitarian is Rawls (1971, 1993, 2001). Among other liberal egalitarians we would include Dworkin (2000, which includes work first published in the 1980s) and Walzer (1985). Some key discussions of the ideas of liberal egalitarians are Anderson 1999, Arneson 1989, 2000, B. Barry 1989, 1995, 2001, G.A. Cohen 1989, 2000, Sen 1992 and Van Parijs 1995. Among self-styled liberals whose views are in some ways closer to equality of condition we would include Kymlicka (1995) and Nussbaum (2000).

5. Some relevant sources are Arneson 1989, Clayton and Williams 2002, G. A. Cohen 1989, Daniels 1990, Dworkin 2000, Fraser 1997a, 1997b, Landesman 1983, Levine 1998, ch. 2, Mortimore 1968, Norman 1987, Nussbaum and Sen 1993, Phillips 1999, Rawls 1971, sec. 15, 1993, sec. 5.4, 2001, secs 17, 51, 53, Sen 1982, 1992 and Young 2001a.

6. The five dimensions are chosen for ease of exposition and to provide a coherent framework. Headings 1, 2, 4 and 5 correspond to the classic and ultimately inescapable Weberian trio of class, status and party (Weber 1958), recently adapted by Fraser (1997a, 2000) and Jaggar (1998), although these authors do not distinguish between work and resources under the heading of class/redistribution and they tend to blur the differences between what we call dimensions and contexts (see Chapter 4). The second, fourth and fifth dimensions broadly correspond to the three parts of Rawls's two principles (1971, 1993, 2001) and to the more radical positions taken by Nielsen (1985) and Norman (1987). Phillips (1999) distinguishes between economic and political equality, including both status and power in the latter. One way or another, the five headings cover most of the goods discussed by Walzer (1985). Honneth (1995) brings both the first and third dimension under the heading of recognition. Our discussion is also indirectly influenced by the capabilities approach of Sen (1982, 1992) and Nussbaum (1995a, 2000), especially in respect to emphasizing enabling rather than outcomes and to highlighting the category of love, care and solidarity.

7. There has always been some tension between these beliefs. Some liberal egalitarians, emphasizing equal opportunity and personal responsibility, maintain that individuals who deliberately squander their advantages have no right to a safety net. We think it is more accurate to the liberal egalitarian tradition to distinguish between equal opportunity and the safety net and to acknowledge the tension (see Arneson 2000 for a relevant discussion).

8. A third conception of equal opportunity, which Roemer (1998) calls 'level-the-playing-field', maintains that individuals should not be helped or hampered by any circumstance outside their control. Depending on how it is interpreted, this view of equal opportunity goes well beyond the traditional views of liberal egalitarians in the direction of equality of condition. What it seems to share with

traditional liberal views is a belief that once equal opportunity is in place, major inequalities of condition are legitimate.

9. In fact, liberalism makes several different public/private distinctions. The distinction discussed is the one most relevant to liberal conceptions of equality.

10. The liberal protection of the family as a private sphere has in recent times been used to defend a wider variety of family forms, such as one-parent families and single-sex couples. For arguments that it is incompatible with liberal principles themselves to treat the family as private see Cohen 2000, ch. 9, Nussbaum 2000, ch. 4 and Okin 1989.

11. Rawls himself thinks of the difference principle as more demanding (1993, p. 229), but in the same passage expresses his view that 'a social minimum providing for the basic needs of all citizens' is a 'constitutional essential', while the difference principle is a more controversial claim about 'basic justice' (see also Rawls 2001, pp. 129–30, 158–62). At first glance, Dworkin's (2000) principle of equality of resources seems much more radical than either the anti-poverty principle or the difference principle, and indeed he explicitly distances himself from the anti-poverty position as too subjective and undemanding (p. 3). But what Dworkin means by equal resources is a type of equal opportunity, and his hypothetical insurance market functions as a form of safety net.

12. One way of developing this point is to say that it shows that equal opportunity entails much more equality of resources than liberal egalitarians seem to be committed to, perhaps nearly as much as is involved in equality of condition. But that is not to deny that liberal egalitarians *think* that equal opportunity (or at least an acceptable degree of it: see Rawls 1971, pp. 511–12) is compatible with major inequalities of resources.

13. A few authors have attempted to incorporate love, care and solidarity into broadly liberal egalitarian theories of justice. Walzer (1985) treats love and kinship as a separate sphere, based on freely exchanged love between adults but subject to a 'rule of prescriptive altruism' that expects family members to love and care for each other and so aims to guarantee them 'some modicum of love, friendship, generosity, and so on' (pp. 229, 238). Nussbaum (1995a, p. 84) treats 'being able ... to love, to grieve, to experience longing and gratitude' as one of the basic human functional capabilities that societies ought to support. She argues (2000, esp. chs 1 and 4) for a partial theory of justice that aims at bringing everyone above a minimum threshold of capabilities, and identifies the family as a key social institution for attaining this aim in relation to love and care. Bubeck (1995) maintains that an ethic of care needs to be complemented by considerations of justice and puts forward two principles of justice in care. Kittay (1999, p. 103) suggests that 'the good both to be cared for in a responsive dependency relation if and when one is unable to care for oneself, and to meet the dependency needs of others without incurring undue sacrifices oneself is a primary social good in the Rawlsian sense' which requires a separate principle of justice. She calls for a connection-based conception of equality.

14. On the right to work, an exception is Arneson (1987, 1990), who argues for a right to 'decent' work, but against a right to 'meaningful' work. On the obligation to work, White (2003) is a noticeable exception, arguing for the obligation to perform 'civic labour'. Rawls comments briefly on the obligation to work (2001, sec. 53) and the issue arises explicitly in discussions of basic income (e.g. Baker 1992, Barry 1997, Levine 1998, ch. 1, Van Parijs 1991, 1992, 1995, 2001).

15. Rawls (2001, secs 41–2) criticizes the limitations of the welfare state, contrasting it with both a 'property-owning democracy' and with 'liberal (democratic)

socialism'. In this respect, he is at least partially exempt from the point made in this paragraph. What remains unclear, as with the difference principle itself, is the degree of inequality Rawls considers to be inevitable.

16. Among proponents of equality of condition we would include Baker (1987), Carens (1981), G.A. Cohen (1981, 1989, 1991, 1995, 1997, 2000), Fraser (1989, 1997a, 1997b, 2000), Nielsen (1985), Norman (1987, 1995), Okin (1989), Phillips (1999), Schaar (1967) and Young (1990, 2001a). There are of course many differences among these authors and some of them would reject some of the views we include in this section. Our aim here is to draw together what we see as their most important insights.

17. These oppressive systems include structures that systematically exclude people with impairments from participating fully in their societies and structures that socially construct a division between 'heterosexual' and 'homosexual' persons and privilege the former over the latter. No attempt is made here at a complete list of oppressive relationships and no inferences should be drawn as to their relative importance.

18. As mentioned earlier, our discussion of the dimensions of equality is meant to be relatively neutral among the more radical positions in the 'equality of what?' debate, and particularly between the answers provided by Arneson (1989), G.A. Cohen (1989) and Sen (1992), on the (somewhat debatable) assumption that none of these answers makes too strong a concession to liberal equality of opportunity. One could see the five dimensions as specifying conditions for true equality of opportunity for welfare (Arneson) or for true equality of access to advantage (Cohen) or for true equality of capabilities (Sen).

19. There are useful discussions of this issue in Barry 2001, esp. ch. 7, Galeotti 2002, Hall 2000, Jaggar 1998, Lentin 2003, Nussbaum 2000, Nussbaum and Glover 1995, Nussbaum and Sen 1993, Okin 1999 and Parekh 2000. Placed in the context of the other four dimensions of equality, it should be clear that critical interculturalism is not an invitation to accept inequalities in those other dimensions under the guise of cultural difference, but to develop a conception of recognition that complements those other dimensions of equality. Our perspective is intended to be open-ended enough to accommodate rather different views on specific issues.

20. In this section we are deliberately using 'resources' in a wider sense than that appropriated by Dworkin (2000) for what he calls 'equality of resources', since Dworkin's approach treats resources as a form of private property. The concept is too important to be monopolized by a particular theorist. Bourdieu's definition of 'social capital' is similar to those of Loury (1987) and Coleman (1990, ch. 12), both of whom emphasize that social capital is a benefit to individuals and groups in virtue of the social networks to which individuals or members of groups belong. By contrast, Putnam (1993, ch. 6) emphasizes the public good aspect of social capital, i.e. the benefits to a society generally of having networks of civic engagement. There is also a parallel between Bourdieu's concept of cultural capital and the widely used concept of human capital. The recognition of leisure time as a resource complements the treatment of work as a fifth dimension of equality. Although Wolff (2002) treats environmental factors as aspects of social structure rather than as resources, we prefer to treat them as a kind of resource. But our account is meant to be open enough to allow for different accounts of resources.

21. Some of the problems involved in thinking about work and income are discussed more thoroughly in Baker 1992. By incorporating work into the idea of equality of condition and recognizing that inequalities of work justify compen-

sating inequalities of income, egalitarians can provide an answer to the New Right complaint that resources do not fall from heaven (Nozick 1974) while remaining sceptical about the claim, discussed briefly below, that inequality is necessary for providing incentives (on which see Baker 1987, ch. 9, Carens 1981 and Cohen 1991, 2000, ch. 8).

22. More precisely, substantial inequalities of resources among people with similar needs.

23. As Wolff (2002) points out, a structural change may be a more effective way of promoting equality than a redistribution of resources. But what seems to be happening in such a case is that the structural change alters the value of people's resources; it may also alter their status, personal relationships, power and educational or occupational opportunities.

24. The point about class was made as early as Macpherson's (1973) discussion and never really addressed. The classic gender-based critique of Rawls is Okin 1989; see also Cohen 2000, ch. 9. Rawls's later work (1993, p. xxix; 2001, pp. 64–6, 162–8) briefly acknowledges the issue of gender inequality but in a way that seems to continue to ignore its depth.

25. For more arguments, see Baker 1987, G. A. Cohen 1981, 1989, 1991, 1995, 1997, 2000, Lukes 1977, ch. 5, Nielsen 1985, Norman 1987, Okin 1989 and Young 1990. One general upshot of these arguments is that, contrary to appearances, it is liberal egalitarians who are unrealistic or utopian, because their limited aims are in fact unrealizable in a world marked by severe inequality and because they neglect the real influence of social structures.

26. Some relevant sources for the analysis of this paragraph are Barnes 1991, 2000, Burchardt 2000, Combat Poverty Agency 1994, EIM Business and Policy Research 2001, Finkelstein 1980, Oliver 1990, Shakespeare 1994 and Shakespeare, Gillespie-Sells and Davies 1996.

27. Some relevant sources for the analysis of this paragraph are Barrett 1980, Daly 1989, Delphy and Leonard 1992, Kittay 1999, Mitchell 1984 and Nolan and Watson 1999. See also works cited in Chapters 10 and 11.

28. Some relevant sources for the analysis of these paragraphs are Bourdieu 1984, O'Neill 1992, Phillips 1999 and Young 1990. See also works cited in Chapters 8 and 10.

29. Some of the criticisms made by Wolff (1998) and Anderson (1999) of certain accounts of egalitarianism rely on how those accounts neglect the dimension of respect and recognition. Whether this exposes some degree of conflict between equal respect and equality of resources is a question we cannot pursue here. What is clear is that the structured social inequalities found in most societies typically call for greater equality in both dimensions.

## 3.  The Centrality of Equality: Equality and Other Values

1. The idea of social exclusion can be taken to encompass both poverty (defined as inadequate income) and other forms of deprivation, including lack of access to services, cultural marginalization, exclusion from political participation, social isolation and lack of work and educational opportunities, allowing for a multi-dimensional analysis similar to our treatment of equality in Chapter 2 (cf. Gordon *et al.* 2000, which uses a four-dimensional definition of social exclusion). There are, however, a number of different interpretations of social exclusion, some of which are more multi-faceted – and more egalitarian – than others (Levitas 1998).

2. In this respect our view is similar to what Rawls says about primary social goods, since the dimensions of equality may be said to concentrate on the things and relationships people need for the sake of whatever they aim at. But to say this is not to endorse the view that equality of condition consists in everyone having the same amounts of these primary goods.

3. The discussion of this section is particularly indebted to the work of Cohen (1995); see also Baker 1987, ch. 7, Dworkin 2000, Nielsen 1985, Norman 1987, 1995 and Tawney 1964.

4. This point is reinforced by considering the social limits to growth analysed by Hirsch (1977), generated by the character of positional goods.

5. A similar conclusion is drawn by Dobson (1998).

## 4. Contexts of Egalitarian Change: Social Systems and Social Groups

1. 'Hegemony' refers to dominance over both the practices and ideas of a society (see Gramsci 1971).

2. 'Whereas the genuine place of "classes" is within the economic order, the place of "status groups" is within the social order, that is, within the sphere of the distribution of "honour". From within these spheres, classes and status groups influence one another and they influence the legal order and are in turn influenced by it. But "parties" live in a house of "power"' (Weber 1958, p. 194; see also pp. 180–1).

3. Talcott Parsons was one of the most influential social scientists of the twentieth century. Although his consensualist view of the social system would be rejected by conflict theorists, his conceptualization of the social system as having four major functional goals that it had to realize if it were to survive was highly influential. He claimed that the functional goal of adapting to the environment was realized within the economy; the goal attainment objective (achieving collective goals) was the task of politics; tension management and pattern maintenance was the task of the cultural system; while integrative systems (particularly the law) played a role in maintaining social integration (Parsons 1951; Parsons and Smelser 1956).

4. The discussion in this chapter is indebted to the work of Young and Fraser. The processes that Young (1990) calls the 'five faces of oppression' – exploitation, marginalization, powerlessness, cultural imperialism and violence – are relevant to understanding how systems generate and reinforce inequality, although we do not foreground these ideas in our discussion. Fraser's (1997a) attempt to relate inequalities of recognition and resources to the distinction between what she calls the cultural and politico-economic systems, Young's (1997) critique and Fraser's (1997c) response have all contributed to the analysis we give here.

5. In classical functionalist sociological literature social systems are defined as collectivities with a range of subsystems organized around the functional imperatives of adaptation, goal attainment, pattern maintenance and integration (see note 3 above and Parsons 1951).

6. To say this is not to deny that people themselves play a part in interpreting and defining social systems.

7. Travellers are a nomadic Irish ethnic group. See Chapter 1 for further information.

8. There are also significant differences among people with different types of impairment, as well as between people with single and multiple impairments, and how

the cultural and economic systems treat these differences is an important question. For example, it may be the case that people with mobility impairments have already significantly overcome traditional cultural stereotypes and are more likely to experience inequality as a result of economic rather than cultural factors.

## 5.   Towards Economic Equality

1. There is a substantial body of empirical evidence documenting the extent of such inequalities in Ireland. See for example Cantillon *et al.* 2001, Kirby 2002, Lynch 1999, Nolan 1991 and O'Toole 1997.
2. The figures given are 'purchasing power parity' dollars, i.e. figures reflecting what money can buy rather than market exchange rates. Source: UNDP 2002, Table 1.
3. The Gini co-efficient is a common measure of inequality, ranging from zero (complete equality) to one (complete inequality). For an explanation, see Barr 1993 or Nolan, O'Connell and Whelan 2000. The global figure is from Sutcliffe 2002, p. 32.
4. A recent empirical study indicates that global income inequality fell between 1970 and 1998 (Sala-i-Martin 2002; see also Sutcliffe 2002). This decline in income inequality occurred despite the fact that within-country inequalities and across-countries inequalities have both increased during the period. The explanation for this paradox lies with China (and, to a lesser extent, India) where higher levels of economic growth and increased incomes, compared to the rest of the world, have led to an overall reduction in global income inequality. However, if China continues to catch up, global income inequality is likely to resume its long-term upward trend.
5. This section draws on the work of Barr (1993) and Clark (1998).
6. See Bénabou 1996 and Figini 1999 for excellent overviews of this literature.
7. While the term political economy is a contested concept, in general it is accepted to mean the interaction between economic outcomes and political power and its essence lies in exploring their interconnectedness. Eighteenth- and nineteenth-century political economy (the origin of present day economics) discussed the economy in the context of society, the environment and morality. With the constructing of economics as a 'science' over the twentieth century those broader contexts for examining the economy became marginalized or excluded.
8. Non-cash benefits available to the unemployed also affect incentives to work and assigning them a cash value to include in replacement rate calculations is complex. Recent work undertaken in the US is reviewed in Nolan *et al.* 2000.
9. The Laffer curve plots tax rates against total tax revenues and suggests that above a certain tax rate, total tax revenues will fall instead of rise because of incentive effects. There is little empirical evidence to support the view that this rate, if it exists, is anywhere near the rates currently used in OECD countries.
10. For examples, see Archer 1995, Breitenbach, Burden and Coates 1990, Le Grand and Estrin 1989, Miller 1989, Nove 1991 and Schweickart 1994. Bowles and Gintis (1998) also call for firms that are owned and managed by their workers, although it would be misleading to call their proposal market socialist.
11. We are not proposing Japan as a model egalitarian society, given its record on, for example, gender equality. Rather we are focusing on one aspect of its

economy, namely its consistent ranking as having one of the most equal income distributions.

12. France and Italy also spend a high percentage of GDP on social welfare but their pre-tax income differentials are so high that the post-tax distribution remains fairly unequal. The US, Canada and Australia feature both large differences in market income and minimal transfer spending and unsurprisingly have among the most unequal income distributions in the OECD.

13. For a fuller description of the partnership model see, for example, O'Donnell and Thomas 1998. The community and voluntary sector comprises a variety of non-profit organizations engaged in a wide range of social and economic activities including training, adult education, advocacy and political work with marginalized groups.

14. Over the period of the economic boom welfare payments were increased at more than double the rate of inflation yet they fell behind the increase in earnings and thus contributed to the overall increase in income inequality over the period. The idea of an explicit link to average earnings has been strongly but unsuccessfully advocated by many groups under the review processes of the National Anti-Poverty Strategy.

15. Some discussions of the basic income approach are Arneson 1987, Barry 1997, Levine 1998, ch. 1, Van Parijs 1991, 1992, 1995, 2001 and White 2003.

# 6. The Challenge of Participatory Democracy

1. On the idea of equality of political power, see Brighouse 1996, 2001 and Armstrong 2003.

2. Some key discussions are Bachrach and Botwinick 1992, Barber 1984, Graham 1986, Held 1996, Pateman 1970 and Thompson 1970. Fung and Wright's (2003) model of 'empowered participatory governance' is an important recent discussion although some of the cases it is applied to involve fuller participation than others.

3. Some other interesting consultative exercises are deliberative polls (Fishkin 1991, 1995; Fishkin and Luskin 1999) and the Participatory Rural Appraisal process described by Larkin (1997). On some of the problems and pitfalls, see Button and Mattson 1998.

4. Here we are trying to bring together a number of contributions on democratic communication, especially Barber 1984, Dryzek 2000, Knight and Johnson 1997, Mansbridge 1999, Phillips 1999, Sanders 1997, Walzer 1999 and Young 1996, 2000, chs 1–2, 2001b.

5. As Mansbridge (1999, 2003) points out, a great deal of political communication occurs in private, and there are occasions when negotiation proceeds more effectively behind closed doors. Where transparency or publicity matters most is at the stage at which final, binding decisions are made.

6. These authors are largely inspired by Rawls (1993) and Habermas (1996a, esp. chs 7–8, 1996b) and include Benhabib (1996), Bohman (1996, 1998), J. Cohen (1989, 1996, 1998), Cohen and Rogers (2003), Cooke (2000), Elster (1986, 1998), Freeman (2000) and Gutmann and Thompson (1996). On the public sphere see also Fraser 1989, 1997a, Mansbridge 1999 and Young 2000, ch. 5.

7. It is also worth noting that theorists of deliberative democracy vary considerably in their confidence in the ability of ordinary citizens to deliberate, a point

reflected in their relative neglect of the importance of socially representative participation in the process of deliberation (see Elster 1998; Gargarella 1998).

8. The following discussion overlaps in many ways with Dahl 1989.

9. A good review of the US data is Delli Carpini and Keeter 1996. Verba, Schlozman and Brady (1995, ch. 4) provide evidence of the 'civic' motivations of political activists.

10. For some helpful advice on meetings in social change organizations, see Bobo, Kendall and Max 2001, ch. 12. On Porto Alegre and Kerala see, respectively, Baiochhi 2003 and Thomas Isaac and Heller 2003.

11. Our model of accountable representation is similar to those of Williams (1998) and Young (2000, ch. 6).

12. A number of institutional devices have been surveyed by Elster (1993). We concentrate here on those particularly relevant to developing a more participatory democracy.

13. Classic discussions of consociational regimes are Lijphart 1977 and 1984. Some useful critical discussions are Barry 1975, Bogaards 1998 and McRae 1997.

14. It should be noted that Ireland is far from a fully neocorporatist system (see, e.g., Siaroff 1999), but has the advantage of being our 'local' example. For the Irish model see O'Donnell and Thomas 1998.

15. An interesting variation on this point is the way in which electoral majorities in Porto Alegre and Kerala have used their power to create the space within which deliberative decision-making can take place (Abers 1998; Fung and Wright 2003).

16. For similar surveys see Phillips 1995, Williams 1998, ch. 7 and Young 2000, ch. 4 sec. 6. It should be emphasized that none of this discussion presupposes that subordinate groups are politically homogeneous, but only that their members have a broadly shared experience of subordination.

17. In the 1999–2000 election cycle, the Republican Party raised $715.7m while the Democratic Party raised $520.4m (data from the Federal Election Commission: http://www.fec.gov). In the 2002 general election, Fianna Fáil spent €3.57m compared to Fine Gael's €2.34m and Labour's €1.1m; each of the other parties spent less than €600 000 (data from the Standards in Public Office Commission, http://www.sipo.gov.ie, which also has details of the legislative provisions). The Bipartisan Campaign Reform Act (BCRA) 2002 is a substantial reform of the US federal system; at the time of writing, a legal challenge was pending in the Supreme Court. Up-to-date information is available from the Campaign Legal Center (http://www.campaignlegalcenter.org).

18. For information about the Citizen Traveller campaign see the Irish Traveller Movement website (http://www.itmtrav.com/citizentrav.html). The report used to justify the end of funding was published by the Department of Justice, Equality and Law Reform (2002).

## 7.  Equality, the Legal System and Employment Law

1. The Canadian Charter of Rights and Freedoms places some general limits on interpretation by directing judges to construe it 'in a manner consistent with the preservation and enhancement of the multicultural heritage of Canadians' (section 27). Similarly, under section 39 of the South African Constitution, when interpreting the Bill of Rights, a court, tribunal or forum '(a) must promote the values that underlie an open and democratic society based on human dignity, equality and freedom; (b) must consider international law; and (c) may consider foreign law.'

2. Traditionally an *amicus curiae* ('friend of the court') was an 'impartial' bystander whose expertise was called upon to assist courts in their deliberations, a position that continues to represent third party participation in Irish litigation. Courts in other countries now admit briefs that advocate particular interests (Whyte 2002, pp. 97–9). With respect to the US see Kearney and Merrill 2000; for the UK position and comparative material see Justice/Public Law Project 1996; on Australia see Williams 2000. Under section 8 (h) of the Human Rights Commission Act 2000, the Irish Human Rights Commission may apply to act as *amicus* in cases involving or concerned with the human rights of any person. Liberty to intervene is at the discretion of the courts.

3. See for example the briefs submitted by the Canadian women's rights organization, LEAF (http://www.leaf.ca).

4. Kearney and Merrill (2000, p. 750) observe that 'amicus briefs filed by institutional litigants and by experienced lawyers – filers that have a better idea of what kind of information is useful to the Court – are generally more successful than are briefs filed by irregular litigants and less experienced lawyers'.

5. Judicial notice provides for an exception to the general rule that all facts in issue must be proved by evidence presented to the court (Davis 1955; L'Heureux-Dubé 1994; MacCrimmon 1998; Tapper 1995, pp. 70–9). In *Moge* v. *Moge* (1992), 43, RFL (3d) 345, a Canadian judge employed the doctrine of judicial notice to highlight the feminization of poverty endemic to post-divorce situations. For further examples from that jurisdiction see Boyle and MacCrimmon 2001. On the contextual approach to legal interpretation employed by the Canadian judiciary see Sugunasiri 1999.

6. The distinction between 'adjudicative' and 'legislative' facts drawn by Davis (1955) distinguishes between facts that relate to the specific parties to litigation and those that concern general policy considerations. The Supreme Court of Canada has defined legislative facts as 'those that establish the purpose and background of legislation, including its social, economic and cultural context' (*Danson* v. *Ontario (A.G.)* [1990] 2 S.C.R. 1086 at 1099).

7. Although the conceptual underpinnings of anti-discrimination laws are by no means clearly articulated (Barnard and Hepple 2000; Collins 2003; Fredman 2001), equal opportunity is their most plausible aim. It is explicitly endorsed by the EU: see Article 2(4) of Directive 76/207 and *Kalanke* v. *Freie Hansestadt Bremen*, Case C-450/93 [1995] ECR I-3051.

8. See for example *Zuchner* v. *Handelskrankenkasse (Erstazkasse) Bremen*, Case 77/95 [1996] ECR I-5689 and *Drake* v. *Chief Adjudication Officer*, Case 150/85 [1986] ECR 1995 on the scope of Article 2 EC Directive 79/7.

9. In *Bettray* v. *Staatssecretaris van Justitie*, Case 344/87 [1989] ECR 1621; [1991] CMLR 459, the Court of Justice held that the definition of 'worker' under Article 18 of the EC Treaty did not include the applicant, who was employed under the Dutch Social Employment Scheme, because the aim of that scheme was to rehabilitate and prepare individuals for employment in the wider labour market. By analogy people with disabilities who work in sheltered employment are not 'workers' either.

10. See for example *Van Roosmalen* v. *Bestuur von de Bedrijfsvereniging voor de Gezondheid*, Case 300/84 [1986] ECR 3097.

11. The boundary between the two models is crossed largely at the level of remedies, so for example a finding of indirect discrimination may result in a direction that the employer institute an affirmative action programme or reasonably accommodate the employee involved.

12. See for example section 2 (1) of the Irish Employment Equality Act 1998.

13. *Commission* v. *Italy*, Case 163/82 [1983] ECR 3273.
14. The principle stems from the US Supreme Court's decision in *Griggs* v. *Duke Power Co.* 401 U.S. 424 (1971) where it struck down reliance on general ability testing and high school diplomas as job requirements because of the disproportionate negative impact these had on African-American workers. As early EU legislative enactments did not define indirect discrimination, development of the principle in the context of gender was left to the European Court of Justice, in *Jenkins*, Case 96/80 [1981] ECR 911 and *Bilka Kaufhaus* v. *Weber*, Case 170/84 [1986] ECR 1607. Indirect discrimination features in sections 19(4), 22, 29 and 31 of the Irish Employment Equality Act 1998.
15. The main EU law authority is *Bilka Kaufhaus* v. *Weber*, Case 170/84 [1986] ECR 1607. There the Court held that employers could pay part-time workers less than their full-time counterparts in order to encourage full-time work. Certain positions may also attract higher rates of pay, notwithstanding any discriminatory effects, where the market dictates that the requisite workers are in short supply (see for example *Enderby* v. *Frenchay Health Authority*, Case C-127/92 [1993] ECR I-5535).
16. The comparator may be actual or hypothetical depending on the context. In the context of equal pay for men and women, the use of a hypothetical male comparator was rejected by the European Court of Justice in *Macarthys Ltd.* v. *Smith*, Case 129/79 [1980] ECR 1275, although a woman may compare herself with an immediate predecessor in the post. There is no need for any comparator in cases of discrimination on the grounds of pregnancy (*Dekker*, Case C-177/88 [1990] ECR I-3941). Section 6 of the Irish Employment Equality Act opened up the possibility of a hypothetical comparator being employed in cases other than those relating to pay. A person can claim that they were treated less favourably than someone from a comparable group *would have been treated* (see for example *Barry* v. *Board of Management (Aisling Project), Virgin Mary Schools* (DEC-E2001-031)). Under EU law the burden of proof shifts to the employer once a prima facie case of discrimination is made out (see Article 4, Directive 97/80).
17. In a decision concerning Directive 79/7/EEC the Court of Justice held that the principle of equal treatment between men and women in matters of social security could only be satisfied by levelling up when applied retrospectively. However, in relation to prospective applications of the principle, the Irish state could opt either to level up or level down (*McDermott and Cotter* v. *Minister for Social Welfare*, Case 286/85 [1987] ECR 1453).
18. See decisions of the US Supreme Court to that effect in *Regents of University of California* v. *Bakke* 438 U.S. 265 (1978); *Adarand Constructors Inc.* v. *Pena* 115 S. Ct. 2097 (1995). That approach can be contrasted with judgments issued by the Canadian judiciary. According to LaForest J. in *Eldridge* v. *British Columbia (Attorney General)* [1997] 3 S.C.R. 624, 'the purpose of s. 15(1) of the *Charter* is not only to prevent discrimination by the attribution of stereotypical characteristics to individuals, but also to ameliorate the position of groups within Canadian society who have suffered disadvantage by exclusion from mainstream society'. In the context of affirmative action, Ely (1980, p. 170) distinguishes between racial classifications on the basis of their underlying purpose; positive applications should not attract heightened judicial scrutiny because a white legislature will not discriminate against itself. But the limits of his representation-reinforcement model of judicial review came to the fore in *Richmond* v. *J.A. Croson Co.*, 488 U.S. 469 (1989), when the Supreme Court cited his work to buttress application of strict scrutiny to an affirmative action programme because a bare majority of the Richmond city council members were black (*ibid.*, p. 495).

19. These measures are variously known as 'affirmative action', 'positive action', 'positive discrimination' or 'employment equity' measures. While positive action is generally thought of in terms of workforce quotas, it can take various forms including public procurement clauses and such outreach measures as encouraging members of an under-represented group to apply for a position or preferring them for training. One primary distinction is whether such programmes are mandated or voluntary. Some states *require* designated employers to use positive action policies, for example South Africa (Chapter III, Employment Equity Act 1998, No. 55) and Canada (Employment Equity Act 1995), while others merely *provide immunity from prosecution for discrimination* to employers who wish to implement such steps, as in the case of Ireland (Employment Equality Act 1998, sections 24(1) and 33). European Union provisions are also enabling rather than compulsory (see Article 141(1) of the EC Treaty re gender and Article 5 of the Race Directive). Although constitutions tend not to recognize positive action, it is envisaged by section 15(2) of the Canadian Charter and the equality guarantee of the South African Constitution (ch. 2, section 9(2)). On South Africa see further Grant and Small 2001.
20. For an example of the test applied by the European Court of Justice, see *Abrahamsson and Anderson* v. *Fogelqvist*, Case C-407/98 [2000] ECR I-5539. US courts rely on similar tests called rational basis, strict and intermediate scrutiny tests (see Eskridge 2002, pp. 2250–300).
21. Case law of the European Court of Justice on positive action includes the decisions in *Kalanke* v. *Freie Hansestadt Bremen*, Case C-450/93 [1995] ECR I-3051; *Marschall* v. *Land Nordrhein-Westfalen*, Case C-409/95 [1997] ECR I-6363; *Badeck & Ors* v. *Landesanwalt beim Staatsgerichtshof des Landes Hessen*, Case C-158/97 [2000] ECR I-1875; *Abrahamsson and Anderson* v. *Fogelqvist*, Case C-407/98 [2000] ECR I-5539. Decisions of the US Supreme Court include *Regents of University of California* v. *Bakke* 438 U.S. 265 (1978); *Richmond* v. *J.A. Croson Co.*, 488 U.S. 469 (1989); *Adarand* v. *Pena* 115 S. Ct. 2097 (1995).
22. *Personnel Admin.* v. *Feeney*, 442 U.S. 256, 279 (1979).
23. EC Directive 2000/78, Art. 5; Employment Equality Act 1998, section 35 (Ireland); Disability Discrimination Act 1996, section 6 (UK); Americans with Disabilities Act 1990, 42 U.S.C. §§ 12101–12213 (1994 & Supp. IV 1998) (ADA). For a comparative analysis see Quinn, McDonagh and Kimber 1993. Reasonable accommodation is applied to all grounds of discrimination under Chapter III of South Africa's Employment Equity Act 1998.
24. See for example the US Family and Medical Leave Act 1993, 29 U.S.C. §§ 2601–2654 (1994) and discussion by Colker (1997).
25. *British Columbia (Public Service Employee Relations Commission)* v. *British Columbia Government and Service Employees Union* [1999] 3 S.C.R. 3.
26. See for example Chapter III of the South African Employment Equity Act 1998 and Part VI of the Irish Employment Equality Act 1998.
27. These orders could form a part of the inter-branch dialogue provided for in some countries' constitutional arrangements; see generally Tushnet 2003.

## 8.   Equality and Education

1. In 1999, 115.4 million children of school age were out of school throughout the world, of whom 56 per cent were girls (UNESCO 2002, p. 16).

2. See Bourdieu 1986 for a discussion of the different forms of capital.
3. This is not to suggest that the distribution issue in education is purely a class issue; it is not. The failure to provide the resources for all types of social groups to avail fully of education, be it women availing of technological or scientific education, or disabled people or migrant workers being able to participate equally with others in education, is essentially a distributive problem. However, because the generative cause of the inequality that the latter groups experience in education is not in the first instance economic but cultural (see Chapter 4), we concentrate on class here.
4. The habitus refers to the socially patterned matrix of preferences and dispositions that are developed across social classes. The habitus of particular classes produces a series of durable, transportable dispositions of mind and body, most of which are learned unconsciously. These provide an unconscious and internalized roadmap for action which the individual defines and regulates continually (see Bourdieu 1984; Bourdieu and Passeron 1977).
5. Although much of the discussion here will focus on schools, many of the equality issues raised apply in equal measure to colleges of further and higher education, and in particular to universities.
6. The terms used for grouping students vary cross-culturally. In the US, 'tracking' is used to refer to the practice of dividing students into vocational or academic groups or bands. In other countries, 'streaming', 'setting' and 'banding' are used to refer to similar processes, particularly where these take place within a given school, varying according to whether students are grouped differently for different subjects (setting) or across all subjects (streaming and banding). What is generally called 'ability grouping' is a misnomer, as most grouping is based on measured levels of attainment. For a more detailed discussion of the conceptual and institutional problems associated with grouping see Lynch and Lodge 2002, pp. 64–86.
7. The Irish state provides most of the funding for socially selective fee-paying schools (catering for 7 per cent of the population at second level). This is one of the more blatant examples internationally of how privilege is underwritten by the state.
8. In Ireland these include the School Inspectorate and the National Council for Curriculum and Assessment (NCCA), where teachers themselves are centrally involved. The subject associations representing different groups of teachers (in Gaeilge, English, Mathematics, etc.) also exercise considerable influence, as do teachers' trade unions.
9. Gardner (1983, 1999) has identified at least eight core intelligences: linguistic, logical-mathematical, musical, bodily-kinaesthetic, spatial, interpersonal, intra-personal and naturalist.
10. Bourdieu and Passeron (1977) refer to the cultural products offered in school as cultural arbitraries to indicate the highly arbitrary way in which they are selected and assessed. In particular, they highlight the social class biases in what is taught, to whom, when and how.
11. It is appreciated that the personal intelligences as defined by Gardner (1983) are not synonymous with Goleman's (1995) concept of emotional intelligence, but there is a considerable overlap between the two.
12. This is not to suggest that such work should be gendered, merely that historically this has been the case.
13. To say this is not to deny that most of the abuse and emotional harm that is done to people takes place within the home.

14. There is a vast literature on the cognitive, affective and pedagogical principles that should underpin social justice related education. This work has its origins in very different intellectual traditions including developmental psychology, feminist, anti-racist and multicultural education, black and ethnic studies, Freirean-inspired critical pedagogy and the Deweyian tradition of experiential learning. A useful synopsis of these approaches is provided in Adams, Bell and Griffin 1997. One of the best known examples of an alternative school that was deeply committed to the principles of respect for difference was Summerhill (Ackerman *et al.* 1970; Neill 1962). Another programme designed specifically to educate about difference was the Education for Mutual Understanding Programme in Northern Ireland (Smith and Robinson 1992, 1996).

## 9.   Emancipatory Research as a Tool of Change

1. While positivism here refers primarily to quantitative studies, much of qualitative research operates out of similar principles in its research design (Jayaratne and Stewart 1995; Oliver 1992).
2. In his analysis of the wealth of Irish households, Nolan (1991) noted that one of the biggest problems in examining wealth distribution was the lack of accurate and comprehensive data.
3. Feminists are not immune to this problem either, as oppressions of class, colour or ethnicity have often been either ignored in feminist debates or analysed in a way that is far from emancipatory (for critiques of such practices see Byrne 1992; Collins 1990; Davis 1982; Lugones and Spelman 1985; McDonagh 2000; O'Neill 1992, 2000).
4. There has been very little independent research funding available to the social sciences in Ireland. Although state aid for social science research was substantially increased in 1998, the research fund of the Irish Social Science Research Council (SSRC) was only in the region of £100 000 (€127 000) per annum as recently as the mid-1990s. While some of the international research foundations did offer grants to Irish researchers, there was no major foundation within Ireland sponsoring social scientific research. Up to the end of the millennium therefore, the bulk of the money available for social science research was available for commissioned studies for state-sponsored projects. Such funding provided the core funding for the work of the Economic and Social Research Institute (ESRI) and the Educational Research Centre (ERC) (Drumcondra). The lack of funding for basic research meant that much of the work undertaken was of an applied nature, frequently designed to answer a specific policy query for the funder. Such a system is heavily biased in favour of empirical (especially quantitative) research in the positivist tradition, as exemplified by the published work of the ESRI and the ERC.
5. The European Community Household Panel Survey and the Irish Household Budget Survey are examples of this type of research. National databases on poverty and related issues are collected through these surveys.
6. The scope for creating massive databases on people of both a quantitative and qualitative nature has been greatly enhanced by computer developments in recent years. The ability of researchers to colonize the life worlds of those who are marginalized is likely to increase considerably unless the research process is democratized.
7. At the Irish Conference on Civil and Social Rights in the European Union (Dublin, 7–8 May 1997), a number of working class community activists criti-

cized one of the speakers for making no attempt to communicate his academic ideas in accessible language (the audience included community activists, researchers, policy-makers and administrators). The speaker dismissed the criticism on the grounds that it was only possible to communicate (*sic*) his ideas in a particular type of language.

8. An example of how academics may inadvertently structure the exclusion of marginalized groups occurred at a conference organized in Trinity College Dublin on 18 July 1997 on 'Travellers, Society and the Law'. All the lecturers were professionals and there was no space in the programme for the Travellers' perspective. In addition, the fee for the day was £100 (€127), so it was only those with access to resources who could attend.

9. We have had direct experience of this in our own research in equality studies. Dialogues with various research participants about the design of a study and the interpretation of its data led to attempts by powerful interests in education to exclude certain questions from the study at the outset and to frame the interpretation in ways that would conceal particular inequalities at the write-up stage (see the discussion of the research process in Lynch and Lodge 2002).

10. Some of the objectives of Learning Partnerships can be pursued through other ways of collaborating with local communities. For example, the postgraduate programme in Equality Studies at University College Dublin gives priority to recruiting students with equality-related experience as a way of increasing dialogue between marginalized groups and the university, disseminating academic knowledge and skills throughout these groups and facilitating social change. The Certificate in Equality Studies and its associated Qualifier programme aim to share knowledge with people with limited academic credentials and to enable them to proceed to postgraduate study in equality studies.

11. Statutory agencies like the Equality Authority in the Republic of Ireland and the Equality Commission in Northern Ireland already exercise such functions to some degree.

## 10. Class, Gender and the Equality Movement

1. The critique of Marxism in this section is indebted to Cohen (1995, 2000). The original model was set out in popular form by Marx and Engels in the *Communist Manifesto* (1848) and we concentrate here on its core assumptions or paradigm. Subsequent generations of Marxists developed and adapted the theory to deal with many of the issues we raise and much of what we say in this part of the book is indebted to their thinking.

2. See Cohen 1995 and Lukes 1985. There is a substantial literature on whether Marx had moral objections to capitalism, whether these included the claim that capitalism was unjust and, if so, what the injustice consisted in (see Kymlicka 2002, ch. 5 for a summary). We are concerned here with the dominant, explicit view of the Marxist paradigm and not with the finer points of Marx scholarship.

3. This definition is adapted from discussions in Alvarez 1997, Giugni 1998 and Tarrow 1998a.

4. A range of anti-egalitarian movements has recently emerged in Ireland, a number of which are overtly anti-feminist and often anti-woman. These include AMEN, a men's rights group that defines its position largely in terms of its opposition to women's rights, the Youth Defence Movement and Human Life International (and their various offshoots), both of which are opposed to reproductive rights

for women, and the Immigration Control Platform which is explicitly xenophobic and anti-immigrant.

5. For lively accounts of the anti-capitalist movement see Bircham and Charlton 2001, Kingsnorth 2003, Klein 2002 and Notes from Nowhere 2003.

6. The most blatant recent Irish example of how the state can silence dissent was the withdrawal of funding for the Citizen Traveller campaign mentioned in Chapter 6.

7. The claim that movements have contributed in some way to the changes set out in the next few paragraphs is better documented in some cases than in others. A full justification for the claim would involve much more detailed research on social and political change than we have to hand. What we say here, therefore, expresses our considered judgements as observers rather than empirically proven effects.

8. The number of 'consistently poor' individuals fell from 14.5 per cent in 1994 to 5.5 per cent in 2000. The revised target is 2 per cent (Combat Poverty Agency 2003a, pp. 6–10).

9. A number of scholars attribute rising economic inequality to the failure of the neocorporatist strategy of social partnership to deliver a fair return to workers for their increased productivity in a period of economic boom in the late 1990s and early 2000s in particular (Allen 2000; O'Hearn 2002). Others suggest that the partnership model has brought some gains to socially vulnerable groups (Nolan, O'Connell and Whelan 2000).

10. In the OECD, the proportion of paid women workers who are part-time varies from 11 per cent in Finland to 30 per cent in Ireland, 44 per cent in the UK and 67 per cent in the Netherlands, with a figure of over 20 per cent for most countries (CSO 2002, Table 1; Lewis 2001, p. 61).

11. In the Irish civil service alone, there are 1200 different grades. The wages and salaries of each grade are tied to other grades (Kavanagh 1996).

12. One of the clearest examples of how organizational power works to the advantage of particular workers was the privatization of a number of nationalized industries and mutual societies in Ireland in the late 1990s. Senior managers were strategically positioned to maximize gains for themselves, even though in formal social class terms they were wage earners without assets in the companies in question.

13. The study, involving 1500 second-level students, asked them to name the occupations of both parents and in a separate question to assign themselves to a class group. While most middle class students (as classified according to accepted social scientific class schema) assigned themselves to the 'correct' social class, this was not true of students who were formally defined as working class. Only 21.6 per cent of those in the semi-skilled and unskilled group defined themselves as working class. Middle class identity was positively appropriated by these same students with 70 per cent of the two groups defining themselves as middle class. In contrast, 90 per cent of those in the professional/managerial class defined themselves as middle class with 30 per cent defining themselves as upper middle class.

14. The ideology of meritocracy is also deeply and implicitly respected in academic work, for example in work by Goldthorpe, Breen and other social mobility theorists that implicitly equates social mobility for a given class with a move towards equality, a liberal egalitarian perspective (Breen and Rottman 1995; Goldthorpe, Llewellyn and Payne 1980).

15. Under the Belfast Agreement, members of the Northern Ireland Assembly must designate themselves as Nationalist, Unionist or other. Key decisions must have support from both the nationalist and unionist blocs (Strand 1, clause 5(d)).

16. Self-employed farmers and relatives assisting comprised 39 per cent of the paid male labour force in 1926 declining to 33 per cent in 1961; agricultural labourers comprised 14 per cent throughout that period. Even as late as 1961, over 41 per cent of the male labour force were employed in the agricultural sectors of the economy, mostly as small farmers and agricultural labourers (Rottman *et al.* 1982, p. 46). In 1926, just over 18 per cent of males were employed outside agriculture as skilled, semi-skilled or unskilled manual workers, increasing only to 27 per cent by 1961. For women, the largest single occupational group at the foundation of the state was domestic workers (Ó hOgartaigh 1999). Women's industrial employment grew steadily from 1922 to 1936. At that time a combination of Roman Catholic teaching and a male backlash in Fianna Fáil and the trade union movement succeeded in passing legislation that excluded women from certain industries (Allen 1997, pp. 58–9). This brought about enforced domestication and accelerated emigration for many. It is often forgotten that in the hundred years from 1871 to 1971 female emigration exceeded male emigration (Ó hOgartaigh 1999, citing Travers). The stability of the class and occupational structure from the 1920s to the late 1950s was maintained at the cost of mass emigration, mostly from the agricultural sector (Breen, Hannan and Wheelan 1990, p. 54). From the 1960s onwards, there was a significant rise in white collar jobs, but the manual working class hardly grew at all. Thus by 1985, 55 per cent of all employees were employed in professional, salaried, managerial and other forms of non-manual employment and only 29 per cent in manual employment (*ibid.*, pp. 56–9).

17. Only 12 per cent of the seats in the Dáil (lower house of the national parliament) and 15 per cent of those in local authorities are held by women (Galligan 1998, 2000). Over 85 per cent of employers are men, most large corporations are controlled by men and over 90 per cent of farm holders are men (O'Connor 1998). Men are also significantly over-represented in senior positions across different sectors of employment (Ruane and Sutherland 1999). By contrast, over 73 per cent of part-time workers are women, and women are over-represented among low paid workers and among those living in poverty (Nolan and Watson 1999).

18. In this chapter we will not examine the ways in which the gender order creates stratifications between men, although we agree with Connell (1995) that these are profound and of considerable political significance.

19. In the Republic of Ireland women are very actively involved in a host of both statutory and non-governmental bodies focused on promoting equality, including the Carers' Association, the Combat Poverty Agency, the Community Workers Co-operative, the Debt and Development Coalition, the Equality Authority, the Human Rights Commission, the Irish Council for Civil Liberties, the Irish Penal Reform Trust, Meitheal (a radical community development organization), the National Consultative Committee on Racism and Interculturalism, the National Disability Authority and the National Women's Council of Ireland. Within Northern Ireland women have played a crucial role in the community development field and in drafting the PAFT guidelines that underpinned the equality provisions of the Belfast Agreement of 1998, as well as in exercising authority through the Northern Ireland Equality Commission and through the Women's Coalition political party.

20. See the National Women's Council of Ireland *Strategic Work Plan 2002–2005* (2002) and similar plans by women in Northern Ireland.

## 11.  Ideology and Resistance

1. This is widely recognized in sociological literature (see, for example, Habermas 1984 on communicative action and Bourdieu and Passeron 1977 on the significance of symbolic violence in education).

2. Empirical evidence from the UK on how the ideology of neoliberalism was systematically promulgated and institutionalized during the 17 years of Tory rule in the 1980s and 1990s, changing the British welfare state from one of the most respected in Europe to one of the most questioned, is an indication of how ideologies are real political forces that can frame practice even within the confines of capitalism itself (Hall 1988). Within the Irish republic, pervasive Roman Catholic and nationalist ideologies have framed not only its constitution, but also its legislation, much of which was deeply misogynistic (Allen 1997). The systematic move by conservative political interests in the US to fund right-wing think tanks and academics since the early 1990s indicates the enormous importance they ascribe to ideological forces (see Callahan 1999; Covington 1997). The top 20 conservative think tanks spent US $1bn from 1990 to 2000.

3. The New Labour message presents autonomous bourgeois subjectivity as an ideal choice, offering freedom without dependence. The price for success is individual responsibility and a life of self-reinvention (Walkerdine, Lucey and Melody 2001).

4. While the anti-globalization movement has the potential to mobilize globally against international trade agreements, its potential for being the sole mobilizing force for ideological resistance in the national politics of Western European countries and the US (who are the ultimate beneficiaries of such agreements) would seem to be much more limited.

5. Thompson (1990, pp. 60–7) outlines how ideologies function in sociological terms. He identifies five general modes of ideological operation. *Legitimation* is the presentation of certain sets of social relations as rational, universal and inevitable. *Dissimulation* involves concealing substantive interests through the use of euphemisms, etc. *Unification* involves the development of symbols of unity such as standard languages, flags, emblems, etc. *Fragmentation* refers to the practice of presenting the opposition as diverse and disorganized as well as being a threat to what is defined as a common-sense view of the world. Finally, *reification* involves presenting a passing or transitory state of affairs as inevitable and natural so that any challenge is presented as unthinkable.

6. Touraine (1965, 1966) has identified three key principles or defining features of social movements. The *principe d'identité* refers to its identity, the self definition of the movement of what it is, and on behalf of whom it speaks; the *principe d'opposition* refers to its adversary, its political enemy; while the *principe de totalité* refers to the societal goals or its vision of the kind of future social order it would wish to attain. What we are talking about here is the *principe de totalité* of the equality movement.

7. We are indebted for clarification on this point to our colleague Ger Moane, of the Psychology Department, UCD.

8. In the long term, however, it is arguable that a society that fails to reproduce itself, or makes the cost of reproduction prohibitive through the commercialization and marginalization of care work, will eliminate the source of its own profitability in the form of a purchasing public.

9. The use of the derogatory term 'feminazis' to label feminists in the Irish print media in the early twenty-first century is itself indicative of deep hostility to

gender equality and to the new political agendas that feminism brings to the political table.

10. There are parallels here between what happened within labour-based political parties in several European countries and what happened in the women's movement in the late twentieth century. From the 1970s onwards, parties of the left largely ignored the growing disenchantment among the declining, but politically powerful, old working class in urban areas who did not make the cut in terms of social mobility. The rise of racism and fascism in Europe in the late twentieth century is undoubtedly one response to the sense of disenchantment with left politics that arose from the failure of the left to deliver, especially to lower paid unskilled and semi-skilled workers, in terms of educational opportunities, standards of living and quality of life. The rise of Thatcherism in the UK also drew on this type of disenchantment (see Hall 1988).

11. 34 per cent of all Irish women are full-time at home (CSO 2002). Women with children under 16 or in full-time education and under 18 do receive child benefit payments (currently €126 per month for first and second children and €157 for each additional child) but this does not give them a significant amount of economic independence.

12. Only recently have the terms of the debate about care work begun to change in Ireland. The National Women's Council of Ireland (NWCI) in particular has started to define the issues in more feminist terms. The Community Platform (representing a wide range of groups belonging to the major new left-of-centre social movements in Ireland) has also adopted an equality framework that promotes affective equality, as has the National Economic and Social Forum, although neither of the latter bodies has accorded the same status to emotional work as the NWCI.

13. The participation rate of women in employment in Ireland is now slightly higher (47.5 per cent) than the EU average (47 per cent) (CSO 2002). While other societies have adapted to these transitions by either socializing child care or making extensive provision for parental or maternity leave, Ireland does not have a state infrastructure of child care and parental leave comparable to that in Northern Europe. There is also a considerable difference between public service workers and private sector workers in the operation of voluntary arrangements.

# 12.   Strategic Issues for the Equality Movement

1. In addition to the specific references made in this chapter, our thinking on this issue has been influenced by Abramsky (2001), Alinsky (1971), Brecher and Costello (1998), Brecher, Costello and Smith (2000), Castells (1997), Cohen (1995, 2000), the Community Workers Co-operative (1998), Donaghy (2002), Epstein (1991), Fox and Starn (1997), Gamson (1990), Giugni, McAdam and Tilly (1998), Gorz (1982), Habermas (1996a), Klein (2000, 2001), Klinkner and Smith (1999), Kriesi *et al.* (1995), Liddy (2002), Marcos (2001), McAdam, McCarthy and Zald (1996), Piven and Cloward (1977), Scott (1985), Tarrow (1998a), Unger (1997) and Walby (2001).

2. Examples of tactical discussions are Alinsky 1971, Bobo, Kendall and Max 2001 and Shaw 2001.

3. As a result of constitutional provisions and litigation, abortion is legal in Ireland only to save the life of a pregnant woman. The 2002 referendum concerned a

proposal to exclude the risk of suicide as a ground for abortion. For an account see Kennedy 2002.

4. The three possible responses here are closely related to the five relationships canvassed by Hanagan (1998). One of his options (articulation) is assumed as inappropriate and two others (alliance, independence) are treated as equivalent.

5. We are not suggesting that Nader founded the Green Party; it was, however, a central aim of his candidacy to build support for that party (Sifry 2002).

6. For a brief recent overview, see Farrell 2000, ch. 7; for a recent account of third parties in the US, see Sifry 2002. The tendency towards two parties is far from being an iron law but it is an understandable feature of plurality electoral systems. The rapid development of some socialist parties in the early twentieth century was facilitated by a concurrent expansion of the electorate; a similar opportunity exists in democratizing situations (e.g. the PT in Brazil) but no longer pertains in countries with a long period of universal suffrage.

7. The problem can be side-stepped in US states whose electoral laws permit candidates to be nominated by more than one party, allowing progressive parties like the Working Families Party of New York (http://www.workingfamilies-party.org) to co-nominate selected Democratic candidates and to demonstrate support for egalitarian policies without playing into the hands of Republicans. See Sifry 2002, chs 9–11, for a fuller discussion.

8. STV voting systems are explained in many introductions to electoral systems, e.g. Dummett 1997. What Americans call IRV is called the alternative vote system in Britain and preferential voting in Australia.

9. A similar point can be made about some smaller parties of the left that seem to use every public gathering as a recruitment fair. For a lively expression of this criticism and a position that is much less accommodating to mainstream parties than the present chapter, see SchNEWS 2001.

10. Szasz (1994, p. 179, n. 32) writes: 'From various interviews, it seems that there is some distrust and tension between the traditional environmental organizations and the new toxics [*sic*] movement organizations. What strikes the outsider, however, is that in spite of the mutual distrust and disapproval, the two types of environmentalism have, in practice, worked out a very effective division of labour.'

11. State funding is often mentioned by equality activists in Ireland as a factor that silences and softens criticism, but we are not aware of published evidence of this effect. This problem is discussed in the US context by Bobo, Kendall and Max (2001), who advise against using the same organization for both service delivery and direct action campaigning (pp. 12, 21, 277) and review a number of fund-raising strategies (ch. 21).

# Bibliography

Abercrombie, Nicholas, Stephen Hill and Bryan S. Turner (1980) *The Dominant Ideology Thesis* (London: Allen & Unwin).

Abercrombie, Nicholas, Stephen Hill and Bryan S. Turner, eds (1990) *Dominant Ideologies* (London: Unwin Hyman).

Abers, Rebecca (1998) 'From Clientelism to Cooperation: Local Government, Participatory Policy, and Civic Organizing in Porto Alegre, Brazil', *Politics & Society* 26, 511–37.

Abraham, David (1996) 'Liberty without Equality: The Property-Rights Connection in a "Negative Citizenship" Regime', *Law and Social Inquiry* 21, 1–65.

Abramsky, Kolya, ed. (2001) *Restructuring and Resistance: Diverse Voices of Struggle in Western Europe* (UK: published by editor).

Acheson, Donald, chair (1998) *Independent Inquiry into Inequalities in Health: Report* (London: Stationery Office).

Acker, Joan (1990) 'Hierarchies, Jobs, Bodies: A Theory of Gendered Organisations', *Gender and Society* 5, 390–407.

Acker, Joan (1992) 'The Future of Women and Work: Ending the Twentieth Century', *Sociological Perspectives* 35, 53–68.

Ackerman, Nathan W., Louise Bates Ames, Sylvia Ashton-Warner, Bruno Bettelheim, Claude Brown, John Culkin, Erich Fromm, Paul Goodman, Fred Hechinger, John Holt, Eda J. Le Shan, Ashley Montagu, Ernst Papanek, Max Rafferty, Michael Rossman and Goodwin Watson (1970) *Summerhill: For and Against* (New York: Hart Publishing).

Adams, Maurianne, Lee Anne Bell and Pat Griffin, eds (1997) *Teaching for Diversity and Social Justice: A Source Book* (New York: Routledge).

Aghion, Philippe and Patrick Bolton (1997) 'A Theory of Trickle Down Growth and Development', *Review of Economic Studies* 64, 151–72.

Ahmed, Waqar I.U. and Trevor A. Sheldon (1993) '"Race" and Statistics', in M. Hammersley, ed., *Social Research: Philosophy, Politics and Practice* (London: Sage), 124–30.

Albert, Michael (2003) *Parecon: Life After Capitalism* (London: Verso).

Alexander, Herbert E. and Shiratori Rei, eds (1994) *Comparative Political Finance Among the Democracies* (Boulder, CO: Westview Press).

Alinsky, Saul D. (1971) *Rules for Radicals: A Practical Primer for Realistic Radicals* (New York: Random House).

Allardt, Erik (1993) 'Having, Loving, Being: An Alternative to the Swedish Model of Welfare Research', in Nussbaum and Sen 1993, 88–94.

Allen, Kieran (1997) *Fianna Fáil and Irish Labour: 1926 to the Present* (London: Pluto Press).

Allen, Kieran (2000) *The Celtic Tiger: The Myth of Social Partnership* (Manchester: Manchester University Press).

Allen, Kieran (2003) 'Neither Boston Nor Berlin: Class Polarisation and Neo-Liberalism in the Irish Republic', in Coulter and Coleman 2003, 56–73.

Allen, Mike (1998) *The Bitter Word: Ireland's Job Famine and its Aftermath* (Dublin: Poolbeg Press).

Althusser, Louis (1971) *Lenin and Philosophy and Other Essays*, tr. Ben Brewster (New York: Monthly Review Press).

Altman, Andrew (1986) 'Legal Realism, Critical Legal Studies, and Dworkin', *Philosophy and Public Affairs* 15, 205–35.

Alvarez, Sonia E. (1997) 'Reweaving the Fabric of Collective Action: Social Movements and Challenges to "Actually Existing Democracy" in Brazil', in Fox and Starn 1997, 83–117.

Amer, Mildred L. (2003) *Membership of the 108th Congress: A Profile*. CRS Report RS21379 (Washington: Congressional Research Service). http://www.senate.gov/reference/resources/pdf/RS21379.pdf (27 March 2003).

Anderson, Elizabeth S. (1999) 'What is the Point of Equality?', *Ethics* 109, 287–337.

Apple, Michael W. (1991) 'Introduction' to Lather 1991, vii–xi.

Apple, Michael W. (2001) *Educating the 'Right' Way: Markets, Standards, God, and Inequality* (New York: RoutledgeFalmer).

Apple, Michael W. and James A. Beane, eds (1999) *Democratic Schools: Lessons from the Chalk Face* (Buckingham: Open University Press).

Archard, David (1993) *Children: Rights and Childhood* (London: Routledge).

Archard, David (2003) *Children, Family and the State* (Aldershot: Ashgate).

Archard, David and Colin M. MacLeod, eds (2002) *The Moral and Political Status of Children: New Essays* (Oxford: Oxford University Press).

Archer, Louise, Robert Gilchrist, Merryn Hutchings, Carole Leathwood, David Phillips and Alistair Ross (2002) *Higher Education and Social Class: Issues of Inclusion and Exclusion* (London: Falmer Press).

Archer, Peter (2001) 'Public Spending on Education, Inequality and Poverty', in Cantillon *et al.* 2001, 197–234.

Archer, Robin (1995) *Economic Democracy: The Politics of Feasible Socialism* (Oxford: Oxford University Press).

Armor, Jody David (1997) 'Diversity of Opinions: Hype and Reality in Affirmative Action', *University of Colorado Law Review* 68, 1173–99.

Armstrong, Chris (2003) 'Some Reflections on Equality of Power', *Imprints* 7, 44–53.

Arneson, Richard J. (1987) 'Meaningful Work and Socialism', *Ethics* 97, 517–45.

Arneson, Richard J. (1989) 'Equality and Equal Opportunity for Welfare', *Philosophical Studies* 56, 77–93.

Arneson, Richard J. (1990) 'Is Work Special? Justice and the Distribution of Employment', *American Political Science Review* 84, 1127–47.

Arneson, Richard J. (2000) 'Luck Egalitarianism and Prioritarianism', *Ethics* 110, 339–49.

Arrighi, Giovanni (2002) 'The African Crisis: World Systemic and Regional Aspects', *New Left Review* 2/15, 5–36.

Atkinson, A.B. and John Micklewright (1989) 'Turning the Screw: Benefits for the Unemployed 1979–88', in A. Dilnot and I. Walker, eds, *The Economics of Social Security* (Oxford: Oxford University Press), 17–51.

Atkinson, A.B., Lee Rainwater and Timothy M. Smeeding (1995) *Income Distribution in the OECD Countries: Evidence from the Luxembourg Income Study* (Paris: OECD).

Austen, Siobhan (1999) 'Norms of Inequality', *Journal of Economic Issues* 33, 435–43.

Bachrach, Peter and Aryeh Botwinick (1992) *Power and Empowerment: A Radical Theory of Participatory Democracy* (Philadelphia: Temple University Press).

Baiochhi, Gianpaolo (2003) 'Participation, Activism, and Politics: The Porto Alegre Experiment', in Fung and Wright 2003, 45–76.

Baker, John (1987) *Arguing for Equality* (London: Verso).

Baker, John (1992) 'An Egalitarian Case for Basic Income', in Van Parijs 1992, 101–27.

Baker, John (2003) 'Poverty and Equality: Ten Reasons Why Anyone Who Wants to Combat Poverty Should Embrace Equality as Well', in *Poverty and Inequality:*

*Applying an Equality Dimension to Poverty Proofing* (Dublin: Equality Authority and Combat Poverty Agency), 12–25.

Baker, John and Richard Sinnott (2000) 'Simulating Multi-Option Referendums in Ireland: Neutrality and Abortion', *Irish Political Studies* 15, 105–25.

Baker, Robert (1979) '"Pricks" and "Chicks": A Plea for "Persons"', in S. Bishop and M. Weinzweig, eds, *Philosophy and Women* (Belmont, CA: Wadsworth), 21–6.

Baland, Jean-Marie and Jean-Philippe Platteau (1998) 'Wealth Inequality and Efficiency in the Commons, Part II: The Regulated Case', *Oxford Economic Papers* 50, 1–22.

Ball, Carlos A. (1996) 'The Making of a Transnational Capitalist Society: The Court of Justice, Social Policy, and Individual Rights under the European Community's Legal Order', *Harvard International Law Journal* 37, 307–88.

Ball, Stephen J. (1981) *Beachside Comprehensive: A Case-Study of Secondary Schooling* (Cambridge: Cambridge University Press).

Ball, Stephen J. (1987) *The Micro-Politics of the School: Towards a Theory of School Organisation* (London: Methuen).

Ball, Stephen J. (1989) 'Micro-Politics versus Management', in S. Walker and L. Barton, eds, *Politics and the Processes of Schooling* (Milton Keynes: Open University Press), 218–41.

Ball, Stephen J. (1997) 'Good School/Bad School: Paradox and Fabrication', *British Journal of Sociology of Education* 18, 317–35.

Ball, Stephen J., Richard Bowe and Sharon Gewirtz (1995) 'Circuits of Schooling: A Sociological Exploration of Parental Choice of School in Social Class Contexts', *Sociological Review* 43, 52–78.

Ballard, Keith, ed. (1999) *Inclusive Education: International Voices on Disability and Social Justice* (London: Falmer Press).

Bandes, Susan (1990) 'The Negative Constitution: A Critique', *Michigan Law Review* 88, 2271–347.

Barber, Benjamin (1984) *Strong Democracy* (Berkeley, CA: University of California Press).

Bardhan, Pranab, Herbert Gintis and Samuel Bowles (2000) 'Wealth Inequality, Weak Constraints and Economic Performance', in A.B. Atkinson and F. Bourguignon, eds, *Handbook on Income Distribution* (Amsterdam: North Holland), 541–604.

Barnard, Catherine (2000) *EC Employment Law*, 2nd edition (Oxford: Oxford University Press).

Barnard, Catherine and Bob Hepple (2000) 'Substantive Equality', *Cambridge Law Journal* 59, 562–85.

Barnes, Colin (1991) *Disabled People in Britain and Discrimination* (London: Hurst and Co.).

Barnes, Colin (1996) 'Theories of Disability and the Origins of Oppression of Disabled People in Western Society', in Barton 1996, 43–6.

Barnes, Colin (2000) 'A Working Social Model? Disability, Work and Disability Politics in the 21st Century', *Critical Social Policy* 65, 441–57.

Barnes, Colin, Mike Oliver and Len Barton, eds (2002) *Disability Studies Today* (Cambridge: Polity Press).

Barr, Nicholas (1993) *The Economics of the Welfare State* (London: Weidenfeld and Nicolson).

Barrett, Michèle (1980) *Women's Oppression Today: Problems in Marxist Feminist Analysis* (London: Verso).

Barrett, Michèle (1991) *The Politics of Truth: From Marx to Foucault* (Cambridge: Polity Press).

Barry, Brian (1975) 'Political Accommodation and Consociational Democracy', *British Journal of Political Science* 5, 477–505.

Barry, Brian (1989) *Theories of Justice* (Berkeley, CA: University of California Press).

Barry, Brian (1995) *Justice as Impartiality* (Oxford: Oxford University Press).

Barry, Brian (1997) 'The Attractions of Basic Income', in J. Franklin, ed., *Equality* (London: IPPR), 157–71.

Barry, Brian (2001) *Culture and Equality* (Cambridge: Polity Press).

Barry, Kathleen (1995) *The Prostitution of Sexuality* (New York: New York University Press).

Barry, Ursula and Ann O'Connor (1995) *Women and the Employment Rate in Ireland: The Causes and Consequences of Variations in the Activity and Employment Patterns of Irish Women* (Manchester: Manchester University Press).

Bartlett, Kathleen T. (1990) 'Feminist Legal Methods', *Harvard Law Review* 103, 829–88.

Barton, Len, ed. (1996) *Disability and Society: Emerging Issues and Insights* (London: Longman).

Bastian, Ann, Norm Fruchter, Marilyn Gittell, Kenneth Haskins and Colin Greer (1986) *Choosing Equality: The Case for Democratic Schooling* (Philadelphia: Temple University Press).

Beck, Ulrich (1992) *Risk Society: Towards a New Modernity*, tr. Mark Ritter (London: Sage).

Bell, Abraham and Gideon Parchomovsky (2001) 'Givings', *Yale Law Journal* 111, 547–618.

Bell, Derek (2002) 'How Can Political Liberals Be Egalitarians?', *Political Studies* 50, 703–24.

Bell, Lee Anne (1997) 'Theoretical Foundations for Social Justice Education', in Adams, Bell and Griffin 1997, 3–15.

Bénabou, Roland (1996) 'Inequality and Growth', in B.S. Bernanke and J.J. Rotemberg, eds, *NBER Macroeconomics Annual 1996* (Cambridge, MA: MIT Press), 11–74.

Bendelow, Gillian and Simon J. Williams, eds (1998) *Emotions in Social Life: Critical Themes and Contemporary Issues* (London: Routledge).

Benhabib, Seyla (1992) *Situating the Self* (Cambridge: Polity Press).

Benhabib, Seyla, ed. (1996) *Democracy and Difference: Contesting the Boundaries of the Political* (Princeton: Princeton University Press).

Bennett Demarrais, Kathleen and Margaret Diane Lecompte (1999) *The Way Schools Work: A Sociological Analysis of Education*, 3rd edition (New York: Longman).

Berends, Mark (1991) *High School Tracking and Students' School Orientations* (Madison, WI: National Centre on Effective Secondary Schools).

Berends, Mark (1995) 'Educational Stratification and Students' Social Bonding to School', *British Journal of Sociology of Education* 16, 327–51.

Bernstein, Basil (1971) 'On the Classification and Framing of Educational Knowledge', in M.F.D. Young, ed., *Knowledge and Control: New Directions for the Sociology of Education* (London: Collier-Macmillan), 19–46.

Bernstein, Richard J. (1976) *The Restructuring of Social and Political Theory* (Oxford: Blackwell).

Bernstein, Richard J. (1983) *Beyond Objectivism and Relativism: Science, Hermeneutics, and Praxis* (Oxford: Blackwell).

Beveridge, Fiona, Sue Nott and Kylie Stephen (2000) 'Mainstreaming the Engendering of Policy Making: A Means to an End?', *Journal of European Public Policy* 7, 385–405.

Bircham, Emma and John Charlton, eds (2001) *Anti-Capitalism: A Guide to the Movement* (London: Bookmarks Publications).

Blackmore, Jean (1996) 'Doing Emotional Labour in the Education Market Place: Stories From the Field of Women in Management', *Discourse: Studies in the Cultural Politics of Education* 17, 337–49.

Blackwell, John and Brian Nolan (1990) 'Low Pay: The Irish Experience', in B. Harvey and M. Daly, eds, *Low Pay: The Irish Experience* (Dublin: Combat Poverty Agency), 1–22.

Bloom, Benjamin S. (1956) *Taxonomy of Educational Objectives: The Classification of Educational Goals. Handbook 1: Cognitive Domain* (London: Longman).

Bloom, Benjamin S. (1964) *Taxonomy of Educational Objectives: The Classification of Educational Goals. Handbook 2: Affective Domain* (London: Longman).

Boaler, Jo (1997a) *Experiencing School Mathematics: Teaching Styles, Sex and Setting* (Buckingham: Open University Press).

Boaler, Jo (1997b) 'Setting, Social Class and Survival of the Quickest', *British Educational Research Journal* 23, 575–95.

Bobo, Kim, Jackie Kendall and Steve Max (2001) *Organizing for Social Change: Midwest Academy Manual for Activists*, 3rd edition (Santa Ana, CA: Seven Locks Press).

Bock, Gisela and Susan James, eds (1992) *Beyond Equality and Difference: Citizenship, Feminist Politics, and Female Subjectivity* (London: Routledge).

Bogaards, Matthijs (1998) 'The Favourable Factors for Consociational Democracy: A Review', *European Journal of Political Research* 33, 475–96.

Bohman, James (1996) *Public Deliberation: Pluralism, Complexity, and Democracy* (Cambridge, MA: MIT Press).

Bohman, James (1998) 'The Coming of Age of Deliberative Democracy', *Journal of Political Philosophy* 6, 400–25.

Bolger, Marguerite and Cliona Kimber (2000) *Sex Discrimination Law* (Dublin: Sweet & Maxwell).

Boshara, Ray (2003) 'Wealth Inequality', *The Atlantic Monthly* 291(1), 91–7.

Bottomley, Anne and Joanne Conaghan, eds (1993) *Feminist Theory and Legal Strategy* (Oxford: Blackwell).

Bourdieu, Pierre (1973) 'Cultural Reproduction and Social Reproduction', in R. Brown, ed., *Knowledge, Education and Cultural Change* (London: Tavistock), 71–122.

Bourdieu, Pierre (1984) *Distinction: A Social Critique of the Judgement of Taste*, tr. Richard Nice (London: Routledge & Kegan Paul).

Bourdieu, Pierre (1986) 'The Forms of Capital', tr. Richard Nice, in J.G. Richardson, ed., *Handbook of Theory and Research for the Sociology of Education* (Westport, CT: Greenwood), 241–58.

Bourdieu, Pierre (1987) 'The Force of Law: Toward a Sociology of the Juridical Field', tr. Richard Terdiman, *Hastings Law Journal* 38, 805–53.

Bourdieu, Pierre (1988) *Homo Academicus*, tr. Peter Collier (Cambridge: Polity Press).

Bourdieu, Pierre (1993) *Sociology in Question*, tr. Richard Nice (London: Sage).

Bourdieu, Pierre (1996) *The State Nobility: Elite Schools in the Field of Power*, tr. Lauretta C. Clough (Cambridge: Polity Press).

Bourdieu, Pierre (1998) *Acts of Resistance: Against the Tyranny of the Market*, tr. Richard Nice (Cambridge: Polity Press).

Bourdieu, Pierre (2001) *Masculine Domination*, tr. Richard Nice (Cambridge: Polity Press).

Bourdieu, Pierre and Jean-Claude Passeron (1977) *Reproduction in Education, Society and Culture*, tr. Richard Nice (London: Sage).

Bourdieu, Pierre and Jean-Claude Passeron (1979) *The Inheritors: French Students and Their Relation to Culture*, tr. Richard Nice (Chicago: Chicago University Press).

Bourke, Angela, Siobhán Kilfeather, Maria Luddy, Margaret Mac Curtain, Gerardine Meaney, Máirín Ní Dhonnchadha, Mary O'Dowd and Clair Wills, eds (2002) *The Field Day Anthology of Irish Writing, Volume V: Irish Women's Writing and Traditions* (Cork: Cork University Press).

Bové, José (2001) 'A Farmers' International?', *New Left Review* 2/12, 89–100.

Bowles, Gloria and Renate Duelli Klein, eds (1983) *Theories of Women's Studies* (London: Routledge & Kegan Paul).

Bowles, Samuel and Herbert Gintis (1976) *Schooling in Capitalist America: Educational Reform and the Contradictions of Economic Life* (London: Routledge & Kegan Paul).

Bowles, Samuel and Herbert Gintis (1987) *Democracy and Capitalism: Property, Community, and the Contradictions of Modern Social Thought* (New York: Basic Books).

Bowles, Samuel and Herbert Gintis (1998) *Recasting Egalitarianism: New Rules for Communities, States and Markets,* ed. Erik Olin Wright (London: Verso).

Boylan, M. and P. Lawton (2000) '"I'd be more likely to talk in class if…": How Some Year Eight Students Experience Teacher Questioning and Discussion Strategies', *British Society for Research into Learning Mathematics: Proceedings* 20(3), 7–12.

Boylan, M., P. Lawton and H. Povey (2001) '"I'd be more likely to talk in class if…": Some Students' Ideas About Strategies to Increase Mathematical Participation in Whole Class Interactions', in M. van den Heuvel-Panhhizen, ed., *Proceedings of the 25th Conference of the International Group for the Psychology of Mathematics Education* (The Netherlands: Freudenthal Institute) 2, 201–8.

Boyle, Christine and Marilyn MacCrimmon (2001) 'To Serve the Cause of Justice: Disciplining Fact Determination', *Windsor Yearbook of Access to Justice* 20, 55–84.

Brah, Avtar (1996) *Cartographies of Diaspora: Contesting Identities* (London: Routledge).

Brantlinger, E.A., M. Majd-Jabbari and S.L. Guskin (1996) 'Self-Interest and Liberal Educational Discourse: How Ideology Works for Middle-Class Mothers', *American Educational Research Journal* 33, 571–97.

Brecher, Jeremy and Tim Costello (1998) *Global Village or Global Pillage: Economic Reconstruction from the Bottom Up,* 2nd edition (Cambridge, MA: South End Press).

Brecher, Jeremy, Tim Costello and Brendan Smith (2000) *Globalization from Below: The Power of Solidarity* (Cambridge, MA: South End Press).

Breen, Richard and David B. Rottman (1995) *Class Stratification: A Comparative Perspective* (London: Harvester Wheatsheaf).

Breen, Richard, Damian F. Hannan and Christopher T. Whelan (1990) *Understanding Contemporary Ireland* (Dublin: Gill & Macmillan).

Breitenbach, Hans, Tom Burden and David Coates (1990) *Features of a Viable Socialism* (London: Harvester Wheatsheaf).

Bresnihan, Valerie (1997) 'Irish Political Culture: A Symbolic Analysis'. Ph.D. thesis, University College Dublin.

Brigham, John (1987) 'Right, Rage, and Remedy: Forms of Law in Political Discourse', *Studies in American Political Development* 2, 303–16.

Brighouse, Harry (1996) 'Egalitarianism and Equal Availability of Political Influence', *Journal of Political Philosophy* 4, 118–41.

Brighouse, Harry (2000) *School Choice and Social Justice* (Oxford: Oxford University Press).

Brighouse, Harry (2001) 'Dworkin on Equality of Power', *Imprints* 5, 237–50.

Brock, Gillian, ed. (1998) *Necessary Goods: Our Responsibilities to Meet Others' Needs* (Lanham, MD: Rowman & Littlefield).

Brown, Philip, A.H. Halsey, Hugh Lauder and A.S. Wells (1997) 'The Transformation of Education and Society: An Introduction', in A.H. Halsey, H. Lauder, P. Brown and A.S. Wells, eds, *Education: Culture, Economy and Society* (Oxford: Oxford University Press), 1–44.

Brownmiller, Susan (1975) *Against Our Will: Men, Women and Rape* (New York: Simon and Schuster).

Bruner, Jerome S. (1963) *The Process of Education* (New York: Vintage Books).

Bruner, Jerome S. (1966) *Toward a Theory of Instruction* (New York: W.W. Norton & Co.).

Bryden, Philip L. (1987) 'Public Interest Intervention in the Courts', *Canadian Bar Review* 66, 490–528.

Bubeck, Diemut Elisabet (1995) *Care, Gender, and Justice* (Oxford: Oxford University Press).

Burchardt, Tania (2000) *Enduring Economic Exclusion: Disabled People, Income and Work* (York: YPS and Joseph Rowntree Foundation).

Bureau of Justice Statistics [US] (2003) 'Table 26. Personal Crimes, 2001: Number of Incidents and Victimizations and Ratio of Victimizations to Incidents, by Type of Crime'. http://www.ojp.usdoj.gov/bjs/pub/pdf/cvus/current/cv0126.pdf (18 May 2003).

Button, Mark and Kevin Mattson (1998) 'Public Deliberation and Democracy – What's the Connection?', *The Good Society* 8(2), 17–22.

Buxton, Laurie (1981) *Do You Panic About Maths? Coping with Maths Anxiety* (London: Heinemann).

Byrne, Anne (1992) 'Academic Women's Studies in the Republic of Ireland', *Women's Studies Quarterly* 20(3 & 4), 15–27.

Callahan, David (1999) *$1 Billion for Ideas: Conservative Think Tanks in the 1990s* (Washington: National Committee for Responsive Philanthropy).

Callan, Tim and Brian Nolan (1992) 'Income Distribution and Redistribution', in J.H. Goldthorpe and C.T. Whelan, eds, *The Development of Industrial Society in Ireland* (Oxford: Oxford University Press), 173–203.

Callan, Tim, Brian Nolan, Brendan J. Whelan, Christopher Whelan and James Williams (1996) *Poverty in the 1990s* (Dublin: Oak Tree Press).

Cantillon, Sara, Carmel Corrigan, Peadar Kirby and Joan O'Flynn, eds (2001) *Rich and Poor: Perspectives on Tackling Inequality in Ireland* (Dublin: Oak Tree Press and Combat Poverty Agency).

Cantillon, Sara and Eamon O'Shea (2001) 'Social Expenditure, Redistribution and Participation', in Cantillon *et al.* 2001, 81–109.

Carens, Joseph H. (1981) *Equality, Moral Incentives, and the Market* (Chicago: University of Chicago Press).

Carroll, Steven and Geoffrey Walford (1996) 'A Panic About School Choice', *Educational Studies* 22, 393–407.

Carter, Alan (1999) *A Radical Green Political Theory* (London: Routledge).

Casey, James (2000) *Constitutional Law in Ireland* (Dublin: Sweet & Maxwell).

Castells, Manuel (1983) *The City and the Grassroots: A Cross-Cultural Theory of Urban Social Movements* (Berkeley, CA: University of California Press).

Castells, Manuel (1996) *The Rise of the Network Society* (Oxford: Blackwell).

Castells, Manuel (1997) *The Power of Identity* (Oxford: Blackwell).

CCPI (2001) *Gosselin v. Quebec: Factum of the Charter Committee on Poverty Issues.* http://www.equalityrights.org/ccpi (31 October 2003).

CESR (Center for Economic and Social Rights) (2000) *Economic, Social and Cultural Rights: A Guide to the Legal Framework* (New York: CESR).

Chambers, Richard (1983) *Rural Development: Putting the Last First* (Harlow: Longman).

Chayes, Abram (1976) 'The Role of the Judge in Public Law Litigation', *Harvard Law Review* 89, 1281–316.

Chiu, W. Henry (1998) 'Income Inequality, Human Capital Accumulation and Economic Performance', *The Economic Journal* 108, 44–59.

Chomsky, Noam (2000) *Rogue States* (London: Pluto Press).

Clancy, Patrick (1988) *Who Goes to College* (Dublin: Higher Education Authority).

Clancy, Patrick (1995) *Access to College: Patterns of Continuity and Change* (Dublin: Higher Education Authority).

Clancy, Patrick (2001) *College Entry in Focus: A Fourth National Survey of Access to Higher Education* (Dublin: Higher Education Authority).

Clancy, Patrick, Sheila Drudy, Kathleen Lynch and Liam O'Dowd, eds (1995) *Irish Society: Sociological Perspectives* (Dublin: Institute of Public Administration).

Clark, Barry (1998) *Political Economy: A Comparative Approach*, 2nd edition (London: Praeger).

Clayton, Matthew and Andrew Williams, eds (2002) *The Ideal of Equality* (Basingstoke: Palgrave Macmillan).

Cohen, G.A. (1981) 'Illusions About Private Property and Freedom', in J. Mepham and D. Hillel-Rubin, eds, *Issues in Marxist Philosophy, Volume IV: Social and Political Philosophy* (Brighton: Harvester), 223–42.

Cohen, G.A. (1989) 'On the Currency of Egalitarian Justice', *Ethics* 99, 906–44.

Cohen, G.A. (1991) 'Incentives, Inequality, and Community', in G.B. Peterson, ed., *The Tanner Lectures on Human Values, Volume 13* (Salt Lake City: University of Utah Press), 261–329.

Cohen, G.A. (1995) *Self-Ownership, Freedom and Equality* (Cambridge: Cambridge University Press).

Cohen, G.A. (1997) 'Back to Socialist Basics', in J. Franklin, ed., *Equality* (London: IPPR), 29–47.

Cohen, G.A. (2000) *If You're an Egalitarian, How Come You're So Rich?* (Cambridge, MA: Harvard University Press).

Cohen, Jean and Andrew Arato (1992) *Civil Society and Political Theory* (Cambridge, MA: MIT Press).

Cohen, Joshua (1989) 'Deliberation and Democratic Legitimacy', in A. Hamlin and P. Pettit, eds, *The Good Polity* (Oxford: Blackwell), 17–34.

Cohen, Joshua (1996) 'Procedure and Substance in Deliberative Democracy', in Benhabib 1996, 85–119.

Cohen, Joshua (1998) 'Democracy and Liberty', in Elster 1998, 185–231.

Cohen, Joshua and Joel Rogers (1995) *Associations and Democracy*, ed. Erik Olin Wright (London: Verso).

Cohen, Joshua and Joel Rogers (2003) 'Power and Reason', in Fung and Wright 2003, 237–55.

Cole, Mike, ed. (2000) *Education, Equality and Human Rights* (London: RoutledgeFalmer).

Cole, Mike and Dave Hill (1995) 'Games of Despair and Rhetorics of Resistance: Postmodernism, Education and Reaction', *British Journal of Sociology of Education* 16, 165–82.

Coleman, James S. (1990) *Foundations of Social Theory* (Cambridge, MA: Harvard University Press).

Coleman, Joe (1998) 'Civic Pedagogies and Liberal-Democratic Curricula', *Ethics* 108, 746–61.

Colker, Ruth (1986) 'Anti-Subordination Above All: Sex, Race, and Equal Protection', *New York University Law Review* 61, 1003–66.

Colker, Ruth (1997) 'Pregnancy, Parenting and Capitalism', *Ohio State Law Journal* 58, 61–83.

Collins, Hugh (1982) *Marxism and Law* (Oxford: Oxford University Press).

Collins, Hugh (2003) 'Discrimination, Equality and Social Inclusion', *Modern Law Review* 66, 16–43.

Collins, Janet (2000) 'Are You Talking to Me? The Need to Respect and Develop a Pupil's Self-Image', *Educational Research* 42, 157–66.

Collins, Patricia Hill (1990) *Black Feminist Thought* (New York: Unwin Hyman).

Collins, Randall (1979) *The Credential Society* (New York: Academic Press).

Combat Poverty Agency (1994) *Disability, Exclusion and Poverty* (Dublin: Combat Poverty Agency).

Combat Poverty Agency (2003a) *Working Towards a Poverty-Free Society: Submission to the National Action Plan Against Poverty and Social Exclusion 2003–2005* (Dublin: Combat Poverty Agency).

Combat Poverty Agency (2003b) *Irish Social Expenditure in a Comparative International Context* (Dublin: Combat Poverty Agency).

Community Platform (1997) *Achieving Social Partnership: The Strategy and Proposals of the Community Platform at the Partnership 2000 Negotiations* (Dublin: The Community Platform).

Community Workers Co-operative (1997) *Strategies to Encourage Participation* (Galway: Community Workers Co-operative).

Community Workers Co-operative (1998) *Equality Policies and Social Change* (Galway: Community Workers Co-operative and NICVA).

Conaghan, Joanne (1986) 'The Invisibility of Women in Labour Law: Gender-Neutrality in Model-Building', *International Journal of Sociology of Law* 14, 377–92.

Condren, Mary (1989) *The Serpent and the Goddess: Women, Religion and Power in Celtic Ireland* (San Francisco: Harper & Row).

Connell, Robert W. (1987) *Gender and Power* (Cambridge: Polity Press).

Connell, Robert W. (1993) *Schools and Social Justice* (Philadelphia: Temple University Press).

Connell, Robert W. (1995) *Masculinities* (Cambridge: Polity Press).

Connell, Robert W. (2000) *The Men and the Boys* (Cambridge: Polity Press).

Connolly, Linda (2002) *The Irish Women's Movement: From Revolution to Devolution* (Basingstoke: Palgrave Macmillan).

Conover, Pamela Johnston, Donald D. Searing and Ivor M. Crewe (2002) 'The Deliberative Potential of Political Discussion', *British Journal of Political Science* 32, 21–62.

Conroy, Pauline (2003) 'Employment Policy', in S. Quin and B. Redmond, eds, *Disability and Social Policy in Ireland* (Dublin: University College Dublin Press), 45–56.

Cooke, Maeve (2000) 'Five Arguments for Deliberative Democracy', *Political Studies* 48, 947–69.

Coolahan, John (1981) *Irish Education: Its History and Structure* (Dublin: Institute of Public Administration).

Cormack, Bob and Bob Osborne (1995) 'Education in Northern Ireland: The Struggle for Equality', in Clancy *et al.* 1995, 495–528.

Correa, Carlos M. (2000) *Intellectual Property Rights, the WTO and Developing Countries* (London: Zed Books).

Cotterrell, Roger (1992) *The Sociology of Law: An Introduction*, 2nd edition (London: Butterworths).

Cotterrell, Roger (1995) *Law's Community: Legal Theory in Sociological Perspective* (Oxford: Oxford University Press).

Coulter, Carol (1993) *The Hidden Tradition: Feminism, Women and Nationalism in Ireland* (Cork: Cork University Press).

Coulter, Colin and Steve Coleman, eds (2003) *The End of Irish History: Critical Reflections on the Celtic Tiger* (Manchester: Manchester University Press).

Cover, Robert (1983) 'Foreword: Nomos and Narrative', *Harvard Law Review* 97, 4–68.

Covington, Sally (1997) *Moving a Public Policy Agenda: The Strategic Philanthropy of Conservative Foundations* (Washington: National Committee for Responsive Philanthropy).

Cox, Laurence (1999) 'Structure, Routine and Transformation: Movements from Below at the End of the Century', in C. Barker and M. Tyldesley, eds, *Fifth International Conference on Alternative Futures and Popular Protest: A Selection of Papers from the Conference* (Manchester: Manchester Metropolitan University).

Craven, Matthew (1995) *The International Covenant on Economic, Social, and Cultural Rights: A Perspective on its Development* (Oxford: Oxford University Press).

Crenshaw, Kimberle (1988) 'Race, Reform and Retrenchment: Transformation and Legitimation in Antidiscrimination Law', *Harvard Law Review* 101, 1331–87.

Crenshaw, Kimberle (1989) 'Demarginalizing the Intersection of Race and Sex: A Black Feminist Critique of Anti-Discrimination Doctrine, Feminist Theory and Antiracist Politics', *University of Chicago Legal Forum* 139, 157–60.

Crompton, Rosemary (1998) *Class and Stratification,* 2nd edition (Cambridge: Polity Press).

Cross, Frank B. and Blake J. Nelson (2001) 'Strategic Institutional Effects on Supreme Court Decision-Making', *Northwestern University Law Review* 95, 1437–93.

Crotty, William (1998) 'Democratisation and Political Development in Ireland', in Crotty and Schmitt 1998, 1–26.

Crotty, William and David E. Schmitt, eds (1998) *Ireland and the Politics of Change* (London: Longman).

Crowley, Niall (1997) 'Participating in the National Economic and Social Forum', in Community Workers Co-operative 1997, 64–6.

Crozier, Gill (1997) 'Empowering the Powerful: A Discussion of the Interrelation of Government Policies and Consumerism with Social Class Factors and the Impact of this upon Parent Interventions in Their Children's Schooling', *British Journal of Sociology of Education* 18, 187–200.

CSO (Central Statistics Office) [Ireland] (2002) *Quarterly National Household Survey, Second Quarter* (Dublin: Central Statistics Office).

Cullen, Mary and Maria Luddy, eds (1995) *Women, Power and Consciousness in Nineteenth Century Ireland* (Dublin: Attic Press).

Dahl, Robert A. (1985) *A Preface to Economic Democracy* (Berkeley, CA: University of California Press).

Dahl, Robert A. (1989) *Democracy and Its Critics* (New Haven: Yale University Press).

Daly, Mary (1978) *Gyn/Ecology: The Metaethics of Radical Feminism* (London: Women's Press).

Daly, Mary (1984) *Pure Lust: Elemental Feminist Philosophy* (London: Women's Press).

Daly, Mary (1989) *Women and Poverty* (Dublin: Combat Poverty Agency).

Daly, Mary, ed. (2001) *Care Work: The Quest for Security* (Geneva: International Labour Office).

Daniels, Norman (1990) 'Equality of What: Welfare, Resources, or Capabilities?', *Philosophy and Phenomenological Research* 50 (Supplement), 273–96.

Dasgupta, Modhurima (2002) 'Social Action for Women? Public Interest Litigation in India's Supreme Court', *Law, Social Justice & Global Development Journal* 1. http://elj.warwick.ac.uk/global/issue/2002–1/dasgupta.htm (13 November 2003).

Davies, Bronwyn (1996) *Power/Knowledge/Desire: Changing School Organisation and Management Practices* (Canberra: Department of Employment, Education, Training and Youth Affairs).

Davies, Scott (1995) 'Leaps of Faith: Shifting Currents in Critical Sociology of Education', *American Journal of Sociology* 100, 1448–78.

Davis, Angela (1982) *Women, Race and Class* (London: Women's Press).

Davis, Dennis M., Patrick Macklem and Guy Mundlak (2002) 'Social Rights, Social Citizenship, and Transformative Constitutionalism: A Comparative Assessment', in J. Conaghan, R.M. Fischl and K. Klare, eds, *Labour Law in an Era of Globalization* (Oxford: Oxford University Press), 511–34.

Davis, Dennis, Matthew Chaskalson and Johan De Waal (1996) 'Democracy and Constitutionalism: The Role of Constitutional Interpretation', in D. van Wyk, J. Dugard, B. de Villiers and D. Davis, eds, *Rights and Constitutionalism: The New South African Legal Order* (Oxford: Clarendon Press), 1–130.

Davis, Kenneth (1955) 'Judicial Notice', *Columbia Law Review* 55, 945–84.

Day, Shelagh and Gwen Brodsky (1996) 'The Duty to Accommodate: Who Will Benefit?', *Canadian Bar Review* 75, 433–73.

de Koning, Korrie and Marion Martin, eds (1996) *Participatory Research in Health* (London: Zed Books).

De Sousa Santos, Boaventura (1998) 'Participatory Budgeting in Porto Alegre: Toward a Redistributive Democracy', *Politics & Society* 26, 461–510.

Deegan, Mary Jo and Nancy A. Brooks, eds (1985) *Women and Disability: The Double Handicap* (New Brunswick, NJ: Transaction Books).

Delli Carpini, Michael X. and Scott Keeter (1996) *What Americans Know About Politics and Why It Matters* (New Haven: Yale University Press).

Delphy, Christine and Diana Leonard (1992) *Familiar Exploitation: A New Analysis of Marriage and Family Life* (Cambridge: Polity Press).

Department of Justice, Equality and Law Reform [Ireland] (2002) *Value for Money and Management Audit of the Citizen Traveller Campaign and the Preparation of a Report on Financial Position: Final Report* (Dublin: Department of Justice, Equality and Law Reform). http://www.justice.ie (18 May 2003).

Devall, Bill and George Sessions (1985) *Deep Ecology: Living as if Nature Mattered* (Layton, UT: Gibbs Smith).

Devine, Dympna (2000) 'The Exercise of Power in Children's Experiences of School', *Irish Educational Studies* 19, 189–206.

Devine, Fiona (1992a) *Affluent Workers Revisited* (Edinburgh: Edinburgh University Press).

Devine, Fiona (1992b) 'Social Identities, Class Identity and Political Perspectives', *Sociological Review* 40, 229–52.

Devine, Pat (1988) *Democracy and Economic Planning* (Cambridge: Polity Press).

Devlin, Bernie, Stephen E. Fineberg, Daniel. P. Resnick and Kathryn Roeder, eds (1997) *Intelligence, Genes and Success: Scientists Respond to 'The Bell Curve'* (New York: Springer-Verlag).

Devlin, Richard F. (2001) 'Jurisprudence for Judges: Why Legal Theory Matters for Social Context Education', *Queen's Law Journal* 27, 161–205.

Dewey, John (1916) *Democracy and Education* (New York: Macmillan).

Dewey, John (1950) *Experience and Education* (New York: Macmillan).

Di Torella, Eugenia Caracciolo and Annick Masselot (2000) 'Pregnancy, Maternity and the Organisation of Family Life: An Attempt to Classify the Case Law of the Court of Justice', *European Law Review* 26, 239–60.

Dilnot, Andrew (1992) 'Social Security and the Labour Market', in E. McLaughlin, ed., *Understanding Unemployment: New Perspectives on Active Labour Market Policies* (London: Routledge), 126–43.

Dobson, Andrew (1998) *Justice and the Environment: Conceptions of Environmental Sustainability and Dimensions of Social Justice* (Oxford: Oxford University Press).

Donaghy, Gerard (2002) 'Autonomous/Non-Governmental Organisation: A Strategy for Egalitarian Counter-Globalisation'. Master of Equality Studies thesis, University College Dublin.

Donaghy, Tahnya Barnett (2003) 'Mainstreaming: Northern Ireland's Participative-Democratic Approach'. Occasional Paper No. 2 (Belfast: Centre for Advancement of Women in Politics School of Politics, Queen's University Belfast).

Dorf, Michael C. (2002) 'Equal Protection Incorporation', *Virginia Law Review* 88, 951–1024.

Douglas, James William Bruce (1964) *The Home and the School: A Study of Ability and Attainment in the Primary School* (London: MacGibbon & Kes).

Dowie, Mark (1995) *Losing Ground: American Environmentalism at the Close of the Twentieth Century* (Cambridge, MA: MIT Press).

Dowling, Teresa (1991) 'Inequalities in Preparation for University Entrance: An Examination of the Educational Histories of Entrants to University College Cork', *Irish Journal of Sociology* 1, 18–30.

Drew, Eileen (1990) *Who Needs Flexibility? Part-Time Working, the Irish Experience* (Dublin: Employment Equality Agency).

Drew, Eileen (1999) *Gender Imbalance in Irish Civil Service Grades at Higher Executive Officer Level* (Executive Summary) (Dublin: Institute of Public Administration).

Drudy, P.J. and Michael Punch (2001) 'Housing and Inequality in Ireland', in Cantillon *et al.* 2001, 235–61.

Dryzek, John S. (1996) 'Political Inclusion and the Dynamics of Democratization', *American Political Science Review* 90, 475–87.

Dryzek, John S. (2000) *Deliberative Democracy and Beyond: Liberals, Critics, Contestations* (Oxford: Oxford University Press).

Duff, Andrew (1993) 'Towards a Definition of Subsidiarity', in A. Duff, ed., *Subsidiarity within the European Community* (London: Federal Trust for Education and Research), 7–32.

Dummett, Michael (1984) *Voting Procedures* (Oxford: Oxford University Press).

Dummett, Michael (1997) *Principles of Electoral Reform* (Oxford: Oxford University Press).

Dunant, Sarah, ed. (1994) *The War of the Words: The Political Correctness Debate* (London: Virago).

Duncan, William (1996) 'The Constitutional Protection of Parental Rights', in Government of Ireland 1996, 612–26.

Duncombe, Jean and Dennis Marsden (1996) 'Extending the Social: A Response to Craib', *Sociology* 30, 155–8.

Duncombe, Jean and Dennis Marsden (1998) '"Stepford Wives" and "Hollow Men": Doing Emotion Work, Doing Gender, and Authenticity in Intimate Heterosexual Relationships', in Bendelow and Williams 1998, 211–27.

Dworkin, Andrea (1981) *Pornography: Men Possessing Women* (London: Women's Press).

Dworkin, Ronald (2000) *Sovereign Virtue: The Theory and Practice of Equality* (Cambridge, MA: Harvard University Press).

Eagleton, Terry (1994) 'Ideology and Its Vicissitudes in Western Marxism', in Zizek 1994, 179–226.

EIM Business and Policy Research (2001) *The Employment Situation of People with Disabilities in the European Union* (Brussels: European Commission, Directorate-General for Employment and Social Affairs).

Electoral Commission [New Zealand] (2003) 'New Zealand's Electoral System'. http://www.elections.org.nz/elections/esyst/index.html (18 May 2003).

Electoral Commission of India (1999) 'The Electoral System of India'. http://www.eci.gov.in/infoeci/elec_sys/elecsys_fs.htm (20 May 2003).

Elster, Jon (1986) 'The Market and the Forum: Three Varieties of Political Theory', in J. Elster and A. Hylland, eds, *Foundations of Social Choice Theory* (Cambridge: Cambridge University Press), 103–32.

Elster, Jon (1993) 'Majority Rule and Individual Rights', in S. Shute and S. Hurley, eds, *On Human Rights: The Oxford Amnesty Lectures 1993* (New York: Basic Books), 175–216.

Elster, Jon, ed. (1998) *Deliberative Democracy* (Cambridge: Cambridge University Press).

Ely, John Hart (1980) *Democracy and Distrust: A Theory of Judicial Review* (Cambridge, MA: Harvard University Press).

Emerson, Peter (1994) *The Politics of Consensus* (Belfast: De Borda Institute).

Engels, Friedrich [1845] *The Origin of the Family, Private Property and the State* (London: Lawrence and Wishart, 1940).

EOC (Equal Opportunities Commission) [UK] (2000) *Women and Men in Britain: The Work–Life Balance* (Manchester: Equal Opportunities Commission). http://www. eoc.org.uk/cseng/research/wm_work_life_balance.pdf (18 May 2003).

Epp, Juanita Ross and Ailsa M. Watkinson (1996) *Systemic Violence: How Schools Hurt Children* (London: Falmer Press).

Epstein, Barbara (1991) *Political Protest and Cultural Revolution* (Berkeley, CA: University of California Press).

Epstein, Debbie and Richard Johnson (1994) 'On the Straight and Narrow: The Heterosexual Presumption, Homophobias and Schools', in D. Epstein, ed., *Challenging Lesbian and Gay Inequalities in Education* (Buckingham: Open University Press), 197–230.

Epstein, Debbie, Sarah O'Flynn and David Telford (2003) *Silenced Sexualities in Schools and Universities* (Stoke-on-Trent: Trentham Books).

Erikson, Robert and Jan O. Jonsson, eds (1996) *Can Education Be Equalized? The Swedish Case in Comparative Perspective* (Boulder, CO: Westview Press).

Eskridge, William N. (2002) 'Some Effects of Identity-Based Social Movements on Constitutional Law in the Twentieth Century', *Michigan Law Review* 100, 2062–407.

Esping-Andersen, Gøsta (n.d.) 'Unequal Opportunities and Social Inheritance', in M. Corak, ed., *The Dynamics of Intergenerational Income Mobility* (Cambridge: Cambridge University Press), forthcoming.

Ethnic Majority (2003) 'African, Hispanic (Latino), and Asian Americans in Politics'. http://www.ethnicmajority.com/political.htm (18 May 2003).

European Commission (1999) *Transformation of Labour and the Future of Labour Law in Europe* (Luxembourg: Office for Official Publications of the European Communities).

Evans, Geoffrey (1992) 'Is Britain a Class-Divided Society? A Re-Analysis and Extension of Marshall et al's Study of Class Consciousness', *Sociology* 26, 233–58.

Ewick, Patricia and Susan S. Silbey (1998) *The Common Place of Law: Stories from Everyday Life* (Chicago: University of Chicago Press).

Fagan, G. Honor (1995) *Culture, Politics and Irish School Dropouts* (London: Bergin and Garvey).

Fahey, Tony, Helen Russell and Emer Smyth (2000) 'Gender Equality, Fertility Decline and Labour Market Patterns among Women in Ireland', in Nolan, O'Connell and Whelan 2000, 244–67.

Fanning, Bryan, Angela Veale and Dawn O'Connor (2001) *Beyond the Pale: Asylum-Seeking Children and Social Exclusion in Ireland* (Dublin: Irish Refugee Council).

Farrell, David M. (2000) *Electoral Systems: A Comparative Introduction* (Basingstoke: Palgrave – now Palgrave Macmillan).

FCZB (Frauen Computer Zentrum Berlin) (2003) *European Database – Women in Decision-Making.* http://www.db-decision.de/English (18 May 2003).

Feldman, Alice (2001) 'Transforming Peoples and Subverting States', *Ethnicities* 1, 147–78.

Figini, Paolo (1999) 'Inequality and Growth Revisited'. Trinity Economic Paper 99/2 (Dublin: Department of Economics, Trinity College Dublin).

Finch, Janet (1983) *Married to the Job: Wives' Incorporation in Men's Work* (London: Unwin Hyman).

Finkelstein, Victor (1980) *Attitudes and Disabled People: Issues for Discussion* (New York: World Rehabilitation Fund).

Firestone, Shulamith (1970) *The Dialectic of Sex: The Case for Feminist Revolution* (New York: William Morrow & Co.).

Fishkin, James S. (1991) *Democracy and Deliberation: New Directions for Democratic Reform* (New Haven: Yale University Press).

Fishkin, James S. (1995) *The Voice of the People: Public Opinion and Democracy* (New Haven: Yale University Press).

Fishkin, James S. and Robert C. Luskin (1999) 'The Quest for Deliberative Democracy', *The Good Society* 9(1), 1–9.

Fitzgerald, Eithne (2001) 'Redistribution Through Ireland's Welfare and Tax Systems', in Cantillon *et al.* 2001, 151–96.

Fitzsimons, Patrick (2002) 'Neo-Liberalism and Education: The Autonomous Chooser', *Radical Pedagogy* 4(2). http://radicalpedagogy.icaap.org/content/issue4_2/04_fitzsimons.html (24 November 2003).

Flynn, Leo (1999) 'The Implications of Article 13 EC – After Amsterdam, Will Some Forms of Discrimination Be More Equal Than Others?', *Common Market Law Review* 36, 1127–52.

Focus Point (1993) *Briefing Document on Homelessness and Housing to the New Dáil* (Dublin: Focus Point).

Folbre, Nancy (1994) *Who Pays for the Kids? Gender and the Structures of Constraint* (London: Routledge).

Folbre, Nancy (2001) 'Accounting for Care in the United States', in Daly 2001, 175–191.

Folbre, Nancy, ed. (1996) *The Economics of the Family* (New York: Edward Elgar).

Forster, Michael F. (2000) 'Trends and Driving Factors in Income Distribution and Poverty in the OECD Area'. Labour Market and Social Policy Occasional Papers No. 42 (Paris: OECD).

Fortin, Nicola M. and Thomas Lemieux (1997) 'Institutional Change and Rising Wage Inequality: Is There a Linkage?', *Journal of Economic Perspectives* 11, 77–95.

Foucault, Michel (1977) *Language, Counter-Memory, Practice: Selected Essays and Interviews*, tr. Donald F. Bouchard and Sherry Simon (Oxford: Basil Blackwell).

Foucault, Michel (1980) *Power/Knowledge: Selected Interviews and Other Writings, 1972–1977*, tr. Colin Gordon (Brighton: Harvester Press).

Foucault, Michel (1991) *Discipline and Punish: The Birth of the Prison*, tr. Alan Sheridan (Harmondsworth: Penguin).

Fox, Richard G. and Orin Starn, eds (1997) *Between Resistance and Revolution: Cultural Politics and Social Protest* (New Brunswick, NJ: Rutgers University Press).

Francis, Becky (1998) *Power Plays: Children's Construction of Gender, Power and Adult Work* (Stoke-on-Trent: Trentham Books).

Fraser, Nancy (1989) *Unruly Practices: Power, Discourse, and Gender in Contemporary Social Theory* (Cambridge: Polity Press).

Fraser, Nancy (1997a) *Justice Interruptus: Critical Reflections on the 'Post-Socialist' Condition* (Princeton: Princeton University Press).

Fraser, Nancy (1997b) 'Social Justice in the Age of Identity Politics', in G.B. Peterson, ed., *The Tanner Lectures on Human Values, Volume 19* (Salt Lake City: University of Utah Press), 1–67.

Fraser, Nancy (1997c) 'A Rejoinder to Iris Young', *New Left Review* 1/223, 126–9.

Fraser, Nancy (2000) 'Rethinking Recognition', *New Left Review* 2/3, 107–20.

Fraser, Nancy and Linda Gordon (1997) 'A Genealogy of "Dependency"', in Fraser 1997a, 121–49.

Frazer, Elizabeth (1999) *The Problems of Communitarian Politics* (Oxford: Oxford University Press).

Fredman, Sandra (1996) 'The Poverty of Equality: Pensions and the ECJ', *Industrial Law Journal* 25, 91–109.

Fredman, Sandra (2000) 'Judging Democracy: The Role of the Judiciary under the Human Rights Act 1998', *Current Legal Problems* 53, 99–129.

Fredman, Sandra (2001) 'Equality: A New Generation?', *Industrial Law Journal* 30, 145–68.

Freeman, Alan D. (1978) 'Legitimizing Racial Discrimination Through Anti-discrimination Law: A Critical Review of Supreme Court Doctrine', *Minnesota Law Review* 62, 1049–95.

Freeman, Samuel (2000) 'Deliberative Democracy: A Sympathetic Comment', *Philosophy and Public Affairs* 29, 371–418.

Freire, Paulo (1972) *Cultural Action for Freedom* (Harmondsworth: Penguin).

Freire, Paulo (1998) *Pedagogy of the Oppressed,* tr. Myra Bergman Ramos, Twentieth Anniversary edition (New York: Continuum).

French, Sally (1997) 'Changing Disability Research'. Public Lecture, Equality Studies Centre, University College Dublin, 14 February.

Friedan, Betty (1963) *The Feminine Mystique* (New York: W.W. Norton & Co.).

Fung, Archon (2003) 'Deliberative Democracy, Chicago Style: Grassroots Governance in Policing and Public Education', in Fung and Wright 2003, 111–43.

Fung, Archon and Erik Olin Wright (2003) *Deepening Democracy: Institutional Innovations in Empowered Participatory Governance* (London: Verso).

Galanter, Marc (1974) 'Why the "Haves" Come Out Ahead: Speculations on the Limits of Legal Change', *Law & Society Review* 9, 95–160.

Galeotti, Anna Elisabetta (2002) *Toleration as Recognition* (Cambridge: Cambridge University Press).

Gallagher, Michael, Michael Laver and Peter Mair (2001) *Representative Government in Modern Europe: Institutions, Parties, and Governments,* 3rd edition (Singapore: McGraw Hill).

Galligan, Yvonne (1998) 'The Changing Role of Women', in Crotty and Schmitt 1998, 107–21.

Galligan, Yvonne (2000) *The Development of Mechanisms to Monitor Progress in Achieving Gender Equality in Ireland.* Report commissioned by the Department of Justice, Equality and Law Reform (Dublin: Stationery Office).

Galligan, Yvonne and Rick Wilford (1998) 'Women's Political Representation', in Y. Galligan *et al.*, eds, *Contesting Politics: Women in Ireland, North and South* (Boulder, CO: Westview Press), 130–48.

Gambetta, Diego (1987) *Were They Pushed or Did They Jump?* (Cambridge: Cambridge University Press).

Gamoran, Adam, Martin Nystrand, Mark Berends and Paul C. LePore (1995) 'An Organizational Analysis of the Effects of Ability Grouping', *American Educational Research Journal* 32, 687–715.

Gamson, William A. (1990) *The Strategy of Social Protest,* 2nd edition (Belmont, CA: Wadsworth).

Gamson, William A. (1998) 'Social Movements and Cultural Change', in Giugni, McAdam and Tilly 1998, 57–77.

Gamson, William A. and David S. Meyer (1996) 'Framing Political Opportunity', in McAdam, McCarthy and Zald 1996, 275–90.

Gardner, Howard (1983) *Frames of Mind: The Theory of Multiple Intelligences* (New York: Basic Books).

Gardner, Howard (1991) *The Unschooled Mind: How Children Think and How Schools Should Teach* (New York: Basic Books).

Gardner, Howard (1993) *Multiple Intelligences: The Theory in Practice* (New York: Basic Books).

Gardner, Howard (1999) *Intelligence Reframed: Multiple Intelligences for the 21st Century* (New York: Basic Books).

Gargarella, Roberto (1998) 'Full Representation, Deliberation, and Impartiality', in Elster 1998, 260–80.

Geras, Norman (1989) 'Our Morals: The Ethics of Revolution', in R. Miliband, L. Panitch and J. Saville, eds, *Socialist Register 1989: Revolution Today* (London: Merlin Press), 185–211.

Gewirtz, Sharon, Stephen J. Ball and Richard Bowe (1995) *Markets, Choice and Equity in Education* (Buckingham: Open University Press).

Giddens, Anthony (1998) *The Third Way: The Renewal of Social Democracy* (Cambridge: Polity Press).

Gilkerson, Christopher P. (1992) 'Poverty Law Narratives: The Critical Practice and Theory of Receiving and Translating Client Stories', *Hastings Law Journal* 43, 861–945.

Giroux, Henry (1983) *Theory and Resistance in Education* (London: Heinemann).

Giugni, Marco G. (1998) 'Introduction: Social Movements and Change: Incorporation, Tranformation, and Democratization', in Giugni, McAdam and Tilly 1998, xi–xxvi.

Giugni, Marco G. and Florence Passy (1998) 'Contentious Politics in Complex Societies: New Social Movements between Conflict and Cooperation', in Giugni, McAdam and Tilly 1998, 81–107.

Giugni, Marco G., Doug McAdam and Charles Tilly, eds (1998) *From Contention to Democracy* (Lanham, MD: Rowman & Littlefield).

GLEN (Gay and Lesbian Equality Network) and Nexus Research (1995) *Poverty: Lesbians and Gay Men. The Economic and Social Effects of Discrimination* (Dublin: Combat Poverty Agency).

Glyn, Andrew and David Miliband, eds (1994) *Paying for Inequality: The Economic Cost of Social Injustice* (London: Rivers Oram Press).

Goffman, Erving (1968) *Asylums: Essays on the Social Situation of Mental Patients and Other Inmates* (Harmondsworth: Penguin).

Goldthorpe, John H., Catriona Llewellyn and Clive Payne (1980) *Social Mobility and Class Structure in Modern Britain* (Oxford: Oxford University Press).

Goleman, Daniel (1995) *Emotional Intelligence* (New York: Bantam Books).

Goleman, Daniel (1998) *Working With Emotional Intelligence* (New York: Bantam Books).

Goodin, Robert E., ed. (1996) *The Theory of Institutional Design* (Cambridge: Cambridge University Press).

Goodman, Alissa and Andrew Shephard (2002) *Inequality and Living Standards in Great Britain: Some Facts.* IFS Briefing Note No. 19 (London: Institute for Fiscal Studies).

Gordon, David, Ruth Levitas, Christina Pantazis, Demi Patsios, Sarah Payne, Peter Townsend, Laura Andelman, Karl Ashworth, Sue Middleton, Jonathan Bradshaw and Julie Williams (2000) *Poverty and Social Exclusion in Britain* (York: Joseph Rowntree Foundation).

Gorz, André (1982) *Farewell to the Working Class: An Essay on Post-Industrial Socialism*, tr. Mike Sonenscher (London: Pluto Press).

Government of Ireland (1995) *Report of the Task Force on the Travelling Community* (Dublin: Stationery Office).

Government of Ireland (1996) *Report of the Constitution Review Group* (Dublin: Stationery Office).

Government of Ireland (1997) *Sharing in Progress: National Anti-Poverty Strategy* (Dublin: Stationery Office).

Gowran, Sandra (2000) 'Minority Sexualities in Education: The Experiences of Teachers'. Master of Equality Studies thesis, University College Dublin.

Grabham, Emily (2002) 'Law v Canada: New Directions for Equality under the Canadian Charter?', *Oxford Journal of Legal Studies* 22, 641–61.

Graham, Keith (1986) *The Battle of Democracy: Conflict, Consensus, and the Individual* (London: Wheatsheaf).

Gramsci, Antonio (1971) *Selections from the Prison Notebooks of Antonio Gramsci*, ed. and tr. Quintin Hoare and Geoffrey Nowell-Smith (London: Lawrence and Wishart).

Grant, Evadné and Joan G. Small (2001) 'Disadvantage and Discrimination: The Emerging Jurisprudence of the South African Constitutional Court', *Northern Ireland Legal Quarterly* 51, 174–97.

Grass, Günter and Pierre Bourdieu (2002) 'The "Progressive" Restoration: A Franco-German Dialogue', *New Left Review* 2/14, 63–77.

Green, Andy (1997) *Education, Globalization and the Nation State* (Basingstoke: Macmillan – now Palgrave Macmillan).

Green, Andy (2003) 'Education, Equality and Social Cohesion: A Comparative Approach'. Paper presented at the 1st GENIE conference, *Globalisation(s), Identity(s) and Europe(s) in Education in Europe*, Nicosia, Cyprus, 10–12 July.

Green, Philip (1985) *Retrieving Democracy* (London: Methuen).

Grofman, Bernard and Lisa Handley (1992) 'Preconditions for Black and Hispanic Congressional Success', in W. Rule and J.F. Zimmerman, eds, *United States Electoral Systems: Their Impact on Women and Minorities* (New York: Praeger), 31–9.

Guha, Ramachandra (1997) 'The Environmentalism of the Poor', in Fox and Starn 1997, 17–39.

Gutmann, Amy (1987) *Democratic Education* (Princeton: Princeton University Press).

Gutmann, Amy and Dennis Thompson (1996) *Democracy and Disagreement* (Cambridge, MA: Harvard University Press).

Habermas, Jürgen (1970) *Toward a Rational Society: Student Protest, Science and Politics*, tr. Jeremy J. Shapiro (Boston: Beacon Press).

Habermas, Jürgen (1971) *Knowledge and Human Interests*, tr. Jeremy J. Shapiro (Boston: Beacon Press).

Habermas, Jürgen (1984) *The Theory of Communicative Action, Volume 1: Reason and the Rationalization of Society*, tr. Thomas McCarthy (Cambridge: Polity Press).

Habermas, Jürgen (1996a) *Between Facts and Norms: Contributions to a Discourse Theory of Law and Democracy*, tr. William Rehg (Cambridge, MA: MIT Press).

Habermas, Jürgen (1996b) 'Three Normative Models of Democracy', in Benhabib 1996, 21–30.

Hacker, Andrew (1992) *Two Nations: Black and White, Separate, Hostile, Unequal* (New York: Charles Scribner's Sons).

Hakim, Catherine (1995) 'Five Feminist Myths About Women's Employment', *British Journal of Sociology* 46, 429–56.

Hall, Stuart (1988) *The Hard Road to Renewal* (London: Verso).

Hall, Stuart (2000) 'Conclusion: The Multi-Cultural Question', in B. Hesse, ed., *Un/Settled Multiculturalism: Diasporas, Entanglements, 'Transruptions'* (London: Zed Books), 209–41.

Hallam, Susan and Inji Toutounji (1996) 'What Do We Know About Grouping Pupils by Ability?', *Education Review* 10(2), 62–70.

Halsey, Albert H. (1994) 'Sociology as Political Arithmetic', *British Journal of Sociology* 45, 427–44.

Hamelink, Cees J. (1994) *The Politics of World Communication: A Human Rights Perspective* (London: Sage).

Hamelink, Cees J. (1995) *World Communication: Disempowerment and Self-Empowerment* (London: Zed Books).

Hammersley, Martyn (1992) 'On Feminist Methodology', *Sociology* 26, 187–206.

Hammersley, Martyn (1995) *The Politics of Social Research* (London: Sage).

Hanafin, Joan, Michael Shevlin and Marie Flynn (2002) 'Responding to Student Diversity: Lessons from the Margin', *Pedagogy, Culture and Society* 10, 409–24.

Hanagan, Michael (1998) 'Social Movements: Incorporation, Disengagement, and Opportunities – A Long View', in Giugni, McAdam and Tilly 1998, 3–30.

Hanley, Eric and Matthew McKeever (1997) 'The Persistence of Educational Inequalities in State-Socialist Hungary: Trajectory-Maintenance versus Counter-Selection', *Sociology of Education* 70, 1–18.

Hannan, Damian F. and Maura Boyle (1987) *Schooling Decisions: The Origins and Consequences of Selection and Streaming in Irish Post-Primary Schools* (Dublin: ESRI).

Hannan, Damian F., Emer Smyth, James McCullagh, Richard O'Leary and Dorren McMahon (1996) *Coeducation and Gender Equality: Exam Performance, Stress and Personal Development* (Dublin: Oak Tree Press).

Hardiman, Niamh (1998) 'Inequality and the Representation of Interests', in Crotty and Schmitt 1998, 122–43.

Hardiman, Niamh (2000) 'Social Partnership, Wage Bargaining and Growth', in Nolan, O'Connell and Whelan 2000, 286–309.

Harding, Sandra (1986) *The Science Question in Feminism* (Milton Keynes: Open University Press).

Harding, Sandra (1991) *Whose Science? Whose Knowledge?* (Milton Keynes: Open University Press).

Harding, Sandra (2003) 'Knowledge and Politics: Three Feminist Issues'. Paper presented at *Feminist Knowledge and Politics: A Research Symposium*, University College Cork, 4–5 April.

Harding, Sandra, ed. (1987) *Feminism and Methodology: Social Science Issues* (Milton Keynes: Open University Press).

Hargreaves, Andy (2000) 'Mixed Emotions: Teachers' Perceptions of their Interactions with Students', *Teaching and Teacher Education* 16, 811–26.

Hargreaves, Andy (2001) 'Emotional Geographies of Teaching', *Teachers College Record* 103, 1056–80.

Harlow, Carol (1999) 'Access to Justice as a Human Right: The European Convention and the European Union', in P. Alston, ed., *The EU and Human Rights* (Oxford: Oxford University Press), 187–213.

Harlow, Carol and Richard Rawlings (1992) *Pressure Through Law* (London: Routledge).

Harré, Rom (1981) 'The Post-Empiricist Approach and its Alternative', in Reason and Rowan 1981, 3–17.

Harris, Angela (1990) 'Race and Essentialism in Feminist Legal Theory', *Stanford Law Review* 42, 581–616.

Harris, Cheryl I. (1993) 'Whiteness as Property', *Harvard Law Review* 106, 1710–76.

Harris, Ron (2000) *Industrializing English Law* (Cambridge: Cambridge University Press).

Harris, Simon (1990) *Lesbian and Gay Issues in the English Classroom* (Milton Keynes: Open University Press).

Harsanyi, John C. (1976) *Essays on Ethics, Social Behavior, and Scientific Explanation* (Dordrecht: D. Reidel).

Harstock, Nancy (1998) *The Feminist Standpoint Revisited and Other Essays* (Boulder, CO: Westview Press).

Hatcher, Richard (1998) 'Class Differentiation in Education: Rational Choices?', *British Journal of Sociology of Education* 19, 5–24.

Hayek, F.A. (1976) *Law, Legislation and Liberty: The Mirage of Social Justice* (London: Routledge & Kegan Paul).

Hays, Sharon (1996) *The Cultural Contradictions of Motherhood* (New Haven: Yale University Press).

Heady, Christopher (1993) 'Optimal Taxation as a Guide to Tax Policy: A Survey', *Fiscal Studies* 14, 15–41.

Heath, Anthony, Roger Jowell and John Curtice (1985) *How Britain Votes* (Oxford: Pergamon).

Held, David (1996) *Models of Democracy,* 2nd edition (Cambridge: Polity Press).

Held, Virginia, ed. (1995) *Justice and Care: Essential Readings in Feminist Ethics* (Boulder, CO: Westview Press).

Hendriks, Aart C. (2000) 'Disability as a Prohibitive Ground for Discrimination: Different Definitions – Same Problems – One Way Out?'. Paper presented at *From Principle to Practice: An International Disability Law and Policy Symposium,* Washington, 22–26 October.

Henwood, Doug (2002) 'Not Such a Good Year, 2001', *Left Business Observer* 103.

Hepple, Bob (1990) 'Discrimination and Equality of Opportunity – Northern Irish Lessons', *Oxford Journal of Legal Studies* 10, 408–21.

Heron, James (1981) 'Philosophical Basis for a New Paradigm', in Reason and Rowan 1981, 19–36.

Herr, Kathryn and Gary Anderson (1997) 'The Cultural Politics of Identity: Student Narratives from Two Mexican Secondary Schools', *Qualitative Studies in Education* 10, 45–61.

Heywood, Mark (2003) 'Contempt or Compliance? The TAC Case after the Constitutional Court Judgment', *ESR Review* 4(1). http://www.communitylaw-centre.org.za (31 October 2003).

Hirsch, Fred (1977) *Social Limits to Growth* (London: Routledge & Kegan Paul).

Hirst, Paul (1994) *Associative Democracy* (Cambridge: Polity Press).

Hobson, Barbara, ed. (2000) *Gender and Citizenship in Transition* (Basingstoke: Macmillan – now Palgrave Macmillan).

Hochman, Harold M. and James D. Rodgers (1969) 'Pareto Optimal Redistribution', *American Economic Review* 59, 542–57.

Hochschild, Arlie (1983) *The Managed Heart: Commercialization of Human Feeling* (Berkeley, CA: University of California Press).

Hochschild, Arlie (1989) *The Second Shift: Working Parents and the Revolution at Home* (Harmondsworth: Penguin).

Hoey, Pat (2000) *Students with Disabilities in Higher Education: Initial Findings of the Survey on Provision for Students with Disabilities in Higher Education for the Academic*

*Year 1998/99*. Report prepared on behalf of the Higher Education Authority (Dublin: AHEAD).

Honneth, Axel (1995) *The Struggle for Recognition: The Moral Grammar of Social Conflicts,* tr. Joel Anderson (Cambridge: Polity Press).

hooks, bell (1984) *Feminist Theory from Margin to Center* (Boston: South End Press).

hooks, bell (1994) *Teaching to Transgress: Education as the Practice of Freedom* (London: Routledge).

hooks, bell (2000) *All About Love* (New York: William Morrow & Co.).

Horgan, Goretti (2001) 'Changing Women's Lives in Ireland', *International Socialism, Quarterly Journal of the Socialist Workers' Party (Britain)* No. 91, 53–91.

Hughes, Bill (2002) 'Disability and the Body', in Barnes, Oliver and Barton 2002, 58–76.

Human Rights Commission [Ireland] (2003) *Promoting and Protecting Human Rights in Irish Society: A Plan for 2003–2006* (Dublin: Human Rights Commission).

Human Rights Watch (2002) *World Report 2002: Events of 2001* (New York: Human Rights Watch).

Humphreys, Eilís and Gerry Jeffers (1999) *Pointing to the Future: Some Second-Level Students' Perceptions of the Points System.* Commission on the Points System Research Paper No. 2 (Dublin: Stationery Office).

Humphries, Beth (1997) 'From Critical Thought to Emancipatory Action: Contradictory Research Goals', *Sociological Research Online* 2(1). http://www.socres-online.org.uk/socresonline/2/1/3.html (18 May 2003).

Humphries, Beth and Carole Truman, eds (1994) *Rethinking Social Research* (Aldershot: Avebury).

Hunt, Paul (1996) *Reclaiming Social Rights: International and Comparative Perspectives* (Aldershot: Dartmouth).

Hyland, J.L. (1995) *Democratic Theory* (Manchester: Manchester University Press).

ILGA (International Lesbian and Gay Association) (2003) *World Legal Survey.* http://www.ilga.org/Information/legal_survey/Summary information/countries_where_same_sex_acts illegal.htm (18 May 2003).

Illich, Ivan (1970) *Deschooling Society* (New York: Harper & Row).

ILO (International Labour Organization) (1941) *Constitution* as amended to include the Declaration Concerning the Aims and Purposes of the ILO. http://www.ilo.org/public/english/about/iloconst.htm (18 May 2003).

ILO (International Labour Organization) (1998) *Declaration on Fundamental Principles and Rights at Work.* http://www.ilo.org/public/english/standards/decl/declaration/text/index.htm (18 May 2003).

ILO (International Labour Organization) (1999) *Report of the Director-General: Decent Work.* http://www.ilo.org/public/english/standards/relm/ilc/ilc87/rep-i.htm (18 May 2003).

ILO (International Labour Organization) (2001) *Report of the Director-General: Reducing the Decent Work Deficit–A Global Challenge.* http://www.ilo.org/public/english/standards/relm/ilc/ilc89/rep-i-a.htm (18 May 2003).

ILO (International Labour Organization) (2002) *Key Indicators of the Labour Market 6. Hours of Work.* http://www.ilo.org/public/english/employment/strat/kilm/kilm06.htm (18 May 2003).

Immergut, Ellen M. (1995) 'An Institutional Critique of Associative Democracy', in Cohen and Rogers 1995, 201–6.

Inglis, Tom (1998) *Moral Monopoly: The Rise and Fall of the Catholic Church in Modern Ireland* (Dublin: University College Dublin Press).

Irish Commission for Justice and Peace (1998) *Re-Righting the Irish Constitution: The Case for New Social and Economic Rights* (Dublin: Irish Catholic Bishops' Conference).

Iyer, Nitya (1993) 'Categorical Denials: Equality Rights and the Shaping of Social Identity', *Queen's Law Journal* 19, 179–207.

Jackman, Martha and Bruce Porter (1999) 'Women's Substantive Equality and the Protection of Social and Economic Rights Under the Canadian Human Rights Act', in Status of Women Canada, *Women and the Canadian Human Rights Act: A Collection of Policy Research Reports* (Ottawa: Status of Women Canada), 43–112.

Jackson, Brian (1964) *Streaming: An Education System in Miniature* (London: Routledge & Kegan Paul).

Jaggar, Alison M. (1998) 'Sexual Equality as Parity of Effective Voice', *Journal of Contemporary Legal Issues* 9, 179–202.

Jayaratne, Toby E. and Abigail J. Stewart (1995) 'Quantitative and Qualitative Methods in the Social Sciences: Feminist Issues and Practical Strategies', in J. Holland, M. Blair and S. Sheldon, eds, *Debates and Issues in Feminist Research and Pedagogy* (Clevedon: Multilingual Matters in association with the Open University), 217–34.

Jeffers, Gerry (2002) 'Transition Year Programme and Educational Disadvantage', *Irish Educational Studies* 21(2), 47–64.

Jeffrey, M. (1998) 'Not Really Going to Work? Of the Directive on Part-Time Work, Atypical Work and Attempts to Regulate It', *Industrial Law Journal* 27, 193–213.

Jencks, Christopher, Lauri Perman and Lee Rainwater (1988) 'What is a Good Job? A New Measure of Labor-Market Success', *American Journal of Sociology* 93, 1322–57.

Jenkins, Patricia H. (1997) 'School Delinquency and the School Social Bond', *Journal of Research in Crime and Delinquency* 34, 337–67.

John, Pippa (1996) 'Damaged Goods: An Interpretation of Excluded Pupils' Perception of Schooling', in E. Blyth and J. Milner, eds, *Exclusion from School: Multi-Professional Approaches to Policy and Practice* (London: Routledge), 159–82.

Johnson, Paul (1994) 'Taxes and Benefits, Equality and Efficiency', in Glyn and Miliband 1994, 160–80.

Jolls, Christina (2001) 'Anti-Discrimination and Accommodation', *Harvard Law Review* 115, 642–99.

Jones, Charles (1999) *Global Justice* (Oxford: Oxford University Press).

Jones, Mary (1988) *These Obstreperous Lassies: A History of the IWWU* (Dublin: Gill & Macmillan).

Joshi, Barbara R. (1982) *Democracy in Search of Equality: Untouchable Politics and Indian Social Change* (Atlantic Heights, NJ: Humanities Press).

Justice/Public Law Project (1996) *A Matter of Public Interest: Reforming the Law and Practice on Interventions in Public Interest Cases* (London: Justice).

Kairys, David, ed. (1998) *The Politics of the Law: A Progressive Critique,* 3rd edition (New York: Basic Books).

Kanter, Rosabeth Moss (1977) *Men and Women of the Corporation* (New York: Basic Books).

Kariya, Takehiko and James E. Rosenbaum (1999) 'Bright Flight: Unintended Consequences of Detracking Policy in Japan', *American Journal of Education* 107, 210–30.

Katz, Michael (1971) *Class, Bureaucracy and Schools* (New York: Praeger Publishers).

Kavanagh, Aileen (1997) 'The Quest for Legitimacy in Constitutional Interpretation', *Irish Jurist* 32, 195–216.

Kavanagh, Sandra (1996) 'A Review of Equality of Opportunity in the Irish Civil Service with Reference to Women'. Master of Equality Studies thesis, University College Dublin.

Keane, John (1993) 'Democracy and the Media – Without Foundations', *Political Studies* 40 (Special Issue), 116–29.

Kearney, Joseph D. and Thomas W. Merrill (2000) 'The Influence of Amicus Curiae Briefs on the Supreme Court', *University of Pennsylvania Law Review* 148, 743–855.

Keck, Margaret E. and Kathryn Sikkink (1998) *Activists Beyond Borders: Advocacy Networks in International Politics* (Ithaca, NY: Cornell University Press).

Kelly, Alison (1985) 'The Construction of Masculine Science', *British Journal of Sociology of Education* 6, 133–54.

Kelly, Mary (1996) *Educational Television: Emancipatory Education and the Right to Learn Project* (Dublin: Radio Telefis Eireann and Equality Studies Centre).

Kennedy, David (1998) 'Legal Education as a Training for Hierarchy', in Kairys 1998, 54–75.

Kennedy, Fiachra (2002) 'Abortion Referendum 2002', *Irish Political Studies* 17, 114–28.

Kenworthy, Lane (1995) 'Equality and Efficiency: The Illusory Tradeoff', *European Journal of Political Research* 27, 225–54.

Keppel, Kenneth G., Jeffrey N. Pearcy and Diane K. Wagener (2002) 'Trends in Racial and Ethnic-Specific Rates for the Health Status Indicators: United States, 1990–98', *Healthy People Statistical Notes* 23 (Hyattsville, Maryland: National Center for Health Statistics).

Kilpatrick, Claire (2002) 'Emancipation Through Law or the Emasculation of Law? The Nation-State, the EU and Gender Equality at Work', in J. Conaghan, R.M. Fischl and K. Klare, eds, *Labour Law in an Era of Globalization* (Oxford: Oxford University Press), 489–509.

King, Patricia M. and Karen Strohm Kitchener (1994) *Developing Reflective Judgement: Understanding and Promoting Intellectual Growth and Critical Thinking in Adolescents and Adults* (San Francisco: Jossey-Bass).

Kingsnorth, Paul (2003) *One No, Many Yeses: A Journey to the Heart of the Global Resistance Movement* (London: Free Press).

Kirby, Peadar (2002) *The Celtic Tiger in Distress: Growth with Inequality in Ireland* (Basingstoke: Palgrave Macmillan).

Kittay, Eva Feder (1999) *Love's Labor: Essays on Women, Equality, and Dependency* (New York: Routledge).

Klare, Karl (1979) 'Law Making as Praxis', *Telos* 40, 123–35.

Klare, Karl (1998) 'Legal Culture and Transformative Constitutionalism', *South African Journal of Human Rights* 14, 146–87.

Klein, Naomi (2000) *No Logo* (London: Flamingo).

Klein, Naomi (2001) 'Reclaiming the Commons', *New Left Review* 2/9, 81–9.

Klein, Naomi (2002) *Fences and Windows: Dispatches from the Front Lines of the Globalization Debate* (London: Flamingo).

Klinkner, Philip A. and Rogers M. Smith (1999) *The Unsteady March: The Rise and Decline of Racial Equality in America* (Chicago: University of Chicago Press).

Knell, Markus (1999) 'Social Comparisons, Inequality and Growth', *Journal of Institutional and Theoretical Economics* 155, 6664–95.

Knight, Jack and James Johnson (1997) 'What Sort of Political Equality Does Deliberative Democracy Require?', in J. Bohman and W. Rehg, eds, *Deliberative Democracy: Essays on Reason and Politics* (Cambridge, MA: MIT Press), 279–319.

Korpi, Walter and Joakim Palme (2003) 'New Politics and Class Politics in the Context of Austerity and Globalization: Welfare State Regress in 18 Countries, 1975–95', *American Political Science Review* 97, 425–46.

Kriesi, Hanspeter (1995a) 'Alliance Structures', in Kriesi *et al.* 1995, 53–81.

Kriesi, Hanspeter (1995b) 'The Dynamics of Protest Waves', in Kriesi *et al.* 1995, 111–42.

Kriesi, Hanspeter (1996) 'The Organizational Structure of New Social Movements in a Political Context', in McAdam, McCarthy and Zald 1996, 152–84.

Kriesi, Hanspeter, Ruud Koopmans, Jan Willem Duyvendak and Marco G. Giugni, eds (1995) *New Social Movements in Western Europe: A Comparative Analysis* (London: UCL Press).

Kroll, Luisa and Lea Goldman, eds (2003) 'Billionaires: Survival of the Richest', *Forbes* online edition. http://www.forbes.com/free_forbes/2003/0317/087.html (18 May 2003).

Kubitschek, Warren N. and Maureen T. Hallinan (1998) 'Tracking and Students' Friendships', *Social Psychology Quarterly* 61, 1–15.

Kuhn, Thomas (1961) *The Structure of Scientific Revolutions* (Chicago: Chicago University Press).

Kuznets, Simon (1955) 'Economic Growth and Income Inequality', *American Economic Review* 45, 1–28.

Kymlicka, Will (1995) *Multicultural Citizenship: A Liberal Theory of Minority Rights* (Oxford: Oxford University Press).

Kymlicka, Will (2000) *Politics in the Vernacular: Nationalism, Multiculturalism, and Citizenship* (Oxford: Oxford University Press).

Kymlicka, Will (2002) *Contemporary Political Philosophy: An Introduction,* 2nd edition (Oxford: Oxford University Press).

L'Heureux-Dubé, Claire (1994) 'Re-Examining the Doctrine of Judicial Notice in the Family Law Context', *Ottawa Law Review* 26, 551–77.

Labov, William (1972) *Language in the Inner City: Studies in the Black English Vernacular* (Philadelphia: University of Pennsylvania Press).

Lacey, Nicola (1998) *Unspeakable Subjects: Feminist Essays in Legal and Social Theory* (Oxford: Hart).

Laclau, Ernesto and Chantal Mouffe (1985) *Hegemony and Socialist Strategy: Towards a Radical Democratic Politics,* tr. Winston Moore and Paul Cammack (London: Verso).

Lakoff, Robin (1977) 'Language and Women's Place', in J. English, ed., *Sex Equality* (Englewood Cliffs, NJ: Prentice-Hall), 220–30.

Landesman, Bruce M. (1983) 'Egalitarianism', *Canadian Journal of Philosophy* 13, 27–56.

Lane, Jan-Erik (1996) *Constitutions and Political Theory* (Manchester: Manchester University Press).

Lareau, Annette (1989) *Home Advantage: School Class and Parental Intervention in Elementary Schools* (London: Falmer Press).

Larkin, Katherine (1997) 'Local Participation in Village and Urban Renewal', in Community Workers Co-operative 1997, 50–3.

Lash, Scott and John Urry (1987) *The End of Organised Capitalism* (Cambridge: Polity Press).

Lather, Patti (1986) 'Research as Praxis', *Harvard Educational Review* 56, 257–77.

Lather, Patti (1991) *Getting Smart: Feminist Research and Pedagogy with/in the Postmodern* (New York: Routledge).

Le Grand, Julian and Saul Estrin, eds (1989) *Market Socialism* (Oxford: Oxford University Press).

Lenin, V.I. [1902] *What is to Be Done? Burning Questions of Our Movement,* tr. J. Fineberg and G. Hanna; ed. V.J. Jerome (New York: International Publishers, 1969).

Lentin, Ronit (1993) 'Feminist Research Methodologies – A Separate Paradigm? Notes for a Debate', *Irish Journal of Sociology* 3, 119–38.

Lentin, Ronit (2003) '"Intercultural" Education for the University of Tomorrow?', in R. Lentin, ed., *Working and Teaching in a Multicultural University* (Dublin: Department of Sociology, Trinity College Dublin), 7–22. http://www.tcd.ie/Sociology/mphil/dwnl/teaching+working.pdf (18 May 2003).

Leposky, M. David (1998) 'The Charter's Guarantee of Equality to People with Disabilities – How Well Is It Working?', *Windsor Year Book of Access to Justice* 16, 155–214.

Lerner, Gerda (1986) *The Creation of Patriarchy* (New York: Oxford University Press).

Levine, Andrew (1995) 'Democratic Corporatism and/versus Socialism', in Cohen and Rogers 1995, 157–66.

Levine, Andrew (1998) *Rethinking Liberal Equality: From a 'Utopian' Point of View* (Ithaca, NY: Cornell University Press).

Levitas, Ruth (1998) *The Inclusive Society? Social Exclusion and New Labour* (Basingstoke: Macmillan – now Palgrave Macmillan).

Lewis, Gail (2000) *'Race', Gender, Social Welfare: Encounters in a Postcolonial Society* (Cambridge: Polity Press).

Lewis, Jane (2001) 'Legitimizing Care Work and the Issue of Gender Equality', in Daly 2001, 57–75.

Liddy, Margaret (2002) 'The Agenda of the Anti-Capitalism Movement: Convergence or Diversity?'. Master of Equality Studies thesis, University College Dublin.

Lijphart, Arend (1977) *Democracy in Plural Societies: A Comparative Exploration* (New Haven: Yale University Press).

Lijphart, Arend (1984) *Democracies: Patterns of Majoritarian and Consensus Government in Twenty-One Countries* (New Haven: Yale University Press).

Lindblom, Charles E. (1988) *Democracy and Market Systems* (Oslo: Norwegian University Press).

Lister, Ruth (2000) 'Dilemmas in Engendering Citizenship', in Hobson 2000, 33–83.

Llewellyn, Karl N. (1960) *The Bramble Bush: On Our Law and Its Study* (Dobbs Ferry, NY: Oceana Publications).

Lobel, Jules (1998) 'The Political Tilt of the Separation of Powers', in Kairys 1998, 591–616.

Loeb, Paul Rogat (1999) *Soul of a Citizen: Living with Conviction in a Cynical Time* (New York: St. Martin's Press – now Palgrave Macmillan).

Loughlin, Martin (2000) *Swords and Scales: An Examination of the Relationship Between Law and Politics* (Oxford: Hart).

Loury, Glenn C. (1987) 'A Dynamic Theory of Racial Income Differences', in P.A. Wallace and A.M. LaMond, eds, *Women, Minorities, and Employment Discrimination* (Lexington, MA: Lexington Books), 153–86.

Loyal, Steve (2003) 'Welcome to the Celtic Tiger: Racism, Immigration and the State', in Coulter and Coleman 2003, 74–94.

Lugones, María C. and Elizabeth V. Spelman (1985) 'Have We Got a Theory for You! Feminist Theory, Cultural Imperialism and the Demand for the "Women's Role"', *Women's Studies International Forum* 6, 573–81.

Lukács, Geog (1971) *History and Class Consciousness: Studies in Marxist Dialectics*, tr. Rodney Livingstone (London: Merlin Press).

Lukes, Steven (1977) *Essays in Social Theory* (London: Macmillan).

Lukes, Steven (1985) *Marxism and Morality* (Oxford: Oxford University Press).

Lupton, Deborah (1998) *The Emotional Self: A Sociocultural Exploration* (London: Sage).

Lynam, Siobhán (1997) 'Democratising Local Development: The Experience of the Community Sector in its Attempts to Advance Participatory Democracy'. Master of Equality Studies thesis, University College Dublin.

Lynch, Kathleen (1987) 'Dominant Ideologies in Irish Educational Thought: Consensualism, Essentialism and Meritocratic Individualism', *Economic and Social Review* 18, 101–22.

Lynch, Kathleen (1989) 'Solidary Labour: Its Nature and Marginalisation', *Sociological Review* 37, 1–14.

Lynch, Kathleen (1997) 'The Relationship between Equality Studies and Cognate Disciplines: Women's Studies, Development Studies and Disability Studies'. Unpublished working paper (Dublin: Equality Studies Centre).

Lynch, Kathleen (1999) *Equality in Education* (Dublin: Gill & Macmillan).

Lynch, Kathleen (2000) 'Research and Theory on Equality in Education', in M. Hallinan, ed., *Handbook of Sociology of Education* (New York: Plenum Press), 85–105.

Lynch, Kathleen and Anne Lodge (1999) 'Essays on School', in Lynch 1999, 217–59.

Lynch, Kathleen and Anne Lodge (2002) *Equality and Power in Schools: Redistribution, Recognition and Representation* (London: RoutledgeFalmer).

Lynch, Kathleen and Cathleen O'Neill (1994) 'The Colonisation of Social Class in Education', *British Journal of Sociology of Education* 15, 307–24.

Lynch, Kathleen and Claire O'Riordan (1998) 'Inequality in Higher Education: A Study of Class Barriers', *British Journal of Sociology of Education* 19, 445–78.

Lynch, Kathleen and Eithne McLaughlin (1995) 'Caring Labour and Love Labour', in Clancy *et al.* 1995, 250–92.

Lyons, Maureen, Kathleen Lynch, Sean Close, Emer Sheerin and Philip Boland (2003) *Inside Classrooms: The Teaching and Learning of Mathematics in Social Context* (Dublin: Institute of Public Administration).

McAdam, Doug (1996) 'The Framing Function of Movement Tactics: Strategic Dramaturgy in the American Civil Rights Movement', in McAdam, McCarthy and Zald 1996, 338–55.

McAdam, Doug, John D. McCarthy and Mayer N. Zald, eds (1996) *Comparative Perspectives on Social Movements* (Cambridge: Cambridge University Press).

McAleese, Dermot and Dominic Burke (2000) 'Policy Objectives for a Regional Economy', in J. O'Hagan, ed., *The Economy of Ireland* (Dublin: Gill & Macmillan), 50–76.

McCaffrey, Colum (1992) 'Political Communication and Broadcasting: Theory, Practice and Reform'. Ph.D. thesis, University College Dublin.

McCann, May, Séamas Ó Síocháin and Joseph Ruane, eds (1994) *Irish Travellers: Culture and Ethnicity* (Belfast: Institute of Irish Studies, Queen's University Belfast).

McChesney, Robert W. (1998) 'The Political Economy of Global Communication', in R.W. McChesney, E.M. Wood and J.B. Foster, eds, *Capitalism and the Information Age: The Political Economy of the Global Communication Revolution* (New York: Monthly Review Press), 1–26.

McChesney, Robert W. and John Nichols (2002) *Our Media, Not Theirs: The Democratic Struggle Against Corporate Media* (New York: Seven Stories Press).

MacCrimmon, Marilyn T. (1998) 'Fact Determination: Common Sense Knowledge, Judicial Notice and Social Science Evidence', *International Commentary on Evidence*. http://www.law.qub.ac.uk/ice/papers/judicial1.html (19 November 2003).

McCrudden, Christopher (1996) 'The Constitutionality of Affirmative Action in the United States: A Note on Adarand Constructors Inc v Pena', *International Journal of Discrimination Law* 1, 369–76.

McCrudden, Christopher (1998) 'Merit Principles', *Oxford Journal of Legal Studies* 18, 543–79.

McCrudden, Christopher (1999) 'Mainstreaming Equality in the Governance of Northern Ireland', *Fordham International Law Journal* 22, 1696–775.

McCullagh, Ciaran (1995) 'Getting the Criminals We Want: The Social Production of the Criminal Population', in Clancy *et al.* 1995, 410–31.

McDonagh, Rosaleen (2000) 'Talking Back', in A. Byrne and R. Lentin, eds, *(Re)searching Women: Feminist Research Methodologies in the Social Sciences in Ireland* (Dublin: Institute of Public Administration), 237–46.

McDonnell, Patrick (2003) 'Educational Policy', in S. Quin and B. Redmond, eds, *Disability and Social Policy in Ireland* (Dublin: University College Dublin Press), 28–44.

McGlynn, Clare (2000) 'Pregnancy, Parenthood and the Court of Justice in Abdoulaye', *European Law Review* 25, 654–62.

McGrath, Daniel J. and Peter J. Kuriloff (1999) '"They're Going to Tear the Doors Off This Place": Upper-Middle Class Parent Involvement and the Educational Opportunities of Other People's Children', *Educational Policy* 13, 603–29.

Mackay, Fiona (2001) *Love and Politics: Women Politicians and the Ethics of Care* (London: Continuum).

MacKinnon, Catherine A. (1987) *Feminism Unmodified: Discourses on Life and Law* (Cambridge, MA: Harvard University Press).

MacKinnon, Catherine A. (1990) 'Legal Perspectives on Sexual Difference', in Rhode 1990, 213–25.

McLaren, Peter (1995) *Critical Pedagogy and Predatory Culture: Oppositional Politics in a Postmodern Era* (London: Routledge).

McLaren, Peter (2000) *Che Guevara, Paulo Freire and the Pedagogy of Revolution* (Lanham, MD: Rowman & Littlefield).

McLaughlin, Eithne (1991) *Social Security and Community Care: The Case of the Invalid Care Allowance.* Department of Social Security Research Report No. 4 (London: Stationery Office).

McLaughlin, Eithne (1994) 'Employment, Unemployment and Social Security', in Glyn and Miliband 1994, 145–59.

McLean, Iain (1987) *Public Choice: An Introduction* (Oxford: Blackwell).

McLeod, Douglas B. (1992) 'Research on Affect in Mathematics Education: A Reconceptualization', in D.A. Grouws, ed., *Handbook of Research on Mathematics Teaching and Learning* (New York: Macmillan), 575–96.

McMinn, Joanna (2000) 'The Changers and the Changed: An Analysis of Women's Community Education Groups in the North and South of Ireland'. Ph.D. thesis, University College Dublin.

Macpherson, C.B. (1973) 'Rawls's Models of Man and Society', *Philosophy of the Social Sciences* 3, 341–7.

McRae, Kenneth D. (1997) 'Contrasting Styles of Democratic Decision-Making: Adversarial versus Consensual Politics', *International Political Science Review* 18, 279–95.

Madeley, John (2000) *Hungry for Trade: How the Poor Pay for Free Trade* (London: Zed Books).

Madison, James [1787–88] 'Number 10. Factions: Their Cause and Control', in A. Hamilton, J. Jay and J. Madison, *The Federalist Papers,* ed. Andrew Hacker (New York: Washington Square Press, 1964), 16–24.

Mahon, Evelyn (1998) *Women in Crisis Pregnancy* (Dublin: Stationery Office).

Mahony, Pat and Christine Zmroczek, eds (1997) *Class Matters: 'Working Class' Women's Perspectives on Education* (London: Taylor and Francis).

Malamud, Deborah C. (1997) 'Values, Symbols, and Facts in the Affirmative Action Debate', *Michigan Law Review* 95, 1668–714.

Mansbridge, Jane (1983) *Beyond Adversary Democracy,* 2nd edition (Chicago: University of Chicago Press).

Mansbridge, Jane (1995a) 'A Deliberative Perspective on Neocorporatism', in Cohen and Rogers 1995, 133–47.

Mansbridge, Jane (1995b) 'Does Participation Make Better Citizens?', *The Good Society* 5(2), 1–7.

Mansbridge, Jane (1996) 'Using Power/Fighting Power: The Polity', in Benhabib 1996, 46–66.

Mansbridge, Jane (1999) 'Everyday Talk in the Deliberative System', in S. Macedo, ed., *Deliberative Politics: Essays on Democracy and Disagreement* (Oxford: Oxford University Press), 211–39.

Mansbridge, Jane (2003) 'Practice – Thought – Practice', in Fung and Wright 2003, 175–99.

Marcos, Subcomandante (2001), interviewed by Gabriel García Márquez and Roberto Pombo, 'The Punch Card and the Hourglass', *New Left Review* 2/9, 69–79.

Marshall, Gordon, Adam Swift and Stephen Roberts (1997) *Against the Odds? Social Class and Social Justice in Industrial Societies* (Oxford: Oxford University Press).

Marshall, Gordon, Howard Newby, David Rose and Carolyn Volger (1988) *Social Class in Modern Britain* (London: Hutchinson).

Martin, Marion (1994) 'Developing a Feminist Participative Research Framework: Evaluating the Process', in Humphries and Truman 1994, 123–45.

Martin, Marion (1996) 'Issues of Power in the Participatory Research Process', in de Koning and Martin 1996, 82–93.

Marx, Karl and Friedrich Engels [1848] *Manifesto of the Communist Party*, tr. Samuel Moore and Friedrich Engels, in K. Marx and F. Engels, *Selected Works, Volume I (1845–59)* (Moscow: Progress Publishers, 1969), 98–137.

Mason, A. and A. Palmer (1995) *Queerbashing: A National Survey of Hate Crimes Against Lesbian and Gay Men* (London: Stonewall).

Matsuda, Mari J. (1987) 'Looking to the Bottom: Critical Legal Studies and Reparations', *Harvard Civil Rights–Civil Liberties Law Review* 22, 323–99.

Mee, John and Kaye Ronayne (2000) *Partnership Rights of Same Sex Couples* (Dublin: Equality Authority).

Meier, Deborah and Paul Schwarz (1999) 'Central Park East Secondary School', in Apple and Beane 1999, 30–47.

Melucci, Alberto (1985) 'The Symbolic Challenge of Contemporary Movements', *Social Research* 52, 789–816.

Melucci, Alberto (1996) *Challenging Codes: Collective Action in the Information Age* (Cambridge: Cambridge University Press).

Menkel-Meadow, Carrie (1996) 'The Trouble with the Adversary System in a Postmodern, Multicultural World', *William and Mary Law Review* 38, 5–44.

Michelman, Frank (1987) 'Possession vs. Distribution in the Constitutional Idea of Property', *Iowa Law Review* 72, 1319–50.

Mies, Maria (1983) 'Towards a Methodology for Feminist Research', in Bowles and Klein 1983, 117–39.

Mill, Harriet Taylor [1851] 'The Enfranchisement of Women', in J.S. Mill and H.T. Mill, *Essays on Sex Equality,* ed. Alice S. Rossi (Chicago: Chicago University Press, 1970), 89–121.

Mill, John Stuart [1861] *Representative Government*, in J.S. Mill, *On Liberty and Other Essays*, ed. John Gray (Oxford: Oxford University Press, 1991), 203–467.

Mill, John Stuart [1869] *The Subjection of Women*, in J.S. Mill, *On Liberty and Other Essays*, ed. John Gray (Oxford: Oxford University Press, 1991), 469–582.

Miller, David (1976) *Social Justice* (Oxford: Oxford University Press).

Miller, David (1989) *Market, State and Community: Theoretical Foundations of Market Socialism* (Oxford: Oxford University Press).

Miller, David (1997) *Principles of Social Justice* (Cambridge, MA: Harvard University Press).

Millett, Kate (1970) *Sexual Politics* (Garden City, NY: Doubleday).

Minnich, Daniel J. (2003) 'Corporatism and Income Inequality in the Global Economy: A Panel Study of 17 OECD Countries', *European Journal of Political Research* 42, 23–53.

Minow, Martha (1987) 'Interpreting Rights: An Essay for Robert Cover', *Yale Law Journal* 96, 1860–915.

Minow, Martha (1990) *Making All the Difference: Inclusion, Exclusion, and American Law* (Ithaca, NY: Cornell University Press).

Minow, Martha (1992) *Not Only for Myself: Identity, Politics, and the Law* (New York: New Press).

Mitchell, Juliet (1984) *Women: The Longest Revolution* (London: Virago).

Moene, Karl Ove and Michael Wallerstein (1997) 'Pay Inequality', *Journal of Labor Economics* 15, 403–30.

More, Gillian (1996) 'Equality of Treatment in the European Community Law: The Limits of Market Equality', in A. Bottomley, ed., *Feminist Perspectives on the Foundational Subjects of Law* (London: Cavendish), 261–78.

Morgan, David G. (2001) *A Judgment Too Far? Judicial Activism and the Constitution* (Cork: Cork University Press).

Morris, Jenny (1989) *Able Lives: Women's Experience of Paralysis* (London: Women's Press).

Morris, Jenny (1991) *Pride Against Prejudice* (London: Women's Press).

Mortimore, G.W. (1968) 'An Ideal of Equality', *Mind* 77, 222–42.

Mortimore, Peter, Pamela Sammons, Louise Stoll, D. Lewis and R. Ecob (1995) *School Matters: The Junior Years* (London: Paul Chapman).

Mossman, Mary Jane (1986) 'Feminism and Legal Method: The Difference It Makes', *Australian Journal of Law and Society* 3, 30–52.

Mullally, Siobhán (2001) 'Mainstreaming Equality in Ireland: A Fair and Inclusive Accommodation?', *Legal Studies* 21, 99–115.

Mullally, Siobhán and Olivia Smith (2000) *Partnership 2000 Working Group Report on Equality Proofing* (Dublin: Stationery Office).

Muller, Edward N. (1989) 'Distribution of Income in Advanced Capitalist States: Political Parties, Labour Unions, and the International Economy', *European Journal of Political Research* 17, 367–400.

Mulligan, John and Colin Griffin, eds (1992) *Empowerment Through Experiential Learning: Explorations of Good Practice* (London: Kogan Page).

Murphy, Andrew (2000) 'Unravelling a Loaded Dice: An Analysis of the State's Response to the Educational Needs of Young People in Residential Care Who Attended Mainstream School'. M.Soc.Sc. thesis (Social Policy), University College Dublin.

Murphy, Frank, Cathleen McDonagh and Erica Sheehan, compilers and eds (2000) *Travellers: Citizens of Ireland* (Dublin: Parish of the Travelling People).

Murphy, Tim (1998) 'Economic Inequality and the Constitution', in T. Murphy and M. Twomey, eds, *Ireland's Evolving Constitution, 1937–1997: Collected Essays* (Oxford: Hart), 163–81.

Murphy-Lawless, Jo and Patricia Kennedy (2002) *The Maternity Care Needs of Refugee and Asylum Seeking Women* (Swords, Co. Dublin: Northern Area Health Board).

Murray, Jill (1999) 'Normalising Temporary Work', *Industrial Law Journal* 28, 269–75.

Naess, Arne (1973) 'The Shallow and the Deep, Long-Range Ecology Movement: A Summary', *Inquiry* 16, 95–100.

National Women's Council of Ireland (2002) *Strategic Work Plan, 2002–2005* (Dublin: National Women's Council of Ireland).

NAWL (2002) *Brief by the National Association of Women and the Law to the Pay Equity Task Force*. http://www.payequityreview.gc.ca (31 October 2003).

Nedelsky, Jennifer (1991) *Private Property and the Limits of American Constitutionalism* (Chicago: University of Chicago Press).

Nedelsky, Jennifer (1993a) 'The Practical Possibilities of Feminist Theory', *Northwestern University Law Review* 87, 1286–301.

Nedelsky, Jennifer (1993b) 'Reconceiving Rights as Relationship', *Review of Constitutional Studies* 1, 1–26.

Neill, Alexander Sutherland (1962) *Summerhill: A Radical Approach to Education* (London: Gollancz).

Nelson, Julie A. (1996) *Feminism, Objectivity and Economics* (London: Routledge).

Nice, Julie A. (2000) 'Equal Protection's Antinomies and the Promise of a Co-Constitutive Approach', *Cornell Law Review* 85, 1392–425.

Nielsen, Kai (1985) *Equality and Liberty: A Defense of Radical Egalitarianism* (Totowa, NJ: Rowman & Allanheld).

Noddings, Nel (1992) *The Challenge to Care in Schools* (New York: Teachers College Press).

Nolan, Brian (1991) *The Wealth of Irish Households* (Dublin: Combat Poverty Agency).

Nolan, Brian and Dorothy Watson (1999) *Women and Poverty in Ireland* (Dublin: Oak Tree Press and Combat Poverty Agency).

Nolan, Brian, Bertrand Maitre, Donal O'Neill and Olive Sweetman (2000) *The Distribution of Income in Ireland* (Dublin: Combat Poverty Agency).

Nolan, Brian, Philip J. O'Connell and Christopher T. Whelan (2000) *Bust to Boom? The Irish Experience of Growth and Inequality* (Dublin: Institute of Public Administration).

Norman, Richard (1987) *Free and Equal* (Oxford: Oxford University Press).

Norman, Richard (1995) *Studies in Equality* (Aldershot: Avebury).

Norris, Pippa (1993) 'Conclusions: Comparing Legislative Recruitment', in J. Lovenduski and P. Norris, eds, *Gender and Party Politics* (London: Sage), 309–30.

Notes from Nowhere, eds (2003) *We Are Everywhere: The Irresistible Rise of Global Anticapitalism* (London: Verso).

Nott, Sue (2000) 'Accentuating the Positive: Alternative Strategies for Promoting Gender Equality', in F. Beveridge, S. Nott and K. Stephen, eds, *Making Women Count: Integrating Gender into Law and Policy-Making* (Aldershot: Ashgate), 247–76.

Nove, Alec (1991) *The Economics of Feasible Socialism Revisited* (London: Unwin).

Nowlin, Christopher (2001) 'Should Any Court Accept the "Social Authority" Paradigm?', *Canadian Journal of Law and Jurisprudence* 14, 55–77.

Nozick, Robert (1974) *Anarchy, State, and Utopia* (New York: Basic Books).

NSPCC (2003) *Summary of Child Protection Register Statistics 2001*. http://www.nspcc.org.uk/inform/Statistics/Protect2001.asp (18 May 2003).

Nussbaum, Martha C. (1995a) 'Human Capabilities, Female Human Beings', in Nussbaum and Glover 1995, 61–104.

Nussbaum, Martha C. (1995b) 'Emotions and Women's Capabilities', in Nussbaum and Glover 1995, 360–95.

Nussbaum, Martha C. (2000) *Women and Human Development: The Capabilities Approach* (Cambridge: Cambridge University Press).

Nussbaum, Martha C. and Amartya Sen, eds (1993) *The Quality of Life* (Oxford: Oxford University Press).

Nussbaum, Martha C. and Jonathan Glover, eds (1995) *Women, Culture and Development: A Study of Human Capabilities* (Oxford: Oxford University Press).

O'Connor, Íoe and Laura Szalacha (2000) *A Queer Quandary: The Challenges of Including Sexual Difference within the Relationships and Sexuality Education Programme* (Dublin: LOT/LEA).

O'Connor, Pat (1998) *Emerging Voices: Women in Contemporary Irish Society* (Dublin: Institute of Public Administration).

O'Connor, Pat (2000a) 'Changing Places: Privilege and Resistance in Contemporary Ireland', *Sociological Research Online* 5(3). http://www.socresonline.org.uk/5/3/o'connor.html (24 November 2003).

O'Connor, Pat (2000b) 'Ireland: A Man's World?', *Economic and Social Review* 31, 81–102.

O'Connor, Pat (2001) 'A Bird's Eye View...Resistance in Academia', *Irish Journal of Sociology* 10, 86–104.

O'Donnell, Rory and Damian Thomas (1998) 'Partnership and Policy-Making', in S. Healy and B. Reynolds, eds, *Social Policy in Ireland: Principles, Practice and Problems* (Dublin: Oak Tree Press), 117–46.

O'Donovan, Katherine (1989) 'Engendering Justice: Women's Perspectives and the Rule of Law', *University of Toronto Law Journal* 39, 127–48.

O'Hearn, Denis (2002) *The Atlantic Economy: Britain, the US and Ireland* (Manchester: Manchester University Press).

Ó hOgartaigh, Margaret (1999) 'Far From Few: Professional Women in Ireland, 1880–1930'. Ph.D. thesis, University College Dublin.

O'Mahony, Paul (1997) *Mountjoy Prisoners: A Sociological and Criminological Profile* (Dublin: Stationery Office).

O'Neill, Cathleen (1992) *Telling It Like It Is* (Dublin: Combat Poverty Agency).

O'Neill, Cathleen (2000) 'Naming Our Own World: Making a Case for Feminist Research', in A. Byrne and R. Lentin, eds, *(Re)searching Women: Feminist Research Methodologies in the Social Sciences in Ireland* (Dublin: Institute of Public Administration), 105–18.

O'Neill, John (1999) 'Economy, Equality and Recognition', in Ray and Sayer 1999, 76–91.

Ó Riain, Seán and Philip J. O'Connell (2000) 'The Role of the State in Growth and Welfare', in Nolan, O'Connell and Whelan 2000, 310–39.

O'Toole, Francis (1997) *Tax from a Low Income Perspective* (Dublin: Combat Poverty Agency).

Oakes, Jeannie (1985) *Keeping Track: How Schools Structure Inequality* (New Haven: Yale University Press).

Oakes, Jeannie and Gretchen Guiton (1995) 'Matchmaking: The Dynamics of High School Tracking Decisions', *American Educational Research Journal* 32, 3–33.

Oakley, Ann (1981) 'Interviewing Women: A Contradiction in Terms', in Roberts 1981, 30–61.

OECD (1998) *Education at a Glance* (Paris: OECD, Centre for Educational Research and Innovation).

Offe, Claus (1984) *Contradictions of the Welfare State* (London: Hutchinson).

Offe, Claus (1985) 'New Social Movements: Challenging the Boundaries of Institutional Politics', *Social Research* 52, 817–68.

Offe, Claus (1995) 'Some Skeptical Considerations on the Malleability of Representative Institutions', in Cohen and Rogers 1995, 114–32.

Okin, Susan Moller (1989) *Justice, Gender, and the Family* (New York: Basic Books).

Okin, Susan Moller with respondents (1999) *Is Multiculturalism Bad for Women?*, ed. Joshua Cohen, Martin Howard and Martha C. Nussbaum (Princeton: Princeton University Press).

Okun, Arthur M. (1975) *Equality and Efficiency: The Big Tradeoff* (Washington: Brookings Institution).

Oliver, Mike (1990) *The Politics of Disablement* (Basingstoke: Macmillan – now Palgrave Macmillan).

Oliver, Mike (1992) 'Changing the Social Relations of Research Production', *Disability, Handicap and Society* 7, 1011–114.

Packwood, Tim (1988) 'The School as a Hierarchy', in Westoby 1988, 74–86.

Paechter, Carrie (1998) *Educating the Other: Gender, Power and Schooling* (London: Falmer Press).

Pakulski, Jan and Malcolm Waters (1996) 'The Reshaping and Dissolution of Social Class in Advanced Society', *Theory and Society* 25, 667–91.

Papadopoulos, Yannis (2003) 'Co-operative Forms of Government: Problems of Democratic Accountability in Complex Environments', *European Journal of Political Research* 42, 473–501.

Parekh, Bhikhu (1993) 'A Case for Positive Discrimination', in B. Hepple and E. Szyszczak, eds, *Discrimination: The Limits of the Law* (London: Mansell), 261–80.

Parekh, Bhikhu (2000) *Rethinking Multiculturalism: Cultural Diversity and Political Theory* (Basingstoke: Macmillan – now Palgrave Macmillan).

Parry, Geraint, George Moyser and Neil Day (1992) *Political Participation and Democracy in Britain* (Cambridge: Cambridge University Press).

Parsons, Talcott (1951) *The Social System* (London: Routledge & Kegan Paul).

Parsons, Talcott and Neil J. Smelser (1956) *Economy and Society* (London: Routledge & Kegan Paul).

Pateman, Carole (1970) *Participation and Democratic Theory* (Cambridge: Cambridge University Press).

Penman, Robyn (1987) 'Regulation of Discourse in the Adversary Trial', *Windsor Yearbook of Access to Justice* 7, 3–20.

Pennock, J. Roland (1979) *Democratic Political Theory* (Princeton: Princeton University Press).

Phelan, Anne M. (2001) 'Power and Place in Teaching and Teacher Education', *Teaching and Teacher Education* 17, 583–97.

Phillips, Anne (1992) 'Democracy and Difference: Some Problems for Feminist Theory', *Political Quarterly* 63, 79–90.

Phillips, Anne (1993) 'Must Feminists Give Up on Liberal Democracy?', *Political Studies* 40 (Special Issue), 68–82.

Phillips, Anne (1995) *The Politics of Presence* (Oxford: Oxford University Press).

Phillips, Anne (1999) *Which Equalities Matter?* (Cambridge: Polity Press).

Phillips, Anne, ed. (1987) *Feminism and Equality* (Oxford: Blackwell).

Piaget, Jean (1950) *The Psychology of Intelligence*, tr. Malcolm Piercy and D.E. Berlyne (London: Routledge & Kegan Paul).

Piaget, Jean (1970) *Science of Education and the Psychology of the Child*, tr. Derek Coltman (New York: Orion Press).

Pitkin, Hanna Fenichel (1967) *The Concept of Representation* (Berkeley, CA: University of California Press).

Piven, Frances Fox and Richard A. Cloward (1977) *Poor People's Movements: Why They Succeed, How They Fail* (New York: Pantheon).

Pomeroy, Eva (1999) 'The Teacher–Student Relationship in Secondary School: Insights from Excluded Students', *British Journal of Sociology of Education* 20, 465–82.

Popper, Karl (1966) *The Open Society and Its Enemies, Volume I: The Spell of Plato*, 5th edition (London: Routledge & Kegan Paul).

Porter, Bruce (2000) 'Judging Poverty: Using International Human Rights Law to Refine the Scope of Charter Rights', *Journal of Law & Social Policy* 15, 117–34.

Post, Robert C. and Reva B. Siegel (2000) 'Equal Protection by Law: Federal Antidiscrimination Legislation after Morrison and Kimel', *Yale Law Journal* 100, 441–522.

Postman, Neil and Charles Weingartner (1969) *Teaching as a Subversive Activity* (New York: Dell Publishing Company).

Przeworski, Adam (1998) 'Deliberation and Ideological Domination', in Elster 1998, 140–60.

Putnam, Robert D. with Robert Leonardi and Raffaella Y. Nanetti (1993) *Making Democracy Work: Civic Traditions in Modern Italy* (Princeton: Princeton University Press).

Putterman, Louis, John E. Roemer and Joaquim Silvestre (1998) 'Does Egalitarianism Have a Future?', *Journal of Economic Literature* 36, 861–902.

Quinn, Gerard (1989) 'The Nature and Significance of Critical Legal Studies', *Irish Law Times* 7, 282–90.

Quinn, Gerard (2000) 'Rethinking the Nature of Economic, Social and Cultural Rights in the Irish Legal Order', in C. Costello, ed., *Fundamental Social Rights: Current European Legal Protection and the Challenge of the EU Charter on Fundamental Rights* (Dublin: European Movement), 35–54.

Radin, Margaret Jane (1989) 'Reconsidering the Rule of Law', *Boston University Law Review* 69, 781–819.

Rae, Douglas, Douglas Yates, Jennifer Hochschild, Joseph Morone and Carol Fessler (1981) *Equalities* (Cambridge, MA: Harvard University Press).

Rawls, John (1971) *A Theory of Justice* (Oxford: Oxford University Press).

Rawls, John (1993) *Political Liberalism* (New York: Columbia University Press).

Rawls, John (1999) *The Law of Peoples* (Cambridge, MA: Harvard University Press).

Rawls, John (2001) *Justice as Fairness: A Restatement* (Cambridge, MA: Harvard University Press).

Ray, Larry and Andrew Sayer, eds (1999) *Culture and Economy after the Cultural Turn* (London: Sage).

Reason, Peter, ed. (1988) *Human Inquiry in Action: Developments in New Paradigm Research* (London: Sage).

Reason, Peter and John Rowan, eds (1981) *Human Inquiry: A Sourcebook of New Paradigm Research* (Chichester: John Wiley and Sons).

Reay, Diane (1996) 'Insider Perspectives or Stealing the Words Out of Women's Mouths: Interpretation in the Research Process', *Feminist Review* 53, 57–73.

Reay, Diane (1998a) 'Rethinking Social Class: Qualitative Perspectives on Class and Gender', *Sociology* 32, 259–75.

Reay, Diane (1998b) *Class Work: Mothers' Involvement in Their Children's Primary Schooling* (London: UCL Press).

Reay, Diane (2000) 'A Useful Extension of Bourdieu's Conceptual Framework? Emotional Capital as a Way of Understanding Mothers' Involvement in Their Children's Education', *Sociological Review* 48, 568–85.

Reay, Diane and Stephen J. Ball (1997) '"Spoilt for Choice": The Working Classes and Educational Markets', *Oxford Review of Education* 23, 89–101.

Rees, Daniel I., Laura M. Argys and Dominic J. Brewer (1996) 'Tracking in the United States: Descriptive Statistics from the NELS', *Economics of Education Review* 15, 83–9.

Reid, Madeleine (2003) *Legal Review 2002* (Dublin: ODEI, The Equality Tribunal).

Rhode, Deborah L. (1989) *Justice and Gender* (Cambridge, MA: Harvard University Press).

Rhode, Deborah L. (1991) 'Feminist Critical Theories', in K.T. Bartlett and R. Kennedy, eds, *Feminist Legal Theory: Readings in Law and Gender* (Boulder, CO: Westview Press), 333–50.

Rhode, Deborah L. (2001) 'Access to Justice', *Fordham Law Review* 69, 1785–819.

Rhode, Deborah L., ed. (1990) *Theoretical Perspectives on Sexual Difference* (New Haven: Yale University Press).

Ritchie, Stephen M., Donna L. Rigano and R. John Lowry (2000) 'Shifting Power Relations in the "Getting of Wisdom"', *Teaching and Teacher Education* 16, 165–77.

Rist, Ray (1970) 'Student Social Class and Teacher Expectations: The Self-Fulfilling Prophesy in Ghetto Education', *Harvard Educational Review* 40, 411–51.

Roberts, Helen, ed. (1981) *Doing Feminist Research* (London: Routledge & Kegan Paul).

Roemer, John E. (1994) *A Future for Socialism* (London: Verso).

Roemer, John E. (1996) *Equal Shares: Making Market Socialism Work,* ed. Erik Olin Wright (London: Verso).

Roemer, John E. (1998) *Equality of Opportunity* (Cambridge, MA: Harvard University Press).

Rofes, Eric (1989) 'Opening up the Classroom Closet: Responding to the Educational Needs of Gay and Lesbian Youth', *Harvard Educational Review* 59, 443–53.

Rooney, Eilish (2002) 'Community Development in Times of Trouble: Reflections on the Community Women's Sector in the North of Ireland', *Community Development Journal* 37, 33–46.

Rottman, David B., Damian F. Hannan, Niamh Hardiman and Miriam Wiley (1982) *The Distribution of Income in the Republic of Ireland: A Study in Social Class and Family-Cycle Inequalities.* General Research Series No. 109 (Dublin: ESRI).

Rousseau, Jean-Jacques [1762] *Émile*, tr. Barbara Foxley (London: Dent, 1911).

Royall, Frédéric (2000) 'Collective Actions and Disadvantaged Groups in Ireland and France 1987–99: The Case of the Unemployed', *Irish Political Studies* 15, 83–103.

Ruane, Frances and J.M. Sutherland (1999) *Women in the Labour Force* (Dublin: Employment Equality Agency).

Rule, Wilma and Joseph F. Zimmerman, eds (1994) *Electoral Systems in Comparative Perspective: Their Impact on Women and Minorities* (Westport, CT: Greenwood).

Ryan, Anne B. (2003) 'Contemporary Discourses of Working, Earning and Spending: Acceptance, Critique and the Bigger Picture', in Coulter and Coleman 2003, 155–74.

Sabel, Charles F. (1996) *Ireland: Local Partnerships and Social Innovation* (Paris: OECD).

Said, Edward W. (1991) *Orientalism: Western Conceptions of the Orient* (Harmondsworth: Penguin).

Said, Edward W. (1993) *Culture and Imperialism* (London: Chatto and Windus).

Sala-i-Martin, Xavier (2002) 'The Disturbing "Rise" of Global Income Inequality'. NBER Working Paper No. w8904 (Cambridge, MA: National Bureau of Economic Research). http://www.nber.org/papers/w8904 (18 May 2003).

Sanders, Lynn M. (1997) 'Against Deliberation', *Political Theory* 25, 347–76.

Savage, Mike (2000) *Class Analysis and Social Transformation* (Buckingham: Open University Press).

Savage, Mike, Gaynor Bagnall and Brian Longhurst (2001) 'Ordinary, Ambivalent and Defensive: Class Identities in the Northwest of England', *Sociology* 35, 875–92.

Sayer, Andrew (1995) *Radical Political Economy: A Critique* (Oxford: Blackwell).

Sayer, Andrew (1997) 'Contractualisation, Work and the Anxious Classes', in J. Holmer and J. Carsson, eds, *Work, Quo Vadis? Rethinking the Question of Work* (Aldershot: Ashgate), 47–78.

Sayer, Andrew (2000) 'Equality and Moral Economy'. Paper presented at the *Equality Studies Centre 10th Anniversary Conference*, University College Dublin, 15 December.

Sayer, Andrew (2002) 'What Are You Worth? Why Class is an Embarrassing Subject', *Sociological Research Online* 7(3). http://www.socresonline.org.uk/7/3/sayer.html (18 November 2002).

Scase, Richard (1992) *Class* (Buckingham: Open University Press).

Schaar, John H. (1967) 'Equality of Opportunity, and Beyond', in J.R. Pennock and J. Chapman, eds, *Nomos IX: Equality* (New York: Atherton Press), 228–49.

Scheiwe, Kirsten (1994) 'EC Law's Unequal Treatment of the Family: The Case Law of European Court of Justice on Rules Prohibiting Discrimination on the Grounds of Sex and Nationality', *Social and Legal Studies* 4, 243–65.

Schepple, Kim Lane (1992) 'Just the Facts, Ma'am: Sexualised Violence, Evidentiary Habits, and the Revision of Truth', *New York Law School Review* 37, 123–72.

Schmitter, Philippe C. (1995) 'The Irony of Modern Democracy and the Viability of Efforts to Reform Its Practice', in Cohen and Rogers 1995, 167–83.

SchNEWS (2001) *Monopolise Resistance? How Globalise Resistance Would Hijack Revolt* (Brighton: SchNEWS). http://www.schnews.org.uk/monopresist/monopoliseresistance/index.htm (18 May 2003).

Schweickart, David (1994) *Against Capitalism* (Cambridge: Cambridge University Press).

Scott, Craig and Patrick Macklem (1992) 'Constitutional Ropes of Sand or Justiciable Guarantees? Social Rights in a New South African Constitution', *University of Pennsylvania Law Review* 141, 1–148.

Scott, James C. (1985) *Weapons of the Weak: Everyday Forms of Peasant Resistance* (New Haven: Yale University Press).

Sen, Amartya (1982) 'Equality of What?' in A. Sen, *Choice, Welfare and Measurement* (Oxford: Blackwell), 353–69.

Sen, Amartya (1985) *Commodities and Capabilities* (Amsterdam: North-Holland).

Sen, Amartya (1988) *On Ethics and Economics* (Oxford: Blackwell).

Sen, Amartya (1992) *Inequality Reexamined* (Oxford: Oxford University Press).

Sen, Amartya (1999) *Development as Freedom* (Oxford: Oxford University Press).

Sennett, Richard and Jonathan Cobb (1993) *The Hidden Injuries of Class,* 2nd edition (London: Faber).

Sevenhuijsen, Selma (1998) *Citizenship and the Ethics of Care: Feminist Considerations on Justice, Morality and Politics* (London: Routledge).

Shakespeare, Tom (1994) 'Cultural Representation of Disabled People: Dustbins for Disavowal?', *Disability & Society* 9, 283–99.

Shakespeare, Tom, Kath Gillespie-Sells and Dominic Davies (1996) *The Sexual Politics of Disability: Untold Desires* (London: Cassell).

Shapiro, Ian (1996) *Democracy's Place* (Ithaca, NY: Cornell University Press).

Shavit, Yossi and Hans-Peter Blossfeld, eds (1993) *Persistent Inequality: Changing Educational Attainment in Thirteen Countries* (Boulder, CO: Westview Press).

Shaw, Randy (2001) *The Activist's Handbook: A Primer,* updated edition (Berkeley, CA: University of California Press).

Sheppard, Colleen (2001) 'Of Forest Fires and Systemic Discrimination: A Review of British Columbia (Public Service Employee Relations Commission) v. B.C.G.S.E.U.', *McGill Law Journal* 46, 533–59.

Sheridan, Kyoto (1998) 'Japan's Economic System', in K. Sheridan, ed., *Emerging Economic Systems in Asia: A Political and Economic Survey* (St. Leonards, NSW: Allen & Unwin), 9–44.

Sherlock, Ann (1991) 'Constitutional Litigation in Ireland', *International and Comparative Law Quarterly* 40, 425–37.

Shirlow, Pete (2003) 'Northern Ireland: A Reminder from the Present', in Coulter and Coleman 2003, 192–207.

Shor, Ira (1992) *Empowering Education: Critical Teaching for Social Change* (Chicago: Chicago University Press).

Shor, Ira, ed. (1987) *Freire for the Classroom: A Sourcebook for Liberatory Teaching* (Portsmouth, NH: Boynton/Cook).

Siaroff, Alan (1999) 'Corporatism in 24 Industrial Democracies: Meaning and Measurement', *European Journal of Political Research* 36, 175–205.

Sifry, Micah L. (2002) *Spoiling for a Fight: Third-Party Politics in America* (New York: Routledge).

Simon, Brian (1978) *Intelligence, Psychology and Education: A Marxist Critique,* 2nd edition (London: Lawrence and Wishart).

Siraj-Blatchford, Iram (1995) 'Critical Social Research and the Academy: The Role of Organic Intellectuals in Educational Research', *British Journal of Sociology of Education* 16, 205–20.

Skeggs, Beverley (1997) *Formations of Class and Gender: Becoming Respectable* (London: Sage).

Skilbeck, Malcolm with the assistance of Helen Connell (2000) *Access and Equity in Higher Education: An International Perspective on Issues and Strategies* (Dublin: Higher Education Authority).

Smart, Carol (1989) *Feminism and the Power of the Law* (London: Routledge).

Smith, Alan and Alan Robinson (1992) *Education for Mutual Understanding: Perceptions and Policy* (Coleraine: University of Ulster).

Smith, Alan and Alan Robinson (1996) *Education for Mutual Understanding: The Initial Statutory Years* (Coleraine: University of Ulster).

Smith, Dorothy E. (1987) *The Everyday World as Problematic: A Feminist Sociology* (Milton Keynes: Open University Press).

Smith, Dorothy E. (1998) 'The Underside of Schooling: Restructuring, Privatization and Women's Work', *Journal for a Just and Caring Education* 1, 11–29.

Smith, Vicki (1993) 'Flexibility in Work and Employment: The Impact on Women', *Research in the Sociology of Organizations* 11, 195–216.

Smyth, Emer (1999) *Do Schools Differ? Academic and Personal Development among Pupils in the Second-Level Sector* (Dublin: Oak Tree Press).

Sørensen, Aage B. and Maureen T. Hallinan (1986) 'The Effects of Ability Grouping on Growth in Academic Achievement', *American Educational Research Journal* 23, 519–42.

Spender, Dale and Elizabeth Spender, eds (1988) *Learning to Lose: Sexism and Education* (London: Women's Press).

Stanley, Liz and Sue Wise (1983) *Breaking Out: Feminist Consciousness and Feminist Research* (London: Routledge & Kegan Paul).

Stern, Vivien (1998) *A Sin Against the Future: Imprisonment in the World* (Harmondsworth: Penguin).

Sternberg, Robert J. (1998) 'Abilities Are Forms of Developing Expertise', *Educational Researcher* 27(3), 11–20.

Stiglitz, Joseph E. (1988) *Economics of the Public Sector*, 2nd edition (New York: W.W. Norton & Co.).

Strainchamps, Ethel (1971) 'Our Sexist Language', in V. Gornick and B. Moran, eds, *Woman in Sexist Society* (New York: Basic Books), 240–50.

Sugunasiri, S.M. (1999) 'Contextualism: The Supreme Court's New Standard of Judicial Analysis and Accountability', *Dalhousie Law Journal* 22, 126–84.

Sunstein, Cass R. (1987) 'Lochner's Legacy', *Columbia Law Review* 87, 873–919.

Sutcliffe, Bob (2001) *100 Ways of Seeing an Unequal World* (London: Zed Books).

Sutcliffe, Bob (2002) 'A More or Less Unequal World? World Income Distribution in the 20th Century'. HEGOA Working Paper 31 (Bilbao: HEGOA).

Swift, Adam (2000) 'Class Analysis from a Normative Perspective', *British Journal of Sociology* 51, 663–79.

Swift, Adam (2003) *How Not to Be a Hypocrite: School Choice for the Morally Perplexed Parent* (London: Routledge).

Szasz, Andrew (1994) *Ecopopulism: Toxic Waste and the Movement for Environmental Justice* (Minneapolis: University of Minnesota Press).

Szasz, Andrew (1995) 'Progress Through Mischief: The Social Movement Alternative to Secondary Associations', in Cohen and Rogers 1995, 148–65.

Tapper, Colin (1995) *Cross and Tapper on Evidence*, 8th edition (London: Butterworths).

Tarrow, Sidney (1998a) *Power in Movement: Social Movements and Contentious Politics*, 2nd edition (Cambridge: Cambridge University Press).

Tarrow, Sidney (1998b) 'Social Protest and Policy Reform: May 1968 and the *Loi d'Orientation* in France', in Giugni, McAdam and Tilly 1998, 31–56.

Tawney, R.H. (1964) *Equality*, 4th edition, intro. R.M. Titmuss (London: George Allen & Unwin).

Taylor, Neil (1993) 'Ability-Grouping and its Effect on Pupil Behaviour: A Case Study of a Midlands Comprehensive School', *Education Today* 43(2), 14–18.

Taylor, Verta (1995) 'Watching for Vibes: Bringing Emotions into the Study of Feminist Organizations', in M.M. Ferree and P.Y. Martin, eds, *Feminist Organizations: Harvest of the New Women's Movement* (Philadelphia: Temple University Press), 223–33.

Teese, Richard and John Polesel (2003) *Undemocratic Schooling: Equity and Quality in Mass Secondary Education in Australia* (Melbourne: Melbourne University Press).

Terdiman, Richard (1987) Translator's Introduction to Pierre Bourdieu, 'The Force of Law: Toward a Sociology of the Juridical Field', *Hastings Law Journal* 38, 805–53.

Tewari, O.P. (2001) *Law of Elections in India* (Faridabad, Haryana: Allahabad Law Agency).

Therborn, Göran (1980) *The Ideology of Power and the Power of Ideology* (London: Verso).

Thomas Isaac, T.M. and Patrick Heller (2003) 'Democracy and Development: Decentralised Planning in Kerala', in Fung and Wright 2003, 77–110.

Thomas, Vinod, Yan Wang and Xibo Fan (2000) *Measuring Education Inequality: Gini Coefficients of Education* (Washington: World Bank). http://econ.worldbank.org/files/1341_wps2525.pdf (8 September 2003).

Thompson, Dennis F. (1970) *The Democratic Citizen: Social Science and Democratic Theory in the Twentieth Century* (Cambridge: Cambridge University Press).

Thompson, John B. (1984) *Studies in the Theory of Ideology* (Cambridge: Polity Press).

Thompson, John B. (1990) *Ideology and Modern Culture: Critical Social Theory in the Era of Mass Communication* (Cambridge: Polity Press).

Thornton, Margaret (1985) 'Affirmative Action, Merit and the Liberal State', *Australian Journal of Law and Society* 2, 28–40.

Thornton, Margaret (1991) 'The Public/Private Dichotomy: Gendered and Discriminatory', *Journal of Law and Society* 18, 448–63.

Thurow, Lester C. (1980) *The Zero-Sum Society: Distribution and the Possibilities for Economic Change* (New York: Basic Books).

Tilly, Charles (1998) *Durable Inequality* (Berkeley, CA: University of California Press).

Tomlinson, Mike, Tony Varley and Ciaran McCullagh, eds (1988) *Whose Law and Order? Aspects of Crime and Social Control in Irish Society* (Belfast: Sociological Association of Ireland).

Touraine, Alain (1965) *Sociologie de l'Action* (Paris: Seuil).

Touraine, Alain (1966) *La Conscience Ouvrière* (Paris: Seuil).

Tregaskis, Claire (2002) 'Social Model Theory: The Story So Far...', *Disability & Society* 17, 457–70.

Trengrove, Wim (1999) 'Judicial Remedies for Violations of Socio-Economic Rights', *ESR Review* 1(4). http://www.communitylawcentre.org.za (31 October 2003).

Tronto, Joan C. (1993) *Moral Boundaries: A Political Argument for an Ethic of Care* (London: Routledge).

Tushnet, Mark (2003) 'New Forms of Judicial Review and the Persistence of Rights- and Democracy-Based Worries', *Wake Forest Law Review* 38, 813–38.

UN (United Nations) (2002) *Water, Energy, Health, Agriculture and Biodiversity: Synthesis of the Framework Paper of the Working Group on WEHAB* (Johannesburg: World Summit on Sustainable Development).

UNDP (United Nations Development Programme) (1998) *Human Development Report 1998: Consumption for Human Development* (New York: Oxford University Press).

UNDP (United Nations Development Programme) (1999) *Human Development Report 1999: Globalization with a Human Face* (New York: Oxford University Press).

UNDP (United Nations Development Programme) (2002) *Human Development Report 2002: Deepening Democracy in a Fragmented World* (New York: Oxford University Press).

UNESCO (2002) *Education for All: Is the World on Track?* (Paris: UNESCO).

Unger, Roberto (1997) *Politics: The Central Texts*, ed. Zhiyuan Cui (London: Verso).

Ungerson, Clare (2000) 'The Commodification of Care: Current Policies and Future Politics', in Hobson 2000, 173–200.

Ungerson, Clare, ed. (1990) *Gender and Caring: Work and Welfare in Britain and Scandinavia* (London: Harvester Wheatsheaf).

Van Dijk, Teun A. (1998) *Ideology: A Multidisciplinary Approach* (London: Sage).

Van Parijs, Philippe (1991) 'Why Surfers Should Be Fed: The Liberal Case for an Unconditional Basic Income', *Philosophy and Public Affairs* 20, 101–31.

Van Parijs, Philippe (1995) *Real Freedom for All* (Oxford: Oxford University Press).

Van Parijs, Philippe (2001) *What's Wrong with a Free Lunch?* (Boston: Beacon Press).

Van Parijs, Philippe, ed. (1992) *Arguing for Basic Income* (London: Verso).

Varian, Hal R. (1975) 'Distributive Justice, Welfare Economics, and the Theory of Fairness', *Philosophy and Public Affairs* 4, 223–47.

Verba, Sidney, Kay Lehman Schlozman and Henry E. Brady (1995) *Voice and Equality: Civic Voluntarism in American Politics* (Cambridge, MA: Harvard University Press).

Vetterling-Braggin, Mary, Frederick A. Elliston and Jane English, eds (1977) *Feminism and Philosophy* (Totowa, NJ: Littlefield, Adams).

Vlachou, Anastasia (1997) *Struggles for Inclusive Education* (Buckingham: Open University Press).

Vojdik, Valorie K. (2002) 'Gender Outlaws: Challenging Masculinity in Traditionally Male Institutions', *Berkeley Women's Law Journal* 19, 68–121.

Voss, Kim (1996) 'The Collapse of a Social Movement: The Interplay of Mobilizing Structures, Framing, and Political Opportunities in the Knights of Labor', in McAdam, McCarthy and Zald 1996, 227–56.

Waerness, Kari (1984) 'The Rationality of Caring', *Economic and Industrial Democracy* 5, 185–211.

Wainwright, Hilary (1994) *Arguments for a New Left: Answering the Free-Market Right* (Oxford: Blackwell).

Wainwright, Hilary (2003) *Reclaim the State: Experiments in Popular Democracy* (London: Verso).

Walby, Sylvia (1990) *Theorizing Patriarchy* (Oxford: Blackwell).

Walby, Sylvia (2001) 'From Community to Coalition: The Politics of Recognition as the Handmaiden to the Politics of Equality in an Era of Globalization', *Theory, Culture and Society* 18, 113–35.

Walkerdine, Valerie (1989) *Counting Girls Out: Girls and Mathematics* (London: Virago).

Walkerdine, Valerie and Helen Lucey (1989) *Democracy in the Kitchen: Regulating Mothers and Socialising Daughters* (London: Virago).

Walkerdine, Valerie, Helen Lucey and June Melody (2001) *Growing Up Girl: Psychosocial Explorations of Gender and Class* (Basingstoke: Palgrave Macmillan).

Walzer, Michael (1985) *Spheres of Justice* (Oxford: Blackwell).

Walzer, Michael (1999) 'Deliberation, and What Else?', in S. Macedo, ed., *Deliberative Politics: Essays on Democracy and Disagreement* (Oxford: Oxford University Press), 58–69.

Wang, Margaret C. and Geneva D. Haertel (1995) 'Educational Resilience', in M.C. Wang, M.C. Reynolds and H.J. Walberg, eds, *Handbook of Special and Remedial Education Research and Practice* (Oxford: Pergamon), 159–92.

Ward, Eilís (1999) 'NGOs and Irish Foreign Policy: A Reconceptualisation'. Paper presented at the *PSAI Annual Conference*, Wexford, 8–10 October.

Ward, Ian (2001) 'Beyond Constitutionalism: The Search for a European Political Imagination', *European Law Journal* 7, 24–40.

Ward, Margaret (1995) *In Their Own Voice: Women and Irish Nationalism* (Dublin: Attic Press).

Watt, Philip (1997a) 'Tenant Participation in Estate Management', in Community Workers Co-operative 1997, 48–9.

Watt, Philip (1997b) 'The Community Platform', in Community Workers Co-operative 1997, 67–9.

Weber, Max (1958) 'Class, Status, Party', in H.H. Gerth and C. Wright Mills, eds and trs, *From Max Weber: Essays in Sociology* (New York: Oxford University Press), 180–95.

Weede, Erich (1990) 'Democracy, Party Government and Rent-Seeking as Determinants of Distributional Inequality in Industrial Societies', *European Journal of Political Research* 18, 515–33.

Weiler, Kathleen (1988) *Women Teaching for Change: Gender, Class and Power* (Boston: Bergin and Harvey Press).

Weiner, Gaby (1994) *Feminisms in Education: An Introduction* (Buckingham: Open University Press).

Wendell, Susan (1996) *The Rejected Body: Feminist Philosophical Reflections on Disability* (New York: Routledge).

Wesselingh, Anton (1996) 'The Dutch Sociology of Education: Its Origins, Significance and Future', *British Journal of Sociology of Education* 17, 213–26.

West, Robin (1990) 'Progressive and Conservative Constitutionalism', *Michigan Law Review* 88, 641–721.

Westoby, Adam, ed. (1988) *Culture and Power in Educational Organisations* (Milton Keynes: Open University Press).

White, Lucie (1990) 'Subordination, Rhetorical Survival Skills, and Sunday Shoes: Notes on the Hearing of Mrs. G.', *Buffalo Law Review* 38, 1–58.

White, Stuart (2003) *The Civic Minimum: On the Rights and Obligations of Economic Citizenship* (Oxford: Oxford University Press).

Whitty, Geoff and Sally Power (2000) 'Marketization and Privatization in Mass Education Systems', *International Journal of Educational Development* 20, 93–107.

WHO (World Health Organization) (2001) *The World Health Report 2001* (Geneva: WHO).

Whyte, Gerry (2002) *Social Inclusion and the Legal System: Public Interest Law in Ireland* (Dublin: Institute of Public Administration).

Williams, George (2000) 'The Amicus Curiae and Intervener in the High Court of Australia: A Comparative Analysis', *Federal Law Review* 28, 365–402.

Williams, Melissa S. (1998) *Voice, Trust, and Memory: Marginalized Groups and the Failings of Liberal Representation* (Princeton: Princeton University Press).

Williams, Patricia J. (1987) 'Alchemical Notes: Reconstructing Ideals from Deconstructed Rights', *Harvard Civil Rights–Civil Liberties Law Review* 22, 401–33.

Williams, Simon J. and Gillian Bendelow (1998) *The Lived Body: Sociological Themes, Embodied Issues* (London: Routledge).

Winter, Jane (2002) *Human Rights, Human Wrongs: A Guide to the Human Rights Machinery of the United Nations*, 3rd edition (Belfast, London: British Irish Rights Watch, Northern Ireland Human Rights Commission).

Wolff, Jonathan (1998) 'Fairness, Respect, and the Egalitarian Ethos', *Philosophy and Public Affairs* 27, 97–122.

Wolff, Jonathan (2002) 'Addressing Disadvantage and the Human Good', *Journal of Applied Philosophy* 19, 207–18.

Wollstonecraft, Mary [1792] *A Vindication of the Rights of Woman,* ed. Carol H. Poston (New York: W.W. Norton & Co., 1975).

Women's Economic Equality Project (2000) *Proceedings of the Consultation on Women's Economic Equality.* http://www.cesr.org (17 June 2003).

Wood, George H. (1988) 'Democracy and the Curriculum', in L.E. Beyer and M.W. Apple, eds, *The Curriculum: Problems, Politics and Possibilities* (Albany: State University of New York Press), 177–98.

World Bank (2003) *World Development Indicators* (Washington: World Bank).

World Social Forum (2001) 'Charter of Principles'. http://www.forumsocialmundial. org.br (18 May 2003).

World Social Forum (2002) 'Official Statistics for the World Social Forum 2002'. http://www.forumsocialmundial.org.br (18 May 2003).

World Social Forum (2003) 'Who Organizes It'. http://www.forumsocialmundial. org.br (18 May 2003).

Wright, Erik Olin (1985) *Classes* (London: Verso).

Wright, Erik Olin (1997) *Class Counts: Comparative Studies in Class Analysis* (Cambridge: Cambridge University Press).

Yoneyama, Shoko (2000) 'Student Discourse on Tokokyohi (School Phobia/Refusal) in Japan: Burnout or Empowerment?', *British Journal of Sociology of Education* 21, 77–94.

Young, Iris Marion (1989) 'Polity and Group Difference: A Critique of the Ideal of Universal Citizenship', *Ethics* 99, 250–74.

Young, Iris Marion (1990) *Justice and the Politics of Difference* (Princeton: Princeton University Press).

Young, Iris Marion (1995) 'Social Groups in Associative Democracy', in Cohen and Rogers 1995, 207–13.

Young, Iris Marion (1996) 'Communication and the Other: Beyond Deliberative Democracy', in Benhabib 1996, 120–35.

Young, Iris Marion (1997) 'Unruly Categories: A Critique of Nancy Fraser's Dual Systems Theory', *New Left Review* 1/222, 147–60.

Young, Iris Marion (2000) *Inclusion and Democracy* (Oxford: Oxford University Press).

Young, Iris Marion (2001a) 'Equality of Whom? Social Groups and Judgments of Injustice', *Journal of Political Philosophy* 9, 1–18.

Young, Iris Marion (2001b) 'Activist Challenges to Deliberative Democracy', *Political Theory* 29, 670–90.

Yount, Mark (1993) 'The Normalizing Powers of Affirmative Action', in J. Caputo and M. Yount, eds, *Foucault and the Critique of Institutions* (University Park, PA: Pennsylvania State University Press), 191–229.

Zajac, Edward E. (1995) *Political Economy of Fairness* (Cambridge, MA: MIT Press).

Zald, Mayer N. (1996) 'Culture, Ideology, and Strategic Framing', in McAdam, McCarthy and Zald 1996, 261–74.

Zizek, Slavoj, ed. (1994) *Mapping Ideology* (London: Verso).

Zuckerman, Adrian A.S. (1999) 'Justice in Crisis: Comparative Dimensions of Civil Procedure', in A.A.S. Zuckerman, S. Chiarloni and P. Gottwald, eds, *Civil Justice in Crisis: Comparative Perspectives of Civil Procedure* (New York: Oxford University Press), 3–52.

# Index

abortion, 197, 208, 230
academy
  equality studies, 14–18
  operation of power, 169–70
  research methods, 175–8, 183:
    emancipatory research, 184–7;
    working conditions, 176–8
  responses to inequality, 12–14
accountability
  participatory democracy, 105–7
  structures of, 112–13
adoption, 68, 128
affective system, 41, 57–8, 59–60 *see also*
    love, care and solidarity
  equality within, 212, 227–8: core
    political project, 209–11; as
    mobilizing narrative, 219–20
  inequalities within, 59–60, 61–2: and
    other inequalities, 64–5, 66–7;
    and participatory democracy,
    115–17
  neglect of, 57–8, 157–8, 166
  source of inequality, 60, 69
affirmative action, 17, 31, 121, 127, 131,
    135
  limits of, 131–2
Africa, 3, 221
age, 10, 45 *see also* children
  care of aged, 223, 226
  dependency, 220–1
  and life chances, 10
agricultural sector, 205, 206, 240
AIDS, 199, 221
Alinsky, Saul, 243
Allen, Kieran, 205
American Bill of Rights, 29
Americans with Disabilities Act 1990, 11
*amicus curiae* briefs, 123–4, 125
Amnesty International, 6, 7, 244
Amsterdam Treaty, 11
anarchism, 196, 219
animal rights movement, 54–5, 220
anti-discrimination legislation, 118,
    119, 139, 199
  constitutional issues, 137–9

in the workplace, 125–32, 134–7:
    individual justice v. group
    relations, 127–9; limits of positive
    action, 131–2; market relations,
    126–7; problem of symmetry,
    130–1; public/private distinction,
    126–7; reasonable
    accommodation, 133–4; use of
    comparators, 129–30, 132
anti-globalization movement, 193, 195,
    215–16, 220
anti-racism movement, 13, 195
anti-war movement, 197, 242
assessment procedures, 149–51, 152–3,
    188
  cultural imperialism, 154
  power relations, 161
asylum seekers, 6, 10, 97, 184, 199
  research into, 173
Australia, 76, 254 n.12
Austrian School, 80

Ball, Carlos A., 126
bargaining structures, 111–12
Barnes, Colin, 13
Barrett, Michèle, 12
Barry, U. and O'Connor, A., 170
Belfast Agreement 1998, 110–11, 200,
    206
Belgium, 111
Benchmarking Body, 91
Benn, Tony, 234, 236
Bernstein, Basil, 149
Bipartisan Campaign Reform Act 2002
    (US), 255 n. 17
birth rate, 226
bisexuality *see* sexual orientation
Bloom, Benjamin S., 167
bodily-kinaesthetic intelligences, 150,
    153, 157
Bourdieu, Pierre, 36, 171, 176, 212
Bové, José, 240
boycotts, 239
*Brandeis* briefs, 124
Brazil, 4, 231, 235

*Brooks* v. *Canada Safeway,* 131
Brownmiller, Susan, 12
Bubeck, Diemut E., 37
Buckley Report, 91
Bush, George W., 236

Canada, 76, 107, 124, 125, 147, 254
　　n. 12, 258 n. 19
　anti-discrimination laws, 131
　discrimination analysis, 134
　equality guarantee, 121
capabilities, 49–50, 248 n. 3, 248 n. 6,
　　249 n. 13, 250 n. 18
capitalism, 7, 33, 39–40, 52, 57, 135,
　　200, 218
　anti-capitalist movements, 67, 193,
　　　195, 196
　concepts of self, 223
　in education, 145
　equality–efficiency trade-off, 84
　equality legislation, 137
　inequalities within, 58–9, 81: class
　　　system, 205; disability, 67–8;
　　　love, care and solidarity
　　　issues, 222–3
　international, 201–2
　and legal system, 120
　Marxist response to, 191–2
　public/private distinction, 126–7
　status of care work, 226, 227
care work, 7, 19, 76, 245 *see also*
　　affective system; love, care and
　　solidarity
　attitude of women's movement to,
　　　224–6
　commodification of, 222–3, 225–6,
　　　227
　disengaged from labour market, 202,
　　　210
　egalitarian division of, 219–20
　political significance of, 225–6
　socialization of women, 64
　legally unprotected, 127
celebrity culture, 6
Celtic Tiger, 200
Central Park East Secondary School,
　　New York, 153
charitable organizations, 103–4
Charter of Rights and Freedoms,
　　Canada, 121
Chicago, Illinois, 103

child abuse, 6
child care, 6–7, 128, 151, 200, 208, 245
　care and love relations, 221
children
　decision to have children, 82–3, 223
　decline in time spent with, 226
　and legal system, 138
　power of adults over, 35, 39, 66, 68–9
　and research, 184
　supports for, 151
China, 253 n. 4
Chomsky, Noam, 234–5, 236
Citizen Traveller, 116, 262 n. 6
citizenship, 26, 27, 210
　entitlement to, 97
　in participatory democracy, 98,
　　　101–2, 102–4
civil, social and political education
　　(CSPE), 156
civil rights, 29, 38, 48, 219, 238
　and democracy, 97
　legal protection, 11, 121
civil rights movement, 10, 11, 107, 118,
　　193
　direct action, 242
Clamshell Alliance, 240
class *see* social class
classism, 170
cognitive skills, 167
collective wage bargaining, 90
Common Agricultural Policy, 201
communication systems, 213–14
　in participatory democracy, 99–100,
　　　103
communication technologies, 215–16
communism, 219
Community and Voluntary Pillar, 111,
　　112
community development movement,
　　10
community movements, 201, 224
Community Platform, 265 n. 12
community sector, 53, 103, 111, 163,
　　221, 223 *see also* solidarity
　accountability, 112
　and research, 184–6
　rise in, 203
　university involvement, 177–8
　women's struggles, 208
Community Workers Co-operative, 203
commuting, 226

computer literacy, 103
condition, equality of *see* equality of
    condition
Confédération Paysanne, France, 235
conflicts of interest, 110–12
conservatism
    in the academy, 177–8
Conservative Party, 216, 238
consociationalism, 111–12
Constitution of Ireland, 1937, 38, 109
constitutional issues, 109
    anti-discrimination laws, 137–9
consultation mechanisms, 135–6
consumerism, 54, 82, 216
    in education, 147
    equated with identity, 200
cooperative enterprises, 89
coordination of action, 229–32
corporate interests
    and research, 172, 173, 175
corporate welfarism, 90–1
counselling, 164, 222
crime
    positivist research, 173
    white collar, 172
critical interculturalism, 35, 154, 243
critical theory, 15, 18, 169, 171, 175,
    186
cultural capital, 36, 179, 250 n. 20
    and class divisions, 145–6, 203
    and education, 145–6, 151–2
    and research, 179
cultural imperialism, 52, 63–4, 154, 252
    n. 4
    denial of personal intelligences, 157–8
cultural production
    and economic production, 212–13
    role of ideology, 212–18
cultural relativism, 52
cultural system, 41, 57, 59
    inequality within, 59, 61: and
        affective inequality, 64–5; and
        economic inequality, 63; and
        participatory democracy, 115–17;
        and political inequality, 63–4
    role of education, 59, 159–61
    source of inequality, 41, 67–8, 154
curriculum, 146
    bias within, 149–51, 152–3, 168
    care work in, 157–8
    cultural imperialism, 154

democratization of, 163
    need for interculturalism, 160
    power relations, 161

Dáil Éireann, 263 n. 17
Daly, Mary, 12
Day, S. and Brodsky, G., 134
Decent Work, 30
decision-making, 39, 238
    autonomous, 107
    collective, 104–5
    consensual, 109–10, 230: weakness of,
        111–12
    in education, 161
    in legal system, 120–1, 122–3
    in participatory democracy, 100,
        108–13
Declaration on Fundamental Principles
    and Rights at Work, 30
delegate model, 105
deliberative consensus, 109–10
Delphy, C. and Leonard, D., 12
democracy, 16–17, 50, 197 *see also*
    participatory democracy
    deliberative, 100
    in education, 141, 152, 161–3
    and liberalism, 29–30
    in mass communications, 214
    power inequalities, 38–9
    in research, 179, 181–2
    in the workplace, 89, 104
dependency, states of, 37, 210, 220–1
Descartes, René, 166
Development Indicators (World Bank), 77
development studies, 13
devolution, 107–8
dialogical theory building, 182–3
difference *see* diversity
difference principle, 25, 27, 32, 249 n. 11
dimensions of equality, 4–10, 21–46 *see*
    love, care and solidarity; power;
    resources; respect and recognition;
    working and learning
    and education, 143–4
    and equality movement, 194–5, 243–6
    and freedom, 50–1
    and legal order, 138
    and participatory democracy, 96–8
    and social systems, 60–2
    and well-being, 49–50
    and the workplace, 132

direct action, 231, 239–40
disability, 9
  abortion issues, 197
  and cultural system, 59, 67–8
  and equality of resources, 36
  and femininity, 70
  inequalities, 5–6, 44, 67–8, 202:
    education, 146, 147, 148, 149,
    158–9; work, 8, 133; care and
    love, 38, 221; disabled women, 70
  and labour politics, 202–3
  legislation, 11, 118–19, 131, 199
  minority protection, 110, 111
  political representation, 114
  research, 13, 173, 174
  rights, 218–19
  social movement, 194–6
  social v. medical model of, 9, 67–8,
    128
Disability Authority Act 1999, 199
disability studies, 13, 14, 169
disablism, 170
'discontented majority,' 205
discrimination *see* anti-discrimination
    legislation
diversity, 25–6, 34–5, 48, 52–3
  of disabled people, 252 n. 8
  in education, 144, 159–60
  of equality movement, 196–7, 217–18,
    230–1, 237, 243
  and participatory democracy, 113–15
  of women, 14, 69–70, 209
divorce, 208
Drew, Eileen, 170
drug use, 199
Dworkin, Andrea, 12

ecology, 53–4, 55
Economic and Social Research Institute
    (ESRI), 260 n. 4
economic equality, 61
  and economic growth, 82–7
  equality–efficiency trade-off, 84, 88
  routes to improvement of, 87–95:
    market socialism, 88–9; primary
    income approach, 89–95
  social welfare transfers, 84–5
economic migrants, 10
economic system, 39, 41, 54, 57, 58–9
  and anti-discrimination laws, 126,
    130–1

and cultural production, 212–13
  division of labour, 39–40
  inequalities within, 58–9, 60–1,
    199, 202: and affective
    inequality, 64–5, 222–3; and
    cultural inequality, 63; and
    participatory democracy 115–16;
    and political inequality, 62–3;
    survey of, 76–7
  and legal system, 120, 126
  and socio-economic rights, 138–9
  source of inequality, 67
economic theories, 75
  perspectives on inequality, 78–82
Ecuador, 5
education
  and the community, 188
  compulsory, 142–3
  and cultural system, 59, 63, 212–13
  egalitarianism in, 30–1, 40–1, 62,
    140–68: importance of, 141–3
  inequalities within, 8, 66, 68, 143–4:
    disability, 158–9; gender, 44, 152,
    157–8, 166; sexual orientation,
    155; social class, 140–1, 144–51,
    155–6, 204–5
  love, care and solidarity in, 143–4,
    157–8, 164–8
  power in, 39, 143–4, 161–3, 194
  and research, 181, 182
  resources in, 143–54
  respect and recognition in, 154–61
  responses to inequality, 12–14
  role in participatory democracy,
    103–4
  women in, 158, 176, 207, 208
Education Act 1998, 141
Education for Mutual Understanding
    (EMU), 260 n. 14
Educational Research Centre (ERC), 260
    n. 4
efficiency
  definitions of, 78–9
  equality–efficiency trade-off, 84–7
  income redistribution, 90
  market socialism, 88–9
  participatory democracy, 101, 104–5
egalitarianism *see* equality of condition;
    equality movement; liberal
    egalitarianism
electoral systems, 113–15, 115, 236

elites, 102, 170
  and education, 142, 150
  strengthened by egalitarian
      fragmentation, 198
emancipatory research, 18, 19, 169–88
  conditions in which research
      produced, 175–8
  and legal system, 124
  methodology, 178–9: dialogical
      theory building, 182–3; ethical
      issues, 179–81; reciprocity in
      research relationship, 181–2;
      reflexivity, 183
  positivist methodologies, 170–5
  in practice, 183–8
emigration, 263 n. 16
emotional intelligences, 157–8, 164–8
emotional work, 167, 209
  political significance of, 225–6
employers *see also* workplace
  and anti-discrimination laws, 130–1
  defences of, 128–9
employment *see* work
Employment Equality Act 1998
    (Ireland), 11, 199, 200
Employment Equity Act 1998 (South
    Africa), 135
empowered participatory governance,
    102–3
end-of-history mentality, 218
energy resources, 54
Engels, Friedrich, 12, 225
Enlightenment, 170
entrenched rights, 109, 111
environment, 180–1
  abuse of, 201
  environmental values, 56
  and equality issues, 53–5
  legislation, 12
  movements to protect, 47, 211,
      215–16, 220, 234: direct action,
      241
  politics of, 54–5
  resources, 49
environmental justice movement, 54
Equal Rights Amendment, 11
Equal Status Act 2000, 11, 199, 200
equality *see also* dimensions of equality;
      equality movement; inequality
  aspects of, 47–9
  centrality of, 19, 47–56

conceptions of, 16, 22–3
  conflicts with other values, 55–6
  economic perspectives on, 78–82
  and education, 140–68
  equality–efficiency trade-off, 84–7
  and gender, 207–11
  legal guarantees, 137
  and social change, 191–211
  theory of, 18
Equality Action Plans, 186
equality audits, 135
Equality Authority, 11, 261 n. 11
Equality Commission, NI, 136, 200, 261
    n. 11
equality empiricists, 170
equality impact assessments, 125
equality movement, 10–11, 71
  achievements and challenges of,
      199–201
  class politics, 201–7
  current situation, 194–9
  dynamics of resistance, 216–18
  and the environment, 53–5
  funding, 198, 244
  legal strategies, 123–5
  mobilizing ideology, 218–20
  need for solidarity, 198
  as network, 195–7, 230
  objectives, 198–9
  research, 175
  and self-interest, 192–3, 194
  strategic issues, 229–46: coordination,
      229–32; ends and means, 243–6;
      political parties, 232–8;
      radicalism, 236–7, 238–43
  and women's movement, 208–9
equality of condition, 33–42, 46, 55,
    218–19
  in employment, 132–9
  and freedom, 50
  human rights, 48
  justification of, 41–2
  love, care and solidarity, 34, 37–8, 52
  power, 34, 38–9
  resources, 34, 36–7
  respect and recognition, 34–6
  working and learning, 34, 39–41
equality of opportunity, 17, 25–32,
    40–2, 88, 125, 141, 218
  in participatory democracy, 101
  problem of symmetry, 130–1

equality of outcome, 33–4
equality proofing, 200
equality schemes, 136
equality studies, 160
    central questions, 14–18
    resistance to, 177
Equality Studies Centre, UCD, 14, 261
    n. 10
Equality Tribunal, 11
equity, 78–9, 81, 85, 90–1, 129, 135
ethnicity, 7, 45, 52, 196 *see also* racism;
    Travellers
    inequalities, 5–6, 8, 9, 202: education,
        146, 149, 158
    minority protection, 110, 111
    Northern Ireland, 208
    political representation, 38, 114
    research, 13, 174
    social movements, 194–6
European Committee for the Prevention
    of Torture and Inhuman or
    Degrading Treatment or
    Punishment, 6
European Convention on Human
    Rights, 29, 32, 109, 219
European Court of Justice, 125, 127,
    128, 130
European Union (EU), 96, 107, 126,
    199, 206, 240
    atypical workers, 130
    decision-making, 110
    grants, 244
    poverty studies, 173
    social policy, 127
    trade relations, 201
    workers' protection, 210
exclusion
    legal, 122–3
    from politics, 122–3, 234–5
    and research strategies, 187–8
    social, 215, 251 n. 1
    unemployment, 63
experiential knowledge, 174, 187
'expert-bureaucratic' models, 135
'expert' dominance, 66, 124, 160,
    173–5, 179–80, 187–8
exploitation, 80–1, 252 n. 4

Fabianism, 140
failure, feelings of, 165
fair employment, 127

fair equal opportunity, 31, 32, 42
family, 25
    care work in, 28, 157, 221
    democratizing, 99, 103–4
    inequalities within, 60, 64: power, 7,
        39, 68
    private sphere, 26, 35
family-friendly policies, 7, 128, 133–4,
    200, 226 *see also* work–life balance
famine, 201–2, 223
Faure, Edgar, 240
femininity
    and disability, 70
feminism, 118, 215–16, 218–19 *see also*
    women's movement
    academic studies, 12
    attention to care and love work, 28,
        58, 224–5
    backlash against, 209, 224–5
    centrality of emotions, 166
    concepts of self, 223
    emancipatory research, 175, 178
    feminist economics, 75, 76
    fight for education, 140
    legislative change, 119
    and positivism, 171
    and social diversity, 14
    socialist, 12
fertility, control of *see* reproductive
    rights
Fianna Fáil, 116, 255 n. 17, 263 n. 16
Fine Gael, 255 n. 17
Finkelstein, Victor, 13
Finland, 4, 147
Firestone, Shulamith, 12
Foucault, Michel, 161
Framework Directive 2000/78 (EU),
    128–9
France, 7, 202, 203, 235, 254 n.12
    education, 156
    May 1968, 240, 241
Fraser, Nancy, 132, 155
freedom, 29, 47, 50–1, 56, 127
freedom of information legislation, 180
Freeman, Alan D., 129
Freire, Paulo, 125, 160
French Revolution, 50
Friedan, Betty, 12
Friedman, Sandra, 85
functionalism, 15
fundamentalism, 195

funding
 political participation, 108, 115, 116,
  198, 244
 public services, 139
 research, 173, 183
Fung, A. and E.O. Wright, 108

Gamson, William A., 240, 242
Gardner, Howard, 150, 153
gay sexuality *see* sexual orientation
gender, 42, 192, 207–11 *see also* anti-
  discrimination legislation; women
 changing expectations, 225–6
 division of labour, 38, 44–5, 60, 64,
  210: care work, 40, 64, 224–5
 in education, 44, 152, 157–8, 170, 166
 inequalities of, 9, 44–5, 69–70: pay, 5,
  129–30; working hours, 8
General Agreement on Tariffs and Trade
  (GATT), 201
genetically modified foods, 180
Genoa demonstrations, 231
Germany, 147, 184, 202
 disability, 8
 income inequality, 5, 91
Gini co-efficient, 77–8
Giugni, M.G. and Passy, F., 241
globalization, 78, 95, 142, 211, 233 *see
  also* anti-globalization movements
 and education, 144–5
 effects of, 201–2
 of mass media, 214
 new social movements, 215–16
Glyn, A. and Miliband, D., 89
Goleman, Daniel, 157
*Gosselin* v. *Quebec*, 139
government *see* state, the
Gramsci, Antonio, 212
Greece, 7, 76
green politics, 53–4, 235
grind schools, 151
group rights, 33, 109, 132
 *versus* individual justice, 127–9
grouping and tracking, 146, 147–9, 152,
  168, 181

Habermas, Jürgen, 169
Hammersley, Martyn, 171
Hannan, Damian *et al.,* 170
Harstock, Nancy, 216
Harvard University, 153

hazardous waste, 12
health insurance, 86
health services, 5, 139, 180–1, 211, 223
 and research, 181
hermeneutics, 15
Heron, James, 179–80
hierarchy, in education, 162–3, 188
home economics, 157, 166
home ownership, 206
homelessness, 6, 28, 45, 184, 198
 and affective inequality, 64–5
homophobia, 10, 136, 170, 184
 and cultural system, 59
 in education, 155
 and employment, 129
Household Budget Survey, Irish, 77
Housing (Miscellaneous Provisions) Act
  2002, 138
housing policy, 139, 206
human capital, 80–1, 82, 250 n. 20
human goods, 47, 49–50
Human Life International, 261 n. 4
human resource management, 164
human rights, 13, 21–2, 29, 48, 200,
  211, 218–19, 227, 228
 in education, 141, 156, 161–2
 entrenched rights, 109, 111
 legislation, 119, 120
 and liberal egalitarianism, 32
 movements, 195, 220
 opposition to violence, 242
 and research, 169–70, 179–80
Human Rights Commission Act 2000,
  199
Human Rights Watch, 6, 7
Hungary, 7

identities, 203–4, 205
 differentiation based on, 127–8
 multiple, 69
 negative, 205
 'resistance identities', 216–17
 social shifts, 192
ideology
 egalitarianism as mobilizing ideology,
  218–20
 love, care and solidarity as political
  themes, 220–3
 role of, 212–18: dynamics of
  resistance, 216–18; ideology and
  structure, 214–16

Immigration Control Platform, 262 n. 4
immigration policies, 199
incentives, distortion of, 84–6
inclusion, principle of, 48, 92, 243
  in education, 159–61, 168
income inequality, 4–5, 76–8
  and cultural capital, 151, 152
income redistribution, 37, 88, 138–9 *see also* social welfare; taxation
  affirmative action, 132
  primary income approach, 89–95
India, 114–15, 253 n. 4
indigenous peoples, 10, 107
individualism, 52, 203–4, 223, 227
Indymedia, 103
inequality *see also* equality
  generative causes of, 65–70:
    implications for politics, 70–1
  economic perspectives, 80–2
  patterns of, 8–10
  responses to, 10–14
information deficits, 100, 103, 181, 213–14
inhuman and degrading treatment
  protection against, 23, 29, 48
institutional structures
  for achieving equality, 16–17
  effects on love and caring, 28–9, 38
  inequalities within, 57
  need for change, 70–1
  public interest law, 123
*intelligence-fair* testing, 153
intelligence, forms of, 150, 157–8, 165–7
inter-group agreement, 110–11
interculturalism, 35, 154, 160, 233, 243
interdependence, 28, 37, 220–1, 232
interest groups, 59, 105, 219
  *amicus curiae* briefs, 123–4, 125
International Covenant on Civil and Political Rights, 29
International Labour Organization (ILO), 30
International Monetary Fund (IMF), 95, 195
internet, 163, 215
  access to information, 103, 104
interstate organizations
  responses to inequality, 11–12
investment, 5, 80, 81, 82–3, 84, 93–4, 126, 206

Ireland, 19–20, 71, 202 *see also* Travellers
  education, 8, 141, 147, 150, 151, 153, 156
  egalitarian achievements, 11, 199–200
  health spending, 5
  home ownership, 206
  income distribution, 5, 76–7, 85, 86, 91, 111, 112
  legal system, 122–3, 138
  love, care and solidarity, 226
  political spending, 116
  research, 170, 185
  social class in, 205–6
  social partnership, 92–3, 111, 112
  status of children, 68
  wage relativities, 91–3
  women in, 8, 207–8
Irish National Organisation of the Unemployed (INOU), 203, 239
Irish Women United, 208
Italy, 76, 128, 254 n. 12, 257 n. 13

Japan, 4, 5, 95, 147, 151, 166, 204
  economic equality, 90–1
job enrichment, 39–40, 137
job-sharing, 136
judges
  doctrine of judicial notice, 124–5
  judicial decrees, 138
  judicial review, 131
  role of, 120–1, 124–5
  training of, 125
jury service, 108
justice, egalitarian concept of, 52–3
Justice, Equality and Law Reform, Department of, 116

Kanter, Rosabeth Moss, 12
Kelly, Mary, 182, 183
Kerala, India, 103, 104, 116
Keynesianism, 80
King, Martin Luther, 240
King, P.M. and Kitchener, K.S., 160
Kittay, Eva Feder, 37
Klare, Karl, 123
Klinker, P.A. and Smith, R.M., 240–1
Knell, Markus, 82
Korea, 7, 147
Kriesi, Hanspeter, 241
Kuznets, Simon, 82

labour, division of, 39–40, 137
  within equality movement, 245, 246
  gendered, 38, 44–5, 60, 64, 69, 132,
    210
labour market, 192 *see also* work;
    workplace
  care, love and solidarity issues, 224–5
  inequalities within, 87–8: part-time
    work, 8, 130, 202
  reasonable accommodation for
    'difference,' 133–4
  role of education, 142
  'unattached worker', 223
  women in, 202, 207, 210
labour movement, 10, 193, 220
  class divisions, 194
  and social democracy, 234, 235
  and women's movement, 209
Labour Party, Irish, 255 n. 17
Labour Party, UK, 216, 234, 235, 238
Laffer curve, 86
language policy, 38, 63, 109
Lather, Patti, 176, 179
Latin America, 83
Learning Partnerships, 185–6
Leaving Certificate Applied, 153
legal aid, 122–3
legal system, 19, 118 *see also* anti-
    discrimination legislation; judges
  decision-making, 122–3
  inequalities, 59, 118–23
  legal equality, 62
  making more egalitarian, 123–5
  political role of, 119–22, 126
  separation of powers, 100, 123, 138
lesbianism *see* sexual orientation
'level-the-playing-field', 248 n. 8
liberal democracy, 29, 48, 98, 100
liberal economics, 75, 80–2
liberal egalitarianism, 24–32, 35–6, 46
  contradictions of, 42
  equality of what?, 24–5
  and freedom, 50
  and human rights, 32, 48
  justification of, 32
  and meritocracy, 31, 55
  what kind of relationship?, 25–31
libertarianism, 55
life choices, 24, 33–4, 40–1, 42, 51, 136
  and education, 141, 147, 181
  responsibility for, 24, 42

Lindblom, Charles E., 94
linguistic intelligences, 149–51, 157
list systems, 113–14
literacy skills, 8, 141, 143, 213
Local Area Partnerships, 112, 185
local government, 39, 114
  democratizing, 99
  provision for Travellers, 199
  revitalization of, 107
Loeb, Paul Rogat, 244
love, care and solidarity, 24–5, 28–9, 46,
    49, 52–3
  and affective equality, 59–60, 61–2,
    209, 219–20
  attitude of women's movement to,
    224–6
  commodification of, 222–3
  cynicism about love, 221–2
  and disability, 9, 44
  in education, 143–4, 157–8, 164–8
  within egalitarian movement, 244,
    245
  equality of condition, 34, 37–8
  and gender, 9, 40, 45, 194, 209–11
  and freedom, 51
  inequalities of, 6–7, 60, 64–5
  in participatory democracy, 98,101
  political significance of, 219–23,
    225–6
  and social class, 8–9, 45
  workplace support for, 133–4, 137
Luxembourg, 147
Luxembourg Income Study, 76

Maastricht Treaty, 107
McDonald's, 240
McLaughlin, Eithne, 84–5
Mahon, Evelyn, 170
majority rule, 101, 108–13
Malamud, Deborah C., 132
Malta, 7
Mannheim, Karl, 212
Mansbridge, Jane, 109
Māori people, 115
marginalization, 63–4, 188, 252 n. 4
  community development groups, 203
  in education, 145, 161
  and participatory democracy, 99,
    109–10
  and research, 177–8, 184, 185:
    positivist research, 172–3

marital status, 128–9
market allocation, 78–82
  public/private distinction, 126–7
market socialism, 88–9
Marx, Karl, 57, 192
Marxism, 12, 15, 18, 67, 120, 169, 204
  contrast with social movement
    model, 19, 194, 195
  ideology in, 212
  as model of social change, 191–3
  perspective on inequality, 81
  on political parties, 232
mass media, 19, 68
  control of, 194
  cultural codes, 59, 116, 205, 213,
    215
  portrayal of women's movement,
    224
  power of, 60, 159
  reporting direct action, 239–40
  role in participatory democracy, 103,
    104
maternity leave, 128, 133
mathematics, 167
means of production, ownership of,
  137
media *see* mass media
medicine, 13, 178
*Meiorin,* 134
mental illness, 10
meritocracy, 31, 55, 171, 176, 204–5
Mexico, 235
Mies, Maria, 183–4
migration, 10, 65, 97, 201–2
Mill, Harriet Taylor, 12
Mill, John Stuart, 12
Millett, Kate, 12, 138
minimum entitlements, 25, 27, 28, 30
minimum wage, 199
minorities *see also* ethnicity
  protection of, 109–13, 233
  representation of, 113–15
Minow, Martha, 128
Mitchell, Juliet, 12
moral principles, 13, 79, 109–10, 179,
  191–2, 227
  moral case for equality, 23, 32, 194
  motivational, 193, 227
  in politics, 242, 243–6
  sexual, 68, 155, 217
motivation, ranges of, 193–4

multiculturalism, 34–5
multiple identities, 69
multiple intelligences, 153

Nader, Ralph, 234, 235–7, 236
Naess, Arne, 53
narratives, 216–17
  affective equality as, 219–20, 227
  mobilizing, 218–20
National Anti-Poverty Strategy, 98, 199
National Council for Curriculum and
  Assessment (NCCA), 259 n. 8
National Economic and Social Forum
  (NESF), 115, 199, 265 n. 12
National Women's Council of Ireland
  (NWCI), 208, 230, 265 n. 12
nationalism, 195, 199, 201, 205–6
negative identities, 205
neoclassical economics, 75, 78–9, 86–7,
  95
neoconservatism, 143, 200, 216, 217
neocorporatism, 75, 92
  decision-making, 111–12
  economic agreements, 111
  political representation, 115
neoliberalism, 55, 200, 216
  resistance to, 217, 218
Netherlands, The, 7, 146
New Labour, 216, 238
New Left, 235
New Right, 55, 162
New Zealand/Aotearea, 115
nomination quotas, 114–15
non-governmental organizations, 96,
  107, 185, 231, 244
non-holistic modelling, 78
non-majoritarian voting, 109–10, 111
North–South inequalities, 77–8
Northern Ireland, 107, 235, 260 n. 14
  education, 159–60
  equality legislation, 135–6, 200
  women in, 208, 224
Northern Ireland Act 1998, 135–6, 139,
  200
Northern Ireland Assembly, 206, 262 n.
  15
Northern Ireland Human Rights
  Commission, 200
Norway, 7, 147
nuclear disarmament, 235, 242
nuclear industry, 180

nursing, 164, 178
Nussbaum, Martha C., 49–50

objectivism, culture of, 172, 178
Okun, Arthur M., 84
Oliver, Mike, 13
opportunity *see* equality of
    opportunity
oral traditions, 174
*O'Reilly* v. *Limerick Corporation,* 139

parents, 6–7
    access to research, 181
    involvement in education, 147,
        148–9, 151, 152, 163
    leave entitlements, 128, 133
    power over children, 35, 39, 66, 68–9
Pareto-efficiency, 79, 87
Parsons, Talcott, 57
part-time work, 8, 130, 202
Part-Time Workers Directive, EU, 130
participatory democracy, 19, 198
    arguments for, 100
    dangers of majority rule, 108–13
    devolution, 107–8
    economic, cultural and affective
        inequality, 115–17
    intrinsic obstacles, 101–13
    model of, 98–101
    practicalities of, 104–8
    representation of subordinate groups,
        113–15
    resources needed, 108
    workplace equality, 104, 135–6
*Partnership 2000,* 112
patriarchy, 33, 57, 60, 173, 210, 218
    cause of inequalities, 58, 69, 202
    in education, 157–8, 158
pay
    inequalities, 5, 37, 128–9, 129–30,
        135, 199
    Ireland, 77, 91–3
    wage relativities, 91
    women, 5, 207, 208
peace movements, 193, 234
pensions, 202–3
    ECJ decisions , 130
    and sexual orientation, 68
    tax relief, 86
people-trafficking, 184
perpetrator perspective, 129

personal development, 35–6, 137,
    157–8, 166
    and education, 142
personal intelligences, 165–7
Philippines, 221
Piaget, Jean, 165
Piven, F.F. and Cloward, R.A., 240, 241
Plato, 166
policing, 117, 239
political correctness, 6, 35
political parties, 19, 46, 59, 103, 117,
    246
    financing of, 115–16
    left-wing, 233–8
    in participatory democracy, 106
    radical, 235–7
    self-exclusion from, 234–5
    strategic issues, 229, 232–8
    women in, 208
    working within, 234
politics
    communications industry, 213–4
    disengagement from, 96, 202–3,
        237–8
    emotions in, 164
    finances, 115–16
    identity politics, 203–5
    left-wing, 47, 203, 233–8
    and research, 169, 186
    women in, 208, 209
political system, 41, 57, 59
    equality within, 96–8
    inequalities within, 7, 29–30, 60–1,
        68: and affective inequality, 64–5;
        and cultural inequality, 63–4; and
        economic inequality, 62–3
    international relations, 201–2
    and legal system, 119–22, 123
    source of inequality, 68
Porto Alegre, Brazil, 103, 104, 107, 116,
    195–6, 219
Portugal, 147
positive action *see* affirmative action
positivist methodologies, 169, 170–5
post-Keynesianism, 75, 80
post-Marxism, 75, 80
post-structuralism, 15
postmodernism, 12, 68, 171
poverty, 81
    analysis of, 156
    anti-poverty movements, 195

poverty – *continued*
  positivist research, 172–4
  relief of, 17, 27, 36, 48, 198, 211:
      limitations of, 90; national target,
      199
power relations, 24–5, 29–30, 33, 46, 49
  and disability, 9, 44
  in education, 39, 143–4, 161–3, 194
  equality of condition, 34, 38–9
  and freedom, 50
  and gender, 8–9, 44–5
  and ideology, 213–14
  inequalities of, 7, 59, 113, 194–5:
      within egalitarian movement,
      245, 246; in the workplace, 132
  and political equality, 60–1, 97
  and research, 169–70, 174–5, 180,
      183: positivist research, 172–3
  and social class, 8, 45
Prague demonstrations, 231
pregnancy discrimination, 128
prisoners, 7, 10, 45, 184
  affective inequality, 6, 64–5, 102,
      115–17
private sphere, 26, 27, 35, 119, 126–7
profit maximization, 201
Programme for Appraisal and Fair
      Treatment (PAFT), 200
promotion, 136, 176–7
property developers, 139
property rights, 29, 38, 51, 81, 108, 126
  and anti-discrimination laws, 131
  in Ireland, 206
  legal protection, 121
  and sexual orientation, 68
proportional representation, 113–15, 236
proportionality tests, 131
prostitution, 222
psychoanalysis, 15
public interest law, 123
public/private distinction, 26, 27, 35,
      119, 126–7
public service
  bureaucracies, 117
  expenditure, 5, 139, 199
  salary levels, 92
Putterman, L, Roemer, J.E. and Silvestre,
      J., 87

'quality of life' debate, 220, 226
quota policies, 114–15, 131

racism, 9, 10, 33, 55–6, 135, 169–70,
      192, 198, 241, 265 n. 10 *see also*
      ethnicity; Travellers
  and cultural system, 59
  and economic system, 58
  and employment, 129
  immigration, 199
  source of inequalities, 202
  studies of, 13, 174
radicalism, 229, 236–7, 238–43, 246
rape, 5, 23
rational choice theory, 15
Rawls, John, 25, 27, 31, 32, 42, 94
*Re Article 26 and the Employment Equality
      Bill 1996*, 131
reasonable accommodation, concept of,
      120, 131, 133–4
Reay, Diane, 204
recognition *see* respect and recognition
reflexivity, 171, 174, 176, 179, 183, 227
  subjective, 187
refugees, 6, 10, 221
regional government, 107
regional partnerships, 107
relationships and sexuality education,
      157–8, 166
religion, 96
  and cultural system, 59, 213
  and education, 140, 157, 158
  love of neighbour, 220
  oppression of, 35, 59
  and participatory democracy, 103–4
  power in, 39
  and workplace equality, 135
replacement ratio, 85
representatives, political, 7
  facilitated by employers, 108
  in participatory democracy, 99, 105–7
reproductive rights, 82–3, 197, 208, 225
research, 18, 167, 205 *see also*
      emancipatory research
  choice of topics, 169
  democratization of, 163
  'hit and run model', 174
  influence of funding, 173, 183
  objectivism, 172
  perspective of 'experts', 66, 124, 160,
      173–5, 179–80, 187–8
  in physical sciences, 180–1
  power relations within, 174–5
  reciprocity in, 181–2

rights of participants, 179–80
working conditions for, 176–8
research coalitions, 183–5, 186, 188
residents' associations, 96, 103–4
resistance, dynamics of, 216–18
resources, 24–5, 27, 46, 48, 51
  for consultation mechanisms, 136
  and disability, 9, 36, 44
  and economic equality, 60–1, 76
  within egalitarian movement, 198,
    230, 244
  equality of condition, 34, 36–7
  and freedom, 51
  and gender, 9, 44
  inequalities of, 4–5, 113, 194–5: in
    education, 143–54, 158, 159, 168;
    in politics, 97
  for participatory democracy, 108
  and research, 173, 181, 183
  role of state in allocation, 78, 79–81
  and social class, 8, 45
respect and recognition, 24–5, 25–7, 46,
    49, 194–5
  and cultural equality, 61
  and disability, 9, 44
  in education, 144, 154–61, 168
  within egalitarian movement, 243–4
  equality of condition, 34–6
  and gender, 8–9, 44–5
  and freedom, 51
  inequalities of, 5–6, 113: in the
    workplace, 132
  and social class, 8, 45
'rights' discourse, 119, 133, 161
Roemer, John E., 88–9
Ruane, F. and Sutherland, J.M., 170

Savage, Mike, 204
School Inspectorate, 259 n. 8
schools *see* education
Seattle demonstrations, 231
Second World War, 192
sectarianism, 208
segregation
  of disability, 158–9
  educational, 154
  occupational, 129–30
  residential, 107
selection and assessment, 146–7, 152,
    168
  power relations, 161

self-employment, 93, 205, 206
self-interest, 194, 203–4, 227
  Marxism reliant on, 192–3
Sen, Amartya, 16
separation of powers, 100, 123, 138
services sector, 202, 222
sex industry, 222
sexism, 5–6, 169–70
  and employment, 129
  harassment, 198
sexual orientation
  inequalities, 5, 9–10, 45, 63, 67, 68,
    128–9, 194–6: in education,
    155
  legislation, 11, 199
  marginalization, 101
  minority protection, 110, 111
  queer studies, 13
  political representation, 114
  and research, 184
  social movements, 10, 193
Shaw, Randy, 235
Shor, Ira, 160
Sierra Leone, 77
Sign Language, 63
Skeggs, Beverley, 204
slavery, 29, 238
Smith, Adam, 95
social capital, 36, 62–3, 203, 250 n. 20
social change, 191–211
  and class politics, 201–7
  dynamics of resistance, 216–18
  models of, 191–4
  role of ideology, 212–18
  social movement model, 242–3
social class, 10, 25–7, 102, 192, 196
  class politics, 201–7
  divisions within, 67, 203
  education about, 153, 160
  inequalities, 5, 8–9, 27, 33, 45, 50:
    education, 142, 143, 144–54,
    115–6; research into, 170, 171,
    172–4
  in Ireland, 205–6
  mobility, 204–5
  shift in identities, 192
social conditioning, 78–9, 125, 140–1
social context evidence, 124
social democracy, 24, 219, 220, 234,
    235
social economics, 75

social employment, 127
social groups, 8–10
  access to legal system, 124
  applying framework to, 42–6
  locating causes of inequality, 65–70
  and solidarity, 52
social institutions, 41, 60, 91–4, 142
  reform of, 16–7, 19, 31, 38, 70–1,
    98–9, 118,134–7
social justice, 48–9, 121, 227
social movements, 19, 201, 232, 236
  direct action, 241
  dual strategies, 240–1
  model of social change, 193–4, 195,
    211, 242–3
  networks, 230–1
  not all egalitarian, 195
  representativeness of, 197–8
  responses to inequality, 10–11
  strengthened by diversity, 237
social networks, 36, 62–3, 203
social partnership, 77, 111
  commitments to equality, 94–5
  Ireland, 91–3
social policy, EU, 127
Social Science Research Council (SSRC),
  260 n. 4
social sciences, 13, 15, 169–70
  emancipatory research, 178
  positivist research, 171–4
social structures, 33
  democratization of, 98–9
  egalitarian change within, 57–65
  and ideology, 214–16
  implications for politics, 70–1
  inequalities, 38, 65–70, 83
  interactions between, 62–5
  socio-economic rights, 138–9
social welfare, 11–12, 83, 84, 88, 108,
  127, 151, 202–3, 238
  basic income system, 93
  corporate welfarism, 90–1
  and economic equality, 84–5
  legal aid, 122–3
  as proportion of national income, 92–3
  reform, 11–12, 17
socialism, 140, 220
  concepts of self, 223
  and egalitarianism, 16–17, 88–9,
    218–19
  and feminism, 12, 208–9
  support for universal suffrage, 232–3

solidarity, 47, 56, 164–5, 221–2 *see also*
    love, care and solidarity
  and equality, 52–3, 198
South Africa, 4, 135, 138–9, 258 n. 19
South East Asia, 83
South Korea, 7
Spain, 147
sports clubs, 103–4
state, the, 96
  allocation of resources, 78, 79–80
  direct action against, 239–40, 242
  economic role, 58–9
  funding influence of, 139, 173, 198,
    244
  income redistribution, 79–81, 90
  and inequalities, 11–12, 59
  infrastructure funding, 139
  and left-wing parties, 236
  and legislature, 117, 138
  power of, 38, 233
  'rights' discourse, 119
strategic issues, 19, 246
  coordinating action, 229–32
  ends and means, 243–6
  for equality movement, 229–46
  political parties, 229, 232–8
  radicals and moderates, 238–43
strategic pluralism, 229, 232, 246
streaming, 147–9, 152, 181, 205
strikes, 239, 241
  middle class, 205
  right to strike, 238
structural-functionalism, 57
structuralism, 15
student councils, 163
subsidiarity, 107
Summerhill, 260 n. 14
Supiot Report, 137
Sweden, 7, 151
Switzerland, 111, 147
syllabus, 146
  bias within, 150, 152–3, 154, 168
systems theory, 15
Szasz, Andrew, 241

Taiwan, 147
Tarrow, Sidney, 240, 241, 242
Tawney, R.H., 15
taxation, 11–12, 81, 84, 86, 88, 89, 93,
  203
  capital gains tax, 86
  and economic equality, 85–7, 92–3

and economic growth, 83
and housing investment, 206
inefficiencies, 89–90
and sexual orientation, 68
teachers, 156, 158, 160, 168, 181, 188
  power relations, 161–3
temporary work, 130, 202
terms of trade, 201–2
Thatcherism, 216, 265 n. 10
therapy, 222
'Third Way', 216
Third World, 77–8
toleration, 26, 27, 34–5, 48
  religious, 10, 26, 29
torture *see* inhuman and degrading
    treatment
trade relations, 126, 201–2
trade unions, 96, 103, 108, 203, 231
  decision-making, 112
  direct action, 241
  economic role, 58–9
  in participatory democracy, 103–4
  women in, 208
training *see* education
transformation *see* social change
transformative action, 137–9, 169
  research coalitions, 186
Transition Year Programme, 153
transnational corporations, 195, 201,
    233, 240
transnational democracy, 117
transparency, 100
transsexualism *see* sexual orientation
Travellers, 20, 28, 138
  education, 146
  anti-discrimination laws, 199
  inequalities, 9, 63–4, 66, 68
  inter-group agreement, 111
  legal appeals, 118–19
  marginalization, 101
  political funding for, 116
  research, 173, 174
  sites for, 199
Treaty of Rome, 11
trespass, 116, 138
TRIPS agreement, 201
Tronto, Joan C., 37
trustee model, 105

understanding, codes of, 213–14
'undue hardship', 134
unemployment, 67, 182, 202, 211

representation of unemployed, 203
  social exclusion, 63
  unemployment trap, 84–5
unemployment benefit, 89
Union of Concerned Scientists, 240
unitary democracies, 109
United Kingdom (UK), 19, 95, 236,
    238
  child abuse, 6
  equality legislation, 11
  income, 76, 77, 91
  inequalities within, 5, 82: disability, 8
  life prospects, 3–4
  parental employment, 6–7
  racism, 9
  social welfare, 85
  taxation, 86
  working class, 203
United Nations (UN), 96, 142
United States of America (US), 10, 19,
    82, 95, 199, 202, 233, 236
  affirmative action, 132
  African Americans, 4, 7, 8
  civil rights, 10, 11, 107
  communications industry, 214
  constitutional rights, 109, 110
  direct action, 240–1
  education, 151, 153
  electoral system, 114, 116
  equal protection doctrine, 128
  equality legislation, 11
  income distribution, 76, 77, 91, 254
    n. 12
  inequalities within, 4, 5, 94
  Knights of Labor, 240
  legal system, 121, 124
  ownership of wealth, 77
  property rights, 126
  racism, 9
  social movements, 235
  trade relations, 201
  'white flight,' 149
  women's movement, 234
Universal Declaration of Human Rights,
    21, 29, 30, 32, 141, 219
universal suffrage, 26, 232–3, 238
universities, 143, 156, 157, 170, 207
  community involvement, 177–8,
    188
  and emancipatory research, 184–7
Universities Act 1997, 141
utopianism, 216–17

Varian, Hal R., 79
Veblen, Thorstein, 80
Vietnam, 5
violence, 6, 29, 39, 154, 211
    political, 240, 241–2
    protection against, 23
    against women, 9, 45, 184, 199, 224
voluntary sector, 30, 40, 61, 92, 96,
    111–12, 115, 177, 179, 221
voting systems, 110, 113–15

wage agreements, 90, 111, 112
    commitments to equality, 94–5
wages and salaries *see* pay
water quality, 5
wealth
    distribution of, 88, 137
    ownership of, 77
    research into wealthy, 172
Weber, Max, 57
welfare state, 17, 27, 31, 32, 89, 192,
    238
    democratization of, 104
women *see also* gender
    blamed for own marginalization, 173
    and care work, 64, 128, 225–6:
        devaluation of, 166; unpaid
        labour, 127, 132
    in community sector, 208
    disabled, 70
    diversity of, 14, 69–70, 209
    in education, 158, 176, 207, 208
    inequalities, 5, 35, 69–70
    in Ireland, 8, 207–8
    and labour market, 202, 207, 210
    literacy rates, 8
    in Northern Ireland, 208, 224
    political participation of, 7, 101,
        113–14, 208, 209
    research into, 173
    subordination of the feminine, 157–8
    trafficking of, 184
    violence against, 9, 45, 184, 199, 224
    working class, 204
Women's Coalition, NI, 208, 235
women's movement, 10, 193, 211, 220,
    234 *see also* feminism
    abortion issues, 197
    affective equality in, 212, 220–8
    attitude to caring work, 224–6
    diversity within, 196, 209, 217–18

    egalitarian values, 197
    and equality movement, 208–9
    and labour movement, 209
    portrayal by mass media, 224
    source of equality discourse, 207–11
    in United States, 234
Women's Political Association, 208
women's studies, 12, 169
    research methods, 181–2
    resistance to, 177, 178
Wollstonecraft, Mary, 12
work, 28, 40 *see also* care work; labour,
    division of; labour market
    and affective system, 60
    affirmative action, 131–2
    atypical workers, 130
    casualization of, 220
    commuting time, 226
    gender divisions, 38, 44–5, 60, 64, 69,
        132, 210
    minimum standards, 30
    obligation to work, 40, 249 n. 14
    taxation, 86–7
    towards equality of condition, 132–9
    unpaid, 76, 127
worker-management, 89
Workers' Party, Brazil, 235
working and learning, 24–5, 30–1, 46, 49
    and democracy, 97
    and disability, 8, 9, 44, 133
    equality of condition, 34, 39–41
    and freedom, 51
    and gender, 8, 44–5
    inequalities of, 7–8
    and social class, 8, 45
    work-based learning, 137
    work–life balance, 200, 226 *see also*
        family-friendly policies
working class, 67, 202
    disengaged from politics, 202–3
    divisions within, 192, 194
    identification with, 203–5
    internal contradictions, 205
    Marxist appeal to, 191–2
    negative identity, 156
    and research, 174, 182
Working Families Party of New York,
    266 n. 7
workplace
    conditions of work, 198, 211
    constitutional issues, 137–9

democracy in, 89, 104, 109
equality legislation, 118, 125–32
equality of condition, 134–7
hours of work, 7–8, 136
inequalities in, 30, 63, 68, 94, 132
leave entitlements, 133–4
quotas, 131
reasonable accommodation, 133–4
works councils, 108
World Bank, 95, 195
Development Indicators, 77
World Social Forum (WSF)

Charter of Principles, 195–6, 219, 230–1
World Trade Organization (WTO), 12, 95, 195, 233

xenophobia, 199

Young, Iris Marion, 122
Youth Defence Movement, 261 n. 4

Zapatista movement, 235
Znet, 103